"A bag of gold. DeRouchie, Martin, and Naselli
riches. These three fine scholars examine bibli
angle—definition, methodology, hermeneutics, th
and the use of the Old Testament in the New Test
wonderful entry point into the vast and complex
that lay people, students, pastors, and teachers wo

—Benjamin L. Gladd,
Associate Professor of New Testament,
Reformed Theological Seminary, Jackson, MS

"This is not only a book for professionals and scholars; this is a book that every serious
student of the Bible should own and refer to often. Although it proceeds on the basis of
the evangelical faith, Christians of all persuasions will find this a mine of well-organized,
clearly written, comprehensive, informative, and easy to understand discussions of the
forty questions posed. The matters dealt with are not only relevant to those who focus on
biblical theology as a discipline, but also concern the formation of systematic, historical,
practical, and homiletic theology. The authors have used every means at their disposal
to make this the kind of reference book in which every aspect of biblical theology is presented in a format that makes the information easy to find. I wish I had had a book like
this when—over sixty years ago—I began my own journey in biblical theology."
—Graeme Goldsworthy,
Lecturer Emeritus in Biblical Theology, Old Testament, and Hermeneutics
Moore Theological College, Sydney, Australia

"When people get a taste of biblical theology, it makes them hungry for more. They
wonder where this way of understanding the Bible has been all their lives. They want
to know how they can learn more. I'll be telling them that *40 Questions About Biblical
Theology* is a great place to start and that it will continue to be a terrific resource to keep
coming back to."
—Nancy Guthrie,
Teacher, Biblical Theology Workshops for Women;
Author of *Even Better Than Eden*

"Good biblical theology is needed for a faithful and full reading of the Bible; it is thus essential for Christian living and teaching. *40 Questions About Biblical Theology* provides
the framework and theory by answering questions in bite-sized chapters. Examples of
biblical-theological themes and readings of Bible passages highlight the value of this
approach and draw out the richness of God's Word. More than just an introduction,
DeRouchie, Martin, and Naselli's book also provides a snapshot of the discipline in
2020, with references for the interested reader to chase. This book helps us see how the
whole Bible fits together and points to and is fulfilled in Christ, and as such, is a great
safeguard against moralism. Highly recommended for Christians the world over."
—Peter H. W. Lau,
Researcher and Writer, OMF International;
Old Testament Book Review Editor, *Themelios*

"When three scholars who are committed to the Bible as the inspired Word of God combine efforts to write a book like this, you should not be surprised that you have a landmark product in your hands. Study biblical theology! When well understood, it is like a well-cut diamond that sparkles and bounces the light of Christ on every page of the Bible, leaving you worshipping the God of history as the God of wonders. Get this book, because it not only teaches you biblical theology, but also leaves you with a growing appetite for God's Word."

—Conrad Mbewe, Pastor,
Kabwata Baptist Church, Lusaka, Zambia

"I was thrilled to see Kregel take on the subject of biblical theology in this particular series because the format makes this vitally important subject accessible to readers. I was doubly thrilled to see the trio of profs who wrote it! Pastors will benefit from *40 Questions About Biblical Theology* because it contains important Christ-exalting observations and implications for the church and is written with a pastoral tone throughout. Professors will benefit from it as they look for supplemental texts on the subject. Church members will gain a good understanding of the themes and the redemptive storyline of Scripture. And I wouldn't hesitate handing this book to some inquisitive skeptics, since I find the unity of the Bible to be a powerful apologetic—one that we should not overlook when giving a defense of the faith. May all who read it walk away with a deeper love for Jesus our Savior, who is magnified throughout the pages of Holy Scripture."

—Tony Merida, Pastor for Preaching, Imago Dei Church, Raleigh, NC;
Dean, Grimké Seminary;
Director for Theological Training, Acts 29

"Biblical theology is among the most contested and misunderstood disciplines of biblical and theological study. It is also among the richest and most rewarding. And faithful teaching and preaching of the Bible depends on a clear understanding of biblical theology. This lucid and engaging 40 Questions volume is a comprehensive guide to its definition, presuppositions, major themes, and applications. Highly recommended for students and ministers alike."

—Brian S. Rosner,
Principal, Ridley College, Melbourne, Australia

"DeRouchie, Martin, and Naselli have written a beautifully clear introduction to biblical theology. They explain what biblical theology is, unpack how it works by considering key topics, illustrate it by considering central texts, and apply it to our lives today. We also benefit as readers in having an Old Testament scholar, a New Testament scholar, and a systematic theologian working together on the project. Their interdisciplinary collaboration gives the book both depth and breadth. I recommend enthusiastically this introduction to biblical theology."

—Thomas R. Schreiner,
James Buchanan Harrison Professor of New Testament Interpretation
and Associate Dean, The Southern Baptist Theological Seminary

"What is biblical theology? What does it include? How do we do it? What themes can we better understand from it? How does it help us, as individuals and as the church? Old Testament scholar Jason DeRouchie, New Testament scholar Andy Naselli, and systematic theologian Oren Martin team up to address these questions and more. The result is this valuable, perceptive, and noteworthy volume."

—Christopher W. Morgan,
Dean and Professor of Theology, School of Christian Ministries,
California Baptist University

"Biblical theology can look like a maze with many twists and turns for novices and for experts—if there is an expert in Scripture. With the many intricacies, the more guides one has the better, as with many counselors success is most achievable. Here we have three escorts to lead us through the maze to behold the King in his beauty. These pastor-scholars have composed a primer to biblical theology that answers some of the most puzzling questions in the field. They do not disappoint as ushers into the world of biblical theology, giving us tools to mine the treasures of Christ. I heartily recommend this work."

—Dieudonné Tamfu, Pastor, Bethlehem Baptist Church, Yaoundé, Cameroon;
Assistant Professor of Bible and Theology and Executive
Director of Cameroon Extension Site, Bethlehem College & Seminary

"DeRouchie, Martin, and Naselli present the essence of biblical theology in moving and captivating ways. Though the level of scholarship is high, the question-and-answer format allows one to read and comprehend without difficulty. By defining, comparing, illustrating, and applying biblical theology, the authors magnify the overarching story-line of Scripture in such a vivid way that none can miss it. The book answers the key questions in the discipline and will serve as a foundational textbook. But even more, readers will not escape the intense urge to worship the Triune God as they grow in their understanding of the great salvation that Messiah Jesus has accomplished! DeRouchie, Martin, and Naselli have given us a treasure that needs to be in the hands of pastors, laypersons, and scholars alike."

—Frew Tamrat,
Principal, Evangelical Theological College,
Addis Ababa, Ethiopia

"In every era, the church stands or falls on its knowledge of the triune God from Scripture. Apart from the exposition and application of 'the whole counsel of God,' the church will endlessly drift and wander. This is why the study of biblical theology is so important. Biblical theology is the theological discipline that seeks to understand all that Scripture teaches on its own terms. In this very helpful book, our authors introduce the reader to the study of biblical theology and its importance for the life and health of the church. By thinking through different approaches to biblical theology and then illustrating how biblical theology is done in practice, this book is a valuable resource for all those who want to know Scripture better."

—Stephen J. Wellum,
Professor of Christian Theology,
The Southern Baptist Theological Seminary

"This is an outstanding resource for the study of biblical theology. The question-and-answer format makes it ideal for both classroom instruction and self-study. Not only do the authors define and compare approaches to biblical theology (Parts 1–2), but they also illustrate and apply it (Parts 3–5) from a variety of important angles. DeRouchie, Martin, and Naselli are to be commended for their work in the service of the church."

—Miles V. Van Pelt,
Alan Hayes Belcher Jr. Professor of Old Testament and Biblical Languages,
Director of the Summer Institute for Biblical Languages,
and Academic Dean, Reformed Theological Seminary, Jackson, MS

40 QUESTIONS ABOUT
Biblical Theology

Jason S. DeRouchie
Oren R. Martin
Andrew David Naselli

Benjamin L. Merkle, Series Editor

KREGEL
ACADEMIC

40 Questions About Biblical Theology
© 2020 Jason S. DeRouchie, Oren R. Martin, and Andrew David Naselli

Published by Kregel Academic, an imprint of Kregel Publications, 2450 Oak Industrial Dr. NE, Grand Rapids, MI 49505-6020.

This book is a title in the 40 Questions Series edited by Benjamin L. Merkle. For additional information about the 40 Questions Series, including instructor's resources, visit www.40questions.net.

ISBN 978-0-8254-4560-6, print
ISBN 978-0-8254-6719-6, Kindle
ISBN 978-0-8254-7540-5, epub

Printed in the United States of America

22 23 24 25 26 27 28 29 30 / 7 6 5 4 3 2

From Jason:
For the Joint Heirs Sunday School Class
of Bethlehem Baptist Church, North Campus

From Oren:
For my children—Jonathan, Anna, and Benjamin

From Andy:
For Professor Layton Talbert

Contents

Introduction

The glorious, transcendent God *over us* has graciously "stooped down" to speak to and fellowship *with us* (Gen. 1–2). The Lord who is high and lifted up, who inhabits eternity (Isa. 57:15), is also the Lord who draws near, acts, and speaks in order to establish, sustain, and perfect fellowship with his people. He has spoken to us most supremely by his Son (Heb. 1:1–2), and by his Spirit he has given us his words in Scripture (1 Cor. 2:12–13; 2 Peter 1:20–21)—the very words of life (John 6:68–69; Acts 5:20). Scripture, therefore, is a gift from God, and we hope this book on biblical theology will help you understand it.

But why add to the growing list of books on biblical theology? This book on biblical theology is important for a number of reasons. First, Kregel established this particular series to address various important theological topics in clear and accessible ways for the church. As both professors and pastors, we regularly teach biblical theology, and so an introductory book that concisely yet comprehensively covers various topics in biblical theology will serve our students and churches. Most of all, we long for the living and true God to sanctify his church—the pillar and buttress of truth. Therefore, this book is our attempt to aid in this joyful task, for both our joy and God's glory in Christ.

Second, the Triune God created and called Christians to know him and his saving works in Christ by the Spirit through what he has revealed. God the Holy Trinity is a fountain of life (Ps. 36:9[10]),[1] and this life is characterized by communication and communion. God the Father eternally communicates his life to the Son (John 5:26), who is his Word, image, radiance, and exact imprint (John 1:1; Col. 1:15; Heb. 1:3). Together the Father and Son communicate this life to the Spirit (John 15:26–16:15), who works to give life (John 3:1–8; Titus 3:5) and bring us into this Trinitarian-shaped life of communion. We come to know this life only because the Triune God has revealed it to us in the gospel of Jesus Christ. "No one knows the Son except the Father, and no one knows the Father except the Son and anyone to whom the Son chooses to reveal him" (Matt. 11:27). Thankfully, the Son invites us to come to him

---

1. When the Hebrew and English verse numberings differ, we will include the Hebrew numbering in brackets.

(11:28–30) and sends his Spirit who is from God, that we may understand the things God freely gives us (1 Cor. 2:12). Thus, the Holy Trinity redeems and enables Christians to know him through the works and words he has revealed in his Word. If this is the case, then we must grow in understanding his works and words so that we may better know him—a glorious task that will occupy us for the rest of our lives and, yes, for eternity (indeed, God is just that infinitely glorious and wonderful!).

Third, mining the Scriptures to know the only true God and his saving ways in Christ is the work of apprentices training for eternal life. Biblical theology is an essential path to reach that goal. But biblical theology is not just one way to read the Bible. Because all Scripture is from God and progresses, integrates, and climaxes in Christ—as Christians throughout the ages have confessed—the Bible demands we read it in a certain way. God speaks to his people through his Word and words and, as a result, we must read it according to *what it is* and *how God has structured it*. In other words, it is *God's word* from beginning to end, from Genesis to Revelation, and therefore we must receive and read it accordingly. This reception and reading is the task of biblical theology. This task, however, is not always easy. Why? Perhaps an illustration will help.

As a father of young children, I (Oren) have spent a significant amount of time building (and stepping on!) tiny individual building blocks that, when properly fitted together, form a masterpiece. I have learned (often the hard way) that each stage is crucial in the building process, and that to skip a step for the sake of efficiency often ends in undesirable and frustrating results. Therefore, the builder must carefully progress through the steps. The first thing to do when beginning the building process is to lay out and examine the pieces, which often brings confusion and anxiety as the task awaits—confusion because it initially seems impossible to see how these tiny and diverse pieces will fit together to form the unified whole, and anxiety because of the prospect of time it will take to complete it. As the set grows more complex, the blocks grow in diversity and number, increasing the confusion and anxiety. It is easy to miss the proverbial forest for the trees. Thankfully, however, hidden among the parts is a manual that contains what is needed: a picture and instructions that guide the process toward the goal. And so the builder moves step by step and piece by piece until that picture reaches the grand reality.

Reading and understanding Scripture can often feel like those building sets. The individual parts can at times seem disconnected from the whole, especially when those parts are foreign to us (e.g., culture, language, genres). What is needed, then, is a picture that guides us toward the goal. Thankfully, God has provided such a picture—the glorious gospel of our blessed God (1 Tim. 1:11). And though our knowledge will forever be finite and therefore we will never know exhaustively how each part fits into that glorious whole, we nevertheless can grow by God's grace to become better builders by analyzing and synthesizing the whole canon on its own terms and by trusting that God has truly given us what we need to know him and his saving purposes in Christ. Thus, we have written this book to explain how to better understand God's Word. May we fix our eyes on Jesus as we make our way through it. And may God's grace fuel our efforts to understand and proclaim the whole counsel of God to see the obedience that flows from faith realized among all the nations for the sake of Christ's name (Rom. 1:5).

A couple of notes about this book are in order: (1) Although you may read this book from beginning to end, we wrote it in such a way that you may read a particular question without a knowledge of the other questions. So feel free to look through the table of contents to see if there is a particular question that most interests you (though it may help to read some of the methodological questions first). (2) Although one person is primarily responsible for writing each chapter, the other two authors gave significant feedback on all the material.

Words of Thanks

There are many people whom we should thank for making this book a reality. We wish to thank Ben Merkle, the series editor, and Kregel for allowing us to add this book to an excellent series from which we have greatly benefited.

I (Jason) thank Oren for collaborating with me and Andy and for bringing to this book a pastoral heart that helps others revel in the Triune God. I am grateful to the administrations at both Bethlehem College & Seminary and Midwestern Baptist Theological Seminary for empowering my writing and for celebrating with me an approach to the Old Testament that exalts Christ. I thank my fourth-year MDiv biblical theology students and my co-teacher and coauthor Andy Naselli for engaging thoughtfully, questioning insightfully, and worshipping with me over the beauties of Christ seen in the whole of Scripture. I am grateful to my research assistant Brian Verrett for his careful eye to both form and content and for his numerous thoughtful suggestions regarding the book as a whole. I thank my wife, Teresa, and my six kids for joining me in this great work of academic ministry and for treasuring the God who reveals himself in a Word that progresses, integrates, and climaxes in Jesus. Finally, I thank the Joint Heirs Sunday School class of Bethlehem Baptist Church north campus who came week after week for thirteen years to study the whole counsel of God, to awaken a heart for the nations, and to nurture hope in the gospel from the Old Testament. I dedicate my portion of this volume to you, and I will forever praise the Lord for letting us love, live, and learn together.

I (Oren) thank the trustees and administration of Southern Seminary for granting me a sabbatical in the fall of 2018, during which time the bulk of my part was written. I also thank Jason DeRouchie and Andy Naselli for the privilege of cowriting this book with them. I did not want to write this book alone; your names were first on my list; and your contributions have made it far, far better. Thank you for your friendship, example, encouragement, and feedback. I also thank my wife, Cindy, who is a joyful and faithful Christian, wife, mother, and partner in the gospel. My life is abundantly richer because of her. Lastly, I thank my children—Jonathan, Anna, and Benjamin—to whom I dedicate my portion of this book. As I wrote at the dining room table watching and listening to them play, I was filled with joy because of the gifts they are to me. My hope and prayer is that one day they may read and benefit from this book—but even more, that they would find their supreme joy in Christ, who alone can save and satisfy them.

I (Andy) am grateful to Layton Talbert for introducing me to biblical theology. I'm grateful to Don Carson for mentoring me and modeling how to do biblical theology. I'm grateful to my school, Bethlehem College & Seminary, for encouraging and empowering me to research and write in order to spread a passion for the supremacy of God in all things for the joy of all peoples through Jesus Christ. I'm grateful to Jason DeRouchie for co-teaching a fourth-year graduate course with me on biblical theology for the past five years. And I'm grateful for my wife, Jenni, who enthusiastically supports the research-writing-teaching-shepherding ministry that God has called me to.

Most of all, we wish to thank our great God and Savior Jesus Christ, who has delivered us from the domain of darkness and transferred us to his blessed kingdom where we find both joy and life. May he use this book—shortcomings and all—to help us all to better behold the glory of the Lord and to transform us from one degree of glory to another by the Lord who is the Spirit (2 Cor. 3:18).

PART 1

Defining Biblical Theology

What Do We Mean by "Biblical Theology"?

Andrew David Naselli

Biblical theology is a slippery term that people define in many ways. Edward W. Klink III and Darian R. Lockett present and illustrate five types of biblical theology:[1]

1. historical description (e.g., James Barr)
2. history of redemption (e.g., D. A. Carson)
3. worldview-story (e.g., N. T. Wright)
4. canonical approach (e.g., Brevard Childs)
5. theological construction (e.g., Francis Watson)

People do biblical theology in different ways.[2] The type of biblical theology that we are advocating in this book blends types 2, 3, and 4—as do exegetes such as Geerhardus Vos, D. A. Carson, G. K. Beale, Stephen G. Dempster, T. D. Alexander, Thomas R. Schreiner, James M. Hamilton Jr., Peter J. Gentry, and Stephen J. Wellum. Redemptive history *is* a worldview story, and we analyze that story by studying the literary features of the unified canon.[3]

---

1. See also Andrew David Naselli, *How to Understand and Apply the New Testament: Twelve Steps from Exegesis to Theology* (Phillipsburg, NJ: P&R, 2017), 231–35; and Edward W. Klink III and Darian R. Lockett, *Understanding Biblical Theology: A Comparison of Theory and Practice* (Grand Rapids: Zondervan, 2012).
2. See Question 10 below.
3. We are not convinced that Klink and Lockett rightly present five distinct types of biblical theology. Types 1 and 5 are not properly biblical theology, and types 2–4 belong together. Further, Klink and Lockett do not fairly critique D. A. Carson. See also Darian Lockett, "Limitations of a Purely Salvation-Historical Approach to Biblical Theology," *HBT* 39, no. 2 (2017): 211–31. For a critique of Klink and Lockett (as well as Lockett's article), see

Here's how we understand biblical theology:

- *Shorter definition*: Biblical theology studies how the whole Bible progresses, integrates, and climaxes in Christ.

- *Longer definition*: Biblical theology is a way of analyzing and synthesizing the Bible that makes organic, salvation-historical connections with the whole canon on its own terms, especially regarding how the Old and New Testaments progress, integrate, and climax in Christ.

Let's begin by focusing on four aspects of the longer definition.

Biblical Theology Makes Organic Connections

When you hear the word *organic*, you might think of food that is healthy and expensive. That's not what we're trying to connote when we say "organic." *Organic* relates to how elements harmoniously grow together as parts of a whole.

Think of an apple tree. It starts out as a seed that sprouts and slowly grows into a mature tree that bears apples. The tree has several parts: roots, trunk, branches, leaves, apples. And it's all one tree.

Many themes in the Bible are like that. They start off early in the Bible's storyline as a seed. Then they sprout and slowly grow into a mature tree that bears fruit. Biblical theology studies and synthesizes that growth. It traces that growth by making organic connections, by showing how the parts relate to the whole.

Biblical Theology Makes Salvation-Historical Connections

Salvation history refers to the Bible's redemptive storyline. That storyline moves from creation to the fall to redemption to consummation. God has a multistage plan to save his people from their sins. This is the history of redemption, the story of salvation. It's a true story. It's real history. And biblical theology connects key people and events within it. Biblical theology focuses on the turning points in the Bible's storyline.

There are several overlapping ways to make organic, salvation-historical connections:

1. Trace a theme's salvation-historical progression. For example, trace the theme of *serpent* from Genesis to Revelation.[4]

D. A. Carson, "New Covenant Theology and Biblical Theology," in *God's Glory Revealed in Christ: Essays on Biblical Theology in Honor of Thomas R. Schreiner*, eds. Denny Burk, James M. Hamilton Jr., and Brian Vickers (Nashville: B&H, 2019), 17–31.

4. See Question 23 below.

2. Consider continuity and discontinuity between the covenants. For example, compare and contrast how OT Israel related to the Mosaic law versus how Christians should today.[5]

3. Track promise and fulfillment. For example, work through the fulfillment language (πληρόω, *plēroō*, "fulfill") in the Gospel of Matthew, and connect it to the OT.[6]

4. Trace type and antitype. Typology analyzes how NT persons, events, and institutions (i.e., antitypes) fulfill OT persons, events, and institutions (i.e., types) by repeating the OT situations at a deeper, climactic level in salvation history. For example, in John 6:32–33 Jesus fulfills God's giving manna in the OT by repeating that event at a deeper, climactic level in the history of salvation.[7]

5. Think through how the New Testament uses the Old. Why do NT authors quote or allude to specific OT passages in the way they do?[8]

Those are ways to make organic, salvation-historical connections. That's what biblical theology is all about.

What are some significant themes that biblical theology should trace from Genesis to Revelation? The editors of the *NIV Biblical Theology Study Bible* had to think through that question carefully when they designed that resource.[9] The study Bible's main distinctive is that it focuses on biblical theology, not only in the notes but in a section of essays at the back of the study Bible. The editors decided to include short biblical-theological essays for twenty-five themes:

1. The glory of God
2. Creation
3. Sin
4. Covenant
5. Law
6. Temple
7. Priest
8. Sacrifice

---

5. See Questions 6, 25, and 26.
6. See Question 7.
7. See Questions 8, 27, 29, 32, and 33.
8. See Questions 9 and 31–35.
9. D. A. Carson, ed., *NIV Biblical Theology Study Bible* (Grand Rapids: Zondervan, 2018). D. A. Carson is the general editor; associate editors are Douglas J. Moo, T. D. Alexander, and Richard S. Hess; and Andrew David Naselli is the assistant editor.

9. Exile and exodus
10. The kingdom of God
11. Sonship
12. The city of God
13. Prophets and prophecy
14. Death and resurrection
15. People of God
16. Wisdom
17. Holiness
18. Justice
19. Wrath
20. Love and grace
21. The gospel
22. Worship
23. Mission
24. Shalom
25. The consummation

It's relatively straightforward to study these typological trajectories straight through the canon, but it gets more complicated when you analyze and synthesize how so many of these themes interweave with each other. They are like interconnecting ligaments and tendons that tie the whole Bible together.

Biblical Theology Analyzes and Synthesizes the Whole Canon

You can do biblical theology in many different ways. In addition to the ways above (i.e., the five overlapping ways to make organic, salvation-historical connections), three other ways are noteworthy:

1. Focus on a single book. You could focus on how a single book contributes to whole-Bible biblical theology, or you could focus on how a single theme in one book relates to that theme in the rest of the Bible. For example, focus on seed in Genesis, righteousness in Romans, or wisdom in 1 Corinthians.

2. Focus on a corpus—that is, the collected writings by a single author. For example, focus on love in John's writings (the Gospel of John, 1–3 John, and Revelation) or faith in Paul's thirteen letters. Even a casual Bible reader notices that John says things differently from Paul or Peter. Their emphases differ from and complement one another.

3. Focus on one of the Testaments. For example, focus on kingdom in the NT. If you focus almost exclusively on just one Testament, then that's

called *Old Testament theology* or *New Testament theology*. Those are subsets of whole-Bible biblical theology.

When we refer to *biblical theology*, we mean *whole-Bible* biblical theology. It includes the three approaches above, but it does not stop there. It studies these particular portions *in light of the whole Bible* because biblical theology analyzes and synthesizes the whole canon. (The canon is the collection of sixty-six books that the church recognizes as belonging to the Bible.)

This presupposes, of course, that the entire Bible is God-breathed and therefore unified and reliable. And it requires that you read the Bible as progressive revelation: God progressively revealed the Bible throughout history, so later revelation builds on earlier revelation.

In 2010 one of us interviewed Steve Dempster regarding his excellent book *Dominion and Dynasty: A Biblical Theology of the Hebrew Bible*.[10] Here is how Dempster replied to the question, "Methodologically, what role does the NT play in your OT theology?"

> This is a good question. I try to bracket it out as much as possible, but of course it is there always in my consciousness. Nevertheless, I think it is important to argue with Brevard Childs that the Old Testament must have its own discrete witness. That is why, for example, I use the structure of the Hebrew Bible in my Old Testament theology. In my theology this distinctive structure is an important part of the argument. . . .
>
> To answer the question in another way, I think that if I didn't try to bracket the New Testament out as much as possible, I am sure I wouldn't have stressed the importance of land in my study, which does not seem to be important—at least on the surface—in the New Testament.

While we understand and respect why Dempster answered the question that way, we don't think that we should do biblical theology this way *and stop there*. And Dempster agrees.[11]

---

10. Andrew David Naselli, "Interview with Stephen Dempster on Old Testament Theology," *The Gospel Coalition*, August 5, 2010, http://www.thegospelcoalition.org/blogs/justintaylor/2010/08/05/interview-with-stephen-dempster-on-old-testament-theology; Stephen G. Dempster, *Dominion and Dynasty: A Biblical Theology of the Hebrew Bible*, NSBT 15 (Downers Grove, IL: InterVarsity, 2003).
11. Dempster wrote this to Andy Naselli: "I agree with your assessment. . . . I guess when I say that I try and bracket out the NT understanding first I am certainly not saying that I wish to stay there. I want to read a book on its own first and hear its distinctive voice. But after doing this I have a responsibility and imperative as a Christian scholar to see how this connects to the New Testament and to read the OT in light of the end" (email to Andy Naselli,

It's valuable to think through what God's people at any given stage of history may have thought given the revelation they had received up to that point. But we live now—at this point in salvation history. We have the whole canon. We might temporarily "bracket out" part of the canon as a thought experiment, but at the end of the day, we shouldn't bracket out any part of it. We should read every part of it in light of the whole.[12] When we read any part of the Bible—including the OT—we must read with *Christian* eyes.[13]

So one danger is to focus on the OT in a way that brackets out the NT. But there's an inverse danger: you can focus on the NT in a way that essentially brackets out the OT. You cannot responsibly read the NT apart from the OT. They are inseparable. As D. A. Carson puts it, "There is likely to be something distorted about a string of learned essays and monographs on, say, Paul, if those essays have been written by someone who has not bothered to study intensely Paul's Bible."[14] The single most important literature for understanding the NT is the OT. We must not interpret the NT as though the OT doesn't exist. If we do, we will badly misread the NT.

November 25, 2015, used with permission). To get an idea of how Dempster reads the New Testament as a key for understanding the Old Testament, see Stephen G. Dempster, "From Slight Peg to Cornerstone to Capstone: The Resurrection of Christ on 'the Third Day' according to the Scriptures," *WTJ* 76, no. 2 (Fall 2014): 371–409.

12. See also Brian S. Rosner, "Biblical Theology," in *New Dictionary of Biblical Theology*, eds. T. Desmond Alexander and Brian S. Rosner (Downers Grove, IL: InterVarsity, 2000), 3: "Biblical theology is principally concerned with the overall theological message of the whole Bible. It seeks to understand the parts in relation to the whole and, to achieve this, it must work with the mutual interaction of the literary, historical, and theological dimensions of the various corpora, and with the inter-relationships of these within the whole canon of Scripture."

13. See also D. A. Carson, "Current Issues in Biblical Theology: A New Testament Perspective," *BBR* 5 (1995): 40–41:

> All Christian theologians, including those whose area of specialty is the Old Testament or some part of it, are under obligation to read the Old Testament, in certain respects, with Christian eyes. . . . I acknowledge that certain kinds of historical study of the Old Testament documents must specifically disavow later knowledge in order to ensure accurate historical and theological analysis of the people and of the documents they have left behind. At the same time, no Christian *Alttestamentler* [i.e., Old Testament scholar] has the right to leave the challenge of *biblical* study to the New Testament departments. The Gospel records insist that Jesus himself, and certainly his earliest followers after him, read the Old Testament in christological ways. Jesus berated his followers for not discerning these points themselves. The rationale for such exegesis is multifaceted and complex. But if we are *Christian* theologians, that rationale must be teased out from both ends of the canon.

14. Carson, "Current Issues in Biblical Theology," 34.

Biblical Theology Analyzes and Synthesizes the Whole Canon on Its Own Terms

For biblical theology, the text sets the agenda. That's why the words *on its own terms* are in the definition. This is what distinguishes biblical theology from systematic theology.[15] Biblical theology prioritizes a passage's literary context.[16]

For systematic theology, the text is important, but other factors often set the agenda. It might be a philosophical question (Is God inside or outside time? Do we have a free will?). Or it might be a modern-day controversial ethical issue (What forms of contraception might be acceptable options for Christians? Is *in vitro* fertilization an option for Christians?). Or it could be a pressing personal question (What must I do to be saved? Should a church baptize infants? Does an unborn infant who dies go to heaven?).

We often have questions about an issue and then ask, "What does the Bible teach about that?" That's a legitimate and necessary type of question. But it differs from biblical theology in that for the latter, the literary themes of the text itself are what drive the questions.[17]

For example, imagine taking a college course on William Shakespeare. As you read one of his plays, you would study its literary context—the role that certain passages have within the play and more broadly within all of Shakespeare's published works. What particular themes and motifs are prominent in a particular Shakespeare play? What themes and motifs are prominent throughout his plays? You would inductively read a play, and that careful reading is what should lead you to explore themes that are significant in the play.

As you read the Bible, you inductively discover that certain literary themes are prominent. Some of those themes are ones that people typically don't ask about when they are wondering what the whole Bible teaches about a topic. For example, people don't generally ask what the whole Bible teaches about sonship or about exile and exodus. But those are themes we should be tracing through the Bible because (1) they are so important in passage after passage, and (2) the divine author wants us to see the interconnections.

Biblical theology is historical, organic, and inductive. Systematic theology is relatively ahistorical, universal, and deductive. See figure 1.1, which contrasts the task and nature of biblical theology with systematic theology.

---

15. See Question 13.
16. On literary context, see Jason S. DeRouchie, *How to Understand and Apply the Old Testament: Twelve Steps from Exegesis to Theology* (Phillipsburg, NJ: P&R, 2017), 323–43; Naselli, *Understand and Apply the New Testament*, 188–205.
17. We don't mean to imply that the text *never* sets the agenda for systematic theology. It often can and should. But it often does not, and that's fine. And that's one way it differs from biblical theology.

	Biblical Theology	Systematic Theology
Final Authority	**The Whole Bible**	**The Whole Bible**
Task	Inductively describe what texts say in relation to the whole Bible. Explore how and what each literary genre or canonical unit distinctively communicates.	Deductively describe what the whole Bible teaches (with an objective of engaging and even confronting one's culture). Integrate and synthesize what the Bible's literary genres communicate.
Nature	• Historical and literary • Organic • Inductive • Diachronic (traces how salvation history progresses through time) • Bridging discipline: a little further from culture and a little closer to the biblical text	• Relatively ahistorical • Relatively universal • Relatively deductive • Relatively synchronic (focuses on what is true at a point in time) • Culminating and worldview-shaping discipline: a little closer to culture and a little further from the biblical text

Fig. 1.1. Comparing Biblical Theology and Systematic Theology[18]

Biblical theology must analyze and synthesize the whole canon on its own terms because it prioritizes literary context—the role that a Bible passage plays in its immediate context, section, book, corpus, testament, and the whole Bible. It is the result of careful reading—interpreting text after text by analyzing what the human authors and what the divine author intended to communicate. Biblical theology is essentially whole-Bible, redemptive-historical exegesis—analyzing text after text to discern what the authors intended to communicate. Exegesis draws the meaning out of a text, and biblical theology does that for the entire unified and God-breathed Bible.

Summary

Biblical theology is a way of analyzing and synthesizing the Bible that makes organic, salvation-historical connections with the whole canon on its own terms, especially regarding how the Old and New Testaments progress, integrate, and climax in Christ.

---

18. See also DeRouchie, *How to Understand and Apply the Old Testament*, 397–98; and D. A. Carson, "Systematic Theology and Biblical Theology," in Alexander and Rosner, *New Dictionary of Biblical Theology*, 89–104.

- *Organic connections* refer to how elements harmoniously grow together as parts of a whole.

- *Salvation-historical connections* refer to integrating key people and events within the Bible's storyline.

- Whole-Bible biblical theology analyzes and synthesizes *the whole canon.*

- Biblical theology analyzes and synthesizes the whole canon *on its own terms* because it prioritizes literary context. The task and nature of biblical theology are different than systematic theology.

REFLECTION QUESTIONS

1. What is one of your favorite ways of doing biblical theology? Why?

2. Do you tend to read the OT without Christian eyes? Why?

3. What is a biblical-theological theme that you would like to trace through the Bible?

4. Pick a novel you enjoy reading. How might you analyze and synthesize themes in that novel?

5. In your own words, how does biblical theology differ from systematic theology?

What Is Scripture's Storyline?

Jason S. DeRouchie

Christ fulfilled the Old Testament (Matt. 5:17; Luke: 24:27, 44; John 5:46) by means of a message and ministry related to God's kingdom (Luke 4:43; Acts 1:3). The kingdom relates to God's reign over God's people in God's land for God's glory.[1] And this theme stands at the core of God's purposes from Genesis to Revelation: God reigns, saves, and satisfies through covenant for his glory in Christ.

What Luke tags in Acts 1:3 as a "kingdom" message after Jesus's resurrection, he earlier describes as a message about the Messiah and the mission he would generate. Thus, Jesus "opened [the disciples'] minds to understand the Scriptures, and said to them, 'Thus it is written, that the Christ should suffer and on the third day rise from the dead, and that repentance for the forgiveness of sins should be proclaimed in his name to all nations, beginning from Jerusalem'" (Luke 24:45–47). In Jesus's view, to understand the OT rightly means that one will see a unified message climaxing in the Messiah––his death and resurrection––and in missions, by which God is declaring the intrusion of his eschatological kingdom (cf. Acts 20:25; 26:22–23; 28:23).

When the Old and New Testaments are read alongside one another, at least seven historical stages are apparent in God's kingdom program. The initial five are the foundation that is ultimately fulfilled in the last two. We use the acronym KINGDOM for easy memorization.

---

1. See also Jason S. DeRouchie, "Jesus' Bible: An Overview," in *What the Old Testament Authors Really Cared About: A Survey of Jesus' Bible*, ed. Jason S. DeRouchie (Grand Rapids: Kregel, 2013), 30–41. While Goldsworthy does not front the importance of God's *reign* for understanding *kingdom* language in the NT, he does similarly note that God's kingdom is characterized by "God's people in God's place under God's rule." Graeme Goldsworthy, *The Goldsworthy Trilogy* (Exeter, UK: Paternoster, 2000), 112.

		Kickoff and Rebellion	1. Creation, fall, and flood (ca. ? BC)
Old Testament Narrative History	**K I N G D O M**	Kickoff and Rebellion	1. Creation, fall, and flood (ca. ? BC)
		Instrument of Blessing	2. Patriarchs (ca. (1900–1550 BC)
		Nation Redeemed and Commissioned	3. Exodus, Sinai, and wilderness (ca. 1450–1400 BC)
		Government in the Land	4. Conquest and kingdoms (ca. 1400–600 BC)
		Dispersion and Return	5. Exile and initial restoration (ca. 600–400 BC)
New Testament Narrative History		Overlap of the Ages	6. Christ's work and the church age (ca. 4 BC–AD ?)
		Mission Accomplished	7. Christ's return and kingdom consummation (ca. AD ?–eternity)

Fig. 2.1. God's Kingdom-Building Program at a Glance

The major plot developments through this salvation story are marked by five overlapping covenants, the progression of which detail God's global purposes with humanity. The interrelationship of the covenants is like an hourglass, with the most universal scope occurring at the two ends and the work of Christ at the center. Theologians title the Adamic-Noahic, Abrahamic, Mosaic, and Davidic covenants in light of the covenant head or mediator through whom God entered into a relationship with his chosen ones. The *old* Mosaic covenant

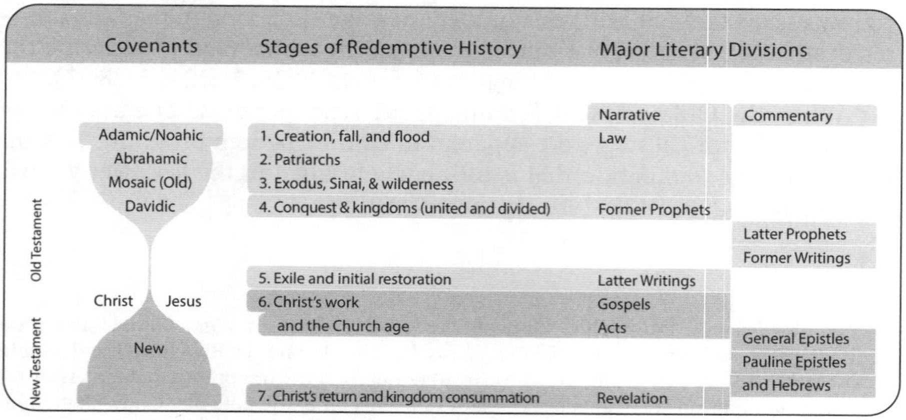

Fig. 2.2. The History of Redemption in the Context of Scripture

and era of punishment contrast with the *new covenant* in Christ, which climaxes all God's purposes in history (see Jer. 31:31–34; Heb. 8:6–13).[2]

Fig. 2.3. God's KINGDOM Program through Images

2. See Question 22.

The entire storyline of Scripture pivots on the person and work of Christ. He is the hub around which all turns and the fulcrum upon which all else is weighed. To him all redemptive history points, and through him God fulfills all previous promises. Scripture develops this messianic plotline by asserting over and over again that everything God does is *for his glory*. "I am the LORD; that is my name; my glory I give to no other" (Isa. 42:8). Yahweh's ultimate goal at every stage in his kingdom program is to display himself as the supreme Savior, Sovereign, and Satisfier of the world, ultimately through his messianic representative. As such, the Bible's grand narrative is *the story of God's glory in Christ*.[3] We will utilize a set of images (found in fig. 2.3) to help communicate the movement in Scripture's grand narrative.

Kickoff and Rebellion (Creation, Fall, and Flood)

God the creator is worthy of highest praise (1 Chron. 29:11; Rev. 4:11). He created humans to image him and commissioned them to display his greatness throughout the world (Gen. 1:26–28). The first couple failed to honor God rightly, and in light of Adam's covenantal headship, God now counts all the rest of humanity as having sinned in Adam (Rom. 5:12, 18–19). We are conceived as condemned sinners under God's just wrath (John 3:36; Eph. 2:1–3), and the result is that all become rebellious and thus fall short of glorifying God as he deserves (Rom. 1:21–23; 3:23). God had called our first parents to heed his voice lest they die (Gen. 2:17), and their rebellion resulted in God's driving them from his presence outside his garden-sanctuary (3:24).

Before subjecting the world to futility (3:16–19; Rom. 8:20–21), the Lord promised to reestablish cosmic order through a human deliverer, who would decisively overcome the curse and the power of evil (Gen. 3:15). The sustained human sin after the fall resulted in the flood (6:7–8), but God preserved a remnant whose hope was in the coming redeemer. He confirmed through Noah his covenant with creation, thus providing a context in which saving grace would become operative (6:12–13, 18; 8:21–9:1, 9–11). At the Tower of

---

3. See John Piper, "The Goal of God in Redemptive History," in *Desiring God: Meditations of a Christian Hedonist*, rev. and exp. (Sisters, OR: Multnomah, 2003), 308–21; cf. Thomas R. Schreiner, "A Biblical Theology of the Glory of God," in *For the Fame of God's Name: Essays in Honor of John Piper*, eds. Sam Storms and Justin Taylor (Wheaton, IL: Crossway, 2010), 215–34.

Babel, however, such mercy was matched by humankind's exalting themselves over God, resulting in Yahweh's punishing humanity once again (11:1–9).

Instrument of Blessing (Patriarchs)

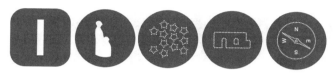

It was to the praise of his glorious grace that God elected and created a people for himself (Jer. 13:11; Isa. 43:6–7; 49:3; Eph. 1:4–6). Of the seventy families dispersed throughout the earth at Babel (Gen. 10:32), God set apart one through whom he would reverse the global curse with blessing. God's glory compelled Abraham to leave Mesopotamia by faith (Acts 7:2; Heb. 11:8), and Yahweh commissioned him:

> Go from your country and your kindred and your father's house to the land that I will show you so that I may make of you a great nation, and may bless you, and may make your name great. And there, be a blessing, so that I may bless those who bless you, and him who dishonors you I may curse. And the result will be that in you all the families of the ground shall be blessed. (Gen. 12:1–3, DeRouchie's translation)

The Abrahamic covenant has two stages. The Mosaic covenant fulfilled stage one: in going to the land, Abraham would become a great nation. The new covenant fulfilled stage two: through one of Abraham's representatives (i.e., the Messiah) displaying a life of blessing rather than curse, some from all the families of the earth would be restored into relationship with their Creator.

Though the patriarch's wife was barren (11:30) and though he realized Yahweh's promises would take a miracle, Abraham believed God could do for him what he could not do on his own, and God counted his faith in the offspring promise as righteousness (15:6; cf. 18:13–14). To exalt his faithfulness and anticipate future mercy, Yahweh vowed to fulfill his land promise to Abraham's offspring (15:17–18) and provided a substitute sacrifice in the place of Isaac (22:12–14). He also reaffirmed that he would bless the nations through a royal representative, now known to be from Judah, who would destroy evil and reestablish world peace (22:17–18; 24:60; 49:8–10). Through him and by means of spiritual adoption, Abraham would become a father of a multitude of nations (Gen. 17:4–6), and the land would expand to lands (22:17; 26:3–4), resulting in Abraham inheriting the world (Rom. 4:13). For such ultimate good, God sent Joseph to Egypt to preserve the children of

Jacob/Israel alive in the midst of famine while they awaited the Promised Land (45:7–8; 50:20, 24–25).

Nation Redeemed and Commissioned (Exodus, Sinai, and Wilderness)

God fulfilled his promises by sustaining and multiplying Israel through four hundred years of Egyptian bondage (Exod. 1:7; cf. Gen. 15:13–14). For the sake of his name and reputation, God brought the plagues on Egypt and redeemed Israel from slavery (Exod. 7:5; 9:15–16; 14:4; 2 Sam. 7:23).

Yahweh gave Israel his old covenant law through Moses in order to mediate his presence and display his holiness among the nations (Exod. 19:5–6). Through lives of radical love overflowing in sustained obedience (Lev. 19:28; Deut. 6:4–5; 10:16–19), Israel could bear witness to the worth and excellencies of God to a watching world (4:5–8). Yahweh would consider their perfect surrender as "righteousness" (6:2, 5), and they would enjoy lasting life (4:1; 8:1; 16:20; cf. Lev. 26:3–13; Deut. 28:1–14). Yahweh provided a means of atonement so that they could be near him, and he identified that his presence alone would distinguish them from the nations (Exod. 33:16; 34:6–9; Lev. 9:3–6; 10:3). He also restated his promise that a royal deliverer would arise from Jacob who would exercise international influence (Num. 24:7–9, 17–19).

Nevertheless, the majority were "stubborn," "rebellious," and "unbelieving" (Deut. 9:6–7, 23–24), and God did not overcome their hard-heartedness (29:4; cf. Rom. 11:7–8). Instead, God foretold that Israel would continue to rebel and suffer exile (Deut. 4:25–29; 31:16–17, 27–29), and God promised to restore Israel in a way that would exalt himself alone as the one who enables his people to love him and do what he commands (4:30–31; 30:3, 6–8).

Government in the Land (Conquest and Kingdoms)

As Israel entered into the land through the conquest, Yahweh exalted himself before the nations as the only true God. In the Canaanite Rahab's words, "Yahweh your God, he is God in the heavens above and on the earth beneath" (Josh. 2:11; cf. 8:24; 1 Sam. 4:8). The Lord was completely faithful to his promises that he had made to Israel (Josh. 21:43–45). As with Adam in Eden, he brought them into a new paradise (Exod. 15:17–18).

Nevertheless, the majority of the people soon forgot Yahweh and progressively became Canaanized: "They abandoned the LORD, the God of their fathers, who had brought them out of the land of Egypt. They went after other gods, from among the gods of the people who were around them, and bowed down to them. And they provoked the LORD to anger" (Judg. 2:12), resulting in their ruin. Without a faithful king, the people did what was right in their own eyes (21:25), and God's word became rare (1 Sam. 3:1). The people sought a king, which God granted, but they wanted one who would replace rather than represent Yahweh (8:7). Ultimately, because the leaders and community refused to listen to God's gracious appeal via his prophets, the united empire was divided (1 Kings 11:11, 13), and both the northern and southern kingdoms came to a ruinous end—exile and a destroyed temple (2 Kings 17:14–15, 18; ch. 25).

In spite of all the darkness and rebellion of Israel's rise and fall, Yahweh graciously renewed his promise of a coming royal redeemer (1 Sam. 2:10). King David foreshadowed this deliverer, and God declared that through David Yahweh would fulfill his universal kingdom purposes (2 Sam. 7:12, 16). One of David's offspring would be God's royal "Son" who would possess and bless the nations and destroy God's enemies (Ps. 2:7–9; 72:17; cf. 2 Sam. 7:14). God would establish and uphold David's throne with justice and righteousness (Isa. 9:7; cf. Luke 1:32). Bearing the name "Israel," this new representative servant-king would "bring back the preserved of Israel" (the people) and be "a light to the nations," thus extending Yahweh's saving reign to the end of the earth (Isa. 49:3, 6). The anticipated savior-king would proclaim Yahweh's end-time reign—the year of his favor and the day of his vengeance (52:7; 61:2). He also, while himself guiltless (50:9; 53:9), would, through a substitutionary death, satisfy God's wrath against sinners and, by his righteousness, "make many to be accounted righteous" (53:5, 10–11; cf. John 11:50–52; Rom. 5:19; 2 Cor. 5:21).

Dispersion and Return (Exile and Initial Restoration)

Yahweh cast Israel from the Promised Land because they failed to live for him and heed his voice (2 Kings 17:7; 2 Chron. 36:16). And from the depths of exile, Daniel pled, "Open your eyes and see our desolations, and the city that is called by your name. For we do not present our pleas before you because of our righteousness, but because of your great mercy. O Lord, hear; O Lord, forgive.

O Lord, pay attention and act. Delay not, *for your own sake*, O my God, because your city and your people are called by your name" (Dan. 9:18–19).

Yahweh is a God whose "steadfast love . . . never ceases" and whose "mercies never come to an end" (Lam. 3:22–23). Out of his boundless kindness, God promised that, in the latter days, "the God of heaven will set up a kingdom that shall never be destroyed" (Dan. 2:44) and that "one like a son of man" would receive "dominion and glory and a kingdom, that all peoples, nations, and languages should serve him" (7:13–14). Hence, *for his own sake*, the Lord would sustain Israel through exile and would ultimately use them as witnesses to his greatness in the world (Isa. 48:9, 11; Ezek. 36:22–23; cf. Acts 1:8).

Yahweh preserved his people. He prevented enemies from annihilating them (i.e., the book of Esther), and he restored them to the land (i.e., Ezra-Nehemiah). He commanded the Jews to rebuild the temple "that I may be glorified" (Hag. 1:8), and he also charged them to honor and fear him as the "great King" over all (Mal. 1:6, 14). But the story of God's glory still waited for its consummation.

While the seventy-year exile that Jeremiah foretold (Jer. 25:12; 29:10; cf. Ezra 1:1; Dan. 9:2) came to an end in relation to Cyrus's decree that the people could return to the land (Isa. 44:26–28; 2 Chron. 36:20–23), the royal servant had yet to arrive who would reconcile sinners to God (Isa. 49:6; 53:11; Dan. 9:24). Numerous features identify that the end of the OT era was not the end of God's kingdom purposes:

- The land had not returned to an Edenic state (Isa. 51:3; Ezek. 36:33–36).

- The nation was not fully reunited (Jer. 23:6; 31:31; Ezek. 37:22), with believing Gentiles in their midst (Isa. 2:2–4; 49:6; Jer. 12:16; 30:8–9).

- The Jews were still slaves (Ezra 9:8–9; Neh. 9:36), and the Davidic king was not yet reigning (Isa. 9:6–7; Jer. 23:5; 30:9; Ezek. 37:24).

- God's people did not enjoy a new covenant of universal, everlasting peace (Isa. 61:8–9; Jer. 31:31–34; 32:40; Ezek. 37:26).

- God's people did not have new inner dispositions to love and obey the Lord (Deut. 30:6, 8; Isa. 2:3; 42:4; Jer. 31:33; 32:39–40; Ezek. 36:26–27).

- God's people did not fully enjoy his presence (Ezek. 36:27; 37:27–28).

Yahweh had not yet fully realized his kingdom purposes. The king who was to bring global blessing still needed to come.

Overlap of the Ages (Christ's Work and the Church Age)

As we move into the NT narrative history, one of the mysterious parts of God's kingdom program was the way Jesus's first coming was as a suffering servant, and only in his second coming would he show himself fully as a conquering king (Heb. 9:28). In his initial appearing, he brought the future into the middle of history. He proclaimed "the year of the LORD's favor," but only later would he bring "the day of vengeance of our God" (Isa. 61:2; cf. Luke 4:19). Today we live in an overlap of the ages: Christ has delivered us from "the present evil age" (Gal. 1:4) yet only in a way that lets us taste "the powers of the age to come" (Heb. 6:5).

Thus, "the sufferings of this present time are not worth comparing with the glory that is to be revealed to us" (Rom. 8:18). As Paul says, "For the grace of God has appeared, bringing salvation for all people, training us to renounce ungodliness and worldly passions, and to live self-controlled, upright, and godly lives in the present age, waiting for our blessed hope, the appearing of the glory of our great God and Savior Jesus Christ" (Titus 2:11–13). Already we have been "born again to a living hope through the resurrection of Jesus Christ from the dead," and that hope points to "an inheritance that is imperishable, undefiled, and unfading, kept in heaven for you, who by God's power are being guarded through faith for a salvation ready to be revealed in the last time" (1 Peter 1:3–5; cf. Eph. 1:3–14). Figure 2.4 attempts to visualize the *already* but *not yet* aspects of the kingdom in this overlap of the ages.

In the fullness of time, "God sent forth his Son" (Gal. 4:4), as the very Word who was God "became flesh and dwelt among us" (John 1:14). And "by sending his own Son in the likeness of sinful flesh and for sin, [God] condemned sin in the flesh, in order that the righteous requirement of the law might be fulfilled in us" (Rom. 8:3–4). The kingdom is *already* here because Jesus came to earth to appease God's wrath toward the sin of Israel and the world. Jesus is the Christ, the promised royal deliver, who came "to give his life as a ransom for many" (Mark 10:45). He is "the Lamb of God, who takes away the sins of the world" (John 1:29), and by his life, death, and resurrection, he inaugurated the new covenant (Luke 22:20; Heb. 9:15) and new creation (2 Cor. 5:17). In the "great exchange" of the ages, God counts every believer's sin to Christ and Christ's righteousness to every believer (Isa. 53:11; Rom. 5:18–19; 2 Cor. 5:21).

Jesus lived for the glory of his Father (John 7:18; 17:4), and his death and resurrection vindicated God's righteousness and exalted God's glory (John

12:27–28; 17:1). "God put forward [Jesus Christ] as a propitiation by his blood . . . so that he might be just and the justifier of the one who has faith in Jesus" (Rom. 3:25–26). "Christ redeemed us from the curse of the law by becoming a curse for us . . . so that in Christ Jesus the blessing of Abraham might come to the Gentiles" (Gal. 3:13–14). God's glory raised Christ from the dead (Rom. 6:4) and through this magnified Christ (Heb. 2:9; 1 Peter 1:21).

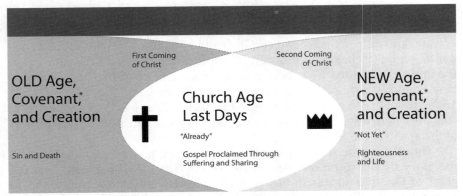

*At one level, the old and new covenants do not overlap, for Jesus "makes the first one obsolete" and "does away with the first in order to establish the second" (Heb. 8:13; 10:9). At another level, however, because the old (Mosaic) covenant represents the age of death in Adam, the writer of Hebrews can add, "And what is becoming obsolete and growing old is ready to vanish away" (8:13), noting that while "the end of the ages" is already upon us (9:26), the consummation of "the age to come" has not yet been realized (6:5; cf. 2 Cor. 3:11).

Fig. 2.4. Redemptive History and the Overlap of the Ages [4]

Jesus and his apostles proclaimed the good news of God's kingdom (Luke 4:43; Acts 1:1–3; 20:25; 28:23), which is nothing less than God's end-time reign manifest through "the glory of God in the face of Jesus Christ" (2 Cor. 4:6; cf. 1 Tim. 1:11). The good news is the message "that Christ died for our sins in accordance with the Scriptures, that he was buried, that he was raised on the third day in accordance with the Scripture, and that he appeared to Cephas, and then to the twelve" (1 Cor. 15:3–5). By means of faith-filled, Spirit-empowered disciples bearing witness to Christ, God's reign and glory have spread from Jerusalem to Judea and Samaria and to the ends of the earth (Acts 1:8). Under Christ's universal authority, the church must make disciples of all nations for the sake of Christ's name, ever trusting the powerful presence of the reigning king to guard his servants and open hearts to the gospel (Matt. 28:18–20; Rom. 1:5).

---

4.   This figure originally appeared in Jason S. DeRouchie, ed., *What the Old Testament Authors Really Cared About: A Survey of Jesus' Bible* (Grand Rapids: Kregel, 2013), 39. Used with permission.

Mission Accomplished (Christ's Return and Kingdom Consummation)

God's mercy, wrath, and power make known "the riches of his glory for vessels of mercy, which he has prepared beforehand for glory" (Rom. 9:22–23). Jesus came to satisfy our deepest longing and to help us see and savor his glory (John 6:35; 17:24). His return will be glorious (Matt. 16:27; 25:31), as we "see the Son of Man coming on the clouds of heaven with power and great glory" (24:30). Only those who "fear God and give him glory" will escape divine wrath when the Son of Man returns to be glorified in his saints (Rev. 14:7; 2 Thess. 1:9–10; cf. Matt. 16:27; 24:30; 25:31; John 17:24).

Even now, those around the throne of the conquering Lion and slain Lamb are declaring him worthy to carry out God's decreed purposes to punish and save (Rev. 5:9–10). And the redeemed mixed multitude will one day cry together, "Salvation belongs to our God who sits on the throne, and to the Lamb!" (7:10). In that day, "[God] will dwell with them, and they will be his people, and God himself will be with them as their God. He will wipe away every tear from their eyes, and death shall be no more, neither shall there be mourning, nor crying, nor pain anymore, for the former things have passed away" (21:3–4). And "the glory of God" will give the city light—a glory that will be localized in none other than "the Lamb" (21:23). And "by its light will the nations walk . . . and there will be no night there" (21:24–25). "No longer will there be anything accursed, but the throne of God and of the Lamb will be in it, and his servants will worship him. . . . They will need no light or lamp or sun, for the Lord God will be their light, and they will reign forever and ever" (22:3, 5).

In view of these realities, Jesus proclaims, "I am the root and the descendant of David, the bright and morning star. . . . Surely I am coming soon" (22:16, 20). And we say with John, "Amen. Come, Lord Jesus!" (22:20).

Summary

Genesis through Revelation reveals a kingdom history that is truly *his-story*—a story of God's glory in Christ. God's kingdom program develops in seven stages. In the first five stages, which detail the OT narrative history, God identifies the problem and makes promises. In the final two stages, God supplies the solution and fulfills those promises. One can remember all seven stages through the acronym KINGDOM:

1. Kickoff and rebellion: Creation, fall, and flood
2. Instrument of blessing: Patriarchs

3. Nation redeemed and commissioned: Exodus, Sinai, and wilderness
4. Government in the land: Conquest and kingdoms
5. Dispersion and return: Exile and initial restoration
6. Overlap of the ages: Christ's work and the church age
7. Mission accomplished: Christ's return and kingdom consummation

All salvation history points to Christ, and he is the decisive one who fulfills all our hopes, to the praise of God's glorious grace.

REFLECTION QUESTIONS

1. What are the four elements to which God's kingdom relates?

2. How do we summarize Scripture's theme that stands at the core of God's purposes from Genesis to Revelation? How would you tweak the statement to be more faithful to the biblical message?

3. Using the KINGDOM acronym, what are the seven stages in God's kingdom program?

4. How might you prove to a friend that "the entire storyline of Scripture pivots on the person and work of Christ"?

5. Supply one example of how *each* of the seven stages in God's kingdom program magnifies God's glory. That is, in what ways does God act *for his own sake* throughout the storyline of Scripture? How should our hearts respond to the role of God's glory from Genesis to Revelation?

How Does Biblical Theology Help Us See Christ in the Old Testament?

Jason S. DeRouchie

The only Bible Jesus had was what we call the OT, and he said that it was about him. Jesus highlighted that his Scriptures bore witness about him (John 5:39); that Abraham saw his day and was glad (8:56); that Moses wrote of him (5:46); that prophets, righteous people, and kings longed for his coming (Matt. 13:17; Luke 10:24); and that everything that the OT said concerning him would be fulfilled (Luke 24:27, 44).[1] Moreover, following his resurrection, Jesus opened the minds of his disciples "to understand the Scriptures, and said to them, 'Thus it is written, that the Christ should suffer and on the third day rise from the dead, and that repentance for the forgiveness of sins should be proclaimed in his name to all nations, beginning from Jerusalem'" (Luke 24:45–47; cf. Acts 1:3, 8; 3:18, 24; 10:43). According to Jesus, when we faithfully "understand the Scriptures," what we will see in the OT is a message of the Messiah—his death and his resurrection—and of the global mission he would generate.

Paul, too, was an OT preacher who saw in his Bible a message of God's kingdom focused on the Messiah and the church he would build (Acts 26:22–23). While preaching from the OT, he "decided to know nothing among [the Corinthian church] except Christ and him crucified" (1 Cor. 2:2). May the Lord raise up more OT preachers in our day who preach like that!

Paul affirmed that the OT initially promised the good news embodied in the person and work of Jesus Christ. As an apostle, he was "set apart for the gospel of God, which he promised beforehand through his prophets in the holy Scriptures, concerning his Son" (Rom. 1:1–3). The NT realizes what the

---

1. See also Jason S. DeRouchie, *How to Understand and Apply the Old Testament: Twelve Steps from Exegesis to Theology* (Phillipsburg, NJ: P&R, 2017), 481–89.

OT first anticipated—the good news that the reigning God would eternally save and satisfy believing sinners through Christ's life, death, and resurrection. The progress from creation to the fall to redemption to consummation is in a very real sense *his*-story, and the gospel we enjoy was anticipated, foreshadowed, and foretold much earlier (cf. John 1:45; 5:39, 46; 8:56; Heb. 11:13; 1 Peter 1:10–11).

God created all things by the Son, through the Son, and for the Son—the one who "is before all things" and in whom "all things hold together" (Col. 1:16–17). "All things" would include the OT, which means that God inspired the initial three-fourths of the Christian Scriptures for the glory of the divine Son. We are supposed to see and celebrate Christ when we read the OT.

To do this faithfully requires a multi-form approach because Jesus fulfills the OT in various ways (Matt. 5:17; Luke 24:44; Acts 13:27, 32–33). The Christian interpreter, therefore, must follow the signals God supplies us in his inerrant and unified Word so as to properly magnify the Messiah and his work. This chapter briefly overviews seven possible ways to see and celebrate Christ in the OT.

Biblical Theology Helps Us See and Celebrate Christ through the Old Testament's Direct Messianic Predictions

Peter stressed, "What God foretold by the mouth of *all* the prophets, that his Christ would suffer, he thus fulfilled" (Acts 3:18). Every one of the prophets from Moses onward anticipated the Messiah's work and mission (3:22–24; 10:43). The OT is loaded with explicit and implicit predictions. "He was wounded for our transgressions; he was crushed for our iniquities; upon him was the chastisement that brought us peace, and with his stripes we are healed" (Isa. 53:5). These words in Isaiah portray a servant of God who would suffer as a substitute for many, and Peter, writing about the Christ, saw this text fulfilled in the person of Jesus: "He himself bore our sins in his body on the tree, that we might die to sin and live to righteousness. By his wounds we have been healed" (1 Peter 2:24). At times, the element of prediction-fulfillment is even more pronounced, as when Micah 5:2 foretells that the royal deliverer would be born in Bethlehem, and then Matthew 2:6 explicitly asserts that it happened just as the prophet wrote. Christ fulfills the OT as the specific focus or goal of direct OT Messianic predictions and redemptive-historical hopes.

Biblical Theology Helps Us See and Celebrate Christ through the Old Testament's Salvation-Historical Story and Trajectories

The OT does a great job creating problems for which Jesus is the solution. Both the Old and New Testaments are framed by the narrative of redemption—a historical plot designed to magnify that God reigns, saves, and satisfies through covenant for his glory in Christ. The entire storyline progresses from creation to the fall to redemption to consummation and highlights the work of Jesus as the decisive turning point in salvation-history.[2] "The Law and the Prophets were until John [the Baptist]; since then the good news of the kingdom of God is preached" (Luke 16:16). "The law was our guardian until Christ came, in order that we might be justified by faith. But now that faith has come, we are no longer under a guardian, for in Christ Jesus you are all sons of God, through faith" (Gal. 3:24–26).

The plotline of the Bible is guided by five major salvation-historical covenants, each of which finds its terminus in Christ and the first four of which are named after the covenant head or mediator (Adamic-Noahic → Abrahamic → Mosaic → Davidic → new).[3] We also see that various themes develop or progress as God gradually reveals more of himself and his ways through biblical revelation. Some of the main ones would include covenant, God's kingdom, law, temple and God's presence, atonement, people of God, and mission, all of which find focus in Jesus. Christ fulfills all of the OT's salvation-historical trajectories.

Biblical Theology Helps Us See and Celebrate Christ by Highlighting How the Old and New Ages, Creations, and Covenants Are Similar Yet Distinct

The progress of the biblical covenants and the history of redemption display numerous points of similarity and contrast, many of which are centered in the person of the divine Son. For example, whereas Adam disobeyed and brought death to all, Christ obeys and brings life to many (Rom. 5:18–19). Whereas God used the blood of bulls and goats to picture atonement in the old covenant, Christ's own substitutionary sacrifice provides the ground for eternal redemption (Heb. 9:11–14). Whereas access to Yahweh's presence in the temple was restricted to the high priest on the Day of Atonement, Christ's priestly work opens the way for all in him to enjoy God's presence (9:24–26; 10:19–22). Whereas the nations needed to come to the tabernacle/temple to encounter the Lord's presence in the old covenant, the Spirit of Christ now empowers the church in its witness to the nations from Jerusalem to the ends of the earth (Matt. 28:18–20; Acts 1:8). The work of Jesus creates both continuities and discontinuities. We can celebrate his work more by identifying the patterns and transformations.

Biblical Theology Helps Us See and Celebrate Christ by Noting How Old Testament Characters, Events, and Institutions Clarify and Anticipate His Person and Work

The author of Hebrews said the OT law was "a shadow of good things to come" (Heb. 10:1). Similarly, Paul asserted that clean and unclean food laws, the various Jewish festivals and monthly sacrificial calendar, and even

---

2. See Questions 2 (DeRouchie's KINGDOM) and 39 §2 (Roberts's progressive King[dom]) for two different ways to summarize Scripture's plotline.
3. See Questions 6 and 22.

the Sabbath were each "a shadow of the things to come, but the substance belongs to Christ" (Col. 2:16–17). In the NT, these anticipations and pointers are called "types" or "examples" that in turn find their counter or fulfillment in Jesus as their ultimate realization. God structured the progressive development of salvation-history in such a way that certain OT characters (e.g., Adam, Melchizedek, Moses, David), events (e.g., the flood, the exodus, the return to the land), and institutions or objects (e.g., the Passover lamb, the temple, the priesthood) bear meanings that clarify and predictively anticipate the life and work of Jesus the Messiah.

Biblical Theology Helps Us See and Celebrate Christ as We Revel in Yahweh's Identity and Activity

You will recall that Jesus said that "no one has ever seen God" the Father except the Son (John 1:18; 6:46), but that "whoever has seen me has seen the Father" (John 14:9). What this means is that when Yahweh becomes embodied in a human form in the OT, we are most likely meeting the preincarnate Son. We see him in the stories of Abraham's third guest (Gen. 18), Jacob's wrestling opponent (Gen. 32:24–30), Joshua's "commander of the army of the LORD" (Josh. 5:13–15), Isaiah's Lord on the throne (Isa. 6:1; John 12:41), Ezekiel's exalted king (Ezek. 1:26), Daniel's "son of man" (Dan. 7:13–14), and the numerous manifestations of the "angel/messenger of the LORD" (e.g., Gen. 16:7–13; 22:11–18; Exod. 3:2; Num. 20:16; 22:22–35).

With this, when we hear Yahweh speaking or acting in the OT as the object of people's faith in the OT, we are seeing the very one who would embody himself in the person of Jesus. The Word who was "in the beginning . . . with God . . . was God" (John 1:1–2). The very Son who would be named Jesus "was in the form of God" (Phil. 2:6), was the very "image of the invisible God" (Col. 1:16), and was "the radiance of the glory of God and the exact imprint of his nature" (Heb. 1:3). Thus, the author of Hebrews could attribute Moses's reproach for *God's* sake as a reproach endured for *Christ*: "He considered the reproach of Christ greater wealth than the treasures of Egypt, for he was looking to the reward" (Heb. 11:26). This is also why Jude could identify Israel's deliverer at the exodus as *Jesus*: "Now I want to remind you . . . that Jesus, who saved a people out of the land of Egypt, afterward destroyed those who did not believe" (Jude 5). Who fought for Israel and rescued them at the exodus? Was it not Yahweh? Yes! And it was *Jesus*![4] When we meet Yahweh in the OT, we are catching glimpses of the divine Son.

---

4. Some manuscripts read "the Lord" rather than Jesus, and English translations like KJV, NASB, NIV follow this tradition. However, I believe reading "Jesus" here has the strongest support from a variety of early witnesses, and the variants are best explained as interpreters struggling with the notion of Jesus acting in history before his incarnation. For a defense of reading "Jesus," see Philipp Bartholomä, "Did Jesus Save the People out of Egypt: A Reexamination of a Textual Problem in Jude 5," NovT 50 (2008): 143–58.

Biblical Theology Helps Us See and Celebrate Christ as We Consider the Ethical Ideals Found in Old Testament Law and Wisdom

The OT is filled with stories of sinners who needed a savior. The Mosaic law pointed to the importance for Christ in the way it identified and multiplied sin (Rom. 3:20; 5:20; cf. 7:7–12; Gal. 3:19), imprisoned the sinful (Rom. 3:19–20; 8:2–3; Gal. 3:10, 13, 22), and showed everyone's need for atonement. The law by its nature, therefore, predicted Christ as "the end of the law for righteousness to everyone who believes" (Rom. 10:4).

Furthermore, Jesus is the perfect embodiment of God's character and the ideal image of dependence, law keeping, wisdom, praise, and perseverance. Paul stressed both that in the law we have "the embodiment of knowledge and truth" (Rom. 2:20) and that "the law is holy, and the commandment is holy and righteous and good" (7:12). The same can be said of Christ, who remained sinless (2 Cor. 5:21; Heb. 4:15; 1 Peter 2:22; 1 John 3:5) and "became to us wisdom from God, righteousness and sanctification and redemption" (1 Cor. 1:30). Figures like Moses, David, and Zechariah anticipated the righteousness displayed through the gospel (Rom. 1:16–17), and it is that righteousness that is bound up in Christ's perfect obedience climaxing in his death on the cross (3:22–26; Phil. 2:8), through which we are justified by faith (Rom. 3:27–30; 5:1). He is "the righteous one" who makes "many to be accounted righteous" (Isa. 53:11; cf. Rom. 5:19), and it is because of the saving righteousness that he brings that he is called, "The LORD is our righteousness" (Jer. 23:6; cf. 2 Cor. 5:21). Jesus incarnated the portrait of the worshipping sufferer and victorious king of the Psalms. He perfectly kept his Father's commandments and abided in his love (John 15:10).

As God's word made flesh, Jesus manifests in his person the essence of every ethical ideal aligned with Yahweh's revealed will, and it is this perfection that is then imputed to believers (Rom. 5:18–19; 8:4; 2 Cor. 5:21; Phil. 3:9). With every law and every wise saying in the OT, we find fodder to magnify the greatness of Christ on our behalf.

Biblical Theology Helps Us See and Celebrate Christ as We Use the Old Testament to Instruct or Guide Others in the Law of Love

The NT authors recognized that the OT law was "imposed until the time of reformation" (Heb. 9:10) and that "the law was our guardian until Christ came. . . . But now that faith has come, we are no longer under a guardian" (Gal. 3:24–25). Nevertheless, Paul had no hesitation declaring that "all Scripture [which in context principally meant the OT] is . . . profitable for teaching, for reproof, for correction, and for training in righteousness" (2 Tim. 3:16). In this context, the apostle could even charge Timothy, "Preach the word" (4:2), urging this Christian pastor to help his people find hope in the gospel mostly from the OT Scriptures (cf. Rom. 1:1–3). For Paul and the other apostles, while the old covenant law and wisdom no longer bore direct authority in the Christian's life, it still bore indirect authority when read through the mediation of Christ. Thus, Paul could say to Timothy about the OT, "From childhood [as a Jew, see Acts 16:1 and 2 Tim. 1:5] you have been acquainted with the sacred writings [i.e., the OT], which are able to make you wise for salvation *through faith in Christ Jesus*" (2 Tim. 3:15, emphasis added). The OT continues to matter for Christians, but we must approach it through the light and lens of Jesus. Jesus's coming unlocks the significance of the OT text, and through him we now have access to a massive amount of Scripture that can encourage us with promises (2 Cor. 1:20; cf. 6:16–7:1) and clarify how to love God and love our neighbor (Rom. 16:25–26; 2 Cor. 3:14).

Some of the OT promises that "find their Yes in [Christ]" (2 Cor. 1:20) are those that predicted how new covenant believers would live out God's law in the day when hearts were circumcised (Deut. 30:6, 8) and when God would put his Spirit in his transformed people (Ezek. 36:27; Jer. 12:16). In that day of restoration, all God's children "shall be taught by the LORD" (Isa. 54:13; cf. John 6:44–45), and having the law written on their hearts, "they shall know [the LORD], from the least of them to the greatest" (Jer. 31:33–34; cf. 1 John 2:20–21, 27).

We who are in Christ are now empowered to keep the "precepts" of the law, as we live with circumcised hearts by the power of the Spirit (Rom. 2:26, 29; cf. 2:14–15; see Deut. 30:10; Ezek. 36:27). We fulfill the law as we love our neighbor (Rom. 13:8–10; cf. Matt. 7:12; Gal. 6:2). Christ is our teacher (Isa. 42:4; 51:4; Matt. 17:5; 28:20), and how he fulfills the law now clarifies for us what it means to follow God (Matt. 5:17–19; cf. 1 Cor. 9:21; James 1:25; 2:8, 12). In Christ we find a new pattern for surrender and service (Phil. 2:5–7; Heb. 12:1–3; 1 Peter 2:21; 1 John 2:6), and in Jesus we experience true pardon (Rom. 3:23–26; 5:8–9, 18–19; 8:3–4; 2 Cor. 5:21), which in turn supplies both power to obey (Rom. 1:16; 6:22; 8:13; 1 Cor. 1:18; 15:10) and promises that motivate this obedience (2 Cor. 1:20; 7:1; 2 Peter 1:4; 1 John 3:3; cf. Isa. 41:10; Phil. 1:6; 1 Thess. 5:23–24; Heb. 13:20–21). When we use the OT to instruct or guide others, we have an opportunity to celebrate the sanctifying work of the divine Son.

Summary

Biblical theology helps us to see and celebrate Christ in the OT in at least seven ways. Not all operate at the same time, but each of these provides readers and teachers of Scripture fresh avenues to make much of Jesus. See and celebrate Christ in the OT by:

- reading the OT's direct messianic predictions;

- considering the OT's salvation-historical story and trajectories;

- recognizing similarities and contrasts between the old and new ages, creations, and covenants;

- identifying OT characters, events, and institutions or objects that clarify and anticipate the person and work of Christ;

- reveling in Yahweh's identity and activity;

- observing how the old covenant law characterizes the nature of perfect righteousness and wisdom; and

- using the OT to instruct or guide others and experiencing the power to love and thus fulfill the law.

REFLECTION QUESTIONS

1. When we rightly "understand the Scriptures," what message should we find in the OT (Luke 24:45–47; cf. Acts 26:22–23)?

2. What did Paul say was "promised beforehand through his prophets in the holy Scriptures" (Rom. 1:2)?

3. What are some of the similarities and contrasts that allow us to see and celebrate Christ in the OT?

4. Why should we see and celebrate Christ when the OT discloses Yahweh's character and acts?

5. How does considering the OT's ethical ideals help us see and celebrate Christ?

How Do the Old and New Testaments Progress, Integrate, and Climax in Christ?

Oren R. Martin

Note the italicized words in how we define biblical theology:

> Biblical theology is a way of analyzing and synthesizing the Bible that makes organic, salvation-historical connections with the whole canon on its own terms, especially regarding *how the Old and New Testaments progress, integrate, and climax in Christ.*[1]

The Holy One has come into our midst speaking his life-giving Word. Before the fall God spoke to Adam and Eve, and quite literally, their lives depended on their trusting—or distrusting—his good word. And after the fall, their only hope was the gracious promise that one day an offspring of the woman would come and victoriously triumph over the lying serpent (Gen. 3:15). Ever since that promise, God has continued to speak to and sustain his people. Reflecting on the long and variegated history of God's people, the author of Hebrews writes, "Long ago, at many times and in many ways, God spoke to our fathers by the prophets" (1:1). Whether to Adam, Noah, Abraham, Moses, Israel, David, or the prophets, God has spoken and has authorized his words to be written down as a witness to his people that they might know him and walk in his ways for his name's sake (Exod. 34:1, 27;

---

1. See Andrew David Naselli, *How to Understand and Apply the New Testament: Twelve Steps from Exegesis to Theology* (Phillipsburg, NJ: P&R, 2017), ch. 9.

Deut. 31:24–29; Isa. 30:8; Jer. 30:1–2; Hab. 2:2). And these words have sustained and given hope to God's people as they have waited for him to fulfill his saving promises.

"But," the author of Hebrews goes on to say, "in these last days he has spoken to us by his Son" (1:2). That is, all prior revelation pointed to something—or rather *someone*—greater. The God who spoke creation into existence has spoken finally and definitely in Jesus Christ, the Word *par excellence*. The One who is God, who was in the beginning with God, has come from God to make him known (John 1:1–18). And, in fulfillment of his OT witness, God by his Spirit of Truth authorized the apostles and prophets to bear witness in writing about the final prophet, the Word, the Lord Jesus Christ (John 15:26–27). It is our task, therefore—indeed our life-giving, joy-producing privilege—to believe and understand the riches of God's Word as he has made it known throughout the history of his saving purposes and as he has guided history toward its goal. This undertaking, then, necessarily involves both analyzing and synthesizing the Old and New Testaments as they progress, integrate, and reach their goal in Christ.

Biblical Theology Must See the Parts in Light of the Whole

But why *must* we both analyze and synthesize the Old and New Testaments as they progress, integrate, and climax in Christ? Unfortunately, Scripture can be examined and taught as though it were a diverse collection of unrelated stories. It is difficult to see how the multifaceted parts fit together to form a unified whole. Is it really possible to understand how, and if, the stories fit together? One can understand and teach each story independently—Adam in the garden, Noah in the ark, Abram going to an unknown destination, Moses leading the people through the wilderness to the Promised Land, David fighting Goliath. Nevertheless, to see how each part contributes to and fits together in light of the whole is often daunting, even unattainable. What we need is a picture that helps guide the reader along, story by story, toward the end. But do the individual stories fit together to form one grand story? Is there such a picture? The answer is found not merely in a picture, but in a person, Jesus Christ.[2]

The person and work of Jesus Christ provide the picture and goal, and each part of the biblical story contributes to the whole of God's saving purposes *in him*. The redemptive saga is indeed *his*-story, and to miss him is to miss the point of the overarching narrative (John 5:37–40). The good news of Jesus Christ is that the eternal Son of God, the second person of the Godhead, who is truly and fully God, became truly and fully man, and through his faithful life, suffering, death, and resurrection accomplished what we could not accomplish for ourselves—salvation from the domain of darkness into his

---

2. See Question 2.

blessed kingdom. This gospel message provides the revelational light shining brightly upon the mysteries once concealed. This story of the One who was and is the form of God, who has taken the form of a servant, reveals that the individual stories fit together to form a glorious picture of why the Old and New Testaments progress, integrate, and climax in Christ. By the illuminating presence of God the Holy Spirit (1 Cor. 2:6–16), then, the reader must labor to see how each part contributes to the whole in order to truly understand the rich, life-saving contours of the grand masterpiece, the gospel of the glory of the blessed God (1 Tim. 1:11).

How Biblical Theology Can See the Parts in Light of the Whole

Given the nature of Scripture, then, biblical theology must analyze and synthesize the Old and New Testaments as they progressively reach their goal in Christ. Scripture is a unity because it is from the one God who has made himself known and has declared the end from the beginning (Isa. 46:10). So, to do biblical theology rightly is not merely to survey the individual parts, but to see how each part fits into the whole of God's redemptive purposes in Christ. Because the Old and New Testaments constitute the whole of God's authoritative Word, they integrate and cohere with one another. This coherence is evident when we study the parts in light of the whole, and the whole makes sense of the individual parts. To analyze and synthesize Scripture well, then, we must study it in context. And we must keep more than one context in mind in order to do justice to all that God has revealed, from beginning to end. When analyzing and synthesizing the Old and New Testaments, it is important to keep in mind the immediate context, the covenantal context, and the canonical or christological context.[3]

> 1. *The Immediate Context.* To begin, we must analyze the immediate context on the grammatical-historical level by discerning elements such as genre and grammar and by making general observations of the text. Key question: What did the (human) author of *this specific passage* intend to communicate?

---

3. Richard Lints explains this process in what he calls the three horizons of redemptive interpretation—the *textual* horizon (immediate context at the grammatical-historical level), the *epochal* horizon (context of the period of revelation), and the *canonical* horizon (context of the entirety of revelation). Richard Lints, *The Fabric of Theology: A Prolegomena to Evangelical Theology* (Grand Rapids: Eerdmans, 1993), 293–311. For a complete unpacking of these three levels at work within the context of biblical interpretation, see Jason S. DeRouchie, *How to Understand and Apply the Old Testament: Twelve Steps from Exegesis to Theology* (Phillipsburg, NJ: P&R, 2017) and Naselli, *How to Understand and Apply the New Testament.*

2. *The Covenantal Context*. Next, we must study a passage in its covenantal context—that is, how it fits in God's sovereign, unfolding purposes, "which he set forth in Christ as a plan for the fullness of time, to unite all things in him, things in heaven and things on earth" (Eph. 1:9–10). God's covenants mark how he personally deals with humanity, and his covenants culminate in the new covenant in Christ.[4] God's revelation progresses because his redemptive purposes develop and unfold as he leads his people out of sin and idolatry into his salvation in Christ Jesus. Key question: How should we understand a particular text *in light of what God had already revealed?* For example, how does the covenant with Noah advance what God promised Adam after the fall, or how does the covenant with Israel at Sinai advance what God promised Abraham, or how does the new covenant in Jeremiah 31 pick up and advance the previous covenants with Moses and David?

3. *The Canonical Context*. Finally, interpreters synthesize the Bible's message when they understand a passage in its final context, the whole God-breathed canon of Scripture, which is fulfilled in the much-anticipated arrival of the person and work of Christ (Gal. 4:4). Key question: How should we understand a passage *in light of all Scripture, in relation to the person and work of Christ?* The process of analyzing and synthesizing how the Old and New Testaments progress, integrate, and climax in Christ is incomplete until we study every passage in its final context, the canon of Scripture, where God discloses the final meaning of his Word.

Scripture declares, then, that God fulfills all of his saving purposes and promises in Christ, which means the task of biblical interpretation is incomplete until it views all the parts in the light of him. For example, Jesus's own person and work provide his disciples the interpretive key for understanding the OT in relation to him (Luke 24:27, 44), and had his opponents rightly understood the words of Moses, they would have believed in Jesus, for Moses wrote of him (John 5:46; cf. Deut. 18:15–22; Acts 4:17–26). In other words, had they truly known and believed God's Word, then they would have seen *in Christ* that God fulfills his promises. Indeed, all the promises of God find their yes *in him* (2 Cor. 1:20). For example, Christ Jesus is the final revelation of God (John 1:14; Heb. 1:1–2), the second and last Adam (Rom. 5:12–21; 1 Cor. 15:45), and Abraham's offspring (Matt. 1:1; Gal. 3:16). He is the true, obedient Son (Matt. 2:15; 3:17; cf. Exod. 4:22; Ps. 89:27[28]) who accomplishes a better exodus from a greater enemy (Col. 1:12–13); the true temple through whom is access to God (John 1:14; 2:18–22); the life-giving vine(yard) who bears

---

4. See Questions 6 and 22.

fruit (John 15:1–11; cf. Isa. 5; Hos. 9:10); and the great high priest and sacrifice of a better covenant (Heb. 7–8). He is David's greater Son and King (Matt. 1:1; 22:41–46; Rom. 1:2–3); the true Shepherd (John 10; Ezek. 34; Ps. 23); the better Solomon in whom are hidden all the treasures of wisdom and knowledge (Matt. 12:42; Col. 2:3); and the great "I Aм" who preexists Abraham (John 8:58; cf. Exod. 3:14). Finally, he is the Lord and Christ who wins the new heaven and new earth, which is brilliantly described in a complex of OT imagery such as a paradisiacal new Eden, new Jerusalem, and cosmological temple that is, in the climax of the covenants, filled with God's presence (Rev. 21–22; Isa. 65:17; 66:22; Ezek. 40–48). So, in this christological light, we must give careful attention to all biblical texts and rightly interpret them within their respective contexts—immediate, covenantal, and canonical. Only then can we reach sound biblical and theological conclusions in the final light of the person and work of Christ.

This framework presupposes that Scripture constitutes a unified text with a developing story that is heading toward an appointed goal to achieve God's saving purposes in Jesus. In other words, not only does God progressively reveal his word in and through history, but also he is guiding it toward his appointed end—the Lord Jesus Christ. Michael Horton is correct when he says that when reading Scripture, "eschatology should be a lens and not merely a locus."[5] That is, eschatology—the study of last things—enters not at the end of theology but at the beginning, for the beginning anticipates the end as we wait for a divine solution to the problem of sin—a serpent-crushing offspring of the woman. Hence, the entire Bible is eschatological since it focuses upon and culminates in the arrival of the King, the Lord Jesus Christ, who ushers in the kingdom of God and fulfills what God intended for humanity and the world. Yet the end is not simply a return to the beginning, for the last Adam undoes the disastrous effects of the first Adam, and through his life, death, resurrection, and ascension, he ushers in a new creation where sin and death will be no more.

If we interpret Scripture in a way that does not lead to Christ, then we have missed the point of God's revelation and have not received it like Jesus himself instructed his disciples to receive it. This does not mean that every passage of Scripture leads to Christ in precisely the same way, but it does mean that every passage of Scripture leads to Christ in some way, which we discover through analyzing and synthesizing every passage in the light of him.

Summary

From beginning to end, the Bible is one book with one story that culminates in Jesus Christ, who ushers in the kingdom of God. Because Scripture

---

5. Michael S. Horton, *Covenant and Eschatology: The Divine Drama* (Louisville: Westminster John Knox, 2002), 5.

is a unified and coherent story, we can—indeed, we must—read each part in light of the whole. We must learn to both analyze and synthesize how the Old and New Testaments progress, integrate, and climax in Christ, in whom all the promises of God find their yes (2 Cor. 1:20).

REFLECTION QUESTIONS

1. How does Jesus Christ fulfill all of God's saving promises?

2. What is involved in the process of analyzing and synthesizing Scripture (see, for example, Gen. 12:1–3 and Gal. 3:8, 14, 16)?

3. In analyzing and synthesizing Scripture, what is lost in focusing on one context to the exclusion of the other(s)

4. How do some of your favorite stories in Scripture connect to the person and work of Jesus Christ?

5. How should the truth that God fulfills his saving promises in Christ strengthen confidence in God?

How Should Biblical Theology Trace a Theme's Salvation-Historical Progression?

Andrew David Naselli

Tracing how a theme progresses from Genesis to Revelation is one of the ways to do biblical theology.[1] There are two basic steps to follow:

1. Locate all the Bible passages that are most relevant for a theme.

2. Trace how a theme develops at turning points in the Bible's storyline.

What follows unpacks those two steps and illustrates them with the theme of work.[2]

Locate All the Bible Passages That Are Most Relevant for a Theme

Tracing a theme throughout the Bible's storyline requires locating all the relevant Bible passages. The first step for finding the relevant passages is to locate every word for that theme and then to examine every passage that includes those words.[3]

To do this for the concept of *work*, one of the most efficient places to start is by a search on "work" in two of the guides in Logos Bible Software: (1) The Bible Word Study Guide displays every Hebrew and Greek word that English

---

1. See Question 1.
2. See also Andrew David Naselli, *How to Understand and Apply the New Testament: Twelve Steps from Exegesis to Theology* (Phillipsburg, NJ: P&R, 2017), 254–57, 325–27.
3. On word studies, see Jason S. DeRouchie, *How to Understand and Apply the Old Testament: Twelve Steps from Exegesis to Theology* (Phillipsburg, NJ: P&R, 2017), 269–96; Naselli, *Understand and Apply the New Testament*, 206–29.

translations render as *work*, and (2) the Topic Guide links to relevant articles on work in your library (e.g., in dictionaries, encyclopedias, and journal articles).

But one must beware the word-concept fallacy. That is, be careful not to draw incorrect inferences based on the data you collect on where particular words occur. You have not necessarily located all of the relevant passages, because a concept may be present in a passage even if key words for that concept are not present. Locating all of the passages that use the terms for a theme is necessary to find relevant passages, but it is not sufficient because sometimes a passage may be addressing a theme without using a word that is tightly associated with that theme. For example, the *concept* of work may be present even though a *word* for work is absent.

Trace How a Theme Develops at Turning Points in the Bible's Storyline

The four big turning points in the Bible's storyline are creation, fall, redemption, and consummation. You could include more depending on the theme and on how detailed you want to be.

When you understand work in light of the Bible's storyline, you can explain why popular views on work are unbiblical:

1. Work is awful.
2. Work is meaningless.
3. Work is everything.
4. Work is money.
5. "Secular" work is inferior to full-time Christian ministry.

Understanding what the Bible teaches about work can dramatically change your perspective on work. For example, it gives meaning to what you might have considered worthless work. In order to understand what the Bible teaches about work, we must understand how work fits into the four big turning points of the Bible's storyline: creation, fall, redemption, and consummation.

How Does a Theme Begin in the Bible's Storyline? (Turning Point: Creation)

A significant whole-Bible theme usually begins in Genesis 1–2. Let's consider the theme of work at creation.

Work is not inherently bad or connected with bad things. Work is inherently good. God himself works, and Adam and Eve worked before they sinned. "Work in the Bible," observes Leland Ryken, "begins with God's work of creation. God's work of creation is obviously not toil. It is more like play or the exuberance of the creative artist. It is joyous and energetic."[4]

---

4. Leland Ryken, *Redeeming the Time: A Christian Approach to Work and Leisure* (Grand Rapids: Baker, 1995), 120.

God created the world in six days and rested on the seventh (Gen. 2:2). He rested not because he was exhausted but to set a pattern for humans, whom he had created on day six.

Genesis 1:26–28 gives what theologians call the *creation mandate* or *cultural mandate*:

> Then God said, "Let us make man in our image, after our likeness. And let them have dominion over the fish of the sea and over the birds of the heavens and over the livestock and over all the earth and over every creeping thing that creeps on the earth."
>
> > So God created man in his own image,
> > in the image of God he created him;
> > male and female he created them.
>
> And God blessed them. And God said to them, "Be fruitful and multiply and fill the earth and subdue it, and have dominion over the fish of the sea and over the birds of the heavens and over every living thing that moves on the earth."

Because God created us in his own image, it's our responsibility to sustain and cultivate God's earth. That's our job. That's our vocation. Our work matters to God.[5]

God gave Adam specific instructions: "The LORD God took the man and put him in the garden of Eden to work it and keep it" (Gen. 2:15). So before sin ever entered the world, humans were working. Adam named all the animals and then set out to cultivate the garden of Eden. Work was a beautiful

---

5. Note from Jason DeRouchie: Historically, the church has often treated the cultural mandate of Genesis 1:26–28 as a general directive for all humanity. While I agree with this at one level, I believe that only humans enjoying God's blessing (rather than curse) can actually fulfill what God is calling for because in the text the commission makes up God's blessing and not a secondary statement. That is, God's stated goal was for humans not simply to fill, sustain, and cultivate the earth, but to do so in a way that reflects, resembles, and represents God on earth. The purpose of the image-bearers is to magnify the One they are imaging. As such, the Tower of Babel and the resulting dispersion did *not* automatically fulfill the original cultural mandate. Instead, it is realized only when surrendered lives display God's holiness—a feature captured most ultimately in the life of Christ (2 Cor. 4:4, 6; Heb. 1:3; Rev. 21:23) and most consummately when God's glory fills the earth as the waters cover the sea (Hab. 2:14; cf. Num. 14:21; Ps. 67:1–7[2–8]; Isa. 11:9). For more on this thesis, see Carol M. Kaminski, *From Noah to Israel: Realization of the Primaeval Blessing after the Flood*, JSOTSup 413 (New York: T&T Clark, 2004); cf. G. K. Beale, *The Temple and Church's Mission: A Biblical Theology of the Dwelling Place of God*, NSBT 17 (Downers Grove, IL: InterVarsity, 2004); Jason S. DeRouchie, "The Blessing-Commission, the Promised Offspring, and the *Toledoth* Structure of Genesis," *JETS* 56, no. 2 (Jun 2013): 227–28.

thing. Adam didn't hate it. It was pure joy. It was a delight. And it didn't involve hardship or strenuous sweat.

At this stage in the Bible's storyline, work was not toil. Work became toil after the fall.

How Does a Theme Develop until Christ? (Turning Point: Fall)

The turning point of the fall in Genesis 3 is significant for a whole-Bible theme. Let's consider how the theme of work develops at this turning point— work under the curse.

Adam and Eve sinned, and the nature of work changed for humans.

> And to Adam he said,
>
> > "Because you have listened to the voice of your wife
> > > and have eaten of the tree
> > of which I commanded you,
> > > 'You shall not eat of it,'
> > cursed is the ground because of you;
> > > in pain you shall eat of it all the days of your life;
> > thorns and thistles it shall bring forth for you;
> > > and you shall eat the plants of the field.
> > By the sweat of your face
> > > you shall eat bread,
> > till you return to the ground,
> > > for out of it you were taken;
> > for you are dust,
> > > and to dust you shall return."
> > > > (Gen. 3:17–19)

So now human work is harder for at least five reasons.

> 1. *Sin.* Humans are sinful. This taints our whole perspective toward work. And now we can abuse work by being lazy, by overworking, and by being greedy, dishonest, and dishonorable.[6] Sometimes the worst part about working is not *what* we are doing but *whom* we have to do it with—fellow sinners who can be annoying and cruel.
>
> 2. *Curse.* The creation itself is cursed as a result of humans' falling (see Rom. 8:19–22). For example, the ground is cursed and now has thorns and thistles. Natural disasters such as tsunamis, earthquakes, and famines eventually enter the picture.

---

6. Ryken, *Redeeming the Time*, 131.

3. *Pain.* Work is painful. Now it takes more effort. It involves sweat. It's toil. It originally was not toil.

4. *Death.* Humans didn't die up to this point. Now work becomes more stressful and challenging as others die and we know that we, too, will eventually die.

5. *Separation.* Humans are now separated from God in a way that we were not before the fall. Adam and Eve enjoyed intimate fellowship with God in their vocations, but God expelled them from the garden of Eden after they fell. Humans have related to God differently ever since then.

Work itself is not evil, and it still has many positive aspects. For example, it has a degree of enjoyment, and it provides for human needs and wants. But it's not what it once was. It's not the way it's supposed to be. "Work is a vexation" (Eccl. 2:23; cf. 3:9; 4:4). As John C. Laansma writes, "Even at its best, work is bitter-sweet."[7]

How Does a Theme Climax in Christ in the Bible's Storyline? (Turning Point: Redemption)

Every significant whole-Bible theme climaxes in the person and work of Jesus the Messiah.[8] Let's consider the theme of work under Christ.

After God makes you alive together with Christ (Eph. 2:5), you should have a radically different perspective on work. You're still under the curse, but you're also under Christ. Kent Hughes explains, "God does not remove the curse and its painful, sweaty toil, but He does replace the meaninglessness."[9] Work is no longer awful, meaningless, everything, or merely a means to make money. Work is noble. Work is service. Work is a calling.

What gives work under the curse the most dignity is that Jesus himself worked. He was a blue-collar carpenter, mason, or smith for most of his life. And then he worked in his earthly ministry that led to the cross:

- "My food is to do the will of him who sent me and to accomplish his work." (John 4:34)

- "My Father is working until now, and I am working." (John 5:17)

---

7. John C. Laansma, "Rest," in *New Dictionary of Biblical Theology*, eds. T. Desmond Alexander and Brian S. Rosner (Downers Grove, IL: InterVarsity, 2000), 728.
8. See Questions 4 and 8.
9. R. Kent Hughes, *Disciplines of a Godly Man*, 2nd ed. (Wheaton, IL: Crossway, 2001), 150.

- "We must work the works of him who sent me while it is day; night is coming, when no one can work." (John 9:4)

So how should you work under Christ? There are at least five ways.

1. *Work heartily and sincerely as for the Lord, not other people* (Eph. 6:5–8; Col. 3:17, 22–24). The key phrases are "to the Lord" or "for the Lord." Fundamentally, you work for the Lord—not for yourself, your family, your company, your bosses, or your coworkers. You work for God. That is distinctive about Christian work.

And when you're working for the Lord, your work is hearty and sincere. It's vigorous and cheerful. It's enthusiastic. It's wholehearted because your primary audience is God, not humans. God cares about your motive for working. The work you do that no other human sees you doing is worth doing well because you're ultimately doing it for God.

2. *Work hard, and don't be lazy.* You're tempted to slack off, to get bored, to cut corners, to be slothful. What does God think about people who work hard versus lazy people? Read some short, pithy sayings in Proverbs.[10]

You must work hard and not be lazy. But you must also beware of another extreme.

3. *Work hard, but don't overwork.* Workaholics have a compulsive and extreme desire to work. People of both sexes and every occupation can be workaholics. Workaholics think about work even when they are not on the job. They are intense, energetic, competitive, and driven. They prefer work to leisure, and they fear failure, boredom, and laziness. They are incapable of setting limits to their work or of saying "no." They do not delegate well, and they demand a lot from both themselves and others. They work hard for unusually long hours and sometimes seven days a week. They don't follow God's pattern to routinely work six days and rest one, and they fail to recognize that the One who never slumbers (Ps. 121:4) "gives to his beloved sleep" as a faith-nurturing gift (127:2).

4. *Work shrewdly, but don't work dishonestly.* In the parable of the shrewd steward (Luke 16:1–13), Jesus does not commend the manager's dishonesty but his shrewdness, his ingenuity, his creativity. God is creative and industrious, and we should imitate him.

---

10. At least fourteen passages from Proverbs specifically address working hard and not being lazy: Prov. 6:6–11; 10:4–5; 12:11, 14, 24; 13:4; 14:23; 19:15; 20:4, 13; 21:25; 22:29; 26:13–16; 28:19.

But in our drive to work shrewdly, we must not work dishonestly, as Paul makes clear in Ephesians 6:5–9 and Colossians 3:22–4:1. In these passages Paul directly addresses the "masters." Employers and managers must treat their employees or those under them justly and fairly because they will give an account to their Master in heaven.

5. *Be ambitious, but don't be greedy.* Dictionaries define *ambition* as a strong desire to do or achieve something, especially a desire for success, wealth, or fame. *Greed* is an intense and selfish desire for wealth, power, or food. Or as Tim Keller puts it, "Greed is not only love of money, but excessive anxiety about it."[11] Ambition can quickly turn to greed, but ambition is not necessarily wrong. Greed is wrong.

How Does a Theme Culminate in Christ at the End of the Bible's Storyline? (Turning Point: Consummation)

Every significant whole-Bible theme not only climaxes in the person and work of Jesus the Messiah. It also culminates in Jesus when he returns to completely defeat his enemies and rescue his people.

What will happen to work after Christ returns? Will we work in the new heaven and new earth? Or will work be a thing of the past? Remember: God works; Adam and Eve worked before the fall; Jesus works; angels work. Why shouldn't we work, too?

The Bible teaches that we will be working forever. The parallels between Genesis 1–3 and Revelation 21–22 are remarkable.[12] One is that humans are vice-regents with God-given dominion. "His servants will serve [λατρεύω, *latreuō*] him" (Rev. 22:3 NIV) and eternally reign (Rev. 22:5). This implies that we will be working. Further, passages that distinguish different levels of future service imply that God's people will be working. For example, in the parable of the ten minas (Luke 19:11–27), the master gives the two faithful servants authority over ten cities and five cities. That's work.

So we will be working forever. But lest this dissipate your excitement for the new heaven and the new earth, remember that when God consummates his saving plan through Jesus, he will reverse the effects of the fall. God will reverse everything that makes work unpleasant:

- *Sin.* We won't be sinful. Our perspective toward work will change.
- *Curse.* The creation itself won't be cursed anymore.
- *Pain.* Work won't be painful. It won't involve sweat. It won't be toil.
- *Death.* We won't ever die again. Work won't be stressful as we know it.

---

11. Timothy Keller, *Counterfeit Gods: The Empty Promises of Money, Sex, and Power, and the Only Hope That Matters* (New York: Dutton, 2009), 56.
12. See Question 35.

- *Separation.* We won't be separated from God. We'll enjoy the kind of intimate fellowship with God that Adam and Eve originally did.

Thinking through work in a biblical-theological way like this helps us think rightly about how we should view and do work now.

Summary

Biblical theology traces a theme's salvation-historical progression in two basic steps. First, locate all the Bible passages that are most relevant for a theme. Second, trace how a theme develops at turning points in the Bible's storyline—especially the turning points of creation, fall, redemption, and consummation.

REFLECTION QUESTIONS

1. Why should you beware the word-concept fallacy?

2. What are the four big turning points in the Bible's storyline?

3. What is a theme you would like to trace from Genesis to Revelation?

4. How would you go about tracing that theme from Genesis to Revelation?

5. How does tracing the theme of work's salvation-historical progression help you view and do work now?

How Should We Consider Continuity and Discontinuity between the Covenants?

Oren R. Martin

To say that the covenants are important throughout Scripture is an un-derstatement.[1] Most Christians acknowledge their significant place in the history of redemption.[2] For example, the covenants played key roles in the early church debates concerning Jew-Gentile relations (e.g., Matt. 22:1–14; Acts 10–11; Eph. 2:11–22), the Judaizers' misapplication of the covenant(s) (Gal. 2–4), the appointing of the Jerusalem council (Acts 15), the strong and the weak (Rom. 14–15), and the relationship of Christians to the Mosaic law (Rom. 4; Gal. 3–4). All of these debates circled around the relationship be-tween the covenants.

To say that covenant is *the* center of Scripture may be an overstatement,[3] but it certainly holds a central place in God's redemptive purposes because it shares in a complex of connections with other important themes (e.g., God, kingdom, people, land). More specifically, the covenants serve as the backbone of and means through which God guides his saving purposes to-ward their goal—the uniting of all things in Christ (Eph. 1:9–10). The key issue, however, is the question of *how* biblical theology should consider con-tinuity and discontinuity between the covenants; this has been the subject of much debate.

---

1. Though there is minor variation in numbers, Peter Gentry's analysis of covenant lists 288 instances. See Peter J. Gentry and Stephen J. Wellum, *Kingdom through Covenant: A Biblical-Theological Understanding of the Covenants*, 2nd ed. (Wheaton, IL: Crossway, 2018), 841.
2. See Questions 18 and 19.
3. See Question 15.

This chapter explores in three steps how biblical theology understands continuity and discontinuity between the covenants. First, we define *covenant*. Second, we explore issues of continuity and discontinuity in covenant theology and dispensationalism. Finally, we introduce a mediating position between covenant theology and dispensationalism.

Covenant Defined

For practical purposes, covenant can be defined as an initiated relationship between (at minimum) two parties that involves mutual obligations between the covenant parties. Though there are a number of covenants between human beings in Scripture (e.g., Abraham and Abimelech in Gen. 21:27, Jacob and Laban in Gen. 31:44, David and Jonathan in 1 Sam. 18:3), the most important covenants for the biblical storyline are those between God and people. Covenant is crucial for defining the Creator-creature relationship.

Scripture presents numerous covenants at crucial times throughout salvation history, which serve to (re)establish God's fellowship with humanity, reverse the curses of Eden, and progressively establish and expand God's kingdom on earth. Each covenant progressively serves as God's means for reaching his ordained end—a consummated kingdom. The table below lists the major covenants:[4]

Covenant	Main Scripture Texts
The Adamic-Noahic covenant	Genesis 1–3, 6–9
The Abrahamic covenant	Genesis 12, 15, 17, 22
The Mosaic covenant	Exodus 19–24,; Deuteronomy
The Davidic covenant	2 Samuel 7; Psalm 89
The new covenant	Jeremiah 31–34; Isaiah 54; Ezekiel 34–39

Issues in Covenant Continuity and Discontinuity

While the covenants played a key role in the early church regarding Jew-Gentile relations, today, especially within evangelical theology, these debates mostly take place between two prevailing theological systems, covenant theology and dispensationalism.[5] While it is more accurate to speak of covenant *theologies* and dispensational *theologies*,[6] one way to diagram the differences is to place them on a spectrum that measures continuity and discontinuity.[7]

---

4. For a similar chart, see Gentry and Wellum, *God's Kingdom through God's Covenants: A Concise Biblical Theology* (Wheaton, IL: Crossway, 2015), 50–51.
5. See Questions 17 and 18.
6. See Questions 17, 18, and 19.
7. Adapted from Jason C. Meyer, "The Mosaic Law, Theological Systems, and the Glory of Christ," in *Progressive Covenantalism: Charting a Course between Dispensational and Covenant Theologies*, eds. Stephen J. Wellum and Brent E. Parker (Nashville: B&H, 2016), 71.

Road of Continuity/Discontinuity

◄——— Continuity   Discontinuity ———►

Theonomy	Covenant Theology	<u>Forms of Dispensationalism</u>
		Progressive-Revised-Classical

While these theological systems agree on what is most important in the Christian faith (e.g., the Trinity, the exclusivity of the person and work of Christ, the *solas* of the Reformation, the gospel, the total truthfulness of Scripture, the return of Christ), the following three issues clarify how they differ.

The Nature of the Abrahamic Covenant

One the one hand, dispensational theology appeals to the unconditional nature of the Abrahamic covenant to be fulfilled in an ethnic, national Israel in the future millennial age. Regardless of how the NT describes the multiethnic church *in Christ* (e.g., chosen, royal priests, temple) or how the church inherits the OT promises (including the land promise that is fulfilled in the new creation), dispensationalism argues that precisely because of the Abrahamic covenant's unconditional nature, God *must* fulfill his promises to ethnic, national Israel in the future. Covenant theology (CT) disagrees with dispensationalism by pointing to the diverse ways in which the NT fulfills the OT, arguing that *through Christ* the church—composed of both Jews and Gentiles—fulfills Israel's identity and purpose as the people of God and, as a result, inherits every promise, including the promise of land that reaches its end in the new heavens and new earth.[8]

In a similar way, but at a different point than dispensationalism, CT appeals to the Abrahamic covenant, specifically the genealogical principle—"to you and your children"—to argue that, as Israel received the old covenant sign of circumcision and was a mixed community composed of both remnant and rebel, the new covenant church (including infants) receives the sign of baptism and is a mixed community composed of both believers and unbelievers. Like dispensationalism, then, CT argues that on the basis of continuity and the unconditional nature of the Abrahamic covenant, the new covenant church is made up of all who received the covenant sign, whether infant or new believer. They hold this view irrespective of the fact that the NT neither commands nor gives one example of infant baptism. Nevertheless, both appeal at different points to the nature of the Abrahamic covenant.

---

8. See Question 29.

The Relationship of the Mosaic Law to Christians

Both theonomy and covenant theology emphasize the tripartite division of the law—moral, civil, and ceremonial.[9] Showing the most continuity, theonomy argues that the moral and civil laws are still authoritative today, whereas the ceremonial laws are not because of Christ's sacrificial atonement.[10] Moving to the right toward more discontinuity, covenant theology argues that the civil and ceremonial laws have been abolished but the moral law remains authoritative. In contrast to both theonomy and covenant theology, dispensationalism in its various forms argues that the Mosaic law has come to an end and that Christians are under the law of Christ, not Moses. This abrogation does not mean, however, that the law is useless, but rather that the laws still apply where Christ and the NT repeats them (e.g., nine of the Ten Commandments, excluding the Sabbath).

The Relationship between Israel and the Church

On the one hand, because of one covenant of grace administered through the different covenants, covenant theology argues that the nature of the church is essentially the same as Israel (continuity)—the relationship being one of extension, substitution, or fulfillment.[11] In other words, even if Romans 9–11 teaches a future restoration for ethnic (but not national) Israel, which some hold in covenant theology, all the promises and blessings of Israel in the OT transfer to the church. On the other hand, the necessary tenant of dispensationalism is the distinction between Israel and the church (discontinuity), both in the present and in the future millennial state. That is, Israel will be restored as a national entity in the Promised Land under her Davidic king and will have a mediatorial role to the nations. Thus, the lines of continuity and discontinuity could not be more evident when it comes to the Israel-church relationship.

---

9. Put simply, theonomy argues that the moral and civil law that God gave to Israel in the OT should be the law in all nations today. For a critique of theonomy, see Thomas R. Schreiner, *40 Questions About Christians and Biblical Law*, 40 Questions Series, ed. Benjamin L. Merkle (Grand Rapids, Kregel, 2010), Question 39.

10. On the moral, civil, and ceremonial law, Francis Turretin writes, "The law given by Moses is usually distinguished into three species: moral (treating of morals or of perpetual duties towards God and our neighbor); ceremonial (of the ceremonies or rites about the sacred things to be observed under the Old Testament); and civil, constituting the civil government of the Israelite people. Francis Turretin, *Institutes of Elenctic Theology*, ed. J. T. Dennison Jr., trans. G. M. Giger (Phillipsburg, NJ: P&R, 1994), 2:145.

11. See, e.g., Herman Bavinck, *Holy Spirit, Church, and the New Creation*, vol. 4 of *Reformed Dogmatics*, ed. John Bolt, trans. John Vriend (Grand Rapids: Baker, 2008), 277–79, 665–67; Charles Hodge, *Systematic Theology* (Grand Rapids: Eerdmans, 1982), 3:548–52; Edmund P. Clowney, *The Church*, Contours of Christian Theology (Downers Grove, IL: InterVarsity, 1995), 42–44; Michael Horton, *Introducing Covenant Theology* (Grand Rapids: Baker, 2006), 129–35; cf. Brent E. Parker, "The Israel-Christ-Church Relationship," in Wellum and Parker, *Progressive Covenantalism*, 39.

Progressive Covenantalism and Continuity and Discontinuity

A more recent mediating position is progressive covenantalism.[12] Here is where it fits on the theological spectrum.[13]

Road of Continuity/Discontinuity

◄—— **Continuity**	**Discontinuity** ——►

Theonomy	Covenant Theology	Progressive Covenantalism	<u>Forms of Dispensationalism</u>
			Progressive-Revised-Classical

We think progressive covenantalism provides a more accurate account of the relationship between the covenants. The various covenants have their divinely appointed place in the unfolding of God's redemptive plan, and they are ultimately fulfilled in the new covenant in Christ in an already–not yet manner. That is, the various components of the covenants reach their goal and end in Christ, who is the last Adam, the obedient Son, the Abrahamic offspring, the law-keeper, the true temple, and the better prophet, priest, and king. As a result, the church of Jesus Christ—composed of both Jews and Gentiles—receives every spiritual blessing in the heavenly places through the Holy Spirit, who is the guarantee of our inheritance to come (Eph. 1:1–14)— the new creation. Thus, the progression of the covenants reveals the unified plan of God that unfolds over time in which he makes a people for his own possession, a kingdom made up of royal priests who will dwell with him in his blessed kingdom under the Lord Jesus Christ. Unlike covenant theology, progressive covenantalism does not major on distinctions between a covenant of works versus a covenant of grace, law versus gospel, or unconditional versus conditional covenants. Rather, God's one plan of redemption progressively unfolds through each covenant, which begins with Adam at creation and culminates in the last Adam, Jesus Christ. Furthermore, tension escalates as the biblical story moves forward until the fullness of time when "God sent forth his Son, born of a woman, born under the law, to redeem us from the curse of the law, so that we might receive adoption as sons" (Gal. 4:4–5).[14]

---

12. See Gentry and Wellum, *Kingdom through Covenant*; Wellum and Parker, *Progressive Covenantalism*. It should be noted that progressive covenantalism is similar to new covenant theology, but that label is not preferred since there are divergent views over the creation covenant, Christ's active and passive obedience, the imputation of Christ's righteousness to believers, and the role of new covenant commands in the Christian life.
13. Taken from Meyer, "Mosaic Law, Theological Systems," 71.
14. The tension between God's promise and the necessity of an obedient partner in the covenant relationship becomes clearer and stronger as the storyline progresses. Ultimately the grace of God—not the obedience of Abraham or his descendants, Israel—remains foundational. To be sure, God will see to it that the demands of the covenant are fulfilled. But if sin is native to fallen humanity, then it is safe to say that the fulfillment of the covenant and, thus, the covenant blessings will be brought about by an obedient one who lies beyond

Furthermore, progressive covenantalism does not see the church as directly extending or fulfilling Israel. Rather, *Christ* is the antitype of Israel, who fulfills Israel's identity, purpose, and mission such that *in Christ* the church inherits all the covenant blessings. In other words, the movement is not Israel → church, but rather (Adam →) Israel → *Christ* → church, with Christ's representative role being central.

When it comes to the Mosaic law, whereas most covenant theologians divide the law into three parts—moral, civil, and ceremonial, progressive covenantalism (along with dispensational theology) rejects this "tripartite" distinction because the biblical authors do not make such distinctions.[15] In fact, in one sense all the commands are moral because they come *from God*. Therefore, Scripture portrays the Mosaic law as a unified whole, all of which relates to Christians *only through Christ*. For example, Hebrews 7:11–12 (NIV) says, "If perfection could have been attained through the Levitical priesthood—and indeed the law given to the people established that priesthood—why was there still need for another priest to come, one in the order of Melchizedek, not in the order of Aaron? For when the priesthood is changed, the law must be changed also." The law and the priesthood are bound up together. If one changes, the other does as well. It is an entire package.[16] So, the center of progressive covenantalism is the person and work of Christ, in whom all the covenants reach their goal.

Summary

The biblical covenants are a crucial means through which God establishes fellowship with his creatures and directs history along in order to fulfill his redemptive purposes. However, it is important to work through the relationship between the covenants and how they progress across Scripture as God fulfills his purposes in Christ. Rather than emphasizing continuity at the expense of discontinuity (covenant theology), or discontinuity at the expense of

---

Abraham's—and Israel's—horizon. The student of Scripture, therefore, must look forward to an obedient covenant partner who will fulfill the conditions of the covenant in order to bring blessing on himself and, through him, to the nations. This tension is crucial for understanding the nature and progression of the covenants as they reach their *telos* in Christ, who inaugurates a new and better covenant in his own blood. That is, when the larger canonical storyline is considered, the conditions are met by God himself when he sends his willing obedient Son—the true seed of Abraham and Son *par excellence*—to fulfill the demands of the covenant. Indeed, all of God's promises find their yes in Christ (2 Cor. 1:20), who will win the blessing of a new creation for all of Abraham's offspring. For more on this point, see Gentry and Wellum, *Kingdom through Covenant*, 663–65.

15. Cf. D. A. Carson, "The Tripartite Division of the Law: A Review of Philip Ross, *The Finger of God*," in *From Creation to New Creation: Essays on Biblical Theology and Exegesis*, eds. Daniel M. Gurtner and Benjamin L. Gladd (Peabody, MA: Hendrickson, 2013), 223–36.

16. For more on this point, see Schreiner, *40 Questions About Christians and Biblical Law*. See also Question 25.

continuity (dispensational theology), progressive covenantalism emphasizes *both* continuity *and* discontinuity.

REFLECTION QUESTIONS

1. Why are the covenants important throughout Scripture?

2. How do the various covenants develop in order to fulfill God's saving purposes in Christ?

3. In what ways does dispensational theology stress discontinuity and covenant theology stress continuity?

4. What problems arise when readers of Scripture misinterpret the relationship of the covenants?

5. In what ways does the Lord Jesus Christ fulfill the covenants?

How Should Biblical Theology Track Promise and Fulfillment?

Andrew David Naselli

Tracking promise and fulfillment is one of the overlapping ways to make organic, salvation-historical connections.[1] It overlaps especially with typology.[2] We illustrate how biblical theology works for key themes and in key passages in parts 3 and 4 below. Here are some examples of key themes we will unpack:

- Question 21: What Role Does "Mystery" Play in Biblical Theology?

- Question 22: What Is a Biblical Theology of the Covenants?

- Question 25: What Is a Biblical Theology of the Law?

- Question 26: What Is a Biblical Theology of the Sabbath?

- Question 27: What Is a Biblical Theology of the Temple?

- Question 29: What Is a Biblical Theology of the Land?

One of the major ways to put the Bible together is to connect what God promises with how he fulfills his promises in Christ.[3] That's why Mark Dever titled his published sermons on every book of the Bible as *Promises Made* and

---

1. See Question 1.
2. See Question 8.
3. Predict-fulfill (e.g., Micah 5:2 predicts that the Messiah would be born in Bethlehem, and Matthew 2 fulfills it) is a subcategory of promise-fulfill.

Promises Kept.[4] That's why Reformed Theology Seminary titled their introductions to the Old and New Testaments as *The Gospel Promised* and *The Gospel Realized.*[5] And that's why the title of Greg Gilbert's conversational commentary on the Bible's storyline is the *Story of Redemption Bible: A Journey through the Unfolding Promises of God.*[6] Some utilize that paradigm as a primary way to present biblical theology.[7]

So how should one go about tracking promise and fulfillment? There are at least three ways.

Study Key Passages Where God Makes Promises

The most significant promises in the Bible for biblical theology are what theologians call *covenants.*[8] There are five major covenants:

1. the Adamic-Noahic covenant (Gen. 1–2; 6; 9)
2. the Abrahamic covenant (Gen. 12; 15; 17; 22)
3. the old, Mosaic, Sinaitic, or Israelite covenant (Exod. 19–31)
4. the Davidic covenant (2 Sam. 7; 1 Chron. 17; Ps. 89)
5. the new covenant (Jer. 31; Ezek. 36; Heb. 7–10)

Those glorious promises aren't the only ones God makes,[9] but everything God promises (both to bless and to curse) connects to those covenants in some way. Those covenants are the backbone of the Bible's storyline. At this point in the history of salvation, all God's promises are already "yes" in Christ but not yet fully realized (cf. 2 Cor. 1:20).[10]

Study Key Passages Where God Fulfills What He Promised

How do the five major covenants (see above) relate to each other? Peter Gentry and Stephen Wellum graphically depict the time and scope of being a member of those covenants (see fig. 7.1):

---

4. Mark Dever, *The Message of the Old Testament: Promises Made* (Wheaton, IL: Crossway, 2006); Mark Dever, *The Message of the New Testament: Promises Kept* (Wheaton, IL: Crossway, 2005).
5. Miles V. Van Pelt, ed., *A Biblical-Theological Introduction to the Old Testament: The Gospel Promised* (Wheaton, IL: Crossway, 2016); Michael J. Kruger, ed., *A Biblical-Theological Introduction to the New Testament: The Gospel Realized* (Wheaton, IL: Crossway, 2016).
6. Greg Gilbert, *ESV Story of Redemption Bible: A Journey through the Unfolding Promises of God* (Wheaton, IL: Crossway, 2018).
7. Thomas R. Schreiner, *New Testament Theology: Magnifying God in Christ* (Grand Rapids: Baker Academic, 2008); Walter C. Kaiser Jr., *The Promise-Plan of God: A Biblical Theology of the Old and New Testaments* (Grand Rapids: Zondervan, 2008).
8. See Question 22.
9. See also John Piper, *Future Grace: The Purifying Power of the Promises of God*, in *The Collected Works of John Piper*, eds. David Mathis and Justin Taylor (Wheaton, IL: Crossway, 2017), 4:13–419.
10. See Question 37.

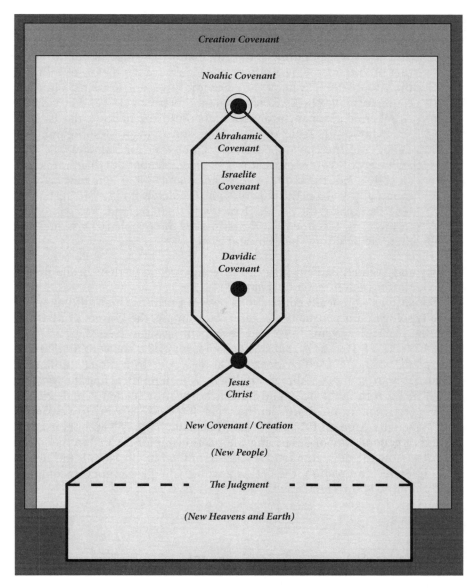

Fig. 7.1. Time versus Scope of Covenant Membership[11]

---

11. Peter J. Gentry and Stephen J. Wellum, *Kingdom through Covenant: A Biblical-Theological Understanding of the Covenants*, 2nd ed. (Wheaton, IL: Crossway, 2018), 673 (used with permission from Jason T. Parry).

Gentry and Wellum explain how to interpret the figure:

> The line corresponding to the Abrahamic covenant is bold to show that both the Israelite and new covenants are the means of fulfilling the Abrahamic covenant. The Davidic covenant is a single line because, formally, the Davidic covenant is between God and David. The Abrahamic covenant promises blessing to the nations, the Israelite covenant locates Israel in the land bridge between Mesopotamia and Egypt, and the Davidic covenant is a charter for humanity. So they all have worldwide implications in principle, but the diagram is specifically about the scope of covenant membership. The new creation eventually replaces the old creation completely. In the Old Testament God first makes the people (Israel) and then the land (Palestine), and in the New Testament God first makes the people (Christians) and then the land (new heavens and earth).[12]

Gentry and Wellum explain how the covenants relate in their brilliant 959-page book *Kingdom through Covenant*.[13]

Sometimes significant connections between promise and fulfillment involve typology. This is usually the case; for example, the Gospel of Matthew says that particular events *fulfill* Old Testament passages (see Matt. 2:17, 23; 3:15; 4:14; 5:17; 8:17; 12:17; 13:35; 21:4; 26:54, 56; 27:9). The verb *fulfill* translates *plēroō* (πληρόω), which does not always refer to a direct fulfillment. Micah 5:2 is an example of direct fulfillment: Micah predicts that the Messiah would be born in Bethlehem, and Jesus is born in Bethlehem (Matt. 2:5–6). But the verb *fulfill* is much broader than that. It means "to bring to a designed end."[14] Douglas Moo and Andrew Naselli explain, "The NT authors use this word as a general way of describing the relationship of the OT to the NT. It describes how the new, climactic revelation of God in Christ 'fills up,' brings to its intended completion, the OT as a whole (the preparatory, incomplete revelation to and through Israel)."[15]

---

12. Gentry and Wellum, *Kingdom through Covenant*, 673.
13. They condense their approach to three hundred pages in Peter J. Gentry and Stephen J. Wellum, *God's Kingdom through God's Covenants: A Concise Biblical Theology* (Wheaton, IL: Crossway, 2015). And Wellum teams up with a pastor to tell the Bible's story in a more popular way: Trent Hunter and Stephen J. Wellum, *Christ from Beginning to End: How the Full Story of Scripture Reveals the Full Glory of Christ* (Grand Rapids: Zondervan, 2018).
14. BDAG 828.
15. Douglas J. Moo and Andrew David Naselli, "The Problem of the New Testament's Use of the Old Testament," in *The Enduring Authority of the Christian Scriptures*, ed. D. A. Carson (Grand Rapids: Eerdmans, 2016), 710.

The Gospel of Matthew's connection to the Old Testament is evident right out of the gate with the opening genealogy.[16] The Gospel of Matthew presents Jesus as the ultimate Davidic king and prophet like Moses. He has ultimate authority. Mark Strauss writes,

> While the Davidic Messiah serves as Matthew's foundational category, it by no means exhausts his messianic portrait of Jesus. As we have seen, for Matthew, Jesus is also the son of Abraham, the Son of God, the Son of Man, the suffering Servant, the new Moses, and the true Israel. What do all of these titles and typologies have in common? All are intimately connected to the Old Testament and to the theme of promise and fulfillment. All point to the coming of the salvation available through Jesus. For Matthew, Jesus fulfills it all: all of God's promises and covenants, to Abraham, Moses, and David. He fulfills the eschatological role of Israel, of the Servant and of the Son of Man. He is the climax of salvation history, the inaugurator of God's reign. It is not quite right to say that Matthew subsumes these other titles and images under that of the Messiah. It is better to say that Matthew's conception of the Messiah broadens to include these Old Testament motifs. Jesus the Messiah does not fulfill just part of Scripture. He fulfills it all.[17]

In the Gospel of Matthew, Jesus fulfills the Old Testament in at least twenty-three specific ways (see fig. 7.2):

Gospel Event in Jesus's Life	Matthew	OT Passage
The virgin birth and name of Jesus	1:22–23	Isa. 7:14; 8:8, 10
Jesus's birthplace, Bethlehem	2:5–6	Mic. 5:2
The flight to Egypt	2:15	Hos. 11:1
The slaying of infants by Herod	2:18	Jer. 31:15
Jesus called a Nazarene ("branch")	2:23	Isa. 11:1; 53:2

---

16. Cf. Mark Alan Minnick, "The Matthean Genealogy and Birth Account of Jesus Christ" (PhD diss., Bob Jones University, 1983), 5: "The thesis of this dissertation is that Matthew selected and arranged the contents of his first chapter in order to answer Jewish questions about Jesus' origins and thus to urge their response to Him as Messiah."

17. Mark Strauss, *Four Portraits, One Jesus: An Introduction to Jesus and the Gospels* (Grand Rapids: Zondervan, 2007), 240.

Gospel Event in Jesus's Life	Matthew	OT Passage
John the Baptist's ministry	3:3; 11:10	Isa. 40:3; Mal. 3:1
The temptation of Jesus	4:1–11	Deut. 6:13, 16; 8:3
The beginning of Jesus's ministry	4:15–16	Isa. 9:1–2
Jesus's healing ministry	8:17; 11:5; 12:17–21	Isa. 53:4; 35:5–6; 42:18; 61:1
Division brought by Jesus	10:35–36	Mic. 7:6
Jesus's gentle style of ministry	12:17–21	Isa. 42:1–4
Jesus's death, burial, resurrection	12:40	Jonah 1:17
Hardened response to Jesus	13:14–15; 15:7–9; 21:33, 42	Isa. 5:1–2; 6:9–10; 29:13; Ps. 118:22–23
Jesus's teaching in parables	13:35	Ps. 78:2
Jesus's triumphal entry	21:5, 9	Isa. 62:11; Ps. 118:26
Jesus's cleansing of the temple	21:13	Isa. 56:7; Jer. 7:11
Jesus as Son and Lord of David	1:1; 22:44	Ps. 110:1
Lament over Jerusalem	23:38–39	Jer. 12:7; 22:5; Ps. 118:26
Judas's betrayal of Jesus	26:15	Zech. 11:12
Peter's denial	26:31	Zech. 13:7
Jesus's arrest	26:54, 56	"The Scriptures, the Prophets"
Judas's death	27:9–10	Zech. 11:12–13; Jer. 32:6–9
Jesus the righteous sufferer	27:34–35, 39, 43, 46, 48	Pss. 22:1, 7–8,18; 69:21

Fig. 7.2. Jesus's Fulfillment of OT Prophecy in Matthew's Gospel[18]

---

18. Andreas J. Köstenberger, L. Scott Kellum, and Charles L. Quarles, *The Cradle, the Cross, and the Crown: An Introduction to the New Testament*, 2nd ed. (Nashville: B&H, 2016), 260. Used with permission.

That highlights the promise-and-fulfillment theme in just *one* New Testament book. But it is prominent throughout the rest of the New Testament. For example, it is especially prominent in Luke-Acts[19] and Hebrews.[20]

Recognize Mystery—the Awe-Inspiring Tension between Promise-and-Fulfill and Hide-and-Reveal

Think of a child you know who loves to read stories.[21] Imagine that the child's birthday is a few months away, and you decide to purchase a birthday present early—a fantasy-adventure novel that the child has never heard of but will *love* to read. Should you tell the child about the gift? You have at least two options.

> 1. Option 1 is the *promise-and-fulfill* strategy. You could drop some hints about the birthday present. You could playfully tantalize the child: "Guess what? I bought you a birthday present that you will love! It's something that you'll love to read. It's an adventure story in an enchanting pretend world." That would simultaneously tantalize the child and encourage them that they will really enjoy what's coming. But the child still won't understand fully what that involves until you give them the book to enjoy.

> 2. Option 2 is the *hide-and-reveal* strategy. You could hide the book somewhere and surprise the child with the book on their birthday. You would plan months in advance to give the child the book, but the child wouldn't know that. The child would learn about your plan only when you give them the book—but not before then. The child wouldn't have a clue what's coming.

What does this have to do with tracking promise and fulfillment in the Bible? The Bible has an awe-inspiring tension between promise-and-fulfill and hide-and-reveal. That's one of the ways to explain how the Bible hangs together, how it coheres, how the New Testament is organically rooted in the Old Testament. This is a fundamental tension in Paul's letters.

---

19. See "The God of Promise, Fulfillment, and Salvation: Synthesis of Texts on the Plan of God," chapter 6 in Darrell L. Bock, *A Theology of Luke and Acts: God's Promised Program, Realized for All Nations*, Biblical Theology of the New Testament (Grand Rapids: Zondervan, 2012), 121–48.
20. See Aubrey M. Sequeira, "The Hermeneutics of Eschatological Fulfillment in Christ: Biblical-Theological Exegesis in the Epistle to the Hebrews" (PhD diss., Southern Baptist Theological Seminary, 2017).
21. See also Naselli, *How to Understand and Apply the New Testament*, 250–54.

1. *Promise-and-fulfill.* In the Old Testament, God promises glorious experiences for his people, and Paul explains that many of those are now fulfilled. D. A. Carson writes, "Paul holds that the old covenant Scriptures anticipate Christ, bear witness to him, prophesy of his coming and of his death and resurrection, and all that flows from it, including the existence of the church as the Jew-and-Gentile people of God who are the true children of Abraham."[22] In other words, Jesus (and all that flows from him) fulfills the Old Testament.

2. *Hide-and-reveal.* Carson notes that according to Paul, "several elements in the gospel, and even the gospel itself, were hidden in the past, and have only been revealed with the coming of Christ."[23] Those glorious truths were hidden in Old Testament times and are only now revealed. Paul calls those hidden truths a *mystery*.[24]

This can get confusing because what *Paul* means by *mystery* isn't what *we* usually mean by *mystery*. For us, *mystery* typically refers to something that is hard to figure out or impossible to understand. It involves secrecy or obscurity. It may involve a person or thing whose identity or nature is puzzling or unknown. So there is a genre of fiction called "mystery novels," often stories that solve a mystery by discovering who committed a murder. That's not what Paul means by *mystery*.

For Paul, *mystery* refers to something that was hidden but that God reveals. It's not something that's puzzling. It's not something that we can solve. The only way that we can know it is for God to reveal it.

The tension is that some of those promises that are now fulfilled are the *same* as what was hidden and is now revealed. That is, they simultaneously fall under both categories. *Promise-and-fulfill* emphasizes continuity, and *hide-and-reveal* emphasizes discontinuity.[25]

For example, that tension appears in Ephesians 3:1–6. On the one hand, the Old Testament promises that God will extend his blessings to the Gentile nations and that Gentiles will turn to the God of Israel and be saved. That's promise and fulfillment. On the other hand, Jews and Gentiles will be an organic unity; believing Gentiles will be on an equal footing with believing Jews. That was hidden, and now it's revealed. Many Christian Jews had no

---

22. D. A. Carson, "Mystery and Fulfillment: Toward a More Comprehensive Paradigm of Paul's Understanding of the Old and New," in *The Paradoxes of Paul*, vol. 2 of *Justification and Variegated Nomism*, eds. D. A. Carson, Peter T. O'Brien, and Mark A. Seifrid, 2 vols., WUNT 2/181 (Grand Rapids: Baker Academic, 2004), 397.
23. Carson, "Mystery and Fulfillment," 397.
24. See Question 21. See also G. K. Beale and Benjamin L. Gladd, *Hidden but Now Revealed: A Biblical Theology of Mystery* (Downers Grove, IL: InterVarsity, 2014).
25. See Question 6.

problem with God's including Gentiles as part of his people *but not as equals.* The Christian Jews assumed that they were more deserving of God's blessings because they were physically descended from Abraham. The mystery in Ephesians 3—the news that God has revealed to us that we could know in no other way—is that Christian Jews and Christian Gentiles are not only part of the same body; they are *equally* part of the same body (cf. Eph. 2:12).

Summary

Biblical theology tracks promise and fulfillment in at least three ways. (1) It studies key passages where God makes promises. (2) It studies key passages where God fulfills what he promised. (3) It recognizes mystery—the awe-inspiring tension between promise-and-fulfill and hide-and-reveal.

REFLECTION QUESTIONS

1. What are the most significant promises in the Bible for biblical theology?

2. What does *fulfill* mean in the Gospel according to Matthew?

3. What does *mystery* have to do with promise and fulfillment?

4. What Bible passage (if you could name only one) are you most interested in studying right now in order to better track promise and fulfillment throughout the Bible?

5. The way the whole Bible fits together is inexhaustibly interesting. How does that make you feel about God?

How Should Biblical Theology Approach Typology?

Andrew David Naselli

Typology analyzes how New Testament persons, events, and institutions (i.e., antitypes) fulfill Old Testament persons, events, and institutions (i.e., types) by repeating the Old Testament situations at a deeper, climactic level in salvation history. David L. Baker helpfully defines terms:

- A *type* is a biblical event, person or institution which serves as an example or pattern for other events, persons or institutions.

- *Typology* is the study of types and the historical and theological correspondences between them.

- The *basis* of typology is God's consistent activity in the history of his chosen people.[1]

Typology includes at least four elements.

Analogy: The Type and Antitype Are Analogous

A type (such as Moses, the exodus, or the sacrificial system) and its antitype (Jesus) correspond in an analogous way. That is, they compare to each other in a significant way. Analogy is the basic starting point. Typology involves *more* than analogy (see below) but not less.

---

1. David L. Baker, *Two Testaments, One Bible: The Theological Relationship between the Old and New Testaments*, 3rd ed. (Downers Grove, IL: InterVarsity, 2010), 180.

Historicity: The Type and Antitype Occur in Real History

Neither a type nor its antitype is allegorical. They occur in actual history. Allegory creates a symbolic world that is not necessarily based on actual history, but typology is always based on actual history.[2] The meaning of an allegory depends on an extra-textual grid,[3] but the meaning of typology depends on historical events that the text narrates and explains.[4] G. K. Beale and D. A. Carson explain,

> Some kind of historical sequence under the providence of a sovereign God is necessary for almost any kind of typological hermeneutic, of course, but there is something more. In Galatians 3, for instance, Paul modifies the commonly accepted significance of the law by the simple expedient of locating it after the Abrahamic promise, which had already established the importance of justification by faith and which had already promised blessing to the Gentiles. Thus instead of asking an atemporal question such as, "How does one please God?" and replying, "By obeying the law," Paul instead insists on reading the turning points of OT history in their chronological sequence and learning some interpretive lessons from that sequence. That sort of dependence on salvation history surfaces elsewhere in the NT (e.g., Rom. 4), and not only in Paul (e.g., Heb. 4:1–13; 7). Thus, eschatological fulfillment has begun with Christ's first advent and will be consummated at his last coming.[5]

Adam is another example. Paul argues that Adam is a type of Christ: Adam is the covenantal head of the original creation, and Christ is the covenantal head

---

2. See also Richard M. Davidson, *Typology in Scripture: A Study of Hermeneutical Τύπος Structures*, Andrews University Seminary Doctoral Dissertation Series 2 (Berrien Springs, MI: Andrews University Press, 1981), 398.

3. See also D. A. Carson, "Mystery and Fulfillment: Toward a More Comprehensive Paradigm of Paul's Understanding of the Old and New," in *The Paradoxes of Paul*, vol. 2 of *Justification and Variegated Nomism*, eds. D. A. Carson, Peter T. O'Brien, and Mark A. Seifrid, 2 vols., WUNT 2/181 (Grand Rapids: Baker Academic, 2004), 404: "Allegorical interpretation, in the contemporary sense of allegory, normally depends on an extra-textual grid, some extra-textual key, to warrant the explanation. Philo happily affirms that Abraham, Isaac, and Jacob are real persons, but he insists that their *meaning* is the 'educational trinity' affirmed by Aristotle—and is it very difficult to see how one can establish that linkage from the text of Genesis or of any other book in the Old Testament."

4. See also Brent E. Parker, "Typology and Allegory: Is There a Distinction? A Brief Examination of Figural Reading," *Southern Baptist Journal of Theology* 21, no. 1 (Spring 2017): 57–83.

5. G. K. Beale and D. A. Carson, introduction to *Commentary on the New Testament Use of the Old Testament*, ed. G. K. Beale and D. A. Carson (Grand Rapids: Baker Academic, 2007), xxvi.

of the new creation (Rom. 5:12–21; 1 Cor. 15:21–22, 45–49).[6] Paul's argument necessarily implies that Adam really existed as the first human being.[7]

Foreshadowing: God Sovereignly Designed the Type to Foreshadow the Antitype

God sovereignly designed types to predictively prefigure Christ, who fulfills the Old Testament. How does authorial intention work here between God and the human authors?[8] The antitype is consistent with what the human author of a type intended to communicate.

Sometimes the human author of a type may be aware that what he writes is prophetically forward looking in a predictive sense. That is, the author is conscious that what he writes is part of a typological trajectory that will climax in the Messiah.

But sometimes the original human author may be unaware that what he writes is part of a typological trajectory that will climax in the Messiah. That typological connection may become evident only *retrospectively*. But the typological connection is one that God sovereignly planned and chose to reveal in his good time:

> Given its *indirect* nature, not only does typology require careful exegesis in its immediate context, but it also may not be fully recognized as a type until later authors pick up the pattern and it becomes more clearly known. Yet in an ontological sense, typology is *in* the text, exegetically discovered, while in the epistemological sense, it is recognized for what it is only as *later* Old Testament authors pick up the pattern. Then in Christ, the veil is removed, and the pattern is finally seen in all its undiminished glory.

In a note, the authors explain:

> Types are *predictive* and *prospective* by nature (ontology) because they are divinely designed. Yet, epistemologically, they are *retrospective* in the sense that later authors recognize the types as God-intended patterns by interbiblical development. If the types are retrospective in an ontological sense, then they are not God-intended but are a mere

---

6. See Joshua M. Philpot, "How Does Scripture Teach the Adam-Christ Typological Connection?," *Southern Baptist Journal of Theology* 21, no. 1 (Spring 2017): 145–52.

7. See also Hans Madueme and Michael Reeves, eds., *Adam, the Fall, and Original Sin: Theological, Biblical, and Scientific Perspectives* (Grand Rapids: Baker Academic, 2014); Guy Prentiss Waters, "Theistic Evolution Is Incompatible with the Teachings of the New Testament," in *Theistic Evolution: A Scientific, Philosophical, and Theological Critique*, eds. J. P. Moreland et al. (Wheaton, IL: Crossway, 2017), 902–7.

8. See Question 14.

analogy of human construction and thus are arbitrary and a form of allegory.[9]

An example of retrospective typology is how Paul uses Isaiah and Job in Romans 11:34–35.[10]

So how do the divine and human authors relate regarding what they intended to communicate? *God may intend more but not less than what the human authors intended to communicate.* If a human author of a type were able to look forward in time and see how a future author interpreted later persons, events, and institutions in light of what he originally wrote, the first human author might respond something like this: "That's beautiful! I didn't fully understand what everything I wrote implies. I wasn't fully conscious of how what I wrote was part of a typological trajectory that climaxes in the Messiah. But now I see that what I wrote is wonderfully consistent with what this later author wrote. Praise God for masterfully designing it that way!"[11]

Paul in 1 Corinthians 10 argues that types are inherently foreshadowing, forward-looking, prospective, prophetic.[12] That's why one Old Testament

---

9. Peter J. Gentry and Stephen J. Wellum, *Kingdom through Covenant: A Biblical-Theological Understanding of the Covenants*, 2nd ed. (Wheaton, IL: Crossway, 2018), 132, and note 64. See also G. K. Beale, *Handbook on the New Testament Use of the Old Testament: Exegesis and Interpretation* (Grand Rapids: Baker Academic, 2012), 14–15:

> By "retrospection" is meant the idea that it was after Christ's resurrection and under the direction of the Spirit that the apostolic writers understood certain OT historical narratives about persons, events, or institutions to be indirect prophecies of Christ or the church. . . . Even when the immediate context of a passage does not indicate that something is being viewed typologically from the OT author's conscious vantage point, the wider canonical context of the OT usually provides hints or indications that the passage is typological. . . . NT writers may interpret historical portions of the OT to have a forward-looking sense in the light of the whole OT canonical context.

> See also R. T. France, "Relationship between the Testaments," in *Dictionary for Theological Interpretation of the Bible*, ed. Kevin J. Vanhoozer (Grand Rapids: Baker Academic, 2005), 669: "This new meaning is not something inherent in the OT texts themselves, so that any objective exegesis, Jewish or Christian, ought properly to perceive it. Rather, it is a new level of relevance, going beyond what the OT writer and the original readers could have perceived, which is now discovered by retrospective reflection in the light of NT events. Typology depends not so much on exegesis of the original meaning as on a theological hindsight informed by commitment to Christ as the climax of God's work of salvation. It proceeds from faith rather than from objective literary analysis."

10. See Question 33.

11. See also Robert L. Plummer, "Righteousness and Peace Kiss: The Reconciliation of Authorial Intent and Biblical Typology," *SBJT* 14, no. 2 (Summer 2010): 54–61; G. K. Beale, "The Cognitive Peripheral Vision of Biblical Authors: J. Gresham Machen Chair Installation Lecture," *WTJ* 76, no. 2 (Dec 2014): 283.

12. See also Andrew David Naselli, "1 Corinthians," in *Romans–Galatians*, vol. 10 of *ESV Expository Commentary* (Wheaton, IL: Crossway, 2020), 302–5.

scholar labels typology as "picture prophecy"—that is, the picture points to something more important, and the picture is not identical to what it points to but illustrates it.[13] And sometimes we can recognize *picture prophecy* only retrospectively. "The most basic of all NT 'hermeneutical axioms,' then, is the authors' conviction that the God who had spoken in the OT continued to speak to them and that it was this final divine context for all of Scripture that determines the meaning of any particular text."[14] This view of typology is based on a foundational interpretational axiom: "God ordered OT history to prefigure and anticipate his climactic redemptive acts, and the NT is the God-breathed record of those redemptive acts."[15]

Escalation: The Antitype Escalates the Type from Shadow to Reality by Climaxing in Jesus

The antitype eclipses the type. The type is but a shadow; the antitype is the substance. As Paul says, "These are a shadow of the things to come, but the substance belongs to Christ" (Col. 2:17). God designed some types to repeat and develop through the progressive covenants before they climaxed in Jesus.[16] "The antitype is *always* greater than the previous types," explains Stephen J. Wellum, "yet escalation across time does *not* occur incrementally from the original type to each installment and then to Christ, as if there is a straight line of increase. Rather escalation fully occurs with Christ's coming."[17]

The Bible is one big story that's all about Jesus. Jesus the Messiah fulfills the Old Testament. The entire Old Testament points to him. He is the climax of every typological trajectory (see Luke 24:27, 44; John 5:39; 2 Cor. 1:20; Heb. 1:1–3).[18] If you interpret the Bible in a way that does not point to Jesus, then you are not interpreting the Bible in the way that Jesus himself said you should. This doesn't mean that every Old Testament or New Testament passage points to Jesus in exactly the same way. But every passage points to Jesus in some way, and biblical theology inductively investigates *how*. Typology is one of the main ways to do that.

---

13. Michael P. V. Barrett, *Beginning at Moses: A Guide to Finding Christ in the Old Testament*, 2nd ed. (Grand Rapids: Reformation Heritage, 2018), 225–74.
14. Douglas J. Moo and Andrew David Naselli, "The Problem of the New Testament's Use of the Old Testament," in *The Enduring Authority of the Christian Scriptures*, ed. D. A. Carson (Grand Rapids: Eerdmans, 2016), 737.
15. Moo and Naselli, "Problem of the New Testament's Use of the Old," 730.
16. See Aubrey M. Sequeira and Samuel C. Emadi, "Biblical-Theological Exegesis and the Nature of Typology," *Southern Baptist Journal of Theology* 21, no. 1 (Spring 2017): 22–25; David Schrock, "From Beelines to Plotlines: Typology That Follows the Covenantal Topography of Scripture," *Southern Baptist Journal of Theology* 21, no. 1 (Spring 2017): 35–56; Gentry and Wellum, *Kingdom through Covenant*, 120–26, 135–37.
17. Gentry and Wellum, *Kingdom through Covenant*, 134–35 (emphasis original).
18. See Question 4.

Interpreting the Bible in a Christ-centered way is not eisegesis. It's exegesis that requires biblical theology. It doesn't creatively make stuff up to imaginatively get to Jesus. It follows themes and trajectories that are right there in the text if God gives you eyes to see them. And when you do see them, you worship God for his wisdom. He breathed out Scripture through individual men who didn't always understand every nuance of typological trajectories to which they were contributing. And the entire finished product brilliantly coheres.

We should interpret the Bible the same way the New Testament authors interpret the Old Testament.[19] The New Testament authors don't get a free pass for wacky interpretations simply because what they wrote is God-breathed. No, they *model* how to interpret any part of the Bible in light of the whole.

Some argue that we can identify a person, event, or institution as a type *only* if the New Testament specifically labels it as a type. For example, Roy B. Zuck, a traditional dispensationalist, asserts, "The New Testament must in some way designate the type and the antitype," and he consequently identifies only seventeen types in the Bible (see fig. 8.1).

Type	Antitype	Scripture
Persons		
1. Melchizedek	Christ's perpetual priesthood	Heb. 7:3, 15–17
2. Aaron	Christ's priestly ministry	Heb. 5:4–5
Events		
3. Passover feast	Christ our sacrifice	1 Cor. 5:7
4. Feast of Unleavened Bread	Believer's holy walk	1 Cor. 5:7–8
5. Feast of Firstfruits	Christ's resurrection a pledge of believers' resurrection	1 Cor. 15:20–23
6. Feast of Pentecost	The coming of the Holy Spirit	Joel 2:28; Acts 2:1–47
7. Feast of Trumpets	Israel's regathering	Matt. 24:21–23
8. Day of Atonement	Israel's national conversion by the blood of Christ	Zech. 12:10; Rom. 11:26–27; Heb. 9:19–28

---

19. Contra Richard N. Longenecker, *Biblical Exegesis in the Apostolic Period*, 2nd ed. (Grand Rapids: Eerdmans, 1999); and Robert L. Thomas, "The New Testament Use of the Old Testament," *MSJ* 13, no. 1 (Spring 2002): 79–98.

Type	Antitype	Scripture
Events		
9. Feast of Tabernacles	God's provision for human need (with Israel in the kingdom)	John 7:2, 37–39
10. Sabbath	The Christian's spiritual rest	Col. 2:17; Heb. 4:3, 9, 11
Things		
11. Tabernacle	Christ, the believer's access to God and basis of fellowship with God	Heb. 8:5; 9:23–24
12. Tabernacle curtain	Christ, the believer's access to God	Heb. 10:20
13. Burnt offering	Christ's offering of himself as the perfect sacrifice	Lev. 1; Heb. 10:5–7; Eph. 5:2
14. Grain offering	Christ's offering of himself as the perfect sacrifice of the highest quality	Lev. 2; Heb. 10:8
15. Fellowship offering	Christ's offering of himself as the basis for fellowship with God	Lev. 3; Eph. 2:14; Col. 1:20
16. Sin offering	Christ's death for the sinner in relation to the guilt of sin	Lev. 4:1–5:13; Heb. 13:11–12
17. Guilt offering	Christ's death as an atonement for the injury of sin	Lev. 5:14–6:7; Heb. 10:12

Fig. 8.1. Types and Antitypes in Scripture according to Zuck[20]

Zuck's approach may seem safe, neat, and tidy, but it is too restrictive. When the author of Hebrews mentions various types related to the tabernacle, he says as an aside, "Of these things we cannot now speak in detail" (Heb. 9:5). That implies that there are typological connections that Scripture does not fully explain. One of the joys of interpreting the Bible is to responsibly trace typological connections by following the example of the New Testament authors—types such as the Noahic flood,[21] the land,[22] and Joseph.[23] Typology

20. Roy B. Zuck, *Basic Bible Interpretation* (Wheaton, IL: Victor, 1991), 179–80.
21. See Scott T. Yoshikawa, "The Prototypical Use of the Noahic Flood in the New Testament" (PhD diss., Trinity Evangelical Divinity School, 2004). The dissertation is a door-stopper at 726 pages.
22. See Question 29.
23. See Samuel Emadi, "Covenant, Typology, and the Story of Joseph: A Literary-Canonical Examination of Genesis 37–50" (PhD diss., Southern Baptist Theological Seminary, 2016).

is not a fancy technique to interpret the Bible but simply the result of drawing out the meaning of Bible passages in light of the whole Bible:

> *Typology can be called contextual exegesis within the framework of the canon since it primarily involves the interpretation and elucidation of the meaning of earlier parts of Scripture by later parts.* . . . Rather than interpreting a text only in the light of its immediate literary context within a book, we are now merely interpreting the passage in view of the wider canonical context. . . . We today cannot reproduce the inspired *certainty* of our typological interpretations as either the OT or NT writers could, but the consistent use of such a method by biblical authors throughout hundreds of years of sacred history suggests strongly that it is a viable method for all saints to employ today.[24]

Summary

Typology includes at least four elements: analogy, historicity, foreshadowing, and escalation. God designed types to foreshadow Jesus.

REFLECTION QUESTIONS

1. Do you agree or disagree that God may intend more but not less than what the human authors intended to communicate? Why?

2. How would you explain what typology is to a child?

3. What is your favorite type in the Bible? Why?

4. What is a type you would like to study further? Why?

5. When you meditate on how God sovereignly designed types to relate to Jesus, how do you feel about God?

---

24. Beale, *Handbook*, 25 (emphasis original).

How Does Biblical Theology Approach Later Scripture's Use of Early Scripture?

Andrew David Naselli

The Old and New Testaments are a single, coherent book.[1] It may seem that they are filled with too many differences to integrate, but they do integrate. God designed them to integrate brilliantly.

Biblical theology's most pivotal concern is how later Scripture uses earlier Scripture. This includes how the Old Testament uses the Old Testament,[2] but most significant is how the New Testament uses the Old.[3] The New Testament may quote or allude to the Old Testament.[4] When a New Testament author quotes or alludes to the Old Testament, you can analyze it in six steps.[5]

---

1. See also Andrew David Naselli, *How to Understand and Apply the New Testament: Twelve Steps from Exegesis to Theology* (Phillipsburg, NJ: P&R, 2017), 174–80, 235–37.
2. See Question 31.
3. See Questions 31–35. The single most helpful introduction to how the NT uses the OT is G. K. Beale, *Handbook on the New Testament Use of the Old Testament: Exegesis and Interpretation* (Grand Rapids: Baker Academic, 2012). See also two reference volumes on the OT in the NT that supplement each other: G. K. Beale and D. A. Carson, eds., *Commentary on the New Testament Use of the Old Testament* (Grand Rapids: Baker Academic, 2007); G. K. Beale, D. A. Carson, Benjamin L. Gladd, and Andrew David Naselli, eds., *Dictionary of the New Testament Use of the Old Testament* (Grand Rapids: Baker Academic, forthcoming). DeRouchie, Martin, and Naselli are contributing articles to the forthcoming *Dictionary*.
4. See Beale, *Handbook*, 29–40. Beale helpfully distinguishes quotations from allusions: "A quotation is a direct citation of an OT passage that is easily recognizable by its clear and unique verbal parallelism" (29), and an allusion is "a brief expression consciously intended by an author to be dependent on an OT passage" (31). It is not that helpful to distinguish echoes from allusions (32–35). For a primer on how many scholars distinguish quotations, allusions, and echoes, see Christopher A. Beetham, *Echoes of Scripture in the Letter of Paul to the Colossians*, BibInt 96 (Leiden: Brill, 2008), 11–40.
5. We are following Beale and Carson, introduction to *Commentary*, xxiv–xxvi. Beale later unpacks this approach in nine steps: Beale, *Handbook*, 41–54.

Study the New Testament Context

Exegete the New Testament passage. This may include investigating at least eight components of exegesis:[6]

1. *Genre.* Establish guidelines for interpreting a passage's style of literature.
2. *Textual criticism.* Establish the original wording.
3. *Translation.* Compare translations.
4. *Greek Grammar.* Understand how sentences communicate by words, phrases, and clauses.
5. *Argument Diagram.* Trace the logical argument by arcing, bracketing, or phrasing.
6. *Historical-Cultural Context.* Understand the situation in which the author composed the literature and any historical-cultural details that the author mentions or probably assumes.
7. *Literary Context.* Understand the role that a passage plays in its whole book.
8. *Word Studies.* Unpack key words, phrases, and concepts.

Study the Old Testament Context

Exegete the Old Testament passage(s). As with studying the New Testament context, this involves investigating multiple components of exegesis.[7] Sometimes you need to reflect on how the Old Testament uses the Old Testament (e.g., how Isaiah uses Exodus).[8]

Study Relevant Uses of the Old Testament Passage in Extrabiblical Jewish Literature

It may be significant to consider how approximately contemporaneous Jewish literature interpreted certain Old Testament texts. We'll spend a bit more space on this step not because it is most important (it's not) but because it is less familiar to most Bible-reading Christians.[9]

What primary Jewish sources might include the most relevant uses of Old Testament passages? Six bodies of Jewish literature are most significant.

> 1. *The Old Testament Apocrypha* is a collection of about fifteen books dating from the third century BC to the first century AD: 1–2 Esdras, Tobit, Judith, Additions to Esther, Wisdom of Solomon, Ecclesiasticus (Sirach), Baruch, Epistle of Jeremiah, Prayer of Azariah and the

---

6. See Naselli, *Understand and Apply the New Testament*, 1–229.
7. See DeRouchie, *Understand and Apply the Old Testament*, 1–343.
8. See Question 31.
9. See also Beale, *Handbook*, 103–32.

Song of the Three Children, Susanna, Bel and the Dragon, Prayer of Manasseh, 1–2 Maccabees. The Roman Catholic and Orthodox churches consider these books canonical, but Jews and Protestants do not.[10]

2. *The Old Testament Pseudepigrapha* is a large and diverse collection of ancient Jewish and Hellenistic writings dating mostly to the intertestamental period. Many of the books use pseudonyms—that is, they claim that their author is a well-known biblical figure such as Enoch, Ezra, Abraham, Isaac, or Jacob.

3. *The Dead Sea Scrolls* is a collection of about 850 Jewish manuscripts (mostly fragments) that shepherds discovered in 1947 in caves in the region of Qumran near the Dead Sea. These scrolls include not only texts from every Old Testament book except Esther but other writings such as commentaries on Old Testament books and other works. These writings are especially significant for understanding a strand of Judaism that probably produced these writings—the Essenes, a group that Josephus describes as existing in Israel during New Testament times.

4. *Philo* was a Hellenistic Jewish philosopher and Old Testament exegete from Alexandria who lived from about 20 BC to AD 50. His most significant writings for biblical studies include his commentaries on Genesis and Exodus, which are filled with allegory. His allegorical hermeneutic can be so creative that it's (sadly) entertaining.

5. *Josephus* was a Jewish historian who lived from about AD 37 to 110. Other than the Bible, Josephus's four books are the single most important source for understanding the Jewish world of the first century: (1) *Life* is his autobiography; (2) *Against Apion* is an apologetic for Judaism; (3) *Antiquities of the Jews* tells the history of the Jews from the creation of the world until the Jewish war against Rome; and (4) *Jewish War* describes the Jewish war against Rome. He is generally (not always) reliable as a historian.

6. *The Targums and rabbinic literature* are windows into how the early Jewish community interpreted the Old Testament. The Targums translate and interpret the Old Testament in Aramaic, and they

---

10. The Old Testament Apocrypha is very different from the New Testament Apocrypha, which includes apocryphal Gospels, letters, and apocalyptic literature that people wrote between the second and sixth centuries AD.

were written down starting around the third century AD. The rabbinic literature (i.e., the Mishnah, Talmuds, and Midrash) collects the teaching of Jewish rabbis or sages. The Mishnah collects oral law; the Palestinian and Babylonian Talmuds are commentaries on the Mishnah; and the Midrash often comments on the Old Testament. But these massively voluminous writings are very difficult to date precisely. It's not clear, for example, whether the Jewish beliefs and practices they describe date back to New Testament times or whether they developed afterward.

So why is extracanonical Jewish literature significant for studying the New Testament? There are many reasons. One of the most significant is that it helps us better understand how the New Testament uses the Old. G. K. Beale and D. A. Carson give five reasons for that:[11]

> They may show us how the OT texts were understood by sources roughly contemporaneous with the NT. In a few cases, a trajectory of understanding can be traced out, whether the NT documents belong to that trajectory or not.

> They sometimes show that Jewish authorities were themselves divided as to how certain OT passages should be interpreted. Sometimes the difference is determined in part by literary genre: Wisdom literature does not handle some themes the way apocalyptic sources do, for instance. Wherever it is possible to trace out the reasoning, that reasoning reveals important insights into how the Scriptures were being read.

> In some instances, the readings of early Judaism provide a foil for early Christian readings. The differences then demand hermeneutical and exegetical explanations; for instance, if two groups understand the same texts in decidedly different ways, what accounts for the differences in interpretation? Exegetical technique? Hermeneutical assumptions? Literary genres? Different opponents? Differing pastoral responsibilities?

> Even where there is no direct literary dependence, sometimes the language of early Judaism provides close parallels to the language of the New Testament writers simply because of the chronological and cultural proximity.

---

11. Beale and Carson, introduction to *Commentary*, xxiv (formatting added).

In a handful of cases, New Testament writers apparently display direct dependence on sources belonging to early Judaism and their handling of the Old Testament (e.g., Jude). What is to be inferred from such dependence?

How should you use those Jewish resources responsibly? Here are six suggestions:

1. *Use literary sensitivity.* Don't rip a passage out of its literary context. Don't pillage extrabiblical texts.

2. *Recognize that the Jewish world was diverse.* Have you ever heard someone say, "The Jews in Paul's day all believed . . . "? It's possible to finish those sentences responsibly, but usually people who talk that way are painting with a brush that is too broad. Groups of people and ideologies are diverse. First-century Judaism was complex and included different ideologies and traditions for different issues.

3. *Beware of parallelomania.*[12] Here's how to become guilty of parallelomania: (1) conclude that some Jewish resources are parallel to a New Testament passage; (2) assume that a direct organic literary connection provided the parallels; and (3) conclude that the flow is in a particular direction—namely, those Jewish resources directly influenced Paul and not vice versa. There's a big difference between the following two statements: (1) "Peter borrowed this idea from . . . ," and (2) "What Peter says here may reflect an idea that also occurs in . . ." The first statement assumes you know that Peter was directly relying on a particular resource. Be careful not to make sweeping conclusions based on just a small handful of alleged parallels.

4. *Specify how a resource helps you better understand the New Testament.* Here are four options listed in order from most common to least common. A Jewish or Greco-Roman resource may (1) reflect the cultural milieu that helps you better understand a New Testament passage, (2) use similar language to that of a New Testament passage, (3) indirectly influence a New Testament passage, or (4) directly influence a New Testament passage.

5. *Be correctable.* Be willing to correct and humbly reform your view. This is important for at least four reasons: (1) The data is incomplete.

---

12. Samuel Sandmel popularized this word. See Samuel Sandmel, "Parallelomania," *JBL* 81, no. 1 (Mar 1962): 1–13.

The resources we are working with are just a sliver of the data for the world of the New Testament. There's so much we don't know. (2) You depend on others to access and interpret the data. (3) You may wrongly read your own historical-cultural assumptions into ancient texts. (4) You probably don't understand these Jewish resources as well as you understand the Bible.

6. *Read the primary sources yourself.* You should definitely use good secondary resources on the historical-cultural context.[13] Those secondary sources are incredibly helpful. They save us a massive amount of time. But don't rely exclusively on secondary sources. It's efficient and wise to start with the secondary sources and let them point you to relevant primary sources. But the secondary sources should be a gateway to the primary sources that you locate and read for yourself.

Study Textual Issues

Textual criticism studies manuscript evidence to establish the original wording. It gathers and organizes data, compares and evaluates variant readings, and reconstructs the transmission history. When studying textual issues for how the NT uses the OT, textual criticism involves two levels:[14]

1. Study textual issues within the Masoretic Text, LXX, and Greek New Testament.[15]

---

13. E.g., Craig A. Evans and Stanley E. Porter, eds., *Dictionary of New Testament Background* (Downers Grove, IL: InterVarsity, 2000); Larry R. Helyer, *Exploring Jewish Literature of the Second Temple Period: A Guide for New Testament Students* (Downers Grove, IL: InterVarsity, 2002); Clinton E. Arnold, ed., *Zondervan Illustrated Bible Backgrounds Commentary: New Testament*, 4 vols. (Grand Rapids: Zondervan, 2002); Everett Ferguson, *Backgrounds of Early Christianity*, 3rd ed. (Grand Rapids: Eerdmans, 2003); Craig A. Evans, *Ancient Texts for New Testament Studies: A Guide to the Background Literature*, 2nd ed. (Peabody, MA: Hendrickson, 2005); George W. E. Nickelsburg, *Jewish Literature between the Bible and the Mishnah: A Literary and Historical Introduction*, 2nd ed. (Minneapolis: Fortress, 2005); John J. Collins and Daniel C. Harlow, eds., *The Eerdmans Dictionary of Early Judaism* (Grand Rapids: Eerdmans, 2010); Joel B. Green and Lee Martin McDonald, eds., *The World of the New Testament: Cultural, Social, and Historical Contexts* (Grand Rapids: Baker Academic, 2013); Craig S. Keener, *The IVP Bible Background Commentary: New Testament*, 2nd ed. (Downers Grove, IL: InterVarsity, 2014); Edwin M. Yamauchi and Marvin R. Wilson, eds., *Dictionary of Daily Life in Biblical and Post-Biblical Antiquity*, 4 vols. (Peabody, MA: Hendrickson, 2014–2016).
14. See also W. Edward Glenny, "The Septuagint and Biblical Theology," *Them* 41, no. 2 (August 2016): 263–78.
15. The Masoretic Text is the received and standard text of the Hebrew Scriptures. A Jewish scribal school called the Masoretes worked on this text from about AD 500 to 1000. The LXX is the Septuagint—the Greek translation of the Hebrew Old Testament.

2. Compare textual issues in the Masoretic Text, LXX, and Greek New Testament with each other. For example, which version of the Old Testament is the New Testament citing?

Sometimes it is controversial whether the New Testament explicitly quotes the Old Testament or merely alludes to it.[16]

This step could just as easily occur as step 1, 2, or 3. What is important is that steps 1–4 all occur before steps 5 and 6, where the "cream" of the study surfaces.

Discern the New Testament Author's Hermeneutical Warrant for Using the Old Testament

The New Testament authors use the Old Testament in a variety of ways. G. K. Beale highlights (and illustrates) twelve:[17]

1. To indicate direct fulfillment of Old Testament prophecy
2. To indicate indirect fulfillment of Old Testament typological prophecy
3. To indicate affirmation that a not-yet-fulfilled Old Testament prophecy will assuredly be fulfilled in the future
4. To indicate an analogical or illustrative use of the Old Testament
5. To indicate the symbolic use of the Old Testament
6. To indicate an abiding authority carried over from the Old Testament
7. To indicate a proverbial use of the Old Testament
8. To indicate a rhetorical use of the Old Testament
9. To indicate the use of an Old Testament segment as a blueprint or prototype for a New Testament segment
10. To indicate an alternate textual use of the Old Testament
11. To indicate an assimilated use of the Old Testament
12. To indicate an ironic or inverted use of the Old Testament

It may initially appear sometimes that a New Testament author irresponsibly cites the Old Testament as a "prooftext"—that is, he selectively quotes a text abstracted from its original context. Those texts require us to carefully think through how the Old and New Testaments integrate. Sometimes a New

---

16. Quoting with precise word-for-word accuracy is a relatively modern ideal. See R. T. France, "Relationship between the Testaments," in *Dictionary for Theological Interpretation of the Bible*, ed. Kevin J. Vanhoozer (Grand Rapids: Baker Academic, 2005), 667–68.
17. See Beale, *Handbook*, 55–93. Cf. Douglas J. Moo and Andrew David Naselli, "The Problem of the New Testament's Use of the Old Testament," in *The Enduring Authority of the Christian Scriptures*, ed. D. A. Carson (Grand Rapids: Eerdmans, 2016), 702–46.

Testament author may implicitly include the larger Old Testament context when he quotes just a small part of it.[18]

Discern How the New Testament Author Theologically Uses the Old Testament

What is the New Testament author doing with the Old Testament? What theological point is he making? For example, what do you conclude when a New Testament passage takes an Old Testament text about God's people under the old covenant and directly applies it to God's people under the new covenant?

Beale explains that the New Testament authors presuppose five significant beliefs that inform how they theologically interpret the Old Testament:[19]

1. There is the apparent assumption of *corporate solidarity* or *representation*.

2. In the light of corporate solidarity or representation, Christ as the Messiah is viewed as representing thew *true Israel* of the OT *and* the true Israel—the church—in the NT.

3. *History is unified* by a wise and sovereign plan so that the earlier parts are designed to correspond and point to the later parts (cf., e.g., Matt. 5:17; 11:13; 13:16–17).

4. The age of *eschatological fulfillment* has come in Christ.

5. As a consequence of the preceding presupposition, it follows that the later parts of biblical history function as the broader context for interpreting earlier parts because they all have the same, ultimate divine author who inspires the various human authors.[20] One deduction from this premise is that Christ is the goal toward which the OT pointed and is the end-time center of redemptive history,

---

18. See also C. H. Dodd, *According to the Scriptures: The Sub-Structure of New Testament Theology* (London: Nisbet, 1952), 126: "The method included, first, the *selection* of certain large sections of the Old Testament scriptures, especially from Isaiah, Jeremiah and certain minor prophets, and from the Psalms. These sections were understood as *wholes*, and particular verses or sentences were quoted from them rather as pointers to the whole context than as constituting testimonies in and for themselves. At the same time, detached sentences from other parts of the Old Testament could be adduced to illustrate or elucidate the meaning of the main section under consideration. But in the fundamental passages it is *total context* that is in view, and is the basis of the argument."

19. Beale, *Handbook*, 95–102 (quoting 96–97, emphasis original).

20. Or more precisely, God inspires the writings (2 Tim. 3:16), and the Holy Spirit carries along the human authors (2 Peter 1:21).

which is the *key to interpreting the earlier portions of the OT and its promises.*

Summary

When a New Testament author quotes or alludes to the Old Testament, you can analyze it in six steps:

1. Study the New Testament context.
2. Study the Old Testament context.
3. Study relevant uses of the Old Testament passage in extrabiblical Jewish literature.
4. Study textual issues.
5. Discern the New Testament author's hermeneutical warrant for using the Old Testament.
6. Discern how the New Testament author theologically uses the Old Testament.

The order of steps 1–4 is not that important. But you should complete steps 1–4 before steps 5–6.

REFLECTION QUESTIONS

1. Why is studying how the New Testament uses the Old Testament so important for biblical theology?

2. What does it mean to study the literary context of a passage?

3. Why might extracanonical Jewish literature be significant for studying the New Testament?

4. What are various hermeneutical warrants for how New Testament authors use the Old Testament?

5. Is there a New Testament passage that quotes or alludes to the Old Testament that you would like to explore? How would you go about studying how that New Testament passage uses the Old Testament?

PART 2

Exploring Method in
Biblical Theology

What Are Different Ways That Evangelicals Do Biblical Theology?

Andrew David Naselli

There are two basic ways to define an evangelical: sociologically or theologically.[1]

1. The sociological approach is descriptive, and most historians adopt it. Who self-identifies as an evangelical?

2. The theological approach is prescriptive, and some theologians adopt it. Who believes the gospel according to the Bible?

We define an evangelical using the theological approach. A narrow way to define the gospel is that Jesus lived, died, and rose again for sinners and that God will save those who turn to and trust Jesus.[2] The people we have in mind who believe that good news presuppose at least three truths: (1) The Bible is God-breathed, entirely true, and our final authority.[3] (2) We must read any part of the Bible in light of the unified, noncontradictory whole. (3) Biblical theology is a fruitful way to read parts of the Bible in light of the whole.[4] Those three presuppositions are important because many biblical scholars reject them and consequently interpret parts of the Bible much differently than we explain

---

1. See Andrew David Naselli, conclusion to *Four Views on the Spectrum of Evangelicalism*, eds. Andrew David Naselli and Collin Hansen, Counterpoints (Grand Rapids: Zondervan, 2011), 209–10.
2. See Andrew David Naselli, *How to Understand and Apply the New Testament: Twelve Steps from Exegesis to Theology* (Phillipsburg, NJ: P&R, 2017), 296–300.
3. See D. A. Carson, ed., *The Enduring Authority of the Christian Scriptures* (Grand Rapids: Eerdmans, 2016).
4. See Question 1.

in this book.[5] As D. A. Carson puts it, "Biblical theology must presuppose a coherent and agreed canon."[6]

Evangelicals do biblical theology in at least three overlapping ways: (1) analyze the message; (2) trace themes; and (3) tell the story.[7] It's ideal to study biblical theology in those three steps: (1) analyze the theological message of each book of the Bible and the message of sections of the Bible; (2) trace central themes through the Bible; and (3) see how it all fits together in the grand storyline. If you start by telling the story without having adequately studied the message and central themes, then you will likely fail to explain important aspects of the story.[8]

These three ways of doing biblical theology are *overlapping* because they are not completely distinct from each other. Some authors combine all three approaches.[9]

Analyze the Message

There are two basic approaches here: (1) analyze the message of the whole Bible, and (2) analyze the message of books or sections of the Bible.

---

5. On the complex history of biblical theology, see Charles H. H. Scobie, "History of Biblical Theology," in *New Dictionary of Biblical Theology*, eds. T. Desmond Alexander and Brian S. Rosner (Downers Grove, IL: InterVarsity, 2000), 11–20; James K. Mead, *Biblical Theology: Issues, Methods, and Themes* (Louisville: Westminster John Knox, 2007).

6. D. A. Carson, "Current Issues in Biblical Theology: A New Testament Perspective," *BBR* 5 (1995): 27.

7. See also Vern Sheridan Poythress, "Kinds of Biblical Theology," *WTJ* 70, no. 1 (Spring 2008): 134–37. On how Edward W. Klink III and Darian R. Lockett present and illustrate five types of biblical theology, see Question 1.

8. See also Andreas J. Köstenberger, "The Promise of Biblical Theology: What Biblical Theology Is and What It Isn't," *Midwestern Journal of Theology* 17, no. 1 (Spring 2018): 12–13.

9. We illustrate the first two approaches to biblical theology below partly by referring to volumes in the New Studies in Biblical Theology series that D. A. Carson edits (published by Apollos and InterVarsity). In the preface to the series, Carson explains, "New Studies in Biblical Theology is a series of monographs that address key issues in the discipline of biblical theology. Contributions to the series focus on one or more of three areas: (1) the nature and status of biblical theology, including its relations with other disciplines (e.g., historical theology, exegesis, systematic theology, historical criticism, narrative theology); (2) the articulation and exposition of the structure of thought of a particular biblical writer or corpus; and (3) the delineation of a biblical theme across all or part of the biblical corpora." See the Gospel Coalition information page on the series: https://www.thegospelcoalition.org/article/new-studies-in-biblical-theology. That webpage links to an Excel spreadsheet that is a master Scripture index for the New Studies in Biblical Theology series. The spreadsheet places an asterisk by each page number where there is a discussion rather than merely a reference or brief comment.

Analyze the Message of the Whole Bible

A book's message is the author's overall task. It is not always the same as its content (what is the author writing about?) or purpose (why is the author writing?). The most comprehensive way to analyze the Bible's overall message is with a whole-Bible biblical theology. This involves studying the literary and theological message of each book and/or section of the Bible.[10]

Analyze the Message of Books or Sections of the Bible

A less comprehensive way to analyze the Bible's message is to focus on parts of the Bible. This includes tracing themes that are part of the literary and theological message of a book or section:[11]

- a book of the Bible[12]

- a section of the Old Testament: for example, Pentateuch,[13] wisdom literature[14]

- each book/section of the Old Testament (i.e., an Old Testament theology)[15]

---

10. E.g., Thomas R. Schreiner, *The King in His Beauty: A Biblical Theology of the Old and New Testaments* (Grand Rapids: Baker Academic, 2013).
11. See especially Alexander and Rosner, *New Dictionary of Biblical Theology*, 113–363.
12. E.g., J. Gary Millar, *Now Choose Life: Theology and Ethics in Deuteronomy*, NSBT 6 (Downers Grove, IL: InterVarsity, 1998); Daniel C. Timmer, *A Gracious and Compassionate God: Mission, Salvation and Spirituality in the Book of Jonah*, NSBT 26 (Downers Grove, IL: InterVarsity, 2011); James M. Hamilton Jr., *With the Clouds of Heaven: The Book of Daniel in Biblical Theology*, NSBT 32 (Downers Grove, IL: InterVarsity, 2014); Peter H. W. Lau and Gregory Goswell, *Unceasing Kindness: A Biblical Theology of Ruth*, NSBT 41 (Downers Grove, IL: InterVarsity, 2016); Brian J. Tabb, *All Things New: Revelation as the Climax of Biblical Prophecy*, NSBT (Downers Grove, IL: InterVarsity, 2019).
13. E.g., John Sailhamer, *The Meaning of the Pentateuch: Revelation, Composition, and Interpretation* (Downers Grove, IL: InterVarsity, 2009).
14. E.g., Richard P. Belcher Jr., *Finding Favour in the Sight of God: A Theology of Wisdom Literature*, NSBT 46 (Downers Grove, IL: InterVarsity, 2018).
15. E.g., Roy B. Zuck, ed., *A Biblical Theology of the Old Testament* (Chicago: Moody, 1991); Paul R. House, *Old Testament Theology* (Downers Grove, IL: InterVarsity, 1998); Stephen G. Dempster, *Dominion and Dynasty: A Biblical Theology of the Hebrew Bible*, NSBT 15 (Downers Grove, IL: InterVarsity, 2003); Eugene H. Merrill, *Everlasting Dominion: A Theology of the Old Testament* (Nashville: B&H, 2006), chs. 12–20; Bruce K. Waltke, with Charles Yu, *An Old Testament Theology: An Exegetical, Canonical, and Thematic Approach* (Grand Rapids: Zondervan, 2007); Jason S. DeRouchie, ed., *What the Old Testament Authors Really Cared About: A Survey of Jesus' Bible* (Grand Rapids: Kregel, 2013).

- a section of the New Testament: for example, Mark;[16] Luke-Acts;[17] John;[18] Paul;[19] James, Peter, and Jude[20]

- each book/section of the New Testament (i.e., a New Testament theology)[21]

Trace Themes

There are two basic approaches here: (1) trace themes through the whole Bible, and (2) trace themes through part of the Bible.

Trace Themes through the Whole Bible

Some evangelicals trace several themes through the whole Bible.[22] Some do this as they tell the story of the Bible: T. Desmond Alexander creatively starts with Revelation 21–22 and works back to show how what precedes connects to how the story culminates,[23] and G. K. Beale shows how the story climaxes in the inaugurated ("already") new creation and culminates in the final ("not yet") new creation.[24]

---

16. E.g., David E. Garland, *A Theology of Mark's Gospel: Good News about Jesus the Messiah, the Son of God*, Biblical Theology of the New Testament (Grand Rapids: Zondervan, 2015).
17. E.g., Darrell L. Bock, *A Theology of Luke and Acts: God's Promised Program, Realized for All Nations*, Biblical Theology of the New Testament (Grand Rapids: Zondervan, 2012).
18. E.g., Andreas J. Köstenberger, *A Theology of John's Gospel and Letters: The Word, the Christ, the Son of God*, Biblical Theology of the New Testament (Grand Rapids: Zondervan, 2009).
19. E.g., Thomas R. Schreiner, *Paul, Apostle of God's Glory in Christ: A Pauline Theology* (Downers Grove, IL: InterVarsity, 2001).
20. E.g., Peter H. Davids, *A Theology of James, Peter, and Jude: Living in the Light of the Coming King*, Biblical Theology of the New Testament (Grand Rapids: Zondervan, 2014).
21. E.g., George Eldon Ladd, *A Theology of the New Testament*, ed. Donald A. Hagner, 2nd ed. (Grand Rapids: Eerdmans, 1993); Zuck, *Biblical Theology of the New Testament*; I. Howard Marshall, *New Testament Theology: Many Witnesses, One Gospel* (Downers Grove, IL: InterVarsity, 2004); Frank Thielman, *Theology of the New Testament: A Canonical and Synthetic Approach* (Grand Rapids: Zondervan, 2005); Craig L. Blomberg, *A New Testament Theology* (Waco, TX: Baylor University Press, 2018).
22. E.g., Charles H. H. Scobie, *The Ways of Our God: An Approach to Biblical Theology* (Grand Rapids: Eerdmans, 2002); Scott J. Hafemann and Paul R. House, eds., *Central Themes in Biblical Theology: Mapping Unity in Diversity* (Grand Rapids: Baker Academic, 2007); Chris Bruno, *The Whole Message of the Bible in 16 Words* (Wheaton, IL: Crossway, 2017).
23. T. Desmond Alexander, *From Eden to the New Jerusalem: An Introduction to Biblical Theology* (Grand Rapids: Kregel, 2008).
24. G. K. Beale, *A New Testament Biblical Theology: The Unfolding of the Old Testament in the New* (Grand Rapids: Baker Academic, 2011). One could classify Beale's New Testament theology as a whole-Bible biblical theology since he spends so much space exegeting key Old Testament texts and connecting them to the New Testament.

Some trace a single prominent theme through the Bible.[25] Prominent themes include the following:

- atonement[26]
- circumcision[27]
- ethnicity[28]
- the city of God[29]
- covenant[30]
- idolatry[31]
- the image of God[32]
- incarnation[33]
- God's glory in salvation through judgment[34]

---

25. See especially Alexander and Rosner, *New Dictionary of Biblical Theology*, 365–863. See also the forthcoming ten volumes in the Essential Studies in Biblical Theology series, edited by Benjamin L. Gladd (InterVarsity), and the Short Studies in Biblical Theology series, edited by Dane Ortlund and Miles Van Pelt (Crossway). On whether there is one overarching theme, see Question 15.
26. E.g., Graham A. Cole, *God the Peacemaker: How Atonement Brings Shalom*, NSBT 25 (Downers Grove, IL: InterVarsity, 2009).
27. E.g., Karl Deenick, *Righteous by Promise: A Biblical Theology of Circumcision*, NSBT 45 (Downers Grove, IL: InterVarsity, 2018); John D. Meade, "Circumcision of Flesh to Circumcision of Heart: The Typology of the Sign of the Abrahamic Covenant," in *Progressive Covenantalism: Charting a Course between Dispensational and Covenant Theologies*, eds. Stephen J. Wellum and Brent E. Parker (Nashville: B&H, 2016), 127–58.
28. E.g., J. Daniel Hays, *From Every People and Nation: A Biblical Theology of Race*, NSBT 14 (Downers Grove, IL: InterVarsity, 2003).
29. E.g., T. Desmond Alexander, *The City of God and the Goal of Creation*, Short Studies in Biblical Theology (Wheaton, IL: Crossway, 2018).
30. E.g., Paul R. Williamson, *Sealed with an Oath: Covenant in God's Unfolding Plan*, NSBT 23 (Downers Grove, IL: InterVarsity, 2007); Thomas R. Schreiner, *Covenant and God's Purpose for the World*, Short Studies in Biblical Theology (Wheaton, IL: Crossway, 2017); Peter J. Gentry and Stephen J. Wellum, *Kingdom through Covenant: A Biblical-Theological Understanding of the Covenants*, 2nd ed. (Wheaton,IL: Crossway, 2018). See Question 22.
31. E.g., G. K. Beale, *We Become What We Worship: A Biblical Theology of Idolatry* (Downers Grove, IL: InterVarsity, 2008).
32. E.g., Richard Lints, *Identity and Idolatry: The Image of God and Its Inversion*, NSBT 36 (Downers Grove, IL: InterVarsity, 2015).
33. E.g., Graham A. Cole, *The God Who Became Human: A Biblical Theology of Incarnation*, NSBT 30 (Downers Grove, IL: InterVarsity, 2013).
34. E.g., John Piper, "The Goal of God in Redemptive History," in *Desiring God: Meditations of a Christian Hedonist*, 3rd ed. (Sisters, OR: Multnomah, 2003), 308–21; James M. Hamilton Jr., *God's Glory in Salvation through Judgment: A Biblical Theology* (Wheaton, IL: Crossway, 2010); Thomas R. Schreiner, "A Biblical Theology of the Glory of God," in *For the Fame of God's Name: Essays in Honor of John Piper*, eds. Sam Storms and Justin Taylor (Wheaton, IL: Crossway, 2010), 215–34.

- kingdom[35]
- land[36]
- law[37]
- marriage[38]
- mystery[39]
- possessions[40]
- prayer[41]
- repentance[42]
- resurrection[43]
- serpent[44]
- shepherd[45]
- temple[46]
- work[47]

---

35. E.g., Christopher W. Morgan and Robert A. Peterson, eds., *The Kingdom of God*, Theology in Community (Wheaton, IL: Crossway, 2012); Jeremy R. Treat, *The Crucified King: Atonement and Kingdom in Biblical and Systematic Theology* (Grand Rapids: Zondervan, 2014); Patrick Schreiner, *The Kingdom of God and the Glory of the Cross*, Short Studies in Biblical Theology (Wheaton, IL: Crossway, 2018).

36. E.g., Oren R. Martin, *Bound for the Promised Land: The Land Promise in God's Redemptive Plan*, NSBT 34 (Downers Grove, IL: InterVarsity, 2015). See Question 29.

37. E.g., Douglas J. Moo, "The Law of Christ as the Fulfillment of the Law of Moses: A Modified Lutheran View," in *Five Views on Law and Gospel*, ed. Wayne G. Strickland, Counterpoints (Grand Rapids: Zondervan, 1996), 319–76 (also 83–90, 165–73, 218–25, 309–15); Thomas R. Schreiner, *40 Questions about Christians and Biblical Law*, 40 Questions (Grand Rapids: Kregel, 2010). See Question 25.

38. E.g., Raymond C. Ortlund, *God's Unfaithful Wife: A Biblical Theology of Spiritual Adultery*, NSBT 2 (Downers Grove, IL: InterVarsity, 1996); Ray Ortlund, *Marriage and the Mystery of the Gospel*, Short Studies in Biblical Theology (Wheaton, IL: Crossway, 2016).

39. E.g., G. K. Beale and Benjamin L. Gladd, *Hidden but Now Revealed: A Biblical Theology of Mystery* (Downers Grove, IL: InterVarsity, 2014). See Question 21.

40. E.g., Craig L. Blomberg, *Neither Poverty nor Riches: A Biblical Theology of Possessions*, NSBT 7 (Downers Grove, IL: InterVarsity, 1999).

41. E.g., J. Gary Millar, *Calling on the Name of the Lord: A Biblical Theology of Prayer*, NSBT 38 (Downers Grove, IL: InterVarsity, 2016).

42. E.g., Mark J. Boda, *"Return to Me": A Biblical Theology of Repentance*, NSBT 35 (Downers Grove, IL: InterVarsity, 2015).

43. E.g., N. T. Wright, *The Resurrection of the Son of God*, Christian Origins and the Question of God 3 (London: SPCK, 2003). See Question 30.

44. E.g., Andrew David Naselli, *The Serpent and the Serpent Slayer*, Short Studies in Biblical Theology (Wheaton, IL: Crossway, 2020). See Question 23.

45. E.g., Timothy Laniak, *Shepherds after My Own Heart: Pastoral Traditions and Leadership in the Bible*, NSBT 20 (Downers Grove, IL: InterVarsity, 2006).

46. E.g., G. K. Beale, *The Temple and the Church's Mission: A Biblical Theology of the Dwelling Place of God*, NSBT 17 (Downers Grove, IL: InterVarsity, 2004). See Question 27.

47. E.g., James M. Hamilton Jr., *Work and Our Labor in the Lord*, Short Studies in Biblical Theology (Wheaton, IL: Crossway, 2017).

Trace Themes through Part of the Bible

Some evangelicals trace a theme or themes not comprehensively through the whole Bible but through only part of the Bible:

- part of a book of the Bible[48]

- a book of the Bible[49]

- a section of the Old Testament[50]

- the Old Testament: a single theme[51] or several significant themes (i.e., an Old Testament theology)[52]

- a section of the New Testament: for example, the Gospels,[53] Luke-Acts,[54] Paul[55]

---

48. E.g., Daniel J. Estes, *Hear, My Son: Teaching and Learning in Proverbs 1–9*, NSBT 4 (Downers Grove, IL: InterVarsity, 1997).

49. E.g., Robert S. Fyall, *Now My Eyes Have Seen You: Images of Creation and Evil in the Book of Job*, NSBT 12 (Downers Grove, IL: InterVarsity, 2002); Peter G. Bolt, *The Cross from a Distance: Atonement in Mark's Gospel*, NSBT 18 (Downers Grove, IL: InterVarsity, 2004); Andreas J. Köstenberger and Scott R. Swain, *Father, Son and Spirit: The Trinity and John's Gospel*, NSBT 24 (Downers Grove, IL: InterVarsity, 2008); W. Ross Blackburn, *The God Who Makes Himself Known: The Missionary Heart of the Book of Exodus*, NSBT 28 (Downers Grove, IL: InterVarsity, 2012); Andrew G. Shead, *A Mouth Full of Fire: The Word of God in the Words of Jeremiah*, NSBT 29 (Downers Grove, IL: InterVarsity, 2012); Andrew T. Abernethy, *The Book of Isaiah and God's Kingdom: A Thematic-Theological Approach*, NSBT 40 (Downers Grove, IL: InterVarsity, 2016).

50. E.g., the temple theme in the Pentateuch: T. Desmond Alexander, *From Paradise to the Promised Land: An Introduction to the Pentateuch*, 3rd ed. (Grand Rapids: Baker Academic, 2012), 119–33, 224–36.

51. E.g., William J. Dumbrell, *Covenant and Creation: An Old Testament Covenant Theology*, 2nd ed. (Milton Keynes, UK: Paternoster, 2013).

52. E.g., Ronald Youngblood, *The Heart of the Old Testament: A Survey of Key Theological Themes*, 2nd ed. (Grand Rapids: Baker, 1998); Merrill, *Everlasting Dominion*, chs. 2–11; Elmer A. Martens, *God's Design: A Focus on Old Testament Theology*, 4th ed. (Eugene, OR: Wipf & Stock, 2015).

53. E.g., Craig L. Blomberg, *Contagious Holiness: Jesus' Meals with Sinners*, NSBT 19 (Downers Grove, IL: InterVarsity, 2005).

54. E.g., Alan J. Thompson, *The Acts of the Risen Lord Jesus: Luke's Account of God's Unfolding Plan*, NSBT 27 (Downers Grove, IL: InterVarsity, 2011).

55. E.g., Thomas R. Schreiner, *The Law and Its Fulfillment: A Pauline Theology of Law* (Grand Rapids: Baker Academic, 1993); Frank Thielman, *Paul and the Law: A Contextual Approach* (Downers Grove, IL: InterVarsity, 1994); Mark A. Seifrid, *Christ, Our Righteousness: Paul's Theology of Justification*, NSBT 9 (Downers Grove, IL: InterVarsity, 2000); David W. Pao, *Thanksgiving: An Investigation of a Pauline Theme*, NSBT 13 (Downers Grove, IL: InterVarsity, 2002); Trevor J. Burke, *Adopted into God's Family: Exploring a Pauline Metaphor*, NSBT 22 (Downers Grove, IL: InterVarsity, 2006); Jason C. Meyer, *The End*

- the New Testament—a single theme[56] or several significant themes (i.e., a New Testament theology)[57]

Tell the Story

Some evangelicals do biblical theology by telling the Bible's grand unfolding story. Graeme Goldsworthy takes this approach in his popular introduction to biblical theology.[58] This approach overlaps with the other two because as you tell the story, you trace central themes and sometimes analyze the message of parts of the Bible or the Bible as a whole. Some follow Goldsworthy, for example, by telling the overall story with God's kingdom as the unifying theme.[59] Nick Roark and Robert Cline do that with fifteen headings:[60]

1. The king creates and covenants.
2. The king curses.
3. The king judges.
4. The king blesses.
5. The king rescues.
6. The king commands.
7. The king leads.
8. The king rules.
9. The king casts out.
10. The king promises.
11. The king arrives.
12. The king suffers and saves.
13. The king sends.
14. The king reigns.
15. The king returns.

---

of the Law: Mosaic Covenant in Pauline Theology, NAC Studies in Bible and Theology 7 (Nashville: B&H, 2009); Brian S. Rosner, *Paul and the Law: Keeping the Commandments of God*, NSBT 31 (Downers Grove, IL: InterVarsity, 2013).

56. E.g., David Peterson, *Possessed by God: A New Testament Theology of Sanctification and Holiness*, NSBT 1 (Downers Grove, IL: InterVarsity, 1995); Murray J. Harris, *Slave of Christ: A New Testament Metaphor for Total Devotion to Christ*, NSBT 8 (Downers Grove, IL: InterVarsity, 1999); Jonathan I. Griffiths, *Preaching in the New Testament: An Exegetical and Biblical-Theological Study*, NSBT 42 (Downers Grove, IL: InterVarsity, 2017).
57. E.g., Donald Guthrie, *New Testament Theology* (Downers Grove, IL: InterVarsity, 1981); Schreiner, *New Testament Theology*.
58. Graeme Goldsworthy, *According to Plan: The Unfolding Revelation of God in the Bible* (Downers Grove, IL: InterVarsity, 1991).
59. E.g., Vaughan Roberts, *God's Big Picture: Tracing the Storyline of the Bible* (Downers Grove, IL: InterVarsity, 2002).
60. Nick Roark and Robert Cline, *Biblical Theology: How the Church Faithfully Teaches the Gospel*, 9Marks (Wheaton, IL: Crossway, 2018), 31–74.

The most helpful biblical theology books for children use a storytelling approach.[61] Adults love a good story, too, and some books present biblical theology by telling the overall story in a theologically informed way.[62] (N. T. Wright is gifted at telling the story in an engaging way,[63] though he earns some thoughtful pushback.[64])

Summary

Evangelicals do biblical theology in three overlapping ways:

1. Analyze the message of books of the Bible, sections of the Bible (e.g., the Pentateuch or Paul's letters), and the whole Bible.

2. Trace themes through books of the Bible, sections of the Bible, and the whole Bible.

3. Tell the Bible's grand story.

REFLECTION QUESTIONS

1. In your own words, what are the three main overlapping ways that evangelicals do biblical theology?

---

61. E.g., David R. Helm, *The Big Picture Story Bible* (Wheaton, IL: Crossway, 2004); Sally Lloyd-Jones, *The Jesus Storybook Bible: Every Story Whispers His Name* (Grand Rapids: Zonderkidz, 2007); Champ Thornton, *God's Love: A Bible Storybook* (Whitakers, NC: Positive Action Bible Curriculum, 2012); James M. Hamilton Jr., *The Bible's Big Story: Salvation History for Kids* (Fearn, Scotland: Christian Focus, 2013); Kevin DeYoung, *The Biggest Story: How the Snake Crusher Brings Us Back to the Garden* (Wheaton, IL: Crossway, 2015).

62. E.g., D. A. Carson, *The Gagging of God: Christianity Confronts Pluralism* (Grand Rapids: Zondervan, 1996), 193–314; D. A. Carson, *The God Who Is There: Finding Your Place in God's Story* (Grand Rapids: Baker, 2010); Sigurd Grindheim, *Introducing Biblical Theology* (London: Bloomsbury T&T Clark, 2013); Chris Bruno, *The Whole Story of the Bible in 16 Verses* (Wheaton, IL: Crossway, 2015); Matthew Y. Emerson, *The Story of Scripture: An Introduction to Biblical Theology* (Nashville: B&H, 2017); Trent Hunter and Stephen J. Wellum, *Christ from Beginning to End: How the Full Story of Scripture Reveals the Full Glory of Christ* (Grand Rapids: Zondervan, 2018).

63. E.g., N. T. Wright, "The Plot, the Plan and the Storied Worldview," in *Paul and the Faithfulness of God*, Christian Origins and the Question of God 4 (London: SPCK, 2013), 1:456–537.

64. E.g., Douglas J. Moo, "*Paul and the Faithfulness of God*," *The Gospel Coalition*, November 6, 2013, https://www.thegospelcoalition.org/reviews/paul-faithfulness-god; Thomas R. Schreiner, "N. T. Wright under Review: Revisiting the Apostle Paul and His Doctrine of Justification," *Credo* 4, no. 1 (2014): 26–56; Simon J. Gathercole, "*Paul and the Faithfulness of God*: A Review," *Reformation21*, July 2014, http://www.reformation21.org/articles/paul-and-the-faithfulness-of-god-a-review.php.

2. What is your favorite way to do biblical theology? Why?

3. How would you state the message of the whole Bible in one sentence?

4. What is a theme that you delight to trace through the Bible? Why?

5. Why might it be dangerous to do biblical theology by telling the story if you have not sufficiently analyzed the message and traced central themes?

What Must We Presuppose to Do Biblical Theology?

Oren R. Martin

To do biblical theology is to interpret the whole Bible as *Christian* Scripture. God revealed Scripture through the biblical authors not for mere historians and textual critics, but for followers of Christ, "for our instruction, that through endurance and through the encouragement of the Scriptures we might have hope" (Rom. 15:4; cf. 1 Cor. 10:11). Christians, then, bring their faith in Christ to the task of biblical theology. As a result, we must read the Bible with certain realities in mind—with faith seeking understanding. Christians must receive and understand according to Christ.

Presuppositions and Biblical Theology

There is no such thing as theology *without* presuppositions. Modern hermeneutics has positively helped readers realize that the interpretive process is never neutral, for numerous factors have affected every person.[1] Influences like parents, upbringing, culture, relationships, education, experiences, tradition, and church background shape how we understand everything, including Scripture. To put it another way, our preunderstandings, beliefs, and ideas influence us every time we seek to observe, understand, and evaluate. The question is not whether we bring assumptions and presuppositions to Scripture, but whether those presuppositions conform to Scripture. It is, therefore, imperative to recognize and evaluate them under the authority

---

1. See, e.g., Kevin Vanhoozer, *Is There a Meaning in this Text? The Bible, The Reader, and the Morality of Literary Knowledge* (Grand Rapids: Zondervan, 1998), chaps. 7–8; Grant R. Osborne, *The Hermeneutical Spiral: A Comprehensive Introduction to Biblical Interpretation*, rev. and exp. (Downers Grove, IL: InterVarsity, 2006), 29.

of God's Word, and then to allow that Word to shape and reshape us. Richard Lints explains,

> Part of the task of theology is to reflect on the one who reads the biblical text. Theology is about God, but it is also about those who have been created in God's image and have become distorted images. A genuine biblical theology will strongly affirm that humans (Christian and non-Christian) are inevitably influenced by their own culture, tradition and experience. Until and unless the evangelical community wrestles more seriously with this fact, they will not overcome the unreflective biases that characterize the evangelical appropriation of the Bible.[2]

To be sure, to identify and defend each interpretive-shaping influence is beyond the scope of this chapter. Nevertheless, Christian presuppositions are justifiable because they are grounded in the Triune God, who has freely made himself known, benevolently created humankind in his image, lovingly acted on humanity's behalf through the person and work of Jesus Christ, and graciously given the gift of his Spirit to those who believe "that we might understand the things freely given us by God" (1 Cor. 2:12).

When doing biblical theology, what we must presuppose includes the commitment to the Triune God, who speaks truthfully and reliably through his Word;[3] the divine and human authorship of Scripture;[4] the possibility of a "whole-Bible biblical theology";[5] and the unity of God's saving plan that progressively unfolds through the Bible's literary diversity.[6] We could devote a whole book to unpacking what we must presuppose in receiving God's Word as *God's* Word, but this chapter briefly develops only some of the themes, shows how they arise from Scripture, and identifies why they are important to faithfully understand and enjoy God's life-giving Word.

---

2. Richard Lints, *The Fabric of Theology: A Prolegomena to Evangelical Theology* (Grand Rapids: Eerdmans, 1993), 27.
3. Scripture coheres and is an established canon of sixty-six books—"a collection of historical texts written over a long period of time, utilizing different literary forms and manifesting diverse perspectives, and as the word of God who spoke and continues to speak through its books." Eckhard J. Schnabel, "Scripture," in *New Dictionary of Biblical Theology*, hereafter *NDBT*, eds. T. Desmond Alexander, Brian S. Rosner, D. A. Carson, and Graeme Goldsworthy (Downers Grove, IL: InterVarsity, 2000), 36.
4. See Question 14 and Timothy Ward, *Words of Life: Scripture as the Living and Active Word of God* (Downers Grove, IL: InterVarsity, 2009).
5. See, e.g., Brian Rosner, "Biblical Theology," in *NDBT*, 3–11.
6. See, e.g., Craig L. Blomberg, "The Unity and Diversity of Scripture," in *NDBT*, 64–72; D. A. Carson, "Unity and Diversity in the New Testament: The Possibility of Systematic Theology," in *Scripture and Truth*, eds. D. A. Carson and John D. Woodbridge (Grand Rapids: Baker, 1992), 65–95.

The God Who Is

Christians must read Scripture as what it is: *God's* Word. Augustine exhorts, "Let us treat scripture like scripture: like God speaking."[7] The task of reading Scripture must have in mind the God who has acted in history and revealed himself in his works and words, especially since those works and words reveal who he is, the Triune God. In other words, if God who is Father, Son, and Holy Spirit had not made himself known, we would neither have knowledge of this Triune God nor his plan "for the fullness of time to unite all things in Christ, things in heaven and things on earth" (Eph. 1:10). A fundamental presupposition for doing biblical theology, then, is that there is a God who has made himself and his purposes known. But who is *this* God, and how has he made himself known? In these last days God has made himself known in his Son by his Spirit (John 1:1–18; Heb. 1:1–2; John 14–16). Fred Sanders explains, "In the fullness of time, God did not give us facts about himself, but gave us himself in the person of the Father who sent, the Son who was sent, and the Holy Spirit who was poured out. These events were accompanied by verbally inspired explanatory words; but the latter depend on the former."[8] As a result, Christians have long confessed that only in Christ by the Spirit do we truly know God.

Biblical theology is possible because of the lively, plentiful, self-communicative character of the true and living God, who has life in himself (Ps. 36:9[10]; cf. John 5:26). As the church has confessed throughout the ages, the eternal life of God (*ad intra*) consists of lively personal relations: the Father's begetting of the Son, the Son's being begotten, and the Spirit's proceeding from the Father and the Son.[9] These relations, or processions, mark God's perfect life and are made known in the (*ad extra*) missions of the sending of the Son (from the Father) and the Spirit (from the Father and the Son).[10] This revelatory, communicative presence makes biblical theology possible and forms the context in which it undertakes its service.

Biblical theology focuses on the God who has freely made himself known, and the discipline is not complete until it reaches its center and goal in God the Son, Jesus Christ, who fulfills God's saving promises, reveals God finally and most fully (John 1:1–18; Heb. 1:1–2), and sends (with the Father) the Holy Spirit to truthfully bear witness about him (John 15:26). In this sense, biblical theology is an exposition of the gospel, which reveals the Triune God and is revealed by the Triune God. So, if the gospel of Jesus Christ shapes

---

7. Augustine, *Sermons* 162C.15.
8. Fred Sanders, *The Triune God* (Grand Rapids: Zondervan, 2016), 41.
9. See Sanders, *Triune God*, ch. 2.
10. See John Webster, *God Without Measure: Working Papers in Christian Theology*, vol. 1: *God and the Works of God* (London: T&T Clark, 2016).

biblical theology, and if the gospel reveals God the Trinity, then biblical theology must presuppose the One God who is Father, Son, and Holy Spirit.

The God Who Speaks and the People Who Listen

Scripture is not only *God's* Word, but God's *Word*. The life-possessing God is the life-giving God who speaks words of life, initially in creation and most fully in Jesus Christ, who is the way, the truth, and the life (John 14:6). Flowing from the first presupposition, then, is that the Triune God speaks and has spoken, which shapes the practice of biblical theology.

The content of biblical theology is God's gracious revelation, which is the self-presentation of God who freely gives himself to us for our greatest joy. It is not merely a record of religious experience with God. Revelation is the way of talking about those words and works in which God makes himself known and present. For example, God speaks to Adam and Eve (Gen. 1–2), Abram (Gen. 12), Moses (Exod. 3), the Israelites at Mt. Sinai (Exod. 19), to and through the prophets (Elijah, Isaiah, Jeremiah, Ezekiel, the Twelve), and finally in the prophet *par excellence*, Jesus Christ, which results in establishing a saving, covenanted fellowship with his creatures. In other words, God is present in and through his living Word.

God's revelation has a purpose. God's goal is not to be a celestial showoff, but to overcome human rebellion and idolatry, alienation and pride, independence and falsehood, and to replace them with true knowledge, worship, love, humility, and fellowship with himself. In the biblical storyline, revelation is not a product of the fall; rather, it precedes redemption and reconciliation, results from God's incomprehensibility, and is possible because God graciously condescends to speak to and be with his people through his Word.

From eternity past, God communicates. "In the beginning was the Word, and the Word was with God, and the Word was God" (John 1:1). The eternal and glorious loving communion of the Father and the Son (John 17:5, 24) is shared by the Holy Spirit, who proceeds from the Father and the Son (John 14:26; 15:26) and searches everything, "even the depths of God" (1 Cor. 2:10). Subsequently, the Spirit of God indwells Christians "that we might understand the things freely given us by God" (2:12). In his goodness, by his free decision, God determined to reveal himself and communicate to his creatures so that we might share in his blessed Triune communion (John 17:20–26). This communication began in the economy of creation with God speaking into existence all things from nothing with a word: "Let there be" (Gen. 1:3, 6, 9, 11, 14, 20, 24, 26, 28, 29). His word is, therefore, independent from creation, powerful, authoritative, effective, and purposeful.

Furthermore, God's Word is good, for it flows from the very nature of God, who simply *is* good (Ps. 135:3) and declares all things good (Gen. 1:4, 10, 12, 18, 21, 25, 31). But rather than take God at his word, Adam and Eve instead listened to another word, the word of the serpent, which brought separation from God and death (Gen. 3). But amid God's judgment of sin (Gen.

3:14–19), he promised to one day provide an offspring from the woman who would triumph over the serpent (3:15), who would come through the line of Abraham (Gen. 12–17; cf. Gal. 3:16). Afterward, through the long and arduous arc of Israel's history, "when the fullness of time had come, God sent forth his Son, born of a woman, born under the law, to redeem those who were under the law, so that we might receive adoption as sons" (Gal. 4:4–5). At each point in history, God's revelation accompanied and interpreted his redemption. In other words, revelation progresses because redemption progresses, from the first exodus to the better exodus in Christ. And this revelation finally came in the Word-made-flesh (John 1:14; Heb. 1:1–2), who dwelt among us to redeem and reconcile us to God. Subsequently, through his once-for-all redemptive work in Christ, God has authorized his NT Word to be written down, which announces and testifies to the living Word, Jesus Christ (2 Peter 1:16–21).

A number of things follow when we understand God's revelation this way. Scripture declares that God has spoken at many times and in many ways (Heb. 1:1). Some of these times and ways include God speaking directly and personally to persons, in visions and dreams, through historical events, in personal experiences, through literary research and labor, and to and through his authorized and commissioned prophets and apostles. And while the notion of revelation is a much broader category than God's written word in Scripture, Scripture is nevertheless a vital component—indeed the supreme verbal manifestation—of God's revelation, for it is the fixed account of God's self-revealing work that testifies to Christ, from beginning to end. Thus, God's written Word is both a fully divine and fully human book,[11] sovereignly designed to serve God's eternal

---

11. The majority of Christians who affirm the total truthfulness of Scripture have upheld that Scripture is the product of both divine and human authorship. The concursive theory, or double-agency discourse, asserts, "God in his sovereignty so superintended the freely composed human writings we call the Scriptures that the result was nothing less than God's words and, therefore, entirely truthful." D. A. Carson, "Recent Developments in the Doctrine of Scripture," in *Hermeneutics, Authority, and Canon*, eds. D. A. Carson and John D. Woodbridge (Eugene, OR: Wipf & Stock, 1986), 45. In other words, Scripture is God's Word in human language. As Scott Swain says, "God condescends to us in covenant communication because God condescends to us in covenant friendship. And friends must speak the same language." Scott R. Swain, *Trinity, Revelation, and Reading: A Theological Introduction to the Bible and Its Interpretation* (London: T&T Clark, 2011), 69. For some, the idea that God speaks to humanity through creaturely language diminishes God's communication. Timothy Ward answers this charge by connecting the Triune God with the creation of human beings in his image. He says, "It is quite reasonable to suppose that [human language] has the ability to speak truly of God, both because it was given to us by a God who speaks within himself as eternally three speaking persons, and also because our possession of language, as made in God's image, is analogous to God's communicative activity. Our language can be made by God to speak truthfully of him because our language has its origin in him and in some way is like his own." Ward, *Words of Life*, 34–35. Furthermore, "God's authorized speech agents are fitting ministers of the Word that he is and fitting instruments of the mission he fulfills" through his Son, "who is at once the personal *agent* of God's word (he is *sent* by God to speak)

purposes in Christ to create, establish, sustain, and perfect covenant fellowship with God the Father through God the Son in God the Spirit.[12]

Since all Scripture is from God, at least five implications follow for doing biblical theology. First, because Scripture is breathed out by God (2 Tim. 3:15–16), from the whole of it down to its very parts, biblical theology is possible because there is a theological and christological unity from beginning to end, from creation in Genesis 1 to the new creation in Revelation 21–22.

But second, the unity of Scripture ought not neglect its diversity. God's revelation is progressive. He did not deliver all of it at one time. Rather, it unfolded over time, through different languages and cultures and genres and people, which requires the reader to take into account such things. Furthermore, through Scripture's rich diversity, God's unfolding redemptive plan culminates in the person and work of Jesus Christ (Gal. 4:4–7), and those who belong to Christ by faith possess the Spirit who enables them to understand and receive God's Word, for "we have received not the spirit of the world, but the Spirit who is from God, that we might understand the things freely given us by God. And we impart this in words not taught by human wisdom but taught by the Spirit, interpreting spiritual truths to those who are spiritual" (1 Cor. 2:12–13).

Third, Christians can have confidence that God's Word is completely true and reliable in everything it speaks (Ps. 119:60; John 17:17), for it testifies to and is fulfilled in the One who is the truth (John 14:6). And because the truth is in Jesus (Eph. 4:21), God will never deceive or lead us astray. He is trustworthy, and therefore his Word is trustworthy.

Fourth, God's Word is sufficient. God has given us "all things that pertain to life and godliness, through the true knowledge of him who called us to his own glory and excellence" (2 Peter 1:3). God has not given us everything there is to know, but he has given us everything we need to know in order to live for his glory in Christ.

And finally, God's Word is clear. Though human hearts are darkened by sin, those who have trusted in Christ have been born again by the Spirit and given the gift of the Spirit to understand the things he has revealed. This regenerating and renewing work of the Spirit, then, makes it possible to understand and receive Scripture with progressively decreasing distortions. There are, however, some things "that are hard to understand" (2 Peter 3:16). Though the clarity of Scripture is not a claim about every passage in Scripture, it is a claim that the main contours of Scripture are clear because God has ensured it that we may know him (Deut. 29:29) and because God by his Spirit "has

---

and the personal *embodiment* of God's word (he *is* God's speech)" (Swain, *Trinity, Revelation, and Reading*, 2011, 37). In other words, grounding for the possibility of truth, meaning and interpretation is in the Triune God who creates and speaks through and to his image-bearers.

12. See Swain, *Trinity, Revelation, and Reading*, ch. 3.

shone in our hearts to give the light of the knowledge of the glory of God in the face of Jesus Christ" (2 Cor. 4:6). This means that the meaning of Scripture is most clearly disclosed to us in its whole context, the canon of Scripture.[13] This kind of reading "equips us to read the various parts of Scripture in light of the whole and with an eye to Scripture's ultimate communicative goal."[14]

Summary

The task of biblical theology belongs to pilgrims in exile who have not reached their final home, not to those who have arrived.[15] But confidence lies ahead on their journey because God has spoken in Christ and is leading them home by his Spirit. There are no doubt other presuppositions that could be discussed, but the ones this chapter discusses provide a framework for the practice of biblical theology. Because the Triune God speaks and is Lord of his Word, we must approach the Word of the Lord with joy and wonder (Ps. 119:7, 16, 18, 24), humility (Isa. 66:1–2), confidence (Luke 1:4), faith (Rom. 10:17), diligence, and dependence (2 Tim. 2:7, 15). In doing so we will experience great joy, for in him are the words of life (John 6:68–69; Acts 5:20).

REFLECTION QUESTIONS

1. Why is it important to be aware of our presuppositions when we approach Scripture?

2. What would happen if we approached Scripture with opposite presuppositions (e.g., that God does not exist, that he is distant and uninvolved, that he hasn't spoken, or that Christ doesn't fulfill all of his saving promises)?

3. How does Scripture reveal the Triune God, and the Triune God reveal Scripture?

4. How should we receive God's Word?

5. Why can we approach God's Word with confidence?

---

13. For more on the significance of canon for doing biblical theology, see Question 16. For more on the canon of Scripture in general, see Roger T. Beckwith, "The Canon of Scripture," in *NDBT*, 27–34; Roger T. Beckwith, *The Old Testament Canon of the New Testament Church* (London: SPCK, 1985); Michael Kruger, *The Question of Canon: Challenging the Status Quo in the New Testament Debate* (Downers Grove, IL: InterVarsity, 2013); Edmon L. Gallagher and John D. Meade, *The Biblical Canon Lists from Early Christianity: Texts and Analysis* (Oxford: Oxford University Press, 2017).

14. Swain, *Trinity, Revelation, and Reading*, 110.

15. Swain, *Trinity, Revelation, and Reading*, 10.

How Does Biblical Theology Compare to Other Theological Disciplines?

Oren R. Martin

It is astonishing that the transcendent Lord over us has spoken to us that he might establish covenant fellowship with us, his creatures. Though one day we will meet with God not through Scripture but face-to-face and know him as we are known (1 Cor. 13:12), for we will see him as he is (1 John 3:2), at the present time interpreting the Bible is an active exercise of redeemed saints learning what it means to be children of God in Christ as they follow him to their eternal home. There are, therefore, various tools in this journey that equip us for our destination: exegesis, biblical theology, systematic theology, historical theology, and practical theology.[1] But we should not view these various elements as mechanical steps, with one leading to the other only to leave the previous step(s) behind, which then result in perfect knowledge of God. Rather, each one complements, informs, and shapes the others as we grow in knowing God. Concerning this process, Andrew Naselli writes,

> It's like asking LeBron James how he plays basketball. He doesn't think, "Well, step 1 is that I dribble. Step 2 is that I walk and dribble at the same time," etc. There are so many facets to playing basketball at a high level. That's why basketball players can improve their overall game by focusing on individual areas like dribbling and sprinting and cutting and passing and layups and hook shots and short-range

---

1. Horton qualifies, "Only in the eighteenth century was theological study divided into distinct subdisciplines now familiar in theological education: biblical, systematic, historical, practical, and sometimes also apologetic (philosophical) theology." Michael S. Horton, "Historical Theology," in *Dictionary for Theological Interpretation of the Bible*, ed. Kevin J. Vanhoozer (Grand Rapids: Baker Academic, 2005), 293.

jumpers and free throws and three-pointers and setting screens and boxing out and lifting weights to get stronger and studying strategies to win. But in the heat of the moment during a game, basketball players aren't thinking, "Step 1: do this. Step 2: do that." At that point they're just playing by instinct and employing all of the skills they've developed as best they can. They go with the flow of the game and adjust to their opponents' defensive schemes and strategize how to improve on both ends of the court. . . . So with exegesis and theology.[2]

Similarly, D. A. Carson explains,

It would be convenient if we could operate exclusively along the direction of the following diagram:

Exegesis → Biblical Theology → [Historical Theology] → Systematic Theology

(The brackets around the third element are meant to suggest that in this paradigm historical theology makes a direct contribution to the development from biblical theology to systematic theology but is not itself a part of that line.) In fact, this paradigm, though neat, is naïve. No exegesis is ever done in a vacuum. If every theist is in some sense a

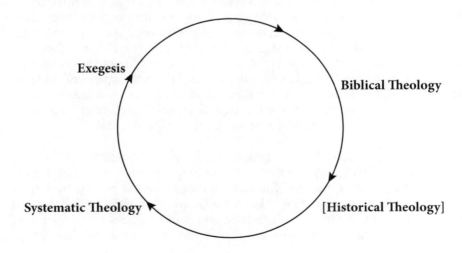

2. Andrew Naselli, *How to Understand and Apply the New Testament: Twelve Steps from Exegesis to Theology* (Phillipsburg, NJ: P&R, 2017), 4. As a native Houstonian, I would prefer Naselli use the Houston Rockets' Hakeem Olajuwon as his example, but his point still carries.

systematician, then he is a systematician *before* he begins his exegesis. Are we, then, locked into a hermeneutical circle, like the following?

No; there is a better way. It might be diagrammed like this:

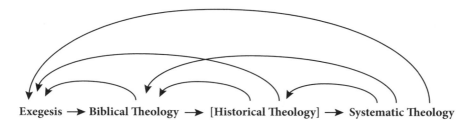

Exegesis ⟶ Biblical Theology ⟶ [Historical Theology] ⟶ Systematic Theology

> That is to say, there are feedback lines (and more lines going forward, for that matter). It is absurd to deny that one's systematic theology affects one's exegesis. Nevertheless, the line of final control is the straight one from exegesis right through biblical and historical theology to systematic theology. The final authority is the Scriptures, and the Scriptures alone.[3]

So each component exercised in communion with the Triune God shapes and informs the others as we pursue with dependence and humility fuller knowledge of God. And as we think over what he has spoken, he will give us understanding (2 Tim. 2:7). With this being said, let's now turn to describe each discipline.

Exegesis

The word *exegesis*, deriving from the Greek verb *exēgeomai*, has a range of meaning that can denote to lead, explain, or expound. For example, in Luke 24:35 two of Jesus's disciples, after seeing and hearing him interpret "in all the Scriptures the things concerning himself" (24:27), "told" the others how he was made known to them. Or, in Acts 21:19, Paul "related" to the other Christians the many things God had done in his mission to take the gospel to the Gentiles. Perhaps the most brilliant expression of this word is found in John 1:18, which says that although no one has ever seen God, the eternal Word who became flesh—Jesus Christ—"has made him known." In other words, we might say that Jesus is the exegesis of God. That is, if you want to see the fullest expression of God and know what he intends, then look to Jesus.

---

3. D. A. Carson, "Unity and Diversity in the New Testament: The Possibility of Systematic Theology," in *Scripture and Truth*, eds. D. A. Carson and John D. Woodbridge (Grand Rapids: Zondervan, 1983), 91–92.

Exegeting Scripture is the process of discovering the meaning of the biblical text in its literary and salvation-historical context through analyzing words and their relations in order to discern what the author intended to communicate. On the one hand, given that Scripture is from God and was revealed and written by the Spirit (2 Tim. 3:16; 2 Peter 1:20–21) through divinely authorized and commissioned people over time, to hear what Scripture says through Moses or Isaiah or Luke or Paul or any other biblical author is to hear what *God* says, for in the end it is *his* Word.[4] There is, therefore, a God-given unity that spans Scripture's pages from beginning to end. On the other hand, because various people gave and wrote this revelation over time, we grow to know and are transformed by the riches of God's written Word only when we mine its rich diversity. As a result, there are various components of exegesis that include analyzing genre, textual criticism, translation, grammar, argument diagram, historical-cultural context, literary context, and word studies.[5] This exegetical process focuses on understanding and receiving the A/author's communicative intent. But exegesis also has larger concerns, for it does not merely deal with isolated texts but also with the relations between them, to which we will now turn.

Biblical Theology[6]

Biblical theology works from individual biblical texts (exegesis) to the entirety of Scripture, giving attention to *how* God revealed Scripture. In making connections between texts, biblical theology allows Scripture to set the agenda and establish its own categories.

Brian Rosner defines biblical theology as "theological interpretation of Scripture in and for the church. It begins with historical and literary sensitivity and seeks to analyze and synthesize the Bible's teaching about God and his relations to the world on its own terms, maintaining sight of the Bible's overarching narrative and Christocentric focus."[7] This definition has some components that are important to unpack in order to properly understand and practice biblical theology.

First, the *nature* of biblical theology is exegesis in light of the completed canon of Scripture, for the final context of every text is the entirety of God's written Word. Scripture comes to us as God's self-attesting Word and

---

4. See Question 14.
5. For an expanded treatment of the nature and process of exegesis, see Jason S. DeRouchie, *How to Understand and Apply the Old Testament: Twelve Steps from Exegesis to Theology* (Phillipsburg, NJ: P&R, 2017), chs. 1–9; and Naselli, *Understand and Apply the New Testament*, chs. 1–8.
6. See also Question 1.
7. Brian Rosner, "Biblical Theology," in *New Dictionary of Biblical Theology*, hereafter *NDBT*, eds. T. Desmond Alexander, Brian S. Rosner, D. A. Carson, and Graeme Goldsworthy (Downers Grove, IL: InterVarsity, 2000), 10 (italics removed from original).

therefore demands that it be interpreted as such. All of Scripture, even though written through the willing agency of human authors, is to be received and understood as God's Word. Apart from the reality of God's self-disclosure in Scripture, the idea of biblical theology becomes an exercise in religious futility. That is, God must have revealed himself *in writing* for doing theology in the true sense to even be possible. As a result, there is a *unity* between the Old and New Testaments that together declare God's unfailing purposes through Christ in this world.

Second, the *mission* of biblical theology is to trace the progressive and organic unfolding of God's revelation in history. God reveals progressively both his presence and his saving acts. He redeems over time (e.g., Gen. 3:15; Exod. 13–14)—not all at once and not all in a uniform way. Rather, his saving comes with strange twists and turns and in separate but related stages. These stages are largely marked by God's major acts and redemptive covenants (e.g., creation, exodus, exile; or the Adamic-Noahic, Abrahamic, Mosaic, Davidic, and new covenants). But the central and final redemptive era of Scripture begins with the incarnation and culminates in the cross work of Jesus Christ. The focal point of biblical theology, then, is not merely how God has revealed himself throughout history, but also how Jesus climactically fulfills all of God's organically related words (cf. Luke 16:16; Gal. 4:4–5; Heb. 1:1–2; 9:24–28). Biblical theology therefore keeps an eye on what came before to better understand the text at hand. But it doesn't stop there, for the final context of every text is the entirety of Scripture that centers on Christ. So biblical theology must pay canonical attention to what comes *before* and *after* a text to understand how it fits into God's final redemptive purposes in Jesus.

For example, when studying the Latter Prophets, one must keep an eye on what came before to make sense of what was happening in that particular historical context.[8] The reason for this attention is that the Latter Prophets explain Israel's history against the backdrop of God's faithfulness and his people's unfaithfulness to his prior covenant(s). Theologically, the prophets proclaim the word of God in the context of the covenant, primarily as the Pentateuch defines it, and Israel's disobedience concludes the promise of covenantal curses as a result of their disobedience (cf. Lev. 26:14–39; Deut. 28:15–68). The Latter Prophets comment on the grand story from creation to exile by showing both the just judgment and free mercy of God. But the

---

8. In the Hebrew canon, the section of the OT referred to as the Prophets falls into two parts: "The Former Prophets consist of Joshua, Judges, Samuel, and Kings, which continue the Torah narrative from the conquest to the exile in Babylon. . . . The Latter Prophets, which begin the second half [of the Hebrew OT], comprise Jeremiah, Ezekiel, Isaiah and the Twelve, which are largely anthologies of prophetic speeches delivered mainly during the time described in the latter part of the book of Kings." Stephen G. Dempster, "Geography and Genealogy, Dominion and Dynasty: A Theology of the Hebrew Bible," in *Biblical Theology: Retrospect and Prospect*, ed. Scott J. Hafemann (Downers Grove, IL: InterVarsity, 2002), 75.

Prophets do not merely point to the past, for God reveals future-oriented events that offer both sobering commentary on Israel's present status as well as the promise of her glorious future. That is, they contribute significantly to the subjects of exile, exodus, people, land, judgment, and salvation. Hence, the Prophets offer foretastes of hope for establishing God's kingdom through his coming Servant-King.

This example is one way of doing biblical theology, but there are other ways as well.[9] Biblical theology can also track words, concepts, and themes across the whole of Scripture (e.g., covenant, kingdom, land, temple) or its parts, whether units of Scripture (e.g., Law, Prophets, Gospels), individual books (e.g., Leviticus, Isaiah, Mark), an authorial collection (e.g., letters of John or Paul), or the Old or New Testaments.[10] What we must stress is that biblical theology is not complete until it addresses the Bible *on its own terms* with its own structures and categories and considers how those structures and categories reach their goal in Christ.

In doing biblical theology, then, it is vital to keep in mind that God is the Lord of history and that redemption moves toward his goal and purposes in the Son, which the Spirit completes (John 14–16). This organic quality of revelation explains both the unity and diversity of Scripture. So, contrary to the idea that variation and diversity in Scripture undermine its authority and truthfulness, its organic nature establishes it. God shaped the human authors through whom he reveals his Word, and God shaped what they wrote, the God-breathed Word, which is completely sufficient for faith and practice (2 Tim. 3:16–17).

Systematic Theology

Biblical theology works intertextually to interpret Scripture on its own terms by tracking how it historically and redemptively unfolds from the beginning (creation in Gen. 1) to the end (new creation in Rev. 21–22). Systematic theology, in contrast, works from Scripture as it makes intrasystematic connections primarily in relation to its source—the Triune God—and secondarily to all things in relation to him.[11] That is, systematic theology preserves the meaning of the terms, structures, and categories in biblical theology, but goes further by transforming those terms into a conceptual framework for people today. It puts all of the conceptual "pieces" together to display the

---

9. See Question 10.
10. Our goal is "whole-Bible biblical theology," which is not merely a theology that is biblical, although it is certainly not less. This phrase picks up on the discipline of biblical theology which, as D. A. Carson says, "even as it works inductively from the diverse texts of the Bible, seeks to uncover and articulate the unity of all the biblical texts taken together, resorting primarily to the categories of those text themselves." D. A. Carson, "Systematic Theology and Biblical Theology," in *NDBT*, 100; see also Rosner, "Biblical Theology," 3–11.
11. See John Webster, "Principles of Systematic Theology," in *The Domain of the Word: Scripture and Theological Reason* (London: T&T Clark, 2012).

anatomy of their relations and proportions. Thus, it connects all reality to the Word and works of God, for "from him and through him and to him are all things" (Rom. 11:36). Flowing from this point, then, systematic theology is ordered around the Word and works of God, which is why most systematic theologies display this kind of logic in their table of contents.

To spell this out, God reveals (doctrine of revelation) who God is (doctrine of the Trinity and his attributes) and what he has created (doctrine of creation and humanity). And, though humanity has sinned against him (doctrine of sin), God the Father has provided a gracious solution by sending God the Son, who became incarnate, who was sent in the likeness of sinful flesh to condemn sin in the flesh by becoming like us in every way yet without sin (doctrines of the person and work of Christ), for us and for our redemption (doctrine of salvation). As a result, God the Father and the Son has graciously sent God the Holy Spirit who indwells, fills, and gifts his people for service (doctrine of the church) until the day when Christ returns to complete what he began by his life, death, resurrection, and ascension and usher in a new creation (doctrine of last things).

By practicing faith seeking understanding, the early fathers of the church were seeking to protect the church against heresy, prepare new converts for baptism and the Lord's Supper, and disciple Christians in the faith. Theology, therefore, was lived. It was not for the theoretical sake of crossing theological t's and dotting doctrinal i's; rather, it was a matter of life and death for the sake of the gospel. Thus, a systematic understanding of the faith attends to the whole of Scripture and seeks to grasp the parts in relation to the whole, where the whole is the completed story of God's relation to the world from the initial act of creation to its final consummation in Christ.[12] As a result, there are a number of important components in systematic theology.

First, it attends to the whole. Scripture is God's Word that tells one story about one King and his kingdom, a King who reigns by covenant over his servant-kings. Moreover, it comes to us through diverse redemptive-historical epochs, various genres, and divinely initiated covenants. Therefore, theology gives sanctified attention and reflection to display how this unified whole relates to all of life lived before God. Furthermore, it seeks to connect the whole to what may be discovered and learned outside of Scripture through God's general revelation. But not only does it attend to the whole of Scripture, it also gives attention to its relations. That is, it not only develops what Scripture teaches about faith, or what Scripture teaches about obedience (works), by looking at how each develops across the canon of Scripture (which is closer to biblical theology), but it also asks, "What is the relation between faith *and* works?" Subsequently, it seeks to account for how faith and works relate in a coherent manner. This relation explains systematic theology's organization. Or to give another example, systematic theology develops what Scripture teaches about God the Father, Son, and

---

12. Kevin J. Vanhoozer, "Systematic Theology," in *DTIB*, 776.

Holy Spirit, but it also asks, "What is the relation between the Father, Son, and Holy Spirit?" At this point theology employs concepts and conceptual tools that provide coherence to what Scripture teaches about God, who is both one (in nature) and three (in person). And lastly, systematic theology gives its attention to proportions. That is, it distinguishes matters that are of "first importance," such as the gospel (1 Cor. 15:3), from other matters of secondary or tertiary importance.[13] So, systematic theology seeks to reflect the Bible's own emphases and priorities in its attention to and presentation of biblical teaching.[14]

Historical Theology

Historical theology analyzes the past for the purpose of living in the present. That is, it examines how the church has understood and lived out God's Word, both faithfully and unfaithfully, in order to gain wisdom and avoid folly. Michael Horton writes,

> While biblical theology draws a line through redemptive history and systematic theology draws a circle demonstrating the intrasystematic coherence of scriptural doctrines, historical theology reminds both that one never steps outside of the hermeneutical circle, simply exegetes Scripture, and discovers its doctrines in abstraction from a communal history of interpretation. In distinction, then, from both biblical and systematic theology, historical theology may be described as the study of the *history of exegesis* (descriptive) rather than the act of biblical exegesis itself (prescriptive). The goal is not to determine what the church is authorized to say, but to determine what the church has in fact said in its dogmatic formulations through their organic development.[15]

At a narrow level, historical theology reminds us of the confession(s) of faith that has been handed down to the saints by way of the ecumenical creeds and councils. In these creeds and councils, God guided his church into truth through the faithful confession of who he is as the Triune God, what he has done for sinners through the person and work of the God-man, Jesus Christ, and how he has given the Holy Spirit to his people in Christ as the guarantee of their future inheritance (Eph. 1:14).[16] While Protestant theology wholeheartedly affirms *sola scriptura* (Scripture alone) as its final and ultimate authority,

---

13. Cf. Gavin Ortlund, *Finding the Right Hills to Die On: Theological Triage in Pastoral Ministry* (Wheaton, IL: Crossway, 2020).
14. Scott R. Swain, "Dogmatics as Systematic Theology," in *The Task of Dogmatics: Explorations in Theological Method*, eds. Oliver D. Crisp and Fred Sanders (Grand Rapids: Zondervan, 2017), 50.
15. Horton, "Historical Theology," *DTIB*, 293.
16. For an accessible introduction to the major creeds and councils, see Justin S. Holcomb, *Know the Creeds and Councils* (Grand Rapids: Zondervan, 2014); for a more in-depth

this does not entail that it lacks other sources with derivative authority insofar as they faithfully summarize what Scripture teaches and proclaim what the church has confessed. Therefore, historical theology serves the church as an important ministerial—but not magisterial—guide.

One may wonder how useful or beneficial historical theology is. While Naselli lists ten benefits,[17] I will briefly give three. First, historical theology guards against *elitism*. The temptation for many is to think that the golden age has arrived, and, as a result, previous generations were inferior or deficient. But in every generation there have been both saints and sinners, and historical theology places every Christian and community at the foot of the cross of Christ.

Second, historical theology guards against *despair*. If one extreme is intellectual or spiritual pride, the other extreme is to think that God is absent in the midst of suffering and hardship. But the history of global Christianity is filled with a long line of Christians who have tasted and seen that the Lord is good. This reminder is helpful to those in the midst of suffering, and it encourages us to persevere in the face of hardship because we know that he who began a good work will complete it at the day of Jesus Christ (Phil. 1:6).

Third, historical theology guards against a naive *biblicism*. No biblical interpreter lives on an island, and God has provided wonderful and gifted guides who have gone before and provided the fruit of their interpretive labors. To exclusively rely on them might be idolatrous, but to disregard them is pretentious. Studying historical theology reminds us of those who have gone before us and interpreted the Word of God for us, so as we consider their way of life, may we imitate their faith (Heb. 13:7).

Practical Theology

If studying the various parts of Scripture (exegesis) as they develop across the canon toward Christ (biblical theology) relate together in a coherent manner (systematic theology), then not only can we learn from the past (historical theology), but we can also gain wisdom to live in the present (practical theology). Kevin Vanhoozer rightly says, "The proper end of the drama of

---

treatment, see Leo Donald Davis, *The First Seven Ecumenical Councils (325–787): Their History and Theology* (Wilmington, DE: Michael Glazier, 1988).

17. Naselli's ten are: (1) It Helps you distinguish between orthodoxy and heresy; (2) It displays the fruit of orthodoxy and heresy; (3) It can foster God-glorifying unity when fellow Christians disagree on nonessential issues; (4) It helps you think globally; (5) It can reveal your theological blind spots; (6) It gives you perspective regarding seemingly novel views; (7) It cultivates humility; (8) It guards you against chronological snobbery; (9) It inspires you; and (10) It reminds you that God sovereignly controls everything for his glory and our good. Naselli, *Understand and Apply the New Testament*, ch. 10.

doctrine is wisdom: lived knowledge, a performance of the truth."[18] That is, in response to God's Word and work, faithful Christian theology is inherently practical, so in this sense it flows from the previous sections. Practical theology asks a particular question, "How do I/we live in the world today?" It therefore deals with preaching, teaching, counseling, singleness, marriage, evangelism, church planting, missions, and so on. In other words, *practical theology is discipleship.*

Furthermore, *practical theology is lyrical.* After God revealed himself to Moses and the Israelites and delivered them from the hands of the Egyptians that they might know that he is the LORD their God (Exod. 6:7), notice what followed: singing (Exod. 15:1–18)! Kelly Kapic writes, "Theology is all about knowing how to sing the song of redemption: to know when to shout, when to mourn, when to be silent and when to hope."[19]

Finally, *practical theology is missional* because Jesus declared, "All authority in heaven and on earth has been given to me. Go therefore and make disciples of all nations, baptizing them in the name of the Father and of the Son and of the Holy Spirit, teaching them to observe all that I have commanded you. And behold, I am with you always, to the end of the age" (Matt. 28:18–20). That commission drove the early church councils as Christians faithfully lived out the Great Commission. They contextualized the Trinity, the incarnate Lord Jesus Christ, and the life-giving Holy Spirit into the thought forms and languages of their day in order to do justice to the teaching of Scripture. And Christians must do this today, from Texas to New England to East Asia to Nigeria—to the uttermost parts of the earth—without compromising the truths of Scripture until that day when people from every tribe and language and people and nation gather around the throne to worship the Lamb who was slain (Rev. 5:9) to take away the sin of the world (John 1:29). So, the goal of theology is both vertical (to love, know, enjoy, worship, and glorify God) and horizontal (love for others).

Summary

God is both our Creator and Redeemer in Christ who has given us his Spirit and Word in order that we might know him. As finite creatures, we will never *fully* possess God's perfect knowledge, for his knowledge is infinitely wonderful and perfect. But because he has graciously spoken in his living Word—Jesus Christ—and his written Word—Scripture—we can *truly* know him. And this knowledge is life (John 17:3). So, may we humbly and joyfully take advantage of all the means he has given us and make it our aim to live the

---

18. Kevin J. Vanhoozer, *The Drama of Doctrine: A Canonical Linguistic Approach to Christian Theology* (Louisville: Westminster John Knox, 2005), 21.

19. Kelly M. Kapic, *A Little Book for New Theologians: Why and How to Study Theology* (Downers Grove, IL: InterVarsity, 2012), 23.

words of Jeremiah 9:23–24: "Thus says the LORD: 'Let not the wise man boast in his wisdom, let not the mighty man boast in his might, let not the rich man boast in his riches, but let him who boasts boast in this, that he understands and knows me, that I am the LORD who practices steadfast love, justice, and righteousness in the earth. For in these things I delight, declares the LORD.'"

REFLECTION QUESTIONS

1. In your own words, how would you describe exegesis, biblical theology, systematic theology, historical theology, and practical theology?

2. How does each discipline shape and inform the others?

3. Why is historical theology important for exegesis, biblical theology, and systematic theology?

4. Why is systematic theology important for fellowship with God?

5. How do specific doctrines shape the Christian life? For example, how should the doctrine of the Trinity shape how a Christian prays (see Eph. 3:14–21)? Or how should the incarnation cultivate humility (see Phil. 2:1–11)?

How Do Biblical Theology and Systematic Theology Differ and Work Together?

Oren R. Martin

The previous chapter describes and compares exegesis, biblical theology, systematic theology, historical theology, and practical theology. This chapter narrows the field by addressing how biblical theology and systematic theology differ and work together. In short, biblical and systematic theology are not foes, but friends, for they partner to form mature disciples of Christ who by his Spirit follow him in every area of life.

To begin, some posit an irreparable chasm that exists between biblical and systematic theology.[1] However, more recent studies in evangelical theology have affirmed what the church has practiced from the beginning—namely, that biblical and systematic theology belong together even if they have not been labeled as such. In fact, the early church practiced something akin to biblical and systematic theology when they responded to various heresies. In other words, there has always been disciplined systematic reflection on the history of redemption as it concerns God and his work in Christ. For example, the early church Trinitarian and Christological debates involved putting the whole canon together in light of the history of salvation as they sought to

---

1. For example, many point to a pivotal address by Johann Phillip Gabler, "An Oration on the Proper Distinction between Biblical and Dogmatic Theology and the Specific Objectives of Each" (1787), reproduced in Ben C. Ollenburger, ed., *Old Testament Theology: Flowering and Future*, 2nd ed., Sources for Biblical and Theological Study 1 (Winona Lake, IN: Eisenbrauns, 2004), 497–506. For a description of this chasm as well as a proposal not to separate what God has joined together, see Kevin J. Vanhoozer, "From Canon to Concept: 'Same' and 'Other' in the Relation between Biblical and Systematic Theology," *Scottish Bulletin of Evangelical Theology* 12, no. 2 (Autumn 1994): 96–124.

answer the questions of who God is, what he has done in redemption, and how Jesus Christ and the Holy Spirit "fit into" his divine identity. They then sought to challenge the contemporary issues of their day, which in one sense is a department of systematic theology, for it involved worldview formation against rival worldviews. On this point Michael Horton writes,

> The doctrine of the Trinity did not fall from heaven all at once but was revealed progressively as God's plan unfolded in history. Biblical theology follows that organic development, while systematic theology pulls these insights in a formal dogma and relates the Trinity to other doctrines in Scripture. If biblical theology is a topographical map, systematic theology is more like a street map, pointing out the logical connection between various doctrines spread throughout the Scripture. Without biblical theology, systematic theology easily surrenders the dynamism of revelation to timeless truths; without systematic theology, biblical theology surrenders the Bible's internal coherence—the relation of the parts to the whole.[2]

Indeed, biblical and systematic theology have been companions from the beginning. What follows, therefore, briefly retraces the previous chapter and then provides a test case in order to show how biblical and systematic theology differ and work together.

Biblical Theology

The previous chapter notes that biblical theology works intertextually by tracking how Scripture develops *on its own terms*. The Bible historically and redemptively unfolds from Genesis to Revelation. From this description, four convictions of biblical theology are worth noting.

First, biblical theology takes into account the unity of God's revelation. Scripture is God's word written, and it reveals his unified plan of redemption from the beginning to end. However, God's redemptive plan did not happen all at once, so his revelation did not come all at once. Rather, "at many times and in many ways, God spoke to our fathers by the prophets" (Heb. 1:1), as he guided them toward his ultimate redemption in Christ. This framework presupposes that Scripture constitutes a unified text with a developing story. God's Word reveals and interprets his redemptive acts that develop across time, from beginning to end. Therefore, biblical theology must keep the redemptive-revelatory and redemptive-historical nature of Scripture in its focus. But not only is God's revelation redemptive-historical, it is also future oriented. That is, it has a divine *goal*. Michael Horton is correct when he says

---

2. Michael S. Horton, *The Christian Faith: A Systematic Theology for Pilgrims on the Way* (Grand Rapids: Zondervan, 2011), 29.

that, when reading Scripture, "eschatology should be a lens and not merely a locus."[3] For example, the promise of the offspring of the woman who would triumph over the serpent (Gen. 3:15) unfolds in diverse and dramatic ways across Scripture until Christ fulfills it. This future-oriented facet of Scripture is rooted in a sovereign God who is moving history along to his appointed ends, both for his redemptive purposes for humanity (penultimate) and for his own glory (ultimate). As a result, biblical theology pays attention to the unity of God's redemptive revelation and reads the parts in light of the whole.

Second, because God's unified revelation came over time, biblical theology gives attention to Scripture's diversity. This diversity is marked by different biblical authors, languages, genres, cultures, epochs, covenants, and Testaments. The diversity of Scripture displays the wonder of God's beauty, but through Scripture's rich diversity is an underlying unity that spans its pages from beginning to end.

Third, biblical theology reads Scripture on its own terms—that is, guided by its own terms, concepts, structures, and categories (e.g., creation, image, covenant, temple). It does not impose extrabiblical categories on the text, but rather lets Scripture set the agenda.[4]

Finally, biblical theology is christological. That is, all revelation *points to and is fulfilled in Christ* (Eph. 1:10). God's past dealings with his people serve as patterns, or types, for his future dealings with his people. Therefore, all OT-era redemptive events, institutions, covenants, persons, and offices point to the final saving event, sacrifice, covenant, person, prophet, priest, and king. Subsequently, the NT authors saw the Lord Jesus Christ as fulfilling or serving as the antitype of these prophetic hopes.[5]

Systematic Theology

Systematic theology attends to the whole of God's revelation and puts all of the conceptual pieces together from biblical theology in order to display the anatomy of their relations. Kevin Vanhoozer describes systematic theology as "an inquiry into the basic concepts of the Christian faith."[6] As a result, there are important components of systematic theology.

First, not only does systematic theology attend to the whole of Scripture and relate it to our world, it also gives attention to Scripture's internal relations. For example, systematic theology not only develops what Scripture teaches about the deity or humanity of Christ by looking at how each develops across Scripture (which is closer to biblical theology), but it also asks, "What is the

---

3. Michael S. Horton, *Covenant and Eschatology: The Divine Drama* (Louisville: Westminster John Knox, 2002), 5.
4. See Question 1.
5. See Question 8.
6. Vanhoozer, "From Canon to Concept," 101.

relation between the deity and humanity of Christ in his (one) person?" As a result, the church has employed terms such as "hypostatic union" to conceptually summarize and capture what Scripture teaches concerning the person of Christ.[7] Furthermore, systematic theology seeks to provide an account of how his deity and humanity relate in a coherent manner, as well as its relation to other doctrines, such as the Trinity or salvation. For this reason, systematic theology employs concepts and conceptual tools that provide coherence to what Scripture teaches about Christ, such as the definitional distinction between person and nature (which is what the church councils achieved).

Second, systematic theology takes into account and is informed by historical theology, for every person approaches the text with certain (confessional) commitments.[8] Theology is neither formulated in a vacuum nor merely theoretical. Rather, it listens to, learns from, analyzes, and incorporates the past in order to know God and make him known in the present.

Finally, systematic theology gives its attention to proportions. That is, it distinguishes matters that are of "first importance," such as the gospel (1 Cor. 15:3) or person of Christ (1 John 4:2–3), from other matters of secondary or tertiary importance (Matt. 23:23; 1 Cor. 1:14–17). Hence, theology seeks to reflect the Bible's own emphases and priorities in its sanctified and disciplined attention to and presentation of biblical teaching.[9]

Working Together for Our Good

Biblical theology gives rise to systematic theology. Graeme Goldsworthy writes,

> From one point of view, biblical theology is what makes dogmatics necessary. If it were not for the progressive nature of revelation, then all texts would stand in the same general relationship to the believer. Dogmatics is the discipline of saying what the total redemptive and revealing activity of God means for us now. It recognizes that all texts do not stand in the same relationship to us now, but that in view of the unity of revelation they do stand in some identifiable relationship to all other texts and therefore to us. Biblical theology examines the diversity within the unity. . . . The dogmatic basis of biblical theology lies in the fact that no empirical datum of exegesis has independent

---

7. See, e.g., Stephen J. Wellum, *God the Son Incarnate: The Doctrine of Christ*, Foundations for Evangelical Theology, ed. John S. Feinberg (Wheaton, IL: Crossway, 2016), ch. 9.
8. Grant R. Osborne, *The Hermeneutical Spiral: A Comprehensive Introduction to Biblical Interpretation*, rev. and exp. (Downers Grove, IL: InterVarsity, 2006), 265–66.
9. Scott R. Swain, "Dogmatics as Systematic Theology," in *The Task of Dogmatics: Explorations in Theological Method*, eds. Oliver D. Crisp and Fred Sanders (Grand Rapids: Zondervan, 2017), 50.

meaning, and no datum of theology or interpretation has independent meaning.[10]

In other words, systematic theology builds on biblical theology in its theological formulations. When systematicians ground their theology in the Bible, they should do so in ways that honor both what it is and how God revealed it. In other words, they should be doing biblical theology. On this point Michael Williams writes,

> The biblical narrative structure, the story of God's relationship with his creation—from Adam to Christ crucified and resurrected to Christ triumphant in the restoration of all things in the kingdom of God—forms the regulative principle and interpretative key for systematic theology no less than it does for biblical theology. This suggests that a systematic theology that is oriented to the biblical narrative and scriptural ways of knowing ought to be redemptive-historically grounded rather than ordered.[11]

Richard Lints sets forth one helpful way to describe this interpretive and theological process—what he calls the three horizons of redemptive interpretation: the *textual* (immediate context at the grammatical-historical level), *epochal* (context of the period of revelation), and *canonical* (context of the entirety of revelation) horizons.[12] In order to reach sound biblical and theological conclusions, interpreters must give equal study to all texts, giving careful attention to the literary genres and rightly interpreting each passage within its respective contexts and overall place in redemptive history and the canon. Similarly, when biblical theologians draw theological conclusions from Scripture (which they should be doing!), they should do so respecting the complex set of historical, philosophical, cultural, and doctrinal issues that attend such conclusions. In other words, they should be doing systematic theology.

Test Case: The Triune God

To give an example, biblical and systematic theology work together to faithfully understand and live before the Triune God. For Moses, the holy

---

10. Graeme Goldsworthy, "'Thus Says the Lord!'—The Dogmatic Basis of Biblical Theology," in *God Who Is Rich in Mercy: Essays Presented to D. B. Knox*, eds. P. T. O'Brien and D. G. Peterson (Grand Rapids: Baker, 1986), 37.

11. Michael Williams, "Systematic Theology as a Biblical Discipline," in *All for Jesus: A Celebration of the 50th Anniversary of Covenant Theological Seminary*, eds. Robert A. Peterson and Sean M. Lucas (Fearn, Ross Shire, UK: Christian Focus, 2005), 199.

12. Richard Lints, *The Fabric of Theology: A Prolegomenon to Evangelical Theology* (Grand Rapids: Eerdmans, 1993), 293–311.

revelation of God out of the midst of the flaming bush prompted him to hide his face, for he was afraid to look at God (Exod. 3:6). In the same way, it is essential that holy reverence and childlike awe be the characteristic of those who witness God revealing himself in his Word as the Triune God.[13]

Biblical theology affirms that God's revelation has a long history that began at creation and continues after the fall until it culminates in Christ. Thus, there is progress and development in the confession of God's existence as we move from the OT to the NT. Israel's confession of the one true God formed the bedrock of its faith. For example, the revelation of God's name most fully and faithfully witnesses to the inexhaustible reality of God's nature (3:13–14). That is, God's name signifies the reality of God's being.[14] It is no wonder, then, why God will not share his glory with another (Isa. 48:11). Passages such as Exodus 20:3 and Deuteronomy 6:4 affirm exclusive monotheism in sharp contrast to the surrounding polytheistic nations. The revelation of God's name and subsequent elaboration of it throughout the OT make clear that he alone is eternal and independent, the cause, creator, and sustainer of all that exists, and unchangeable in his nature, purposes, and character (Exod. 3:14–15; Num. 23:19; Isa. 44:24; Zech. 14:9).

However, the revelation of Yahweh as the one true God is not restricted to the OT. The NT continues the trajectory of the OT by affirming that "the Lord is one" (Mark 12:29) and that "there is no other besides him" (12:32). Paul adds to the biblical witness when he agrees with what the Corinthian Christians know, that idols are not real gods, for "there is one God, the Father, through whom are all things and through whom we exist" (1 Cor. 8:6). Indeed, there is only one way for both Jews and Gentiles to be made right with God, "since God is one" (Rom. 3:30; cf. James 2:19). Moreover, God calls Christians to maintain unity since there is "one Lord . . . one God and Father of all, who is over all and through all and in all" (Eph. 4:5–6). But not only is God's identity unique, he is substantially different than any other being. He possesses invisible attributes, namely, eternal power and divine nature (Rom. 1:20). He is independent, self-existent, and self-sufficient (Acts 17:24–25). He is immortal and invisible (1 Tim. 1:17), blessed, sovereign, and invisible (6:16). Attributes such as these provided fertile ground for Christians throughout every age to affirm that God's reality—his nature, essence, or being—is unique to him, his life. Historic Christian creeds and confessions, therefore, confess God as one.

But even in the OT, Christians have pointed to various references to God in the plural as well as passages where deity is ascribed to various individual persons. The first set of examples includes, most notably, the divine pronouncement in Genesis 1:26, "Let us make man in our image, after our

---

13. Herman Bavinck, *Our Reasonable Faith* (Grand Rapids: Eerdmans, 1956), 143.
14. Scott R. Swain, "Divine Trinity," in *Christian Dogmatics: Reformed Theology for the Church Catholic* (Grand Rapids: Baker, 2016), 83.

likeness." More weight is added to this pronouncement in light of the opening verses of chapter one, where God creates by his word while the Spirit of God is present. As God's revelation progresses, Psalm 33:6 and John 1:1–3 further clarify who this God is (cf. Col. 1:16–17; Heb. 1:1–3). The second set of passages in the OT refers to distinct persons who are assigned divine status. David writes, "The LORD says to my Lord, 'Sit at my right hand until I make your enemies your footstool'" (Ps. 110:1; cf. 45:6–7[7–8]), which the NT writers apply to Christ (Heb. 1:8–9; Matt. 22:41–46; Acts 2:34–35). Closely related are places where various agencies operate on behalf of God and, mysteriously, are identified with God (e.g., Gen. 16:7–13; chs. 18–19; Exod. 3:2–6). Lastly, there are passages throughout the Prophets that bring together the coming of the Lord with a Davidic servant. Furthermore, by the end of the OT, Israel's hope for salvation is anchored in a divine *and* human figure. For example, Isaiah speaks of a worldwide salvation that will come through a divine and human king (9:1–7), Ezekiel speaks of a divine and human shepherd who will feed God's people (34:20–24), and Micah anticipates the time when Israel's ruler and savior, who will be born in Bethlehem, is he whose "origin is from of old, from ancient days" (Mic. 5:2). These mysteries are concealed and unexplained until the opening pages of the NT (e.g., Luke 1:31–34).

So what should we conclude from these passages? On the one hand, caution should be exercised with examples such as these to prove the doctrine of the Trinity solely on OT grounds, for there are alternative interpretations that plausibly affirm both monotheism and orthodox Trinitarianism. On the other hand, the cumulative effect of these passages provide fertile Trinitarian ground for the fullness of time when God would send forth his Son (Gal. 4:4) and, in turn, when the Father with the Son would send the Holy Spirit to bear witness about the Christ. In this time, distinct, divine persons emerge to reveal more fully who God is as Father, Son, and Holy Spirit. Thus, revelation follows redemption, for God works out his grand purposes according to the counsel of his will in Christ (Eph. 1:10–11). As a result, who God is and what he is like is progressively made known so that his people can confess him according to who he reveals himself to be.

While we confess that God is *one*, we also acknowledge that his name belongs to *three* (Matt. 28:19–20). It is largely through the biblical narrative that we identify three distinct, divine persons. That is, it is in the works of God in creation and salvation that we recognize plurality within the Godhead. For example, in Isaiah 48:16 the unidentified speaker ("me") sent by the Lord God—along with his Spirit—is the Servant of the Lord, who also appears in 42:1–13 and 49:1–6. In light of the NT witness, Christians would see this as a reference to the three persons of the Godhead. Passages such as Isaiah 63:10 imply the distinct personality of the Holy Spirit and show God identifying his Spirit with himself (cf. Eph. 4:30). Furthermore, the Spirit's personality and divine presence is expressed with weighty narrative force in his creative hovering over the face of the waters at creation (Gen. 1:2) and in his creative overshadowing of Mary who would bring forth the Son of God, Jesus, in his incarnation (Luke 1:35). Like the Servant of the Lord, the Spirit of the Lord is a distinct, divine person who is also Yahweh.

As the history of redemption unfolds, the NT makes clear that the mystery once concealed is now revealed. The early Christians did not arrive at the doctrine of the Trinity by theological speculation. Rather, they were confronted with the person and work of Jesus Christ, who both claimed to be equal with God (John 10:30) and made good on his claims as he demonstrated his divine authority over nature (Matt. 8:23–27), sickness (9:18–26), sin (Mark 2:1–12), and death (John 11:1–44). With echoes of Genesis 1, John 1 begins, "In the beginning was the Word, and the Word was with God, and the Word was God. He was in the beginning with God. All things were made through him, and without him was not anything made that was made" (1:1–3). Here, the Word is both distinct from God yet identified as God. He is "the only Son from the Father" (1:14), and "the only God, who is at the Father's side, he has made him known" (1:18). He is confessed as "my Lord and my God" (John 20:28), the "image of the invisible God, the firstborn of all creation," who created all things, is before all things, and holds all things together (Col. 1:15–20). Furthermore, he is worshipped alongside God (Rev. 5) and is "the radiance of the glory of God and the exact imprint of his nature, and he upholds the universe by the word of his power" (Heb. 1:3).

Likewise, the Spirit, who is distinct from the Father and the Son, is identified with both Father and Son as God. To the Spirit are attributed works that properly belong to God in creation (Gen. 1:1–2; Ps. 33:6), providence (Ps. 104:30), regeneration (John 3:3–6; Titus 3:5), resurrection (Rom. 8:11), justification (1 Cor. 6:11), indwelling (Rom. 8:9–11), and intercession (8:26–34). To lie to the Holy Spirit is to lie to God (Acts 5:3–4); divine blessing flows from the Father, Son, and Spirit (2 Cor. 13:14); and the Spirit works with the Father and the Son in God's single plan of redemption (John 14:16–16:15; Eph. 1:3–14; 2 Thess. 2:13–15). Lastly, the Spirit shares in the divine attributes such as omniscience (1 Cor. 2:10), omnipresence (Ps. 139:7–10), miracles (Matt. 12:28), and eternity (Heb. 9:14). God is one, and his name belongs to three—Father, Son and Holy Spirit.

As Christianity spread in fulfillment of Jesus's Great Commission, a recurring problem in early trinitarian thought was finding the right words and concepts to proclaim both the unity and triunity of God. As a result, the need for systematic theology grew in order to give conceptual attention to Scripture's relations and proportions. As a result, language was employed to affirm that in his unity, God is one in nature, essence, or being, possessing those attributes or perfections that belong to God alone (e.g., independence, immutability, eternity, omnipresence, simplicity). What is common, therefore, to the Father, Son, and Holy Spirit is the one, simple divine nature (John 10:30), and the nature is shared through the mutual indwelling (i.e., *perichoresis*) of the persons of the Trinity (John 10:38). So, God eternally exists in three persons. The Father is fully God, the Son is fully God, and the Holy Spirit is fully God. Yet there is only one God. The three persons are equal in nature, power, authority, will, and glory, for each share in the one divine essence.

Furthermore, the distinctions of the persons can be viewed from two perspectives: the divine processions (God in himself) and divine missions (God toward us in his works of creation and salvation). First, what distinguishes the persons is their names and relations of origin. That is, the Father eternally begets the Son, the Son is eternally begotten from the Father, and the Holy Spirit eternally proceeds from the Father and the Son (John 1:14; 3:16; 15:26). In other terms, the Father has the personal property of paternity, the Son of filiation, and the Spirit of procession or spiration. These personal properties flow from the biblical witness to give conceptual coherence to the Triune God in the face of various heresies. Second, the divine processions are expressed in the divine missions of creation and salvation, in which each work of God has a threefold cause. That is, mirroring the pattern of the relations of origin, "the Father sends the Son to accomplish his redemptive mission, and the Father, with the Son, sends his Spirit to accomplish his sanctifying mission."[15] So, in creation, God creates the world through the Son in the Spirit (Gen. 1:1–2; John 1:1–3; Col. 1:15–17), and in salvation, God the Father sends his Son— who in obedience became incarnate, suffered, died, and made atonement for sin—to redeem his elect in Christ and to seal them with his Holy Spirit, who is the guarantee of their eternal inheritance, to the praise of his glorious grace (Eph. 1:3–14). Indeed, the good news is that God has graciously opened up his eternal Triune life *to us* in order to become our adoptive Father in Christ by his Spirit *for us*.[16]

Summary

Biblical and systematic theology are not foes, but friends, for they are interdependent activities in the integrated task of knowing and living before God in his world. Biblical theology seeks to interpret the diverse canonical forms on their own terms, while systematic theology seeks to both preserve those canonical forms and transform them into a coherent, conceptual framework for

---

15. Scott R. Swain, "Divine Trinity," in *Christian Dogmatics: Reformed Theology for the Church Catholic*, eds. Michael Allen and Scott R. Swain (Grand Rapids: Baker, 2016), 104.
16. For more on the doctrine of the Trinity, see Herman Bavinck, *Reformed Dogmatics*, vol. 2: *God and Creation* (Grand Rapids: Baker, 2004), ch. 6; Fred Sanders, *The Deep Things of God: How the Trinity Changes Everything*, 2nd ed. (Wheaton, IL: Crossway, 2017); Fred Sanders, *The Triune God*, New Studies in Dogmatics, eds. Michael Allen and Scott R. Swain (Grand Rapids: Zondervan, 2016).

today. In the end, the fixed theological framework of Scripture (biblical theology) gives rise to a theological vision for all of life (systematic theology).[17]

REFLECTION QUESTIONS

1. How do biblical and systematic theology differ?

2. What happens if either biblical theology or systematic theology is neglected?

3. How are the disciplines dependent and mutually informing?

4. In addition to the test case above, can you give other examples (e.g., the person and work of Christ)?

5. How do the disciplines work together to form a theological vision of life?

---

17. For more on moving from a theological framework (biblical theology) to a theological vision (systematic theology), see Lints, *Fabric of Theology*.

What Role Does Authorial Intent Play in Biblical Theology?

Oren R. Martin

Biblical theology is all about knowing God through his life-giving Word. In this sense, then, as Richard Lints says, it must first be about a conversation with God: "This conversation began at creation and took on tragic dimensions at the fall. It became an uncomfortable conversation, for as God revealed himself, fallen humanity appeared that much more wretched in contrast to his glory. But the conversation continued nevertheless, reaching a redemptive climax in the person and work of Christ."[1]

As a result, redemption by faith in Christ brings renewal through the indwelling and illuminating work of his Spirit, who progressively enables his people to become better conversation partners as they are being transformed from one degree of glory to another (2 Cor. 3:18). Biblical theology, then, is about listening—listening to what God has spoken about himself in the person of his Son (Heb. 1:1–2).

Difficulty has arisen, however, in considering the nature of what God has spoken in his Word. More specifically, the Bible has come to us through various human authors in a variety of ways over time (e.g., cultures, languages, genres). This dimension of Scripture is often where biblical interpretation has begun and sometimes ends. However, underlying this remarkable diversity is a God-breathed unity, for it comes *from him* (2 Tim. 3:16). That is, Scripture is both a fully divine and fully human word. As a result, doing biblical theology involves listening to what the various biblical authors have written through their words in order to understand ultimately what the divine author has finally spoken about his Son, the Eternal Word (John 1:1–18; Heb. 1:1–2).

---

1. Richard Lints, *The Fabric of Theology: A Prolegomenon to Evangelical Theology* (Grand Rapids: Eerdmans, 1993), 58.

This chapter, therefore, proceeds in three steps in order to provide a framework for understanding the role of authorial intent in doing biblical theology. First, it gives a theological account of the inspiration of Scripture. Second, it discusses the role of authorial intent in biblical theology. And finally, it provides interpretive controls for doing biblical theology in light of authorial intent.

Authorial Intention and the Nature of Scripture

Christians throughout the ages have affirmed the total truthfulness of God's Word as the product of both divine and human authorship.[2] The dual authorship of Scripture affirms that "God in his sovereignty so superintended the freely composed human writings we call the Scriptures that the result was nothing less than God's words and, therefore, entirely truthful."[3] In other words, Scripture is God's Word in human language.[4] But *what* does this description of Scripture mean, and *how* does God bring it about? This question gets to the heart of the inspiration of Scripture.[5]

The church has often pointed to two crucial and complementary texts to affirm that all Scripture is from God. First, 2 Timothy 3:16 says, "All Scripture is breathed out by God and profitable for teaching, for reproof, for correction, and for training in righteousness." Additionally, 2 Peter 1:20–21 further explains *how* God has given his Word to his people when the apostle writes, "No prophecy of Scripture comes from someone's own interpretation. For no prophecy was ever produced by the will of man, but men spoke from God as they were carried along by the Holy Spirit." However, it is not as though Scripture is *exclusively* the work of the Spirit.[6] As Scott Swain says, "While God is the *primary author* of Holy Scripture, prophets and apostles

---

2. See, e.g., John D. Woodbridge, *Biblical Authority: A Critique of the Rogers/McKim Proposal* (Grand Rapids: Zondervan, 1982); D. A. Carson, ed., *The Enduring Authority of the Christian Scriptures* (Grand Rapids: Eerdmans, 2016).
3. D. A. Carson, "Recent Developments in the Doctrine of Scripture," in *Hermeneutics, Authority, and Canon*, eds. D. A. Carson and John D. Woodbridge (Eugene, OR: Wipf & Stock, 1986), 45.
4. For some, the idea that God speaks to and through humanity in human language diminishes God's authoritative and true communication. See, however, Scott R. Swain, *Trinity, Revelation, and Reading: A Theological Introduction to the Bible and Its Interpretation* (London: T&T Clark, 2011), 70; Timothy Ward, *Words of Life: Scripture as the Living and Active Word of God* (Downers Grove, IL: InterVarsity, 2009), 34–35; E. J. Schnabel, "Scripture," in *New Dictionary of Biblical Theology*, eds. T. Desmond Alexander and Brian S. Rosner (Downers Grove, IL: InterVarsity, 2000), 34–43; Vern S. Poythress, "Divine Meaning of Scripture," *WTJ* 48 (1986): 241–79.
5. I am indebted to Scott Swain for what follows. For more, see Swain, *Trinity, Revelation, and Reading*, 62–71.
6. This is why, for example, previous Scripture can be attributed at times to God as the divine author (e.g., Heb. 3:7) and at other times to the human author (e.g., 4:7).

are *secondary authors*."[7] This reality, however, does not remove the human element(s) throughout Scripture. Again, Swain writes,

> The presence and operation of the Spirit's sovereign lordship in the production of Holy Scripture does not lead to the suppression or overruling of God's human emissaries in their exercise of authorial rationality and freedom. Rather, his sovereign lordship leads to their enlivening and sanctified enablement. The Spirit who created the human mind and personality does not destroy the human mind and personality when he summons them to his service. Far from it. The Spirit sets that mind and personality free from its blindness and slavery to sin so that it may become a truly free, thoughtful, and self-conscious witness to all that God is for us in Christ. He bears *his* lively witness and *therefore* prophets and apostles *also* bear *their* lively witness (John 15:26–27). The Spirit creates a divine-and-human *fellowship*—a common possession and partnership—in communicating the truth of the gospel (John 16:13–15).[8]

Whether through the Law, the Prophets, the Psalms, the Gospels, or the Epistles, the inspiration of Scripture is simply—yet profoundly!—a claim that God by his Spirit, through his perfect wisdom and power, has produced a book that is from God and therefore authoritative, true, clear, and sufficient. Biblical theology, therefore, must take into account the dual authorship of Scripture in order to do full justice to all that God has spoken through the prophets and apostles in Holy Scripture.

Authorial Intention and Biblical Theology

The progressive nature of redemptive-historical revelation given by God and written down by human authors in Scripture entails that the "meaning" of a text develops through the canon until it reaches its fullness in the person and work of Christ.[9] This development is rooted in the text of Scripture as later biblical authors, who "spoke from God as they were carried along by the Holy Spirit" (2 Peter 1:21), interpreted earlier ones in light of God's progressive plan of redemption.[10] The process of understanding the meaning of a text, then, begins with interpreting the immediate grammatical-historical

---

7. Swain, *Trinity, Revelation, and Reading*, 66.
8. Swain, *Trinity, Revelation, and Reading*, 67 (emphasis original).
9. See Kevin Vanhoozer's magisterial work, *Is There a Meaning in This Text? The Bible, the Reader, and the Morality of Literary Knowledge* (Grand Rapids: Zondervan, 1998), in which he robustly relocates meaning in authorial intention that includes the nature of Scripture as a dually authored text.
10. For further elaboration of this point, see Aubrey Sequeira and Samuel C. Emadi, "Biblical-Theological Exegesis and the Nature of Typology," *SBJT* 21, no. 1 (Spring 2017): 11–34.

context, proceeds through the redemptive-historical character of Scripture as it looks back to prior revelation, and reaches its full meaning in the context of the whole canon. This way of interpretation honors the nature of Scripture as both a fully divine and fully human word.

How, then, does this approach to biblical theology fit with the concept of authorial intent? Meaning is not limited exclusively to what the human author intended, but also to what God intended, which becomes clearer as revelation progresses until it reaches its fullness at the canonical level. That is, the nature of Scripture and biblical-theological exegesis must allow for a fuller meaning that does not disagree with or go against what the human author wrote. In fact, it extends and develops it toward its fulfillment in Christ.[11] Douglas Moo and Andy Naselli write,

> When God breathes out his words through human authors, he surely knows what the ultimate meaning of their words will be, but he has not created a double entendre or hidden a meaning in the words that we can uncover only through special revelation. The "added meaning" that the text takes on is the product of the ultimate canonical shape. . . . We can often verify the "fuller sense" that the NT discovers in the OT by reading OT texts as the NT authors do: as part of a completed, canonical whole.[12]

Therefore, in citing the OT, the NT authors through the Holy Spirit were given insight into the divinely intended meaning of earlier Scripture. God's end-time work in Christ and the gift of the Spirit, then, enabled the NT authors to read the OT with new—indeed with Spirit-filled, christological—eyes.[13] This same Holy Spirit, then, regenerates and illumines readers of the

---

11. The category of "mystery" (see, e.g., Rom. 11:25–27; 16:25–27; 1 Corinthians 2; 15:50–55) set forth by Carson, Beale, and others is helpful in grasping this point. Carson writes, "The content of [the] mystery is a component, perhaps even an entailment, of the Christian gospel, and . . . the basic ingredients are grounded in Scripture itself." See D. A. Carson, "Mystery and Fulfillment: Toward a More Comprehensive Paradigm of Paul's Understanding of the Old and the New," in *Justification and Variegated Nomism: The Paradoxes of Paul*, eds. D. A. Carson, Peter T. O'Brien, and Mark A. Seifrid (Tübingen: Mohr Siebeck, 2004), 422; see also G. K. Beale and Benjamin J. Gladd, *Hidden but Now Revealed: A Biblical Theology of Mystery* (Downers Grove, IL: InterVarsity, 2014); and Jared Compton, "Shared Intentions? Reflections on Inspiration and Interpretation in Light of Scripture's Dual Authorship," *Themelios* 33, no. 3 (December 2008): 23–33. See also Question 21 in the present volume. God's ultimate intent in prior revelation was concealed, or "hidden in plain view," until the fullness of time when God's final redemptive purposes are fulfilled and revealed in Christ and written for us in the NT.

12. Douglas J. Moo and Andrew David Naselli, "The Problem of the New Testament's Use of the Old Testament," in *The Enduring Authority of the Christian Scriptures*, ed. D. A. Carson (Grand Rapids: Eerdmans, 2016), 736.

13. Sequeira and Emadi, "Nature of Typology," 15.

canonical Scriptures to understand what God has spoken in his Son, who fulfills his saving promises that have been written down for the eye of faith to see (1 Cor. 2:10–16).

Interpretive Controls for Doing Biblical Theology

This way of understanding the role of authorial intent in biblical theology provides important interpretive controls for understanding the whole counsel of God.

First, biblical theology should make a theological account of the inspiration of Scripture.

Second, biblical theology should consider the progressive stages of revelation along Scripture's covenantal structure that escalate from OT anticipation (concealed) to NT fulfillment (revealed) in the person and work of Christ in the new covenant.[14]

Third, biblical theology should assess how the NT uses the OT.[15]

Fourth, biblical theology should consider typology, which involves authorially intended textual patterns and correspondence(s) between persons, events, and institutions with later persons, events, and institutions.[16] That is, God's past dealings with his people serve as patterns, or types, for his future dealings with his people. For example, OT writers anticipated and looked for, among other things, a new prophet, king, exodus, covenant, land, temple, and city of God. Subsequently, the NT authors saw in Christ and his work the fulfillment, or antitype, of these prophetic hopes, albeit in an already–not yet framework.

Finally, biblical theology should keep the whole canon in view even when studying the various parts. That is, we must read every passage in the context of the completed canon of Scripture since God intended from the beginning that his later words should build on and bring to fulfillment earlier words. In some sense, the whole of the Bible represents one long, diverse but unified process of communication from God.[17]

Summary

God has spoken to and through the biblical writers. In so doing, he has given us a wonderful gift in Scripture. As a result, we must hear, understand, and receive all of it in its grand literary and theological unity and diversity so that we might live in him.

---

14. See Questions 6 and 22.
15. See Question 10; see also G. K. Beale, *Handbook on the New Testament Use of the Old Testament: Exegesis and Interpretation* (Grand Rapids: Baker, 2012); Moo and Naselli, "New Testament's Use of the Old Testament."
16. See Question 8.
17. See Poythress, "Divine Meaning of Scripture," 267–68.

REFLECTION QUESTIONS

1. How should the inspiration of Scripture shape or govern biblical theology?

2. In what ways does Scripture show that it is *from God* (i.e., God-breathed)?

3. How does Scripture display unity? Diversity?

4. How should the fact that Scripture is both fully human and fully divine influence our approach to biblical interpretation?

5. Why are interpretive controls important for doing biblical theology?

Does the Bible Have One Central Theme?

Andrew David Naselli

Does the Bible have a *center*—a single central theme? This issue is an on-going debate among biblical theologians.

Some Biblical Theologians Propose One Central Theme for the Bible

Biblical theologians have proposed many central themes (see fig. 15).

For the Old Testament	For the New Testament	For the Whole Bible
1. communion between God and humans 2. covenant 3. covenant and the new creation 4. the design of God 5. the Deuteronomistic theology of history 6. the election of Israel as God's people 7. the exclusiveness of God as the first commandment expresses 8. geography and genealogy, dominion and dynasty 9. God	1. communion between God and humans 2. covenant 3. the cross and resurrection 4. eschatology 5. faith 6. the glory of God 7. the gospel 8. Jesus the Messiah 9. justification	1. communion between God and humans 2. the covenant faithfulness of God 3. covenant 4. creation and new creation 5. election 6. exodus and new exodus 7. the glory of God in salvation through judgment 8. God 9. grace and obedience

For the Old Testament	For the New Testament	For the Whole Bible
10. God as the Lord	10. the kingdom (or	10. Jesus the Messiah
11. the holiness of God	rulership) of God	11. the kingdom (or
12. the kingdom (or	11. the kingdom of	rulership) of God
rulership) of God	the new creation	12. the people of God
13. the love of God	12. life	13. promise and
14. the mighty acts of God	13. the love of God	fulfillment
15. the presence of God	14. humankind	14. salvation
16. promise	15. mission	15. salvation history
17. righteousness	16. new creation	16. type and antitype
18. righteousness and justice	17. new Jerusalem/	
19. the self-revelation of God	Zion	
in history	18. the people of God	
20. the sovereignty of God	19. the presence of	
21. Yahweh the God of Israel	God	
and Israel the people of	20. promise	
Yahweh	21. reconciliation	
	22. redemption	
	23. temple	
	24. salvation	
	25. salvation history	

Fig. 15.1. Some Proposed Central Themes[1]

One Central Theme for the Bible Seems Reductionistic

Biblical theology demonstrates how the whole Bible exalts Jesus, so in one sense we could say that the central theme of the Bible is Jesus.[2] But simply saying that the theme is Jesus doesn't seem specific enough. The vast majority

1. See also Gerhard F. Hasel, *New Testament Theology: Basic Issues in the Current Debate* (Grand Rapids: Eerdmans, 1978), 140–70; Gerhard F. Hasel, *Old Testament Theology: Basic Issues in the Current Debate*, 4th ed. (Grand Rapids: Eerdmans, 1991), 139–71; Craig L. Blomberg, "The Unity and Diversity of Scripture," in *New Dictionary of Biblical Theology*, eds. T. Desmond Alexander and Brian S. Rosner (Downers Grove, IL: InterVarsity, 2000), 65–66; James M. Hamilton Jr., "The Glory of God in Salvation through Judgment: The Centre of Biblical Theology?," *TynBul* 57, no. 1 (May 2006): 65–70; Gregory K. Beale, *A New Testament Biblical Theology: The Unfolding of the Old Testament in the New* (Grand Rapids: Baker, 2012), 86, 162, 171.

2. See also Graeme Goldsworthy, "Biblical Theology as the Heartbeat of Effective Ministry," in *Biblical Theology: Retrospect and Prospect*, ed. Scott J. Hafemann (Downers Grove, IL: InterVarsity Press, 2002), 284: "The hub of the church and of the life of the believer is Jesus Christ, the crucified and risen Lord. He is not only the hermeneutical center of the whole Bible, but, according to the biblical testimony, he gives ultimate meaning to every fact in

of biblical theologians agree that proposing only one central theme for the Bible is reductionistic. Here's a sampling (in which OT theology and NT theology are subsets of whole-Bible biblical theology):

- D. A. Carson on NT theology: "The quest for the center of NT theology has three challenges. . . . (1) What does 'center' mean, and how might it be discovered? Does it refer to the most common theme, determined by statistical count, or to the controlling theme or to the fundamental theological presuppositions of the NT writers, so far as they may be discerned? Precisely how does one determine what a 'controlling theme' is? Is pursuit of the 'center' legitimate in literature that all sides admit is largely occasional? (2) How does one avoid mere generalities? One might say that the center of NT theology is Jesus Christ, but although at one level that is saying everything at another level it is saying almost nothing. Or one might say (with Dunn) that the fundamental tenet of NT christology is the belief that the predeath Jesus is to be identified with the postresurrection Jesus—but this too is anemic. (3) How shall one avoid the tendency to elevate one book or corpus of the NT and domesticate the rest, putting them on a leash held by the themes of the one, usually the book or corpus on which the biblical theologian has invested most scholarly energy? . . . The pursuit of the center is chimerical. NT theology is so interwoven that one can move from any one topic to any other topic. We will make better progress by pursuing clusters of broadly common themes, which may not be common to all NT books."[3]

- Thomas R. Schreiner on NT theology: "Is there a single center for NT theology? The question of a center has long been debated, and many different centers have been proposed. I think it is safe to say that no alleged center will ever become the consensus. In one sense, having several different centers is useful, as NT theology can be studied helpfully from a number of different perspectives. Since the various perspectives are interlocking and not mutually exclusive, there is a diversity of ways by which the NT can be explored. Furthermore, examining the NT from different angles allows new light to be shed upon the text. Since the subject matter of NT theology is God himself, we

---

the universe. He is thus the hermeneutical principle of all reality." (Thanks to Miles Van Pelt for sharing this quotation with us.)

3. D. A. Carson, "New Testament Theology," in *Dictionary of the Later New Testament and Its Developments*, eds. Ralph P. Martin and Peter H. Davids (Downers Grove, IL: InterVarsity, 1997), 810.

are not surprised to learn that none of our scholarly endeavors ever exhausts the subject matter."[4]

- Schreiner on whole-Bible biblical theology: "By now it is common consensus that no one theme adequately captures the message of the Scriptures. It is not my intention to dispute that hypothesis here, for almost any center chosen tends to domesticate one theme or another. I maintain that there are a number of different ways to put together the story line and theology of the Scriptures that are legitimate. We should not insist, therefore, that one theme captures the whole. Indeed, the word 'center' is ambiguous. Are we talking about the central theme of the story or the ultimate reason for the story?"[5]

- Gerhard F. Hasel on OT theology: "Even the most carefully worked out single center or formula will prove itself finally to be one-sided, inadequate, and insufficient, if not outrightly erroneous, and therefore will lead to misconceptions."[6]

- David L. Baker on OT theology: "No single concept can sum up the meaning of the whole Old Testament nor its relationship to the New."[7]

- Frank Thielman on NT theology: "It is not enough in a description of New Testament theology to discuss only the discrete theological message of each writing or group of writings. It is necessary also to indicate, even if only briefly, how these writings comprise a theological unity. Where do the New Testament Scriptures converge? What issues emerge as most important from reading them together as a single unit? In the interpretation of the New Testament writings proposed here, five issues [i.e., not just one central theme] occupy an especially important place: the significance of Jesus, faith as a response to Jesus, the outpouring of God's Spirit, the church as the people of God, and the consummation of all things."[8]

---

4. Thomas R. Schreiner, *New Testament Theology: Magnifying God in Christ* (Grand Rapids: Baker, 2008), 13.
5. Thomas R. Schreiner, *The King in His Beauty: A Biblical Theology of the Old and New Testaments* (Grand Rapids: Baker, 2013), xii.
6. Hasel, *Old Testament Theology*, 155. Hasel proposes that God is the Old Testament's central theme and that Christ is the New Testament's central theme but that neither may serve as an organizing principle or structure for doing biblical theology. See Hasel, *Old Testament Theology*, 171; Hasel, *New Testament Theology*, 164.
7. David L. Baker, *Two Testaments, One Bible: The Theological Relationship between the Old and New Testaments*, 3rd ed. (Downers Grove, IL: InterVarsity, 2014), 152.
8. Frank Thielman, *Theology of the New Testament: A Canonical and Synthetic Approach* (Grand Rapids: Zondervan, 2011), 681.

- G. K. Beale on OT and NT theology: "It is perhaps best not to speak of 'centers' because, as we will see, such proposals tend to be reductionistic. This kind of suggested scheme for the OT has the same problems as similar proposals for the NT. A focus on a single theme can lead to overlooking other important notions, which sometimes can happen when systematic theological categories are appealed to. Some who are discontented with referring to centers nevertheless eventually end up positing their own center or essential principle. Instead, it is more fitting and suitable to the Bible as narrative and literature to talk of a 'storyline' that is woven throughout the various genres of the OT (historical narrative, prophetic, poetic, wisdom, etc.), from which most other significant ideas are derived and are to be seen as subordinate and explanatory of parts of the storyline."[9]

The only biblical theologian we know of today who argues for one central theme for the whole Bible is our esteemed friend Jim Hamilton, who swings for the fences in his exegetically insightful 640-page biblical theology.[10] If there is one central theme for the Bible, then what Hamilton proposes is viable: "the glory of God in salvation through judgment is the center of biblical theology."[11] The way Hamilton attempts to prove his thesis, however, overstates his case by arguing that the glory of God in salvation through judgment is the theological message of each book and section of the Bible. That seems to flatten the distinctive theological message of each book and section—that is, it seems to force one overarching theme on each book and section the way Cinderella's stepsisters tried to force her little glass slipper on their feet.[12]

The Bible Has a Central Storyline with an Overarching Theological Message

It seems reductionistic to propose only one central theme for the whole Bible, but that does not mean that the diverse Bible lacks theological unity.[13]

---

9. G. K. Beale, *A New Testament Biblical Theology: The Unfolding of the Old Testament in the New* (Grand Rapids: Baker, 2012), 86.
10. James M. Hamilton Jr., *God's Glory in Salvation through Judgment: A Biblical Theology* (Wheaton, IL: Crossway, 2010).
11. Hamilton, *God's Glory in Salvation through Judgment*, 41.
12. See also Stephen G. Dempster, "Review of James M. Hamilton Jr., *God's Glory in Salvation through Judgment*," *9Marks* 8, no. 1 (Feb 2011): 42–48; Eugene H. Merrill, "Review of James M. Hamilton Jr., *God's Glory in Salvation through Judgment*," *BSac* 168, no. 672 (Oct–Dec 2011): 478–79; Preston M. Sprinkle, "Review of James M. Hamilton Jr., *God's Glory in Salvation through Judgment*," *JETS* 54, no. 4 (Dec 2011): 827–29; Andreas J. Köstenberger, "The Present and Future of Biblical Theology," *Them* 37, no. 3 (November 2012): 452–55.
13. Contra non-evangelical biblical theologians who argue that the Bible's diversity is so great that to speak of its unity is preposterous. See also the Roman Catholic scholar Roland E. Murphy, "Once Again—The 'Center' of the Old Testament," *BTB* 31, no. 3 (Fall 2001): 88

The Bible has a central storyline with an overarching theological message. "It is preferable and more sensitive to the Bible as literature to speak of a 'story-line' rather than a single 'center.'"[14]

Paul told the church at Ephesus, "I did not shrink from declaring to you the whole counsel of God" (Acts 20:27). It is possible, therefore, to summarize and unpack the Bible's theological message.[15] So instead of focusing on a single central theme, biblical theologians should focus on accurately integrating the Bible's most prominent themes[16] as they summarize the Bible's (1) central storyline, and (2) overarching theological message.

What Is the Bible's Central Storyline?

The story has four main turning points: creation, fall, redemption, and consummation. The story has three main characters: the Triune God, the people of God, and the enemies of God.

We can tell the story by focusing on a single theme (e.g., God the King[17] or God the Serpent Slayer[18]) or a combination of themes (e.g., kingdom through covenant for God's glory).[19] A multi-thematic approach is more comprehensive. For example, Charles H. H. Scobie identifies four major themes (God's

---

(emphasis added): "A Christian might urge Jesus Christ as the center of the New Testament at least. But this literature cannot be reduced to Jesus Christ as 'center,' without making a mockery of it. One might as well say that God is the center of the Bible, as has been claimed (Hasel: 168)—but this solves nothing. Literature is literature, and theology is thematic. The Old Testament in particular is far too diversified to be curtailed to an essential center/theme, no matter how broad (e.g., presence), or how important (e.g., covenant). *The drive for the unity of the biblical writings fails because the literature has no middle, or unity.* It was composed over a period of centuries, and reflects the most varied circumstances. It is rich in its diversity. The plan of God, the historical design of the God worshiped in both Testaments, is not the same thing as the literature spawned by the people of God. The unity of divine design is not the unity of the literature that gives witness—a variegated witness (Torah, Prophets, Wisdom) to the design itself." For a better approach, see Blomberg, "Unity and Diversity of Scripture," 64–72.

14. Beale, *New Testament Biblical Theology*, 163. Beale recognizes, "Summative storylines are also open to the criticism of being reductionistic, and for the same reasons as proposed centers: (1) one can ask why specific ideas or events are chosen and seen to be more conceptually dominant than other events; (2) furthermore, a plotline approach may not be sufficiently representative, since significant portions of Scripture are not narrative (e.g., wisdom literature, apocalyptic, and epistolary material); (3) whatever themes are chosen are the result of interpreters seeing only what they have been culturally conditioned to see, since many believe that all knowledge is culturally conditioned" (165).

15. See Beale, *New Testament Biblical Theology*, 164; Daniel J. Brendsel, "Plots, Themes, and Responsibilities: The Search for a Center of Biblical Theology Reexamined," *Them* 35, no. 3 (November 2010): 400–412.

16. See Beale, *New Testament Biblical Theology*, 161–84.

17. See Question 10.

18. See Question 23.

19. See Question 19.

order, God's servant, God's people, and God's way), and he groups subthemes beneath each major theme.[20]

Beale summarizes each testament in a single (dense!) sentence, and spends most of his 1,072-page biblical theology unpacking the two following sentences:

> [OT storyline] God . . . progressively reestablishes his new-creational kingdom out of chaos over a sinful people by his word and Spirit through promise, covenant, and redemption, resulting in worldwide commission to the faithful to advance this kingdom and judgment (defeat or exile) for the unfaithful, unto his glory. . . .
>
> [NT storyline] Jesus's life, trials, death for sinners, and especially resurrection by the Spirit have launched the fulfillment of the eschatological already–not yet new-creational reign, bestowed by grace through faith and resulting in worldwide commission to the faithful to advance this new-creational reign and resulting in judgment for the unbelieving, unto the triune God's glory.[21]

Beale argues that the new-creational kingdom theme recapitulates throughout the storyline:

> (1) chaos of precreation state and creation/commission of Adam as king, followed by fall; (2) chaos of deluge and re-creation/commission of Noah, followed by fall (sins of Noah and his sons); (3) chaos of Egyptian captivity and plagues of de-creation, followed by re-creation (at exodus)/commission of Israel (anticipated by commission of patriarchs), followed by fall (golden calf); (4) chaos of captivity in Babylon and in Israel's own land, followed by re-creation/commission of Jesus the true Israel (in his life, death, and resurrection), followed by no fall of Jesus as last Adam, and by successful consummation of initial re-creation in eternal new heaven and earth.[22]

"Throughout this book," Beale explains, "I relate the storyline of the new creation and kingdom to the subject matter of all the major NT corpuses and books."[23] Beale qualifies that he is not proposing one central theme for the whole Bible around which all the major thematic strands of the Bible revolve.[24] Nor is he proposing that storyline as the center of the whole Bible "but rather as

20. Charles H. H. Scobie, *The Ways of Our God: An Approach to Biblical Theology* (Grand Rapids: Eerdmans, 2003), 93–99.
21. Beale, *New Testament Biblical Theology*, 16.
22. Beale, *New Testament Biblical Theology*, 169–70.
23. Beale, *New Testament Biblical Theology*, 170.
24. Beale, *New Testament Biblical Theology*, 61.

the primary strand of the biblical storyline thread, around which other minor or thinner narratival and conceptual strands are woven and are held together."[25]

What Is the Bible's Overarching Theological Message?[26]

Here is how we summarize the theological message of the whole Bible in one sentence: *God reigns, saves, and satisfies through covenant for his glory in Christ.* We can break that down into four parts: content, means, goal, and agent.[27]

> 1. *Content.* What is the Bible about? It reveals God as the supreme king. More specifically, it presents God not only as the one who reigns but who saves and satisfies. God reigns as the sovereign king over everyone (both his people and his enemies) and everything. And God has a special relationship with his people, whom he saves and satisfies. He not only delivers his people from sin and death and hell; he satisfies them with himself.[28] "To the thirsty," says the Alpha and Omega, "I will give from the spring of the water of life without payment" (Rev. 21:6; cf. 22:17).
>
> 2. *Means.* How does God reign, save, and satisfy? God does that through the covenants.[29] The story from creation to consummation progresses through divine-human covenants (Adamic-Noahic, Abrahamic, Mosaic, Davidic, new), and the early church names the

---

25. Beale, *New Testament Biblical Theology*, 87.
26. See also Jason S. DeRouchie, *How to Understand and Apply the Old Testament: Twelve Steps from Exegesis to Theology* (Phillipsburg, NJ: P&R, 2017), 368–69; Andrew David Naselli, *How to Understand and Apply the New Testament: Twelve Steps from Exegesis to Theology* (Phillipsburg, NJ: P&R, 2017), 193, 237.
27. Or frame, form, focus, and fulcrum. See DeRouchie, *Understand and Apply the Old Testament*, 368–70.
28. See John Piper, *Desiring God: Meditations of a Christian Hedonist*, in *The Collected Works of John Piper*, eds. David Mathis and Justin Taylor (Wheaton, IL: Crossway, 2017), 2:11–359.
29. See Question 22. We agree with how Peter J. Gentry and Stephen J. Wellum argue in their 959-page *Kingdom through Covenant*: "We are *not* asserting that the biblical covenants are the center of biblical theology or merely a unifying theme of Scripture. Instead, we assert that *the progression of the covenants* forms the backbone of Scripture's metanarrative, the relational reality that moves history forward according to God's design and final plan for humanity and all creation, and unless we 'put together' the covenants correctly, we will not discern accurately 'the whole counsel of God' (Acts 20:27). [Footnote 2:] We will not discuss the thorny issue of the center of biblical theology. Many proposals have been given, and they all tend toward reductionism. . . . Our claim is more modest: the biblical covenants form the backbone of the Bible's metanarrative, and apart from understanding each covenant in its immediate context and then in relation to its fulfillment in Christ, we will potentially misunderstand the Bible's overall message and misapply Scripture to our lives." Peter J. Gentry and Stephen J. Wellum, *Kingdom through Covenant: A Biblical-Theological Understanding of the Covenants*, 2nd ed. (Wheaton, IL: Crossway, 2018), 31–32 (emphasis original).

two testaments after the contrast between the old (Mosaic) covenant and the new covenant (i.e., the Old and New *Testaments* = covenants).

3. *Goal.* What is the ultimate goal for God to reign, save, and satisfy through covenant? God does it all for his glory: "For from him and through him and to him are all things. To him be glory forever. Amen" (Rom. 11:36).

4. *Agent.* Who accomplishes this grand mission? Jesus the Messiah. The prepositional phrase *in Christ* is not a superfluous add-on to our one-sentence summary. It's everything. The new covenant is a better covenant that Jesus the Messiah mediates. God fulfills his ancient promises in Christ. The Bible is one big story that's all about Jesus. Jesus fulfills the Old Testament. The entire Old Testament points to Jesus (John 5:39; Luke 24:27, 44; 2 Cor. 1:20). Jesus is the climax of God's revelation (Heb. 1:1–3). So if you interpret the Bible in a way that does not point to Jesus, then you are not interpreting the Bible in the way that God himself says you should. This doesn't mean that every Old Testament or New Testament passage points to Jesus in exactly the same way. But every passage points to Jesus in some way, and biblical theology inductively investigates *how*.[30]

Here are seventeen other one-sentence summaries of the Bible's theological message to consider:[31]

1. *Craig L. Blomberg:* God is in the process of recreating the universe, which has been corrupted by sin, and has made it possible for all those and only those who follow Jesus to be a part of the magnificent, eternal community that will result.

2. *Darrell L. Bock:* The Bible tells how the loving Creator God restored a lost humanity and cosmos through reestablishing his rule through Jesus Christ and the provision of life to his honor.

3. *Daniel J. Brendsel:* The triune God is actively engaged in increasing (and incarnating) his presence among his people, a presence that

---

30. See Question 4. See also *Southern Baptist Journal of Theology* 22, no. 3 (Fall 2018); the issue is on preaching Christ from the Old Testament.
31. The source of these sentences (except for those by Brendsel and Rigney) is Dane Ortlund, "What's the Message of the Bible in One Sentence?," *Strawberry-Rhubarb Theology*, January 12, 2011, https://dogmadoxa.blogspot.com/2011/01/whats-message-of-bible-in-one-sentence.html.

entails for his people the responsibility of worship, in the fourfold story of creation, fall, redemption, and consummation.[32]

4. *Mark Dever:* God has made promises to bring his people to himself, and he is fulfilling them all through Christ.

5. *Kevin DeYoung:* A holy God sends his righteous Son to die for unrighteous sinners so we can be holy and live happily with God forever.

6. *John M. Frame:* God glorifies himself in the redemption of sinners.

7. *Scott J. Hafemann:* The Triune God is the beginning, middle, and end of everything, "for from him (as Creator) and through him (as Sustainer and Redeemer) and to him (as Judge) are all things" (Rom. 11:36).

8. *David R. Helm:* Jesus is the promised Savior-King.

9. *Paul House:* [History moves] from creation to new creation through the redemptive work of Father, Son, and Spirit, who saves and changes corrupted people and places for his glory and their good.

10. *R. Kent Hughes:* God is redeeming his creation by bringing it under the lordship of Jesus Christ.

11. *Dane Ortlund:* Despite ongoing rebellion on our part, the holy God of the universe refuses to leave us to wallow in our sin, eventually and climactically becoming one of us, in the moral mud, to restore us to glory, if we will receive his love in trusting contrition.

12. *Ray Ortlund:* The Lover of our souls won't let the romance die, but is rekindling it forever.

13. *Joe Rigney:* Kill the dragon, get the girl![33]

14. *Thomas R. Schreiner:* God reigns over all things for his glory, but we will only enjoy his saving reign in the new heavens and the new earth if we repent and believe in the gospel of Jesus Christ, who is the

---

32. Daniel J. Brendsel, "Plots, Themes, and Responsibilities: The Search for a Center of Biblical Theology Reexamined," *Themelios* 35, no. 3 (November 2010): 412.

33. Rigney coined this phrase shortly after he read Douglas Wilson's one-sentence summary (see below). Rigney started including that tagline to the end of his emails.

crucified and risen Lord and who gave himself on the cross for our salvation.

15. *Erik Thoennes:* The one true God is displaying his glory primarily in redeeming and restoring his fallen creation by fulfilling his covenant promises and commands through the glorious person and atoning work of Christ.

16. *Douglas Wilson:* Scripture tells us the story of how a Garden is transformed into a Garden City, but only after a dragon had turned that Garden into a howling wilderness, a haunt of owls and jackals, which lasted until an appointed warrior came to slay the dragon, giving up his life in the process, but with his blood effecting the transformation of the wilderness into the Garden City.

17. *Robert W. Yarbrough:* He—God in Christ—shall reign forever and ever; so today if you hear his voice, do not harden your heart, but believing the good news take up your cross and follow Jesus.

Summary

Some biblical theologians propose one central theme for the whole Bible, but that seems reductionistic. A better approach is to integrate the Bible's most prominent themes as one summarizes the Bible's (1) storyline, and (2) theological message.

REFLECTION QUESTIONS

1. If you had to identify only one central theme for the whole Bible, what theme would you propose?

2. Which of the seventeen one-sentence summaries above do you like best? Why?

3. What three or four themes do you think are most prominent in the Bible?

4. How would you summarize the Bible's central storyline in a single sentence?

5. How would you summarize the Bible's overarching theological message in a single sentence?

Is the Order of the Canon Significant for Doing Biblical Theology?

Jason S. DeRouchie

Brevard Childs correctly notes, "It is historically inaccurate to assume that the present printed form of the Hebrew and the Christian Bible represent ancient and completely fixed traditions. Actually, the present stability regarding the ordering of the books is to a great extent dependent on modern printing techniques and carries no significant theological weight."[1] Religious communities have been responsible for the *present* order of the biblical books, but we must ask whether historical and theological priority should be given to any one canonical structure over another, most specifically when doing biblical theology. Is the order of the canon significant when it comes to assessing how the whole Bible progresses, integrates, and climaxes in Christ?

A number of factors move us to answer with a qualified "Yes," and our response will come in three stages. First, this study overviews the nature and limits of the biblical canon. Second, it assesses how much canon-consciousness among the ancient Israelite/Jewish communities included not simply which books but also their ordering. Third, it considers ways that canonical arrangement could and should inform a Christian's interpretive conclusions in relation to biblical theology.

The Nature and Limits of the Biblical Canon

The Christian canon is the church's authoritative collection of holy books (Rom. 1:2; 2 Tim. 3:15; 2 Peter 3:16). God authored the whole through human agents (2 Tim. 3:16; 2 Peter 1:21), and it is made up of what we now call the Old and New Testaments. The Protestant OT canon is made up of thirty-nine

---

1. Brevard S. Childs, *Biblical Theology of the Old and New Testaments: Theological Reflection on the Christian Bible* (Minneapolis: Fortress, 1993), 74.

books, and the Jewish Bible is identical with it in content but consists of twenty-four books that are divided and arranged differently.[2] The NT has twenty-seven books with some known variation in the ordering.[3]

Both historically and theologically the concepts of canon and covenant correlate. The essence of canon is bound up in the authoritative written word of a covenant lord.[4] That is, written texts became canonized not by the decision of the recipients but in the light of their source, and we recognize Scripture as canonical (i.e., authoritative) because it is by nature the very word of the living God.[5]

---

2. The Jewish Scriptures pair some of our English Bible books into single volumes (e.g., 1–2 Samuel, 1–2 Kings, the Twelve Minor Prophets, Ezra-Nehemiah, 1–2 Chronicles). At least in the case of the books of Samuel, Kings, and Chronicles, the reason these were later separated into two books appears to be merely pragmatic: the Hebrew Bible used only consonants, and when it was translated into Greek, which included vowels, the books got too long for single scrolls. There are minor variations in the traditions: the Roman Catholic OT has forty-six books (adding Tobit, Judith, Baruch, Ben Sira, Wisdom, and 1–2 Maccabees, with additions to Daniel and Esther), and the Orthodox Church has forty-eight books (adding 1 Esdras and 3 Maccabees). For a full survey of OT canonical lists in the early church with an argument for a closed canon far before the Christian era, see Roger T. Beckwith, *The Old Testament Canon of the New Testament Church and Its Background in Early Judaism* (Grand Rapids: Eerdmans, 1985); Edmon L. Gallagher and John D. Meade, *The Biblical Canon Lists from Early Christianity: Texts and Analysis* (Oxford: Oxford University Press, 2017).

3. For an overview of the evidence with an argument that the NT canon was fixed as early as AD 125, see David Trobisch, *Paul's Letter Collection: Tracing the Origins* (Minneapolis: Fortress, 1994); David Trobisch, *The First Edition of the New Testament* (Oxford: Oxford University Press, 2000); Michael J. Kruger, *Canon Revisited: Establishing the Origins and Authority of the New Testament Books* (Wheaton, IL: Crossway, 2012); Michael J. Kruger, *The Question of Canon: Challenging the Status Quo in the New Testament Debate* (Downers Grove, IL: InterVarsity, 2013); cf. Charles E. Hill, "'The Truth above All Demonstration': Scripture in the Patristic Period to Augustine," in *The Enduring Authority of the Christian Scriptures*, ed. D. A. Carson (Grand Rapids: Eerdmans, 2016), 43–88, esp. 69–72; Gallagher and Meade, *Biblical Canon Lists*.

4. Meredith G. Kline, "The Correlation of the Concepts of Canon and Covenant," in *New Perspectives on the Old Testament*, ed. J. Barton Payne (Waco, TX: Word, 1970), 265–79; Meredith G. Kline, *The Structure of Biblical Authority*, 2nd ed. (Eugene, OR: Wipf & Stock, 1997), 27–44. Similarly, Cole writes, "Canon is a corollary of special revelation and a written canon a corollary of divine inspiration." Graham A. Cole, "Why a Book? Why This Book? Why the Particular Order within This Book? Some Theological Reflections on Canon," in Carson, *Enduring Authority of the Christian Scriptures*, 467.

5. As Webster asserts, "Canonization is thus to be understood as assent rather than authorization, as an act of reception and submission, and as a pledge to be governed by the textual norm given to the church." John Webster, "Canon," *Dictionary for Theological Interpretation of the Bible*, 99. Metzger wrote of the NT canon, "Neither individuals nor councils created the canon; instead they came to recognize and acknowledge the self-authenticating quality of these writings, which imposed themselves as canonical upon the church." Bruce M. Metzger, *The New Testament: Its Background, Growth, and Content*, 3rd ed., rev. and enlarged (Nashville: Abingdon, 2003), 318. Similarly, Hill notes of the

Evidence of Early Canon-Consciousness

A proper view of canon requires understanding that God not only gave us books but progressively shaped a Book (i.e., Scripture as a whole with Old and New Testaments), the meaning of which is influenced by the order and relationship of the parts. We see support for this thesis in the rich canon-consciousness that the ancients bore with respect to the Scripture. Both in and outside the Bible the ancient authors identify a sacred canonical body of material and include lists of biblical books.[6]

First, the concept of canon is evident in the way the Jews spoke of their sacred collection of texts. What we now label the OT they spoke of in various ways. At times, they used one-part titles like "the Law" (e.g., John 10:34; 12:34; Rom. 3:19; 1 Cor. 14:34),[7] "the Holy Scriptures/Writings" (Rom. 1:2; 2 Tim. 3:15),[8] or just "the Scriptures" (Luke 24:45; 1 Cor. 15:3). Other times they employed a two-part designation like "the Law and the Prophets" (Matt. 5:17; 7:12; 11:13; 22:40; Luke 16:16; Acts 13:15; 24:14), "Moses and the Prophets" (Luke 16:29, 31; 24:27; Acts 26:22), or "the Law of Moses and the Prophets" (John 1:45; Acts 28:23).[9] And still other times they adopted a three-part heading like "the Law of Moses and the Prophets and the Psalms" (Luke 24:44), "the Law, the Prophets, and the rest of the books," or "the Book of Moses, the Books of the Prophets and David."[10] The very presence of such designations identifies a high canon-consciousness.

NT canon that the early church "saw themselves not as 'determining' the documents they found most useful, but as 'recognizing' and 'receiving' what God had given through Jesus and his apostles. . . . The attitude—demonstrable in the latter half of the second century, but surely existing earlier—seems to be that Scripture is something given by God and that only he can determine what it is. The role of the church, therefore, is essentially receptive, to recognize what he has given." Charles E. Hill, "The New Testament Canon: *Deconstructio Ad Absurdum?*," *JETS* 52 (2009): 105, 119. For numerous primary source claims that support these sentiments from the first centuries of the Common Era, see Hill, "Truth above All Demonstration," 46–53.

6. Two other clear evidences of canonical consciousness are the Bible's witness to its own authority (e.g., John 10:33–36) and that, as early as the late second or early third centuries AD, scribes used an arrow or wedge-shaped siglum in the margin of manuscripts (called a *diplē*) to distinguish Old and New Testament quotations from other sources that were not part of the canon. For a description, see Hill, "Truth above All Demonstration," 68–69.

7. Cf. 1 Macc. 2:50, 64.

8. Cf. Josephus, *Ag. Ap.* 1.10.

9. Cf. 2 Macc. 15:9; 4: Macc. 18:10; 1QS 1.2–3; 8.15–16; CD 7.15–17; 4QMMT 16.

10. See the prologue to Sirach 1, 8–10, 24–25; 4QMMT 10; cf. Sir 39:1–2; 2 Macc. 2:1, 13. Dempster notes that the difference between the two- and three-part designations is likely only one of preference: "The canon is already tripartite and two designations can be used to describe it, a short form ('Moses and the words of the prophets') and a long form ('Moses, the words of the prophets and David')." Stephen G. Dempster, "From Many Texts to One: The Formation of the Hebrew Bible," in *The World of the Aramaeans*, vol. 1 of *Biblical Studies in Honour of Paul-Eugène Dion*, eds. P. M. Michèle Daviau, John W. Wevers, and Michael Weigl (Sheffield: Sheffield Academic, 2001), 33; cf. Stephen G.

Second, we have a series of early lists of Old and New Testament books that together highlight that certain writings were sacred and that they were viewed in certain groupings and orders. With respect to the OT, two of the earliest lists of the Hebrew Scriptures are Jewish (see fig. 16.1). While they portray two different arrangements, they are both tripartite and together support the conviction that prophecy had temporally ceased after Malachi (see 1 Macc. 9:27; cf. 4:45–6; 14:41) and that long before the NT age what we call the OT was already a fixed canonical standard.[11]

Josephus *Against Apion* 8.37–43 (ca. AD 94–117)	Babylonian Talmud *Baba Bathra* 14b (ca. AD 1–200)	**English Old Testament**
Five Books of Moses	*The Law (assumed)*	*Pentateuch*
Genesis	Genesis	Genesis
Exodus	Exodus	Exodus
Leviticus	Leviticus	Leviticus
Numbers	Numbers	Numbers
Deuteronomy	Deuteronomy	Deuteronomy

Dempster, "The Old Testament Canon, Josephus, and Cognitive Environment," in Carson, *Enduring Authority of the Christian Scriptures*, 338. For a more thorough list of designations, see Beckwith, *Old Testament Canon of the New Testament Church*, 105–9. For more on the development of the three-part designation, see Stephen G. Dempster, "Torah, Torah, Torah: The Emergence of the Tripartite Canon," in *Exploring the Origins of the Bible: Canon Formation in Historical, Literary, and Theological Perspective*, eds. Craig A. Evans and Emanuel Tov (Grand Rapids: Baker Academic, 2008).

11. For more on this reading of the evidence, see, e.g., Sid Z. Leiman, *The Canonization of Hebrew Scripture: The Talmudic and Midrashic Evidence* (Hamden, CT: Archon Books, 1976); Beckwith, *Old Testament Canon of the New Testament Church*; E. Earle Ellis, *The Old Testament in Early Christianity: Canon and Interpretation in the Light of Modern Research*, WUNT 2/54 (Tübingen: Mohr Siebeck, 1991); Andrew E. Steinmann, *The Oracles of God: The Old Testament Canon* (St. Louis: Concordia, 2005); Peter J. Gentry, "The Text of the Old Testament," *JETS* 52 (2009): 19–45; Dempster, "Old Testament Canon, Josephus." Aligning with a late first-century reference in 4 Ezra 14:44–48 that Ezra assembled the Scriptures following the Babylonian exile, early Christian tradition dated the completion of the OT canon to the days of Ezra; see, e.g., Irenaeus, *Haer.* 3.21.2; Clement of Alexandria, *Strom.* 1.22; Tertullian, *Cult. Fem.* 1.3. Jerome's *Prologus Galeatus* notes that, beginning in the third century AD, the early church identified that the Jews had two different enumerations of the same canon—one with twenty-two books and the other with twenty-four. Dempster, "Old Testament Canon, Josephus," 336n43.

Thirteen Books of the Prophets That Include the History of Their Times (possible order)[12]	The Prophets	History
	Joshua	Joshua
	Judges	Judges
	Samuel	Ruth
	Kings	1–2 Samuel
Joshua	Jeremiah	1–2 Kings
Judges-Ruth	Ezekiel	1–2 Chronicles
Samuel	Isaiah	Ezra
Kings	The Twelve	Nehemiah
Isaiah	**The Writings**	Esther
Jeremiah-Lamentations		**Poetry/Wisdom**
Ezekiel	Ruth	
Daniel	Psalms	Job
The Twelve	Job	Psalms
Job	Proverbs	Proverbs
Chronicles	Ecclesiastes	Ecclesiastes
Ezra-Nehemiah (= Esdras)	Song of Songs	Song of Songs
Esther	Lamentations	**Prophets**
		Isaiah
		Jeremiah
Four Remaining Books of Hymns and Instructions (possible order)	Daniel	Lamentations
	Esther	Ezekiel
	Ezra-Nehemiah	Daniel
Psalms	Chronicles	Hosea
Proverbs		Joel
Ecclesiastes		Amos
Song of Songs		Obadiah
		Jonah, Micah, Nahum, Habakkuk, Zephaniah, Haggai, Zechariah, Malachi

Fig. 16.1. The Earliest Jewish Hebrew Bible Lists

The first Hebrew list comes from the Jewish historian Josephus in *Against Apion* 8.37–43 (ca. AD 94–117). He did not register the books themselves, but he spoke of a closed list of twenty-two inspired books that had guided the Jews for centuries and that bore a three-part structure. In alignment with his role as historian, he grouped the biblical books by genre and chronology and apparently used the twenty-two letter Hebrew alphabet to fix his number: the five books of Moses from the beginning to his death, thirteen prophets who recorded history from the death of Moses to the reign of Artaxerxes (likely

---

12. For various other proposals for the arrangements of Josephus's "Prophets," see Gallagher and Meade, *Biblical Canon Lists*, 63–64.

joining Judges-Ruth and Jeremiah-Lamentations), and four remaining books that included various hymns and instructions.[13] Gallagher and Meade note, "Many Jews—all, according to Josephus—received these books as authoritative by the late first century, and it is unlikely that such reception constituted a radical change from the previous situation, especially in the absence of ancient statements disputing the status of these books."[14]

The second Jewish list is *Baba Bathra* 14b, an ancient rabbinic Baraita, a tradition that is in the Jewish oral law but not incorporated into the Mishnah. *Baba Bathra* 14b comes from rabbinic scholars known as the Tannaim, who lived during the first two centuries AD and whose work was later included in the Babylonian Talmud.[15] It lists twenty-four biblical books and also differentiates a three-part structure ("the Law, the Prophets, the Writings"). Here, however, chronology, theology, and literary artistry guide the arrangement,[16] most notably with Ruth and Chronicles being a part of the third division and the historical narrative books (Law, Former Prophets, Latter Writings) framing what can be termed non-narrative "commentary" books (Latter Prophets, Former Writings) (see fig. 16.2)—that is, books whose purpose is not to detail the progress of redemptive history but to explain, interpret, and guide our reading of it.[17] The Major Prophets are out of chronological order (i.e., not Isaiah, Jeremiah, Ezekiel); Ruth is totally separated from its temporal context after Judges; Daniel is not among the Prophets; and Chronicles and Ezra-Nehemiah are in reverse chronological order. The narrative runs chronologically from Genesis to Kings, pauses from Jeremiah to Lamentations, and then resumes from Daniel to Ezra-Nehemiah. Chronicles then recalls the story from Adam to Cyrus's decree that Israel can return. As for the commentary, the Latter Prophets structure the four books largest to smallest, and the Former Writings follow the same pattern, except Ruth prefaces the Psalter and the longer Lamentations follows Song of Songs. The former shift places the Psalter in the context of Davidic hope, and the latter switch allows (1) Jeremiah's writings to frame the whole commentary unit, (2) Solomon's three volumes (Proverbs, Ecclesiastes, and Song of Songs) to remain together, and

---

13. For more on the alphabet as a structuring device, see Dempster, "Old Testament Canon, Josephus," 340.
14. Gallagher and Meade, *Biblical Canon Lists*, 20.
15. Beckwith, *Old Testament Canon of the New Testament Church*, 26–27.
16. Dempster, "Old Testament Canon, Josephus," 339. Dated to around the same time as Josephus's *Against Apion*, 4 Ezra 14:44–48 distinguishes twenty-four books that were for public reading and thus canonical from seventy others that were only for private uses. Similarly, around the second half of the second century, the ascetic, noncanonical Gospel of Thomas represents Jesus's disciples as saying to him, "Twenty-four prophets have spoken in Israel, and they all spoke of you" (Gos. Thom. 52).
17. For this description, see Stephen G. Dempster, *Dominion and Dynasty: A Biblical Theology of the Hebrew Bible*, NSBT 15 (Downers Grove, IL: InterVarsity, 2003), 45–51.

(3) Lamentations to reorient the reader to the exilic context where Kings left off and where the narrative in Daniel resumes.

Law	Former Prophets	Latter Prophets	Former Writings	Latter Writings
Genesis Exodus Leviticus Numbers Deuteronomy	Joshua Judges 1–2 Samuel 1–2 Kings	Jeremiah Ezekiel Isaiah The Twelve	Ruth-Psalms Job Proverbs Ecclesiastes Song of Songs Lamentations	Daniel Esther Ezra-Nehemiah 1–2 Chronicles
Narrative	**Narrative**	**Commentary**	**Commentary**	**Narrative**

Fig. 16.2. The Arrangement of the Hebrew Bible in Baba Bathra 14b

Outside these two lists, we do not find alternative Jewish arrangements of the Hebrew Scripture until much later—in the middle part of the medieval period from the Western Masoretic tradition (e.g., Aleppo Codex, ca. AD 925; Leningrad Codex, ca. AD 1008/9) and then after the medieval period in the sixteenth-century second Rabbinic Bible. Furthermore, of the two early Jewish lists, *Baba Bathra* 14b more closely aligns with the NT's internal testimony regarding the structure of Jesus's Bible and therefore most likely represents the standard listing found at the temple.[18]

Specifically, the Jewish Bible that Jesus and the apostles used bore a three-part structure that included Psalms as the largest and first main book in the third division (with Ruth apparently serving as a preface). Luke 24:44 is evidence of that structure since Jesus appears to use "Psalms" as the title of the whole third division. Also, the biblical evidence suggests that the Bible of the earliest church began with Genesis and ended with Chronicles, just like *Baba Bathra* 14b. When Jesus confronted the Pharisees, he spoke of the martyrdom of the OT prophets "from the blood of Abel to the blood of Zechariah" (Luke 11:51; cf. Matt. 23:35). This is not a simple "A to Z" statement, for Zechariah's name does not begin with the last letter of any biblical language alphabet. Also, it is not strictly a chronological statement, for while Abel was the first martyr (Gen. 4:4, 8), the OT's last martyr with respect to time was Uriah the son of Shemaiah, who died during the reign of Jehoiakim (609–598 BC; see Jer. 26:20–23). Jesus seems to have been speaking canonically by mentioning

---

18. It also most likely testifies to the standard order that Judas Maccabaeus attested to around 164 BC (see 2 Macc. 2:14–15). This would make it the most ancient list of the OT books discovered to date. So, too, Beckwith, *Old Testament Canon of the New Testament Church*, 121–27.

the first and last martyr in the literary structure of his Bible. Specifically, just as Genesis records Abel's murder (Gen. 4:2–8), the end of Chronicles highlights a certain Zechariah who was killed in the temple court during the reign of Joash (835–796 BC; see 2 Chron. 24:20–21).

With respect to the NT, many of the earliest Christian lists, whether Greek or Latin, include both Testaments or just the NT.[19] However, the earliest complete twenty-seven-book record comes in AD 367 in Athanasius's thirty-ninth *Festal Letter* (*Epistula festalis* 39.15–21), in which he identified the canonical NT books so as to distinguish those that did not bear such authority. His registry looks very similar to our present-day English Bible lists, except that he places the seven General/Catholic Epistles (James–Jude) directly after Acts and then includes Hebrews with Paul's letters (also quite common in the East) and places Hebrews before the Pastorals. As early as the second century, however, the church widely accepted the collections of the four Gospels, the seven General Epistles, and Paul's letters (with thirteen in the West and fourteen in the East, +/– Hebrews), along with Acts and Revelation.[20] While it is difficult to assess due to the paucity of evidence for the General Epistles prior to the fourth century AD, Trobisch argues that the NT canon was fixed as early as AD 125 and originally bore the structure that matches Athanasius's list (see fig. 16.3).[21]

---

19. Eusebius records the earliest lists, which date back to a number of comments by Origen in the mid-second century AD (AD 230, 248/249, 250). They together mention the four "Gospels" and then distinguish the "Epistles and Apocalypse," which Eusebius registers as Peter (two), James, Jude, John (plural), Paul (fourteen, including Hebrews), and Revelation (Eusebius, *Hist. eccl.* 6.25.3–6, 7–10). Gallagher and Meade, *Biblical Canon Lists*, also identify Eusebius's own record (*Hist. eccl.* 3.25, AD 325), that of Cyril of Jerusalem (*Catechesis* 4.33–36, AD 350), and the Muratorian Fragment, which likely dates to the late second or early third century. See C. E. Hill, "The Debate over the Muratorian Fragment and the Development of the Canon," *WTJ* 57 (1995): 437–52.
20. Gallagher and Meade, *Biblical Canon Lists*, 30–31.
21. Trobisch, *Paul's Letter Collection*; Trobisch, *First Edition of the New Testament. The Greek New Testament* maintains the early tradition of placing the General Epistles directly after Acts, followed by Paul's Epistles and then Hebrews. Dirk Jongkind, ed., *The Greek New Testament: Produced at Tyndale House, Cambridge* (Wheaton, IL: Crossway, 2017).

  Athanasius also provides twenty-two books in his list of the OT. The only major division he signals is "the Prophets," in which he includes Baruch, Lamentations, and the Letter of Jeremiah and may include with Daniel both Susanna and Bel and the Dragon. Furthermore, he lists seven "books to be read": Wisdom of Solomon, Wisdom of Sirach, Esther, Judith, Tobit, Didache, Shepherd; and four "apocryphal books," which most likely include the Book of Enoch, the Testament of Moses, the Apocalypse of Elijah, and the Ascension of Isaiah. See Gallagher and Meade, *The Biblical Canon Lists from Early Christianity*, 120, 127.

Athanasius of Alexandria *Epistula festalis* 39.15–21 (ca. AD 367)	English New Testament
The Four Gospels	*Gospels*
1. Matthew 2. Mark 3. Luke 4. John	1. Matthew 2. Mark 3. Luke 4. John
5. Acts of the Apostles	5. Acts
Seven Catholic Letters	*Paul's Epistles and Hebrews*
6. James 7. 1–2 Peter 8. 1–3 John 9. Jude	6. Romans 7. 1 Corinthians 8. 2 Corinthians 9. Galatians
Fourteen Letters of Paul [+ Hebrews]	10. Ephesians 11. Philippians
10. Romans 11. 1–2 Corinthians 12. Galatians 13. Ephesians 14. Philippians 15. Colossians 16. 1–2 Thessalonians 17. Hebrews 18. 1–2 Timothy 19. Titus 20. Philemon	12. Colossians 13. 1 Thessalonians 14. 2 Thessalonians 15. 1 Timothy 16. 2 Timothy 17. Titus 18. Philemon 19. Hebrews
21. Revelation of John	*General Epistles*
	20. James 21. 1 Peter 22. 2 Peter 23. 1 John 24. 2 John 25. 3 John 26. Jude
	27. Revelation

Fig. 16.3. The Earliest Full Christian New Testament List (Greek)

The Significance of Canonical Arrangement for Biblical Theology

Much like the book of Psalms, which God inspired over a thousand-year period and which culminated in God's leading editors to shape its final form into five "books," it is possible that we should think about Scripture as a whole in this same way—God not only led individual authors to give us books but also guided editors to give us a book that they progressively shaped in two parts: Old and New Testaments. Canonical consciousness appears to have included arrangement and not just the presence of individual books.[22] Furthermore, when Jesus, Peter, and Paul asserted that their Scriptures declared a unified message about the tribulation and triumph of the Messiah and the mission he would spark (Luke 24:44–47; Acts 3:18, 24; 26:22–23; 1 Peter 1:10–11), their Bible included a number of features related to arrangement that helped proclaim that message in a distinctive way. As we will see, failing to see the significance of this will lead us astray when it comes to engaging in biblical theology.[23] In a quest to read OT Scripture like Jesus and the apostles did, it seems most natural that we would want to read the whole in the tripartite arrangement that shaped their thinking. And there are at least four ways in which arrangement matters when engaging the discipline of biblical theology.

First, a proper biblical-theological method requires that we prioritize the Law of Moses in the OT and the Gospels in the New, for each grouping of books details how God established the foundational covenant (i.e., old and new) that shapes how we understand each Testament. In the OT, all books written after Moses assume the presence of his words in Genesis–Deuteronomy and the covenantal context they describe. What Moses writes guides how later narrators detail Israel's history from the conquest to Jerusalem's demise and through the exile to initial restoration (e.g., Josh. 1:8–9; 2 Kings 17:13–15; Dan. 6:5; Neh. 1:7–9). Furthermore, the story identifies that the faithful kings retained a high-level of canon consciousness (1 Kings 2:3; 2 Kings 22:11), whereas the unfaithful did not (Jer. 36:24), and that the nation's ruin was an act of divine covenantal curse and fully due to Israel and Judah's failure to heed the words of Moses proclaimed through the prophets (2 Kings 17:13–15; Dan. 9:11). The prophets made their indictments, instructions, and predictions

---

22. John Sailhamer, *Introduction to Old Testament Theology: A Canonical Approach* (Grand Rapids: Zondervan, 1995), 249; Dempster, *Dominion and Dynasty*, 28; Rolf Rendtorff, *The Canonical Hebrew Bible: A Theology of the Old Testament* (Leiden: Deo, 2005), 2.

23. In this respect, Dempster writes of Jesus's Bible, "The final compilers of the biblical text ensured that the text was to be understood as a unity. There are not only major groupings of books, but editorial 'splices' that join major groupings of books with each other. Therefore, both theological and literary points are made simultaneously." Dempster, *Dominion and Dynasty*, 31–32. For a developed overview of the types of features Dempster is referring to, see Stephen G. Dempster, "An 'Extraordinary Fact': Torah and Temple and the Contours of the Hebrew Canon, Part 1," *TynBul* 48 (1997): 23–56; Stephen G. Dempster, "An 'Extraordinary Fact': Torah and Temple and the Contours of the Hebrew Canon, Part 2," *TynBul* 48 (1997): 191–218; Dempster, *Dominion and Dynasty*. For a similar approach in the NT, see Matthew Y. Emerson, *Christ and the New Creation: A Canonical Approach to the Theology of the New Testament* (Eugene, OR: Wipf & Stock, 2013). We are not convinced that later editors altered already fixed books but rather positioned them with intentionality and made their new material allude to earlier material, thus allowing for the types of connections Dempster sees.

of punishment or restoration blessing all in light of Moses's Law,[24] and the sages built their prayers and wisdom upon it (e.g., Pss. 1, 19, 119; Prov. 3:1–2; 6:20–23; Eccl. 12:13). Moses's five books give shape to the problems Christ solves, and they formalize or anticipate all of Scripture's covenants. Most biblical-theological themes and most typological shadows originate in the Law. Probably for these reasons, every known canonical list and order begins with the Law.

Furthermore, as recorded in the four Gospels, Jesus's teachings and work shape and clarify all further instruction and supply the lens for faithfully reading Scripture as a whole. Acts and Revelation develop the history of the church by identifying how the reign of God that Christ inaugurated is expanded by means of his Spirit and will culminate in the final judgment and a glorious consummate state (Acts 1:1–3, 8; Rev. 1:4–6). The book of Hebrews opens by asserting its foundation: "In these last days [God] has spoken to us by his Son, whom he appointed the heir of all things. . . . After making purification for sins, he sat down at the right hand of the Majesty on high" (Heb. 1:2–3). Paul knew well the teachings of Christ (e.g., Acts 20:35 with Matt. 10:8; 1 Cor. 7:10 with Matt. 5:32; 1 Tim. 5:18 with Matt. 10:10; Luke 10:7), and he stresses numerous times how his own encounter with the resurrected Jesus reshapes his outlook on all of reality (e.g., Acts 22:14–15; 26:16–18; 1 Cor. 9:1; 15:8; 2 Cor. 3:14; Gal. 1:11–12). While the NT does not explicitly draw on the Gospels at the same rate that the OT draws on Moses's Law, there would be no NT were it not for the life, death, and resurrection of Christ and the Spirit-empowerment his ascension secured. Therefore, taking Scripture on its own terms requires that we use the portrait of Christ in the Gospels as the lens for interpreting the rest of the NT and as the lens for interpreting the Old.

Second, proper biblical-theological method requires reading the biblical story in succession. Historical *narrative* books frame both Jesus's Bible and the NT. The people God used to providentially arrange those books intentionally placed them in chronological succession to clarify God's perspective on how the peoples and events of space and time relate to his kingdom purposes. The story moves from original creation to new creation, from the old, cursed world in Adam to the new, blessed world in Christ.[25] The progress of five

---

24. For indictments and instructions, see, e.g., Isa. 2:3; Jer. 2:8; Ezek. 7:26; Hos. 4:6; Amos 2:4; Hab. 1:4; Zeph. 3:4; Zech. 7:12; Mal. 4:4[3:22]. The oracles of warning/punishment and hope/salvation all grow out of Moses's blessings, curses, and restoration blessings detailed in Leviticus 26 and Deuteronomy 27–32. For a complete list, see Jason S. DeRouchie, *How to Understand and Apply the Old Testament: Twelve Steps from Exegesis to Theology* (Phillipsburg, NJ: P&R, 2017), 48–49.

25. In Emerson's words, "The structure is primarily that of narrative. There is an overarching metanarrative which the Bible's structure brings to light. . . . This narrative is Christologically focused and typically articulated in some form of Creation, Fall, Redemption, Restoration." Emerson, *Christ and the New Creation*, 11–12.

covenants—Adamic-Noahic, Abrahamic, Mosaic, Davidic, new—drives this grand story. All of those covenants progress, integrate, and climax in Christ.[26] Building organic connections within the canon itself requires that we read this redemptive story in succession, with Christ standing as the ultimate end and goal of its history (Matt. 2:15; Gal. 4:4), its law (Matt. 5:17–18; Rom. 10:4), and its promises (Acts 3:18; 2 Cor. 1:20). All Scripture points to Christ, and by fulfilling all previous anticipations, he provides the lens for interpreting the whole. Yet we will only properly see and understand his central role if we read the story in its proper order.

Significantly, the Christian Bible includes more than historical narrative. The *narrative* portions themselves contain various subgenres like commands (e.g., Exod. 20:1–17; Deut. 12–26; Matt. 5:20–7:27; 1 Cor. 14:37), oracles (e.g., Num. 23–24; Heb. 5:11–12; 1 Peter 4:11), blessings and curses (e.g., Lev. 26; Deut. 28; Matt. 25:31–46; Luke 6:20–26), songs (e.g., Exod. 15; Deut. 32; Rev. 5:9–10), riddles (e.g., Judg. 14:14; John 2:19; 16:16–19), parables (e.g., 2 Sam. 12:1–4; Mark 4:3–9), and apocalyptic visions (e.g., Daniel 7; Revelation 1). But also the Scripture includes the Latter Prophets, the Former Writings, the General Epistles, and the Pauline Epistles and Hebrews, four large groupings of poetic, prophetic, and hortatory books that together provide *commentary* on the storyline by informing and guiding our understanding of the broader plotline. As such, we will grasp Scripture's overarching message most clearly when we read the narrative and commentary books in a complementary way.

Third, when we engage in biblical theology, we must account for the shift from Old Testament to New and stay centered on the person and work of Jesus. Scripture teaches that there are only two major redemptive-historical epochs—before and after Christ. "The Law and the Prophets were until John; since then the good news of the kingdom of God is preached" (Luke 16:16; cf. Matt. 11:12). "The law was our guardian until Christ came, in order that we might be justified by faith. But now that faith has come, we are no longer under the guardian" (Gal. 3:24–25). A proper biblical theology requires that we account for how Scripture progresses, integrates, and climaxes in Jesus. What Jesus and the apostles teach in the NT is the basis for what the church must teach (Matt. 17:5; 28:20; Acts 2:42; Eph. 2:20). It is what God revealed through Jesus's death and resurrection that supplies the necessary lens for rightly appropriating the OT as God intended (Rom. 16:25–26; 2 Cor. 3:14; cf. John 2:20–22; 12:13–16).[27] The biblical-theological task requires that we read the OT as the foundation for how Christ in the NT fulfills God's promises,

---

26. See Questions 6 and 22.
27. For more on this, see Charles E. Hill, "God's Speech in These Last Days: The New Testament Canon as an Eschatological Phenomenon," in *Resurrection and Eschatology: Theology in Service of the Church; Essays in Honor of Richard B. Gaffin Jr.*, eds. Lane G. Tipton and Jeffrey C. Waddington (Phillipsburg, NJ: P&R, 2008), 203–54; Hill, "New Testament Canon," 107–13.

and it also requires that we see in Christ the mystery revealed that unlocks the full meaning of the OT (Rom. 16:25–26; 2 Cor. 3:14).

Fourth, doing biblical theology demands that we assess intertextual connections that are always informed by a book's placement, regardless of how one's canon is arranged. As Goswell observes, "Where a biblical book is placed relative to other books inevitably influences a reader's view of the book, on the supposition that juxtaposed books are related in some way and therefore illuminate each other. A prescribed order of books is *de facto* interpretation of the text."[28] For example, following the arrangement of our English Bibles, many Bible reading plans place 1–2 Chronicles directly after 1–2 Kings, which can cause one to feel like the same story is being told, just in different words. However, when 1–2 Chronicles is separated from Kings and placed at the end of the Hebrew Scriptures, its message is naturally viewed as more hopeful, pointing ahead to the fulfillment of the Davidic kingdom promises and the satisfaction in God's presence that the NT realizes through Jesus. Irrespective of what canonical ordering one utilizes, the position in which one reads a given book will likely affect one's biblical theology.

Summary

Douglas Stuart writes, "An orthodox understanding of canonization holds that the contents of the biblical canon are a matter of divine inspiration but that the specific order of the contents may have been left in large measure to human agency."[29] While this common view accounts for the plethora of early orders of books among the lists and manuscripts, it does not account for at least some of the explicit features of the canon itself and the nature of reading, all of which necessitate that biblical theology regard canonical arrangement in at least a qualified way. Along with seeking to approach the Scripture in the arrangement that Jesus and his apostles did, Scripture first requires that we treat the five books of Moses and the four Gospels as foundational for how we interpret the rest of Scripture. Second, we must read in succession the story of salvation recounted in the narrative books, while allowing the messages of the non-narrative commentary books to inform our reading. Third, we must always see the OT as the theological basis of the NT and the NT's revelation of Christ as the goal to which the OT points and the lens through which the

---

28. Gregory Goswell, "Two Testaments in Parallel: The Influence of the Old Testament on the Structuring of the New Testament Canon," *JETS* 56, no. 3 (2013): 459–60. Dempster states, "A particular sequence suggests hermeneutical significance." Dempster, *Dominion and Dynasty*, 34; cf. Rolf Rendtorff, *The Old Testament: An Introduction*, trans. John Bowden (Philadelphia: Fortress, 1991), 290; Emerson, *Christ and the New Creation*, 21.

29. Douglas Stuart, *Hosea–Jonah*, WBC 31 (Dallas: Word, 1987), xliii; cf. Greg Goswell, "The Order of the Books in the Hebrew Bible," *JETS* 51 (2008): 677, 688; Emerson, *Christ and the New Creation*, 21, 29.

OT is read. Fourth, we must recognize that the location of a given book in any canonical structure informs our biblical theological interpretation.

REFLECTION QUESTIONS

1. What is the definition of "canon," and how does the concept of canon correlate with the concept of covenant?

2. What is some evidence for early canon-consciousness that included arrangement?

3. How does knowing that Jesus's Bible was arranged differently than our modern English Bible impact the way you think about your OT?

4. What are four reasons why canonical arrangement matters when doing biblical theology?

5. Jewish tradition witnesses a variety of placements for the book of Ruth—for example, directly following Judges and before Samuel (Josephus, English Bibles), as a preface to Psalms at the head of the Writings (*Baba Bathra* 14b), and directly following Proverbs as the first of the "five scrolls" (Ruth, Song of Songs, Ecclesiastes, Lamentations, Esther) (as in the Leningrad Codex and *Biblia Hebraica Stuttgartensia*). In what ways does placement influence the message and function of the book?

How Does Dispensational Theology Understand Biblical Theology?

Oren R. Martin

Since the mid-nineteenth century, a system for interpreting the Bible known as dispensationalism has influenced how Christians view the doctrines of the church (ecclesiology) and last things (eschatology).[1] Dispensationalism sees the progress of God's plan based upon how the NT uses the term *oikonomia* (see, for example, Gal. 3–4 and Eph. 3), which Charles Ryrie defines as a "distinguishable economy in the outworking of God's purpose."[2] In other words, the various covenants throughout Scripture do not provide the basic framework for its storyline, no matter how important they might be for how God relates to humankind.[3] Rather, the various dispensations reveal the changes in the way God administers his sovereignty over creation through history. Though dispensationalists differ on the ordering of history, it can be summarized in three stages: past (Israel before Pentecost), present (church age), and future (millennium). Kreider writes:

> Dispensationalism views the world as a household run by God. In this household world God is dispensing or administering its affairs

---

1. Svigel presents a helpful, concise, and clear history of dispensationalism and correctly asserts, "Though we can speak in terms of *dispensationalism* as a definable and distinguishable theological movement, we must in some ways also speak of *dispensationalisms* as distinct varieties within a larger species. It is a movement that continues to grow, reproduce, and develop to this day." Michael J. Svigel, "The History of Dispensationalism in Seven Eras," in *Dispensationalism and the History of Redemption: A Developing and Diverse Tradition*, eds. D. Jeffrey Bingham and Glenn R. Kreider (Chicago: Moody, 2014), 93.
2. Charles C. Ryrie, *Dispensationalism*, 2nd ed. (Chicago: Moody, 2007), 33.
3. Glenn R. Kreider, "What Is Dispensationalism? A Proposal," in Bingham and Kreider, *Dispensationalism and the History of Redemption*, 20.

according to His own will and in various stages of revelation in the process of time. These various stages mark off the distinguishably different economies in the outworking of His total purpose, and these economies are the dispensations. The understanding of God's differing economies is essential to a proper interpretation of His revelation within those various economies.[4]

Though there is some level of continuity in God's plan of redemption, *the way* God relates to (his) people differs from one era to the next. The elements of discontinuity do not indicate different ways of salvation, for dispensationalists hold that God always saves by grace through faith in the (promised) Messiah, the Lord Jesus Christ.[5] Furthermore, what is important for dispensationalists is not the number or names of the various dispensations, for there are differences even among them; rather, the importance centers on what the era prior to Christ revealed about God's overarching purposes, specifically God's intention(s) for the nation of Israel. Craig Blaising writes, "Dispensationalists [do] not believe that the dispensation with Israel was simply a 'shadow' of reality revealed in the church; rather, Israel and the church revealed distinct purposes in God's plan."[6] This distinction gets to the heart of dispensationalism.

Varieties of Dispensationalism

Dispensationalism is not monolithic. It has gone through three significant changes in its relatively brief history.[7]

1. *Classical dispensationalism.* Initially, classical dispensationalism (e.g., John Nelson Darby, Lewis Sperry Chafer) emphasized a radical dualism between Israel (God's earthly people) and the church (God's spiritual people). This distinction consisted of two separate redemptive programs, one related to earth (Jews) and the other to heaven (the church). They claimed this dualism is seen in the way the NT distinguishes the kingdom of God and kingdom of heaven, and they also maintained the new covenant in Jeremiah 31 applies

---

4. Kreider, "What Is Dispensationalism?," 34–35.
5. Kreider, "What Is Dispensationalism?," 17, 26. In reply to the charge that dispensationalists hold to different ways of salvation, John Feinberg argues that there is continuity in the basis (work of Christ), requirement (faith), and object (God) of salvation, but discontinuity or changes in the revealed content of salvation. John S. Feinberg, "Salvation in the Old Testament," in *Tradition and Testament: Essays in Honor of Charles Lee Feinberg*, eds. John S. Feinberg and Paul D. Feinberg (Chicago: Moody, 1981), 39–77.
6. Craig A. Blaising, "Dispensation, Dispensationalism," in *Evangelical Dictionary of Theology*, 3rd ed., ed. Daniel J. Treier and Walter A. Elwell (Grand Rapids: Baker Academic, 2017), 248.
7. For a more detailed treatment, see Craig A. Blaising and Darrell L. Bock, *Progressive Dispensationalism* (Grand Rapids: Baker, 1993), 9–56.

only to Israel, not the church. Furthermore, in the future when, God consummates his redemptive plan, the two peoples will remain separate.[8]

2. *Revised or traditional dispensationalism.* Revised dispensationalists (e.g., Charles Ryrie, John Walvoord, New Scofield Reference Bible) modified classical dispensationalism by dropping the cosmological heavenly/earthly language, yet still maintained two distinct anthropological entities—Israel and the church. For example, though the church now partially participates in the new covenant, Israel will experience the full fulfillment of the new covenant in a future earthly millennium, even continuing into the eternal state, when Jesus will sit on and rule from the throne of David.[9] As distinct groups, then, this separation between Israel and the church will continue throughout eternity, even though both parties experience blessings in the new covenant.

3. *Progressive dispensationalism.* Progressive dispensationalists (e.g., Craig Blaising, Darrell Bock, Robert Saucy) see more continuity between Israel and the church when it comes to the various dispensations. They view the various dispensations as ascending stair steps rather than distinct, unrelated eras in which God deals with distinct anthropological groups.[10] That is, they underscore God's one plan of salvation in Christ for Jews and Gentiles and emphasize full spiritual blessings for both groups in the new covenant, which is a step forward in the progressive nature of redemption. Also, they maintain that God has inaugurated his kingdom in the present through the life, death, resurrection, ascension, and session of Christ. God's kingdom, therefore, has *already* broken into history through King Jesus, but it is *not yet* present in its fullness. When Christ comes again, he will finally usher in his saving rule.[11] According to Blaising and Bock,

> Progressives do not view the church as an anthropological category in the same class as terms like Israel, Gentile Nations, Jews, and Gentile people. The church is neither a separate race of humanity (in contrast to Jew and Gentiles) nor a competing nation alongside Israel

---

8. Blaising, "Dispensation, Dispensationalism," 248.
9. Cf. R. Bruce Compton, "Dispensationalism, the Church, and the New Covenant," *Detroit Baptist Seminary Journal* 8 (2003): 3–48.
10. Svigel, "History of Dispensationalism in Seven Eras," 87.
11. Because of the distinction between Israel and the church, dispensationalism typically holds to pretribulational premillennialism, which teaches that Christ's second coming consists of two stages. The first stage is a secret "rapture" (1 Thess. 4:17) when Christ comes *for his saints* to remove the (predominantly Gentile) church before a seven-year period of tribulation. The second stage is when Christ appears and visibly comes *with his saints* after the tribulation to rule the earth as the Davidic King for a thousand years, during which time he fulfills his OT promises to the nation of Israel (e.g., some would argue for rebuilding the temple and reinstituting the sacrificial system for memorial purposes). After the thousand years, final judgment and the new heaven and new earth will come. For more on the different views of last things, see Eckhard Schnabel, *40 Questions About the End Times* (Grand Rapids: Kregel, 2011).

and Gentile nations. . . . The church is precisely redeemed humanity itself (both Jews and Gentiles) as it exists in this dispensation prior to the coming of Christ.[12]

In other words, both Israel and the church are the people of God *in Christ*.

However, though both Jews and Gentiles in Christ presently enjoy these spiritual blessings, there are still "functional distinctions" for national Israel in the millennium, such as the promised land, when Jesus's Davidic reign will be finally consummated.[13] When it comes to God's promises, then, progressive dispensationalists argue four key points:

1. God initially fulfills his OT promises in the ultimate seed, Jesus Christ, the Abrahamic and Davidic promised ruler who fulfills God's saving promises to both Jews and Gentiles.

2. God's inclusion of the Gentiles in the one people of God does not cancel his promises to the nation of Israel.

3. The people of God, both Jew and Gentile, are one in Christ.

4. God will restore the nation of Israel in the future.

Distinctives of Dispensationalism

Despites these differences within dispensationalism, it is possible to distill the pillars of dispensational theology into an essential core.[14] That is, all forms of dispensational theology derive a biblical theology from an interconnected set of convictions.[15] First, the *sine qua non* of dispensationalism is the way it distinguishes between the nation of Israel and the church.[16]

---

12. Blaising and Bock, *Progressive Dispensationalism*, 49.
13. Michael J. Vlach, *Dispensationalism: Essential Beliefs and Common Myths* (Los Angeles: Theological Studies Press, 2008), 12.
14. Blaising and Bock list eight "common features" of dispensationalism, though not all are exclusively unique to it: (1) the authority of Scripture, (2) dispensations, (3) uniqueness of the church, (4) practical significance of universal church, (5) significance of biblical prophecy, (6) futurist premillennialism, (7) imminent return of Christ, and (8) a national future for Israel. Blaising and Bock, *Progressive Dispensationalism*, 13–21.
15. These points have been adapted from John S. Feinberg, "Systems of Discontinuity," in *Continuity and Discontinuity: Perspectives on the Relationship between the Old and New Testaments*, ed. John S. Feinberg (Wheaton: Crossway, 1988), 63–86; and Michael Vlach, "What Is Dispensationalism?" in *Christ's Prophetic Plans: A Futuristic Premillennial Primer*, eds. John MacArthur and Richard Mayhue (Chicago: Moody, 2012), 24–35.
16. Ryrie, *Dispensationalism*, 46; Craig A. Blaising, "Dispensationalism: The Search for Definition," in *Dispensationalism, Israel and the Church*, eds. Craig A. Blaising and Darrell L. Bock (Grand Rapids: Zondervan, 1992), 23. Feinberg notes that while many theological

Second, dispensationalists believe that God must fulfill his unconditional promises in the Abrahamic covenant to the nation of Israel in the future. For example, the promise of land "includes at least the millennial reign of Christ and for some dispensationalists, extends into the eternal state as well."[17] Underlying this belief is the conviction that if "an OT prophecy or promise is made unconditionally to a given people and is still unfulfilled to them even in the NT era, then the prophecy must still be fulfilled to them."[18] Third, dispensationalism believes that proper hermeneutics requires that we interpret Scripture "literally" by employing a limited grammatical-historical approach that focuses on what the human author intended. That is, the NT does not reinterpret or spiritualize the promises to Israel such that they apply to the church.[19] Again, Feinberg writes, "Lack of repetition in the NT does not render an OT teaching inoperative during the NT era so long as nothing explicitly or implicitly cancels it."[20] Feinberg's contention applies to typology as well. In other words, both type and antitype must have their own meaning even if they have a typological relation to the other. As a result, the NT antitype, or fulfillment, does not cancel the meaning of the OT type.[21] Thus, dispensationalists prioritize the Old Testament above the New.[22] On this point Vlach writes,

> An interpreter's testament priority assumptions are especially significant when interpreting how the New Testament authors use the Old

---

systems distinguish Israel from the church in some way, it is the kind of distinction that distinguishes dispensationalism. For Feinberg, what is unique about dispensational thinking is the recognition of four distinct senses of the Abrahamic seed/offspring: (1) biological, ethnic, national; (2) political; (3) spiritual; (4) and typological. This distinction is operative in both Testaments, "coupled with a demand that no sense (spiritually especially) is more important than any other, and that no sense cancels out the meaning and implications of the other senses. The more one emphasizes the distinctness and importance of the various senses, the more dispensational and discontinuity-oriented his system becomes, for the distinct senses necessitate speaking of Israel ethnically, politically, and spiritually, as well as speaking of the church." Feinberg, "Systems of Discontinuity," 72–73. Bruce Ware defines this distinction when he writes, "Israel and the church share theologically rich and important elements of commonality while at the same time maintaining distinct identities." Bruce A. Ware, "The New Covenant and the People(s) of God," in Blaising and Bock, *Dispensationalism, Israel, and the Church*, 92.

17. Blaising, "The Extent and Varieties of Dispensationalism," in Blaising and Bock, *Progressive Dispensationalism*, 21.
18. Feinberg, "Systems of Discontinuity," 76. See also Craig A. Blaising, "The Structure of the Biblical Covenants," in Craig A. Blaising and Darrell L. Bock, *Progressive Dispensationalism* (Grand Rapids: Baker, 1993), 132–34.
19. Robert L. Saucy, *The Case for Progressive Dispensationalism: The Interface between Dispensational and Non-Dispensational Theology* (Grand Rapids: Zondervan, 1993), 30–31.
20. Feinberg, "Systems of Discontinuity," 76.
21. Feinberg, "Systems of Discontinuity," 79.
22. Feinberg, "Systems of Discontinuity," 79.

Testament. Dispensationalists want to maintain a reference point in the Old Testament. They desire to give justice to the original authorial intent of the Old Testament writers in accord with historical-grammatical hermeneutics. Nondispensationalists, on the other hand, emphasize the New Testament as their reference point for understanding the Old Testament.[23]

Thus, dispensationalists distinguish themselves from nondispensationalists by asserting that "the OT be taken on its own terms rather than reinterpreted in the light of the NT."[24] So, for example, if God promised Israel in Ezekiel 40–48 a rebuilding of the temple with the reinstitution of sacrifices, and it is still unfulfilled to them in the NT, then God *must* fulfill that promise to them in the future.[25] For dispensationalists, then, God demonstrates his faithfulness by keeping his promises to the nation of Israel.

Summary
Dispensationalism has significantly changed and progressed since its inception on issues such as biblical interpretation, the relation between the Testaments, the NT use of the OT, the nature of the kingdom, and the relationship between Israel and the church. What remains to be seen, however, is whether or not the NT fulfills the OT in ways that do not reinterpret, spiritualize, or contravene it.[26]

REFLECTION QUESTIONS

1. How would you define dispensationalism?

2. How has dispensationalism developed over time?

3. What are strengths of dispensationalism? What are weaknesses?

4. How does the NT describe the church in relation to Israel (e.g., elect, temple, assembly)?

5. Should Christian interpreters of Scripture prioritize the one Testament over the other—for example, the OT over the NT? Why or why not?

---

23. Vlach, *Dispensationalism*, 17.
24. Feinberg, "Systems of Discontinuity," 75.
25. For a brief response to this argument, see Question 29. For a more comprehensive response, see Oren R. Martin, *Bound for the Promised Land: The Land Promise in God's Redemptive Plan*, NSBT 34 (Downers Grove, IL: InterVarsity, 2015).
26. See Question 19.

How Does Covenant Theology Understand Biblical Theology?

Oren R. Martin

A vital way in which God relates to his creatures is through the biblical covenants.[1] In addition to recognizing the various covenants throughout Scripture, covenant theology develops the concept of covenant into an architectural framework.[2] The Westminster Confession of Faith summarizes this organizational scheme:

> The distance between God and the creature is so great, that although reasonable creatures do owe obedience unto him as their Creator, yet they could never have any fruition of him as their blessedness and reward, but by some voluntary condescension on God's part, which he hath been pleased to express by way of covenant. The first covenant made with man was a covenant of works, wherein life was promised to Adam, and in him to his posterity, upon condition of perfect and personal obedience. Man by his fall having made himself incapable of life by that covenant, the Lord was pleased to make a second, commonly called the covenant of grace: whereby he freely offereth unto sinners life and salvation by Jesus Christ, requiring of them faith in him, that they may be saved; and promising to give unto all those that are ordained unto life his Holy Spirit, to make them willing and able to believe. This covenant of grace is frequently set forth in the Scripture by the name of a Testament, in reference to the death of Jesus Christ the Testator, and to the everlasting inheritance, with all

---

1. See Questions 5 and 22.
2. Like dispensationalism, it is better to speak of covenant *theologies* rather than covenant *theology* since there are variations, some of which will be shown below.

things belonging to it, therein bequeathed. This covenant was differently administered in the time of the law, and in the time of the gospel; under the law it was administered by promises, prophecies, sacrifices, circumcision, the paschal lamb, and other types and ordinances delivered to the people of the Jews, all foresignifying Christ to come, which were for that time sufficient and efficacious, through the operation of the Spirit, to instruct and build up the elect in faith in the promised Messiah, by whom they had full remission of sins, and eternal salvation; and is called, the Old Testament. Under the gospel, when Christ, the substance, was exhibited, the ordinances in which this covenant is dispensed are the preaching of the Word, and the administration of the sacraments of baptism and the Lord's Supper which, though fewer in number, and administered with more simplicity, and less outward glory, yet, in them, it is held forth in more fullness, evidence, and spiritual efficacy, to all nations, both Jews and Gentiles and is called the New Testament. There are not therefore two covenants of grace, differing in substance, but one and the same, under various dispensations. (WCF 7.1–6)

Like dispensationalism, covenant theology is a way of reading the individual parts of Scripture in light of the whole. Its architectural structure highlights the continuity of the covenant of grace, which stretches from Genesis 3:15 to Revelation 22, and under which the other biblical covenants are subsumed. This chapter addresses how covenant theology understands biblical theology through its lenses of three covenants: the covenants of redemption, works, and grace.

The Covenant of Redemption
The covenant of redemption refers to the Triune God's sovereign decree and plan from eternity past that he is accomplishing in history by establishing covenants for his glory. The revelation of God's eternal plan is rooted in biblical texts such as Ephesians 1:3–6:

Blessed be the God and Father of our Lord Jesus Christ, who has blessed us in Christ with every spiritual blessing in the heavenly places, even as he chose us in him before the foundation of the world, that we should be holy and blameless before him. In love he predestined us for adoption to himself as sons through Jesus Christ, according to the purpose of his will, to the praise of his glorious grace, with which he has blessed us in the Beloved.

Thus, as Scott Swain says, the covenant of redemption "concerns the divinely ordained, messianic means whereby the Father, 'for whom and by whom all things exist,' seeks to manifest his glory 'by bringing many sons to glory' (Heb. 2:10)."[3] Herman Bavinck helpfully summarizes the covenant of redemption that is worked out in history in both the covenant of works and the covenant of grace:

> The covenant of grace revealed in time does not hang in the air but rests on an eternal, unchanging foundation. It is firmly grounded in the counsel and covenant of the triune God and is the application and execution of it that infallibly follows. Indeed, in the covenant of grace established by God with humanity in time, human beings are not the active and acting initiators, but it is again the triune God who, having designed the work of re-creation, now brings it about. It is a false perception that God first made his covenant with Adam and Noah, with Abraham and Israel, and only finally with Christ; the covenant of grace was ready-made from all eternity in the pact of salvation of the three persons and was realized by Christ from the moment the fall occurred. Christ does not begin to work only with and after his incarnation, and the Holy Spirit does not first begin his work with the outpouring on the day of Pentecost. But just as the creation is a trinitarian work, so also the re-creation was from the start a project of the three persons. All the grace that is extended to the creation after the fall comes to it from the Father, through the Son, in the Holy Spirit. The Son appeared immediately after the fall, as Mediator, as the second and final Adam who occupies the place of the first, restores what the latter corrupted, and accomplishes what he failed to do. And the Holy Spirit immediately acted as the Paraclete, the one applying the salvation acquired by Christ. All the change that occurs, all the development and progress in insight and knowledge, accordingly, occurs on the side of the creature. In God there is no variation or shadow due to change (James 1:17). The Father is the eternal Father, the Son the eternal Mediator, the Holy Spirit the eternal Paraclete.[4]

Since the Triune God ordains, plans, promises, and executes his redemptive purposes, covenant theology has spoken of an inter-Trinitarian covenant of redemption. Accordingly, Swain characterizes the covenant of redemption by four main features:

---

3. Scott R. Swain, "The Covenant of Redemption," in *Christian Dogmatics: Reformed Theology for the Church Catholic*, eds. Michael Allen and Scott R. Swain (Grand Rapids: Baker, 2016), 16–17.
4. Herman Bavinck, *Reformed Dogmatics*, vol. 3: *Sin and Salvation in Christ*, eds. John Bolt, trans. John Vriend (Grand Rapids: Baker Academic, 2006), 215–16.

1. the will of the Father and of the Son, expressed by way of covenant, regarding

2. the incarnate Son's obedience unto death

3. on behalf of his elect siblings, for whom he serves as redeemer and head, and

4. the eternal glory promised by the Father to the Son as a reward for his incarnate obedience.[5]

For covenant theology, the covenant of redemption "is one of the most profound and assuring expressions of the mutual love and commitment of the Father to the Son in the Spirit in planning and executing God's redemptive degree."[6] Furthermore, it grounds both the covenant of works and covenant of grace in covenant theology.

The Covenant of Works

God initiated the covenant of works at creation with Adam and Eve, who lived in fellowship with God under his rule.[7] God promised righteousness and life if they obeyed and threatened judgment and death if they disobeyed. But Adam rebelled (Gen. 3), and as a result his sin brought judgment and death not only on him but also on his posterity because he was acting as their representative (Rom. 5:12–21). As a result, the Lord exiled Adam and Eve from Eden and the tree of life.

However, the tragic events of the fall were not the end of the story. The good news looked backward, upward, and forward. On the one hand, it looked backward and upward to the Triune God in the covenant of redemption. But on the other hand, it looked forward to the covenant of grace. That is, instead

---

5. Swain, "Covenant of Redemption," 117–18. For more biblical and Trinitarian reasoning to support the covenant of redemption, which includes answers to the charge of tritheism, see Swain, "Covenant of Redemption," 118–22.

6. Swain, "Covenant of Redemption," 123.

7. Though some would argue that we should not employ the term "covenant," it is not improper to see the relationship God initiated in the garden within a covenantal context. When looking at concepts and not strictly words, there is sufficient warrant for calling this relationship a covenant. First, the creation account is framed within a covenantal pattern or framework. That is, there is a title/preamble (Gen. 1:1), historical prologue (1:2–29), stipulations (1:28; 2:16–17), witnesses (1:31; 2:1), and blessings/curses (1:28; 2:3, 17). Second, although the term for "covenant" is not present, the essential relational elements of a covenant are there. God is clearly committed to his image-bearers, even after they disobey him. Third, the Noahic covenant in Genesis 6–9 appears to not be initiating something new but to be confirming for Noah and his descendants God's prior commitment to humanity previously initiated at creation (see also Isa. 24:4–6; Hos. 6:7).

of the covenant of works that says, "Do this and live" (Lev. 18:5; cf. Rom. 10:5), God initiated a gracious covenant that would progress in and through history and culminate in the coming of Christ.[8]

The Covenant of Grace

The eternal purpose of the Triune God is realized in history through the covenant of grace. That is, immediately after the fall, God promised to pour forth his saving grace (Gen. 3:15), which then subsequently unfolded through history. Though there are differences between the covenants with Abraham, Moses, David, and Christ, there is, in substance, one overarching covenant of grace that is ultimately fulfilled in the new covenant in Christ.[9] And while there is continuity in the covenant of grace throughout history, the sending of Christ in his mission and gift of the Holy Spirit at Pentecost have brought a richness of gifts not known and experienced in prior generations.[10]

As a result of the continuity of the covenant of grace, covenant theology views the nature of the church as similar to that of Israel—composed of both believers and unbelievers. Though the church enjoys knowing the Lord in deeper ways through the new covenant in Christ and is by design an international entity, it nevertheless remains a spiritually mixed community. Just as all (male) Israel received the covenant sign (circumcision) but was made up of both believers and unbelievers, so also the church receives the covenant sign (baptism) but is still composed of believers and unbelievers.

One can see, then, a crucial question in the debate over the makeup of the church: What is new in the *new* covenant in Christ? Jeremiah 31:31–34 says,

---

8. For some within covenant theology, the contrast between works and grace definitively distinguishes law and gospel. "Law" refers to the covenant of works (associated with Adam and Sinai), and "gospel" refers to the covenant of grace (associated with Abraham, David, and the new covenant in Christ). For many in covenant theology, this distinction runs like a thread through Scripture and serves as the means through which God will fulfill his saving purposes in Christ. That is, the gracious giving of the law exposes sin and reveals the need for a Savior, who ultimately is Jesus Christ, who kept the law in our place so that God could carry out the covenant of grace. For more on the law-gospel distinction, see Michael S. Horton, *God of Promise: Introducing Covenant Theology* (Grand Rapids: Baker, 2006), 77–110.

9. Some covenant theologians argue that the new covenant is not entirely new, but rather a renewal of the previous covenants. Peter Leithart writes, "The new Davidic dynasty is not a replacement of the old, but a transformation of it. The same is true of the new covenant in relation to the old. It is not as if God changed his mind about how He would structure His relations with His people. God still makes promises, requires obedience, and threatens sanctions against the disobedient. The new covenant is simply the old covenant transformed by the death and resurrection of the covenant Head, Jesus Christ." Peter J. Leithart, *The Kingdom and the Power: Rediscovering the Centrality of the Church* (Phillipsburg, NJ: P&R, 1993), 160–61; see also Meredith G. Kline, *By Oath Consigned: A Reinterpretation of the Covenant Signs of Circumcision and Baptism* (Grand Rapids: Eerdmans, 1975), 75.

10. M. E. Osterhaven, "Covenant Theology," in *Evangelical Dictionary of Theology*, 3rd ed., eds. Daniel J. Treier and Walter A. Elwell (Grand Rapids: Baker, 2017), 216.

Behold, the days are coming, declares the LORD, when I will make a new covenant with the house of Israel and the house of Judah, not like the covenant that I made with their fathers on the day when I took them by the hand to bring them out of the land of Egypt, my covenant that they broke, though I was their husband, declares the LORD. For this is the covenant that I will make with the house of Israel after those days, declares the LORD: I will put my law within them, and I will write it on their hearts. And I will be their God, and they shall be my people. And no longer shall each one teach his neighbor and each his brother, saying, 'Know the LORD,' for they shall all know me, from the least of them to the greatest, declares the LORD. For I will forgive their iniquity, and I will remember their sin no more.

Some covenant theologians assert that Jeremiah was envisioning realities that are still *not yet* for the people of God so that the new covenant community today can still be made up of believers and unbelievers alike.[11] If, however, as Baptists hold, *all* in the new covenant *already* have the law written on their hearts (Jer. 31:33), know the Lord (31:34), and experience the full forgiveness of sin (31:34) through trusting in Christ and receiving the Holy Spirit in regeneration, then there are significant implications for how one views the nature of the church. We know that *all* God's promises find their yes in Christ, who has already decisively fulfilled all OT hopes (2 Cor. 1:20). We also know that the new covenant in Christ "*is enacted* on better promises" than the old (Heb. 8:6) and that Christ "*has perfected* for all time those who are being sanctified" (10:15–18). How one perceives the nature and structure of the new covenant has direct consequences for church membership and the Christian life.[12]

---

11. E.g., Richard L. Pratt Jr., "Jeremiah 31: Infant Baptism in the New Covenant," *Biblical Perspectives* 4, no. 1 (2002), http://thirdmill.org/newfiles/ric_pratt/TH.Pratt.New. Covenant.Baptism.pdf; Richard L. Pratt, "Infant Baptism in the New Covenant," in *The Case for Covenantal Infant Baptism*, ed. Gregg Strawbridge (Phillipsburg, NJ: P&R, 2003), 156–74; Michael Horton, "*Kingdom through Covenant*: A Review," *The Gospel Coalition*, Sept. 13, 2012, https://www.thegospelcoalition.org/reviews/kingdom-covenant-michael-horton.

12. For a critique of the nature of the church in covenant theology, see Peter J. Gentry and Stephen J. Wellum, *Kingdom through Covenant: A Biblical-Theological Understanding of the Covenants*, 2nd ed. (Wheaton, IL: Crossway, 2018). See also Question 24, as well as Samuel E. Waldron, "A Brief Response to Richard L. Pratt's 'Infant Baptism in the New Covenant,'" *Reformed Baptist Theological Review* 2, no. 1 (2005): 105–10; Jason S. DeRouchie, "Counting Stars with Abraham and the Prophets: New Covenant Ecclesiology in OT Perspective," *JETS* 58, no. 3 (2015): esp. 481–85; Jason S. DeRouchie, "Father of a Multitude of Nations: New Covenant Ecclesiology in Old Testament Perspective," in *Progressive Covenantalism: Charting a Course between Dispensational and Covenant Theologies*, eds. Stephen J. Wellum and Brent E. Parker (Nashville: B&H, 2016), esp. 34–38.

Summary

Covenant theology argues that all of God's saving purposes in history serve the eternal covenant of redemption in Christ. In the covenant of works, God established a relationship with humanity in Adam that was typological of the last Adam, who did what Adam and his descendants failed to do. Through Christ's holy, incarnate life, death, burial, resurrection, ascension, and session, he leads his people—both Jew and Gentile—to eternal life. As a result, all in the church are in the new covenant and are baptized; "not only those that do actually profess faith in and obedience unto Christ, but also the infants of one, or both, believing parents, are to be baptized."[13] The overarching covenant of grace, then, explains why there is continuity across redemptive history, a continuity that establishes the nature of the church and its ordinances.

REFLECTION QUESTIONS

1. What is the covenant of redemption?

2. What is the covenant of works?

3. What is the covenant of grace?

4. In covenant theology, what is new about the new covenant?

5. Does OT circumcision correspond to NT baptism? What are other views?

---

13. WCF, 28.4.

How Does Progressive Covenantalism Understand Biblical Theology?

Oren R. Martin

As we have seen in the previous two chapters, various theological systems are rooted in the progression, continuity, and discontinuity between the covenants. On the one hand, dispensational theology emphasizes discontinuity to the extent that Israel and the church are and will remain distinct in certain ways. So, for example, at minimum Israel will retain her distinct national identity in the land in the millennium, and for some, even into eternity. On the other hand, covenant theology emphasizes continuity to the extent that Israel and the church are similar, if not the same with subtle nuances. So, for example, under the old and new covenants the people therein are composed of both elect and non-elect who all receive the covenant sign of circumcision and baptism, respectively.

Recently, however, a new theological system has emerged that aims to be a *via media* between the two: progressive covenantalism.[1] Progressive covenantalism emphasizes both continuity (e.g., one redemptive plan of God, one people of God in Christ who share in the same blessings, both now and forever) and discontinuity (e.g., the newness of the new covenant, the regenerate nature of the church, the fulfillment of circumcision in regeneration, not baptism). This chapter will explore how progressive covenantalism does biblical theology.

---

1. See, e.g., Peter J. Gentry and Stephen J. Wellum, *Kingdom through Covenant: A Biblical-Theological Understanding of the Covenants*, 2nd ed. (Wheaton, IL: Crossway, 2018); Stephen J. Wellum and Brent E. Parker, *Progressive Covenantalism: Charting a Course between Dispensational and Covenant Theologies* (Nashville: B&H Academic, 2016).

Situating Covenant in Scripture's Storyline

Scripture presents numerous covenants at crucial times throughout salvation history, which serve to (re)establish God's fellowship with humanity, reverse the curses of Eden, and progressively establish and expand God's kingdom on earth. The Lord orchestrates each covenant to his ordained end—a consummated kingdom.

God's divinely initiated covenants get to the heart of his gracious plan to make a people for himself. This plan begins with Adam and ends with the people of the last Adam from every tribe and language and people and nation (Rev. 5:9). Perhaps a good way to begin, then, is to place the covenants within the overarching storyline of Scripture.

Scripture begins with an original creation and ends with the description of a more glorious new creation.[2] Between these two accounts lies the history of redemption. God's plan for his people begins with Adam and Eve (Gen. 1–2). The creation account reveals the pattern of the kingdom: God's people in God's place under God's rule.[3] For Adam and Eve to enjoy God and his blessings, they must take God at his word (1:28–30; 2:16–17). However, they despised God's word and instead believed the serpent's, which led to their expulsion from God's blessed presence (ch. 3). As a result, sin and death entered creation and separated humans from God. But his plan did not end, for God made a promise that would, in time, undo the effects of sin by the serpent-crushing offspring of the woman (3:15). The rest of the story, then, focuses on how God will progressively reestablish his kingdom.

Crucial to understanding why Scripture ends with an Eden-like picture is that Eden is depicted as the prototypical place on earth where God dwells with his people. The Lord's original creation reaches its fulfillment in the new heaven and new earth. The beginning inaugurates the consummated vision at the end, and God's new creation at the end brings to fulfillment his design from the beginning. But crucial to observing the (dis)continuity between the historical bookends is the historical line that connects them.

Perhaps one of the most prominent features of the beginning and end of the story is the concept of God's kingdom. Jesus's declaration that "the kingdom of God is at hand" (Mark 1:15) reveals the Lord fulfilling what he promised back in Eden to undo—namely, the effects of sin—by triumphing over the serpent (Gen. 3:15).[4] Furthermore, the importance of the kingdom in Jesus's teaching is apparent by the prominence and place of what he says about the kingdom. When he begins his ministry, Jesus proclaims the arrival of the kingdom, which serves to highlight the fact that it is central to the

---

2. See Question 35.
3. See Graeme Goldsworthy, *According to Plan: The Unfolding Revelation of God in the Bible* (Downers Grove, IL: InterVarsity, 2002).
4. See Question 23.

biblical storyline. Jesus saw his ministry fulfilling OT promises, which he demonstrates by announcing, "The time is fulfilled, and the kingdom of God is at hand; repent and believe in the gospel" (Mark 1:14–15). Jesus did not present a comprehensive biblical theology of the kingdom set within salvation history. Nevertheless, the Gospels reveal that Jesus saw himself acting within and bringing to fulfillment the whole process of God's redemptive purposes. That is, from his humiliation to his glorification, Jesus Christ's life and ministry were fulfilling God's saving promises. Thus, the pattern of God's kingdom provides a framework within which history moves from beginning to end.

One of the most important ways Yahweh reestablishes his reign on earth is through the biblical covenants, for they form the backbone of Scripture and are crucial for understanding its overarching story, from creation to new creation.[5] That is, the biblical covenants chart a course and serve as a unifying theme for the unfolding kingdom drama. Scripture presents numerous covenants at crucial times in salvation history, all of which progressively serve to reverse the curses of Eden and to reestablish with escalation God's visible, universal reign. For this reason, every covenant to some extent involves and advances the promise of Yahweh's rule, people, and place.

Developing Covenant in Scripture's Storyline

A crucial means the Lord uses to accomplish his redemptive ends is the biblical covenants, in which there is both continuity and discontinuity. A cursory overview will establish this point, but this book will provide more detail later.[6] Judgment and death reign after humanity's fall into sin, and the initial sign of Yahweh's reversing of the curse is his covenant with Noah (Gen. 6:18; 9:9–17), which reaffirms what he started with Adam. Noah is God's representative commissioned to rule the earth, be fruitful and multiply, and bring the Lord's blessing to the world (9:1–17). In other words, Noah is an Adam-like figure. But just as Adam failed, so also does Noah (9:18–29). So sin and death continue to reign, and, as a result, Yahweh judges the nations at the Tower of Babel (11:1–9). Yet, God keeps his promise by calling out another—Abram—to fulfill his purposes.

Yahweh's covenant with Abraham provides *the way* in which God will fulfill his creation promises and bless the world. Through Abraham and his offspring Israel, God will bring about universal and international blessing. But how, ultimately, will this blessing come? The answer is through a promised offspring (15:4–5; 22:17–18; cf. Gal. 3). And as Genesis 15 makes clear, God will make good on his promise. By passing between the pieces, Yahweh graciously pledges that he will fulfill his covenant commitment to Abraham

---

5. Gentry and Wellum, *Kingdom through Covenant*, 34. See Question 22.
6. See Question 22.

(Gen. 15:17; cf. Jer. 34:18). The patriarch received God's promise by faith, and the Lord counted his believing as righteousness (Gen. 15:6), which is foundational for the NT authors'—and the Protestant church's—doctrine of justification (Rom. 4; Gal. 3; James 2). And as glorious and gracious as the blessing of justification is (cf. Ps. 32:1–2), this blessing was not the end but only the beginning of the story. With Abraham God sets out in programmatic form his plan to make a people for himself (Gen. 17:8; cf. Rev. 21:3).

However, one problem still remained that Yahweh needed to overcome. As time went on, history repeatedly demonstrated that sin plagued God's people and brought his curses because they disobeyed the (old) Mosaic covenant. Though they were physically circumcised as a sign of belonging to God, what they fundamentally needed was for their hearts to be circumcised (Deut. 30:6). Whether it was Abraham, Isaac, Jacob, Moses, Israel, David, or Solomon, one thing was for sure: the Lord needed to deal with their sin once and for all, for the blood of bulls and goats could not permanently bring the forgiveness of sin (Heb. 10:4). Furthermore, God's commands under the old covenant only exacerbated the problem, for through the law came the knowledge of sin (Rom. 3:20). But thanks be to God, who used the guardianship of the law until Christ came, so that *all* might be justified by faith—both Jew and Gentile (Gal. 3:23–29)—and so that this multiethnic band might become recipients of God's covenant blessings. It is the *new covenant* (Jer. 31:31–34; cf. Isa. 54; Ezek. 36:22–32) in Christ's blood that brings these blessings (Luke 22:20).

In the new covenant there is both continuity and discontinuity with the old covenant that preceded it. We see continuity in that the new covenant involves God's people (Jer. 31:31), emphasizes obedience to God's law (31:33), focuses on offspring (31:36)—particularly on a royal seed (Isa. 55:3; Jer. 33:15–26; Ezek. 37:24–25)—and, in the end, will fulfill the repeated covenant refrain: "I will be their God, and they shall be my people" (Jer. 31:33).

Despite its continuity, however, it is *not* like the previous (old) Mosaic covenant (31:32). First, the new covenant will not be broken (31:32). Israel's history was one of repeated covenant breaking, but in the new covenant Yahweh ensures this will not happen. In fact, look at Jeremiah's use of first-person pronouns that emphasizes God's effectual work: "*I* will put *my* law within them, and *I* will write it on their hearts" (31:33); "*I* will not turn away from doing good to them. And I will put the fear of me in their hearts, that they may not turn from me" (32:40, emphases added). The new covenant discloses this infrangibility in the way Christ kept the law for those who are united to him by faith, resulting in God's counting Jesus's obedience to us (Rom. 5:18–19; 8:4; 2 Cor. 5:21). Furthermore, God's power is *now* guarding members of the new covenant for their future salvation (1 Peter 1:5).

Second, the new covenant transforms the heart and permanently supplies the indwelling of the Spirit so that obedience will flow from the inside out (Jer. 31:33; Ezek. 36:26–27). Rather than writing the law on stones and scrolls and exhorting the people to internalize it, the Lord now writes his law on his people's hearts.

Third, *every* member of the new covenant is regenerate—for they shall *all* know the Lord (Jer. 31:33–34; cf. Isa. 54:13). Whereas under the previous covenants God urged the various members to know and follow him, most did not. However, the new covenant includes only those whom God teaches in the heart and who know him (John 6:44–45; 1 Thess. 4:9; 1 John 2:20–21, 27). "When Christ had offered for all time a single sacrifice for sins, he sat down at the right hand of God. . . . For by a single offering he has perfected for all time those who are being sanctified" (Heb. 10:12, 14).

Finally, all of these new covenant blessings will come *because* God has provided full and final forgiveness of sin (Jer. 31:34; Ezek. 36:29, 33). Through the inauguration of the new covenant, then, God fulfills his promises and secure his redemptive purposes for his people.

The new covenant makes clear that God always finishes what he starts. In fact, the ultimate fulfillment of the divine promises come through a suffering servant, an "ideal Israel." Isaiah 42:6–7 says that Yahweh will give his servant "as a covenant for the people, a light for the nations, to open the eyes that are blind, to bring out the prisoners from the dungeon, from the prison those who sit in darkness." By being a *covenant* (Isa. 42:6; 49:8; 55:3; 59:21), the servant will supply the means through which people will come into a covenant relationship with the Lord. The new covenant is grounded on better promises than the old because God's obedient Son fulfills it (Heb. 8–10).

Implications for Progressive Covenantalism

So what do we learn from the continuity and discontinuity between the covenants? We learn at least four lessons. First, it confronts us with sin and the necessity of salvation by faith in Christ. If we are to be made right with God, we must rely on God's provision of Christ—and Christ alone—for the forgiveness of our sins. Abraham is the father of all who believe, Jew and Gentile. Paul writes, "Now to the one who works, his wages are not counted as a gift but as his due. And to the one who does not work but believes in him who justifies the ungodly, his faith is counted as righteousness" (Rom. 4:4–5). But how does faith come? Faith comes as a gift of God's grace through the proclamation and reception of the word of Christ (3:24–25; 10:17). May God strengthen us, then, to be faithful in proclaiming this gloriously good news to those who need to hear and be set free by it.

Second, since all new covenant members are regenerate, pastors and churches should diligently (though to be sure, imperfectly) work to ensure their church membership includes only those who give a credible profession of faith. (Yes, we are Baptists, and for good reasons!)

Third, all of God's promises, including what he promised Abraham, find their yes in Christ (2 Cor. 1:20). Christ is the mediator of a new covenant, so that those who are called into fellowship with him may receive the promised eternal inheritance (Heb. 9:15). Indeed, all of God's promises reach their goal when Jesus rises from the dead and by this fulfills God's saving plan, which will end in nothing less than a new creation for all of his redeemed people in Christ from every tribe and language and people and nation (Rev. 5:9). And "he will dwell with them, and they will be his people, and God himself will be with them as their God" (21:3).

Finally, how the NT fulfills OT promises strongly influences the progressive covenantal understanding of typology, which sees Christ as the ultimate antitype of all previous types. This conviction distinguishes progressive covenantalism from dispensational theology with respect to the land promises. It also distinguishes progressive covenantalism from covenant theology with respect to the seed promise. The first issue relates to how progressive covenantalists understand eschatology (what the Bible teaches about the end times), and the second issue relates to how they view ecclesiology (what the Bible teaches about the church).

Dispensational Theology and God's Promise of Land

Dispensationalists contend that if God's promises to Israel are unconditional, then national Israel alone must ultimately fulfill them in the future, regardless of how the NT develops the OT declarations.[7] As a result, some progressive dispensationalists, who agree with revised dispensationalists but go beyond them in their understanding of typology, allow the church to typologically fulfill some of the OT promises for Israel. Nevertheless, they assert that, even though the antitype in a real sense fulfills the type, this fulfillment is only partial. That is, though the church initially fulfills OT promises, it does not annul the original OT meaning for Israel. For the issue of land, the progressive dispensationalist view maintains that, although some spiritual aspects are applied to the church, God will still fulfill the territorial aspects of his promise to national Israel in the future. Therefore, the original promises to the nation of Israel must still be kept, even if they apply in partial ways to the church.[8]

Does this view correctly understand how Christ fulfills the OT promises? Although we should commend progressive dispensationalism for attempting to apply the inaugurated eschatology of the NT, for various reasons this view does not correctly account for the already–not yet character of the kingdom or the nature of typological fulfillment in Scripture. First, the way they apply inaugurated eschatology is not accurate *at this point*. While there is an already–not

---

7. See, e.g., John S. Feinberg, "Systems of Discontinuity," in *Continuity and Discontinuity: Perspectives on the Relationship between the Old and New Testaments*, ed. John S. Feinberg (Wheaton, IL: Crossway, 1988), 77–83.

8. This both-and approach is tied to the inaugurated eschatology embraced by progressive dispensationalists.

yet nature to the kingdom in the NT, this eschatological perspective does not *merely* mean that part of the kingdom is present now with the church and part of it (e.g., the physical land) will be present later for national Israel. Instead, the NT shows that Christ has *already* fulfilled *all* of God's saving promises and that these promises are expanding where Christ is present—in the church now, which is one new "man" composed of both Jews and Gentiles in Christ (Eph. 2:11–22), and finally in the consummated new creation.

Second, the NT presents Christ's person and work as both fulfilling and completing OT types. This point distinguishes progressive covenantalism from so-called replacement theology.[9] It is not that the church simply replaces Israel. Rather, Christ represents and fulfills Israel as the true obedient Son, temple, vine, prophet, priest, and king—and then bestows blessings to his people, believing Jews and Gentiles alike. Hence, all who are included *in Christ* receive every spiritual blessing in Christ as they await their future inheritance, the new creation. In other words, believing Israel does not receive less, but more: the whole earth![10]

This interpretation aligns with the way the Bible consistently treats types as eschatologically escalating or intensifying in the progression from type to antitype and from promise to fulfillment. OT types do not merely correspond analogically to the NT antitype, but they serve as "a shadow of the good things to come" (Heb. 10:1; cf. Col. 2:17).[11] At this point, then, though dispensationalists agree that the promises to Israel are fulfilled in the new heaven and new earth, they still want to maintain that God will fulfill his nationalistic promises to Israel only by supplying a geopolitical state to his redeemed Jewish people separate from Gentile Christians in the millennial age. But this is incorrect for two reasons. First, God fulfills all of his promises in relation to Christ and gives them to believing Jews and Gentiles *equally* as the church (Eph. 2:11–22). Second, other types such as prophets, Levitical priests, Davidic kings, circumcision, temple, and sacrifices are not waiting for God to fulfill them in the consummation but instead are already fulfilled, having reached their terminus and *telos* in Christ. They have already arrived at their divinely appointed end, regardless of the already–not yet aspect of Christ's work. In other words, when Christ comes, *he* as the antitype is the true Son,

---

9. See, for example, Michael J. Vlach, *Has the Church Replaced Israel? A Theological Evaluation* (Nashville: B&H, 2010), 104–7.
10. This point does not eliminate, however, the possibility of a future salvation for ethnic Jews (i.e., Rom. 9–11), which some, though not all, adherents from each theological system have believed. For more on this question, see Jared M. Compton and Andrew David Naselli, eds., *Three Views on Israel and the Church: Perspectives on Romans 9–11*, Viewpoints (Grand Rapids: Kregel, 2018). For more on the Christian's relationship to OT promises, see Question 37.
11. For discussion of typology, see Question 8.

prophet, priest, king, vine, temple, covenant, and sacrifice. And such realities should inform our understanding of the promises of land as well.

Covenant Theology and Ecclesiology

Because of the overarching covenant of grace, covenant theology has viewed the church as an extension of Israel.[12] That is, the new covenant community is substantially the same as previous eras, for all the biblical covenants are various administrations of the one covenant of grace. As a result, children born into homes with a Christian parent are baptized into the new covenant. In this way, the new covenant church, like old covenant Israel, remains a "mixed" community composed of both believers and unbelievers who receive the new covenant sign: baptism. Progressive covenantalism disagrees with this view for various reasons.

First, covenant theology does not adequately account for the *newness* of the new covenant.[13] By substantially equating the Abrahamic covenant with the new covenant, one fails to see two distinct progressive eras in which the Abrahamic covenant is fulfilled—"the first national (Gen. 17:7–8) with a genealogical principle as its guide and circumcision as its sign (17:9–13); and the second international with the patriarch's fatherhood being established by spiritual adoption and no longer bound by biology, ethnicity, or the distinguishing mark of circumcision (17:4–6)."[14] In fact, these eras correspond to God's words to Abram in Genesis 12:1–3, where Abram must "go" to the land to be his holy nation (realized under the Mosaic covenant), and then once there "be a blessing" so that all the families of the earth would be blessed (realized in the new covenant in Christ).[15] As redemptive history unfolds, then, God's purposes are fulfilled in Christ, the true seed of Abraham (Gal. 3:16), the one who defeats death by his own death and triumphs over sin and the serpent by his righteous, resurrected life. As a result, he brings blessings to the nations and commissions his disciples to proclaim the good news of Christ, in whom blessing is found. Hence, the superiority of Christ as the true son, seed, and servant is evident, and his new covenant work inaugurates and ushers in a new age of salvation in which the new covenant

---

12. See, e.g., G. K. Beale, *A New Testament Biblical Theology: The Unfolding of the Old Testament in the New* (Grand Rapids: Baker, 2011), 656; Michael Horton, *Introducing Covenant Theology* (Grand Rapids: Baker, 2006), 130–31.

13. See also Question 22.

14. Jason S. DeRouchie, "Father of a Multitude of Nations: New Covenant Ecclesiology in OT Perspective, in *Progressive Covenantalism: Charting a Course between Dispensational and Covenant Theologies*, eds. Stephen J. Wellum and Brent E. Parker (Nashville: B&H, 2016), 34. For an expansion of this argument, see Jason S. DeRouchie, "Counting Stars with Abraham and the Prophets: New Covenant Ecclesiology in OT Perspective," *JETS* 58, no. 3 (2015): 445–85.

15. DeRouchie, "Counting Stars with Abraham," 460.

community, called the church, is no longer the same as the old covenant community. That is, the nature of the church is no longer identified by the physical, genealogical principle but rather is a corporate, spiritual reality established with those united to Christ by faith (Col. 1:11–15). On this point, DeRouchie writes,

> In Christ, spiritual adoption, not physical descent, becomes the mark of the new covenant community. While ethnic distinctions are not eradicated (e.g., Rom. 1:16; 2:9; 9:25–27; cf. Acts 13:46), new covenant membership is grounded solely in "corporate identification" with the Messiah and is no longer assumed simply because of biological connection. In this and many other senses, Christ's new covenant work marks an escalation beyond all previous eras.[16]

To put it another way, circumcision in the old covenant was a shadow of spiritual circumcision in the new (Rom. 2:28–29; cf. Deut. 10:16; 30:6). In this new covenant, God removes old hearts, gives believers in Christ new hearts wrought by the Spirit, thereby causing them to obey his Word (Ezek. 36:26–27), all of which is rooted in the final forgiveness of sin obtained by the better priest and sacrifice, Jesus Christ (Jer. 31: 31–34; Heb. 7–10). As a result, the NT commands believers to be baptized in order to testify that one has died to sin and risen to new life *in Christ*, experienced the new birth and entered into the realities of the new covenant, received the gift and guarantee of the Spirit, joined to the body of Christ, and separated from the world unto God (Acts 2:40–41; Rom. 6:1–11; 1 Cor. 12:12–13; Gal. 2:27–29; Col. 1:11–15).

Second, covenant theology's view of the church and baptism does not adequately account for the relation of typology to the person and work of Christ. For example, G. K. Beale writes, "[Water] baptism is the redemptive-historical and typological *equivalent* to circumcision."[17] This equivalence, however, fails to see the progress, escalation, and fulfillment of all types in their antitype, Jesus Christ. On this point Brent Parker writes,

> Through the chief antitype, Christ, the new covenant community is also Israel's antitype. Israel's experiences (1 Cor. 10:1–11), structures (temple, priesthood) and core identity as God's chosen race, Abraham's seed, and as God's flock were all advance presentations of the eschatological Israel of God (Gal. 6:16). The church is the restored flock of God, the true seed of Abraham (Gal. 3–4; Rom. 4), the new temple, the people of the new exodus, the ultimate chosen

---

16. DeRouchie, "Father of a Multitude of Nations," 36.
17. G. K.Beale, *New Testament Biblical Theology*, 816.

race, royal priesthood (Exod. 19:6; 1 Peter 2:9; cf. Rev 1:4), and holy nation.[18]

In other words, it is those *in Christ by faith* who are children of God, who have put on Christ, who are baptized. And if Christ's, then they are also Abraham's offspring, heirs according to promise (Gal. 3:24–29).

Conclusion
Progressive covenantalism differs from both dispensationalism and covenant theology in crucial ways. First, by virtue of the newness of the new covenant, the nature of the new covenant church is radically different than Israel under the old covenant, for all in the new covenant have their sin forgiven and all have new, circumcised hearts. Second, the land is viewed as a type that Christ antitypically fulfills, first in his person and work as he inaugurates a new age; second in believers as God's new covenant, new creational people (2 Cor. 5:17); and finally in the consummated new creation (Rev. 21–22). Third, both believing Jews and Gentiles as the "one new man" (Eph. 2:11–22) equally receive their promised inheritance and rest in the glorious new creation in Christ (Heb. 3–4), of which the indwelling Holy Spirit is the guarantee (Eph. 1:13–14).

Summary
Our Triune God always keeps his covenant promises. In his ministry, Jesus announced that God was working through *him* to fulfill his ancient promises to redeem and restore from sin and to reestablish his universal and international kingdom. In this age, between the time when Christ inaugurated and will consummate those promises, we live as sojourners and exiles who seek a city that is to come, whose designer and builder is God (1 Peter 2:11; Heb. 11:10; 13:14). We should in faith, therefore, anticipate the ultimate end in our minds, hearts, and words before others until *that* day "when the dwelling place of God is with man. He will dwell with them, and they will be his people, and God himself will be with them as their God" (Rev. 21:3).

REFLECTION QUESTIONS

1. What does the fact that God freely initiates and enters into covenant fellowship with his creatures say about his character?

---

18. Brent E. Parker, "The Israel-Christ-Church Typological Pattern: A Theological Critique of Covenant and Dispensational Theologies" (Ph.D. diss., Southern Baptist Theological Seminary, 2017), 385.

2. How does each covenant advance God's saving purposes in Christ?

3. What is new about the new covenant? Why does humanity need a new covenant?

4. Why is the new covenant in Christ a better covenant (see Heb. 8–10)?

5. How does progressive covenantalism differ from dispensationalism and covenant theology?

PART 3

Illustrating Biblical Theology: Tracing Themes

How Can Fiction Illustrate Biblical Theology? The Case of Harry Potter

Andrew David Naselli

Harry Potter, the seven-book fantasy series by J. K. Rowling, is the best-selling series in history, with more than 500 million copies sold.[1] We are using Harry Potter to illustrate our point because that story is the "shared text" of the twenty-first century.[2] (While some people think Harry Potter is dark literature that Christians should avoid, we are convinced it is filled with implicit and explicit Christian themes.[3])

Harry Potter helps illustrate biblical theology. We're being serious!

The first time I read the books I listened to them with my wife, Jenni. We enjoyed it so much that we read the books again two years later, and the timing was just right. But something happened that we didn't anticipate (though I

---

1. See also Andrew David Naselli, *How to Understand and Apply the New Testament: Twelve Steps from Exegesis to Theology* (Phillipsburg, NJ: P&R, 2017), 238–39. See J. K. Rowling, *Harry Potter and the Sorcerer's Stone* (New York: Levine, 1998); Rowling, *Harry Potter and the Chamber of Secrets* (New York: Levine, 1999); Rowling, *Harry Potter and the Prisoner of Azkaban* (New York: Levine, 1999); Rowling, *Harry Potter and the Goblet of Fire* (New York: Levine, 2000); Rowling, *Harry Potter and the Order of the Phoenix* (New York: Levine, 2003); Rowling, *Harry Potter and the Half-Blood Prince* (New York: Levine, 2005); Rowling, *Harry Potter and the Deathly Hallows* (New York: Levine, 2007).
2. John Granger, "Book Binders: What I Learned about the Great Books and Harry Potter," *Touchstone* 21 (December 2008), http://www.touchstonemag.com/archives/article.php?id=21-10-028-f. *Time Magazine* calls John Granger the "Dean of Harry Potter Scholars": https://techland.time.com/2009/08/28/john-granger-dean-of-harry-potter-scholars-the-nerd-world-interview.
3. See John Granger, *How Harry Cast His Spell: The Meaning behind the Mania for J. K. Rowling's Bestselling Books*, 4th ed. (Carol Stream, IL: Tyndale House, 2006); Jerram Barrs, *Echoes of Eden: Reflections on Christianity, Literature, and the Arts* (Wheaton, IL: Crossway, 2013), 125–46.

should have since I teach biblical theology!). The first time we read the books, we were focusing on their storyline: Who are the characters? What happened? What will happen next? We didn't know where the story was going. We could only anticipate and guess. In our first reading, we were preoccupied with simply following a thrilling story.

But when we read the series for the second time, we were reading it differently. We already knew the characters. We already knew what would happen. We already knew where the story was going. We already knew how the story would end. But do you think that spoiled the second reading? Not at all. It actually made it better.

We loved our second reading right out of the gate in book 1. We immediately started making thematic connections that we missed the first time. We kept stopping to say such things like, "Did you hear that? I totally missed that the first time we read this. Rowling picks up on that theme again in book 3 and then develops it further in books 5 and 7." In other words, we started *tracing thematic trajectories* from book 1 all the way through to book 7. We started marveling at how well Rowling packaged the seven books as a coherent series with an overarching theme and many motifs that she masterfully develops throughout the storyline. (Rowling wasn't bumbling along as she wrote each novel. She masterminded the entire storyline *before* she completed book 1. Sure, there were new details she filled in along the way, but she designed the overall plotline at the beginning.)

The joy we experienced tracing those thematic trajectories is just a small taste of what it's like to read the Bible over and over again. Each time I read straight through the Harry Potter books, I make richer and thicker connections that I didn't see before—themes that are right there in the text but that I didn't have eyes to see my first or second time through.[4]

Once you've read the Bible straight through once, you know its overall plotline. But you can't reread it enough. There's always more to see, more connections to make. That's what biblical theology focuses on: making organic, salvation-historical connections with the whole Bible, especially regarding how the story progresses, integrates, and climaxes in Christ.

This means that once you've read the whole book, you simply can't read it the same way the second time and subsequent times. *You can't help but read any part in light of the whole.* And since the whole Bible is a coherent story, we must read the whole Bible—including the Old Testament—with *Christian* eyes. We live at this stage in the history of salvation, so we should read every bit of the Bible in light of everything God has revealed to us. The New Testament is the

---

4. To clarify, typology is a technical term for a phenomenon in the Bible (see Question 8). Anything like that outside the Bible is simply analogous. The Bible is unique as a divine-human book. Typology within the Bible is historical and something God progressively revealed over the course of fifteen hundred years.

answer key to the Old Testament. We have the answer key! So why would we read the Old Testament as if the New Testament did not exist?

We chose to illustrate this point with Harry Potter, but we could illustrate it with any epic storyline—whether a book or a movie. And the story doesn't even have to be epic. Some books and films are filled with intrigue the first time you watch them—such as those featuring a detective solving a case (e.g., Sherlock Holmes). Or consider movies such as *The Village*, *The Truman Show*, *A Beautiful Mind*, *Inception*, and *Interstellar*. Once you have already seen such a movie and know the basic storyline, if you watch it a second time, you see details that you missed the first time, and you start making thematic connections that you couldn't have made the first time. Once you've watched the movie the first time, you'll never watch it that same way again.

Since the Bible is one big story that is all about Jesus the Messiah, we should be able to read any one part of the Bible in light of the whole. If you don't understand a part of the Bible in light of the whole storyline, then you don't adequately understand that part of the Bible. It'd be like reading just one chapter from book 3 of the Harry Potter series without having read anything else in the seven-book series. You wouldn't be able to understand or appreciate that chapter because you'd be reading it out of context. You couldn't see how it fits into the whole story.

Biblical theology shows how all the seemingly loose threads in the Bible weave together in Jesus. Jesus is the climax and consummation. The story is all about him. And whether the theme is creation or covenant, law or liberty, sin or salvation, happiness or holiness, rest or righteousness, it all climaxes in Jesus.

My wife and I have read the Harry Potter series together three times. We love it. It hasn't gotten old. We'll probably read it again together in the future. But we certainly don't read it every day.

The beautiful thing about the Bible is that it *never* gets old. You can read it *every day* and make connections that you hadn't made before (or you can remind yourself of details and connections that you had forgotten!). It's a special book—a book like no other, a book that God himself wrote. And we have the pleasure of reading it at this stage of salvation history: Jesus the Messiah has come, and he is coming back to consummate his rule. So read every part of the Bible in light of the whole.

Summary

When you read a masterful story like Harry Potter, the first time you read it is special because you are enjoying a spellbinding storyline. But the subsequent times you read the story can be even more significant because you can start tracing thematic trajectories that you were unable to detect in your first reading.

That illustrates how we do biblical theology. As we read the Bible over and over and over, we can better trace thematic trajectories and make connections that the divine author brilliantly designed.

REFLECTION QUESTIONS

1. Name an epic book (or series of books) that you have enjoyed reading more than once. What sort of thematic connections have you made as you have read it again and again?

2. Name an epic film that you have enjoyed watching more than once. What sort of thematic connections have you made as you have watched it again and again?

3. How can you help young children see connections in the Bible?

4. How can you help adults who are new to the Bible (e.g., new converts) see connections in the Bible?

5. In your recent Bible reading and Bible study, what is a fresh way you have appreciated how the whole Bible fits together?

What Role Does "Mystery" Play in Biblical Theology?

Jason S. DeRouchie

The Old and New Testaments relate to each other with both continuity and discontinuity. On the one hand, the NT fulfills what the OT promises (continuity). On the other hand, the NT more fully reveals what the OT at least partially hides (discontinuity).[1] Paul highlights the continuity when he asserts that "the gospel of God . . . concerning his Son" was "promised beforehand through his prophets in the holy Scriptures" (Rom. 1:1–3). But the apostle could also stress discontinuity by identifying his gospel with "the revelation of the mystery [Gk. *mystērion*] that was kept secret for long ages but has now been disclosed and through the prophetic writings has been made known to all nations" (16:25–26). That is, Paul identified that in many ways Jesus's life, death, and resurrection supplied a brighter light and a new lens for reading what was actually there in the OT. So to properly grasp how Scripture progresses, integrates, and climaxes in Christ requires that we read the Bible forward, backward, and then forward again.

Defining Mystery

In the NT, the word *mystery* (*mystērion*) occurs twenty-eight times and is a technical term that refers to an end-time reality that was largely (though not entirely) hidden in the OT but that is now more fully disclosed in the New.[2]

---

1. See especially D. A. Carson, "Mystery and Fulfillment: Toward a More Comprehensive Paradigm of Paul's Understanding of the Old and New," in *The Paradoxes of Paul*, vol. 2 of *Justification and Variegated Nomism*, eds. D. A. Carson, Peter T. O'Brien, and Mark A. Seifrid, 2 vols., WUNT 2/181 (Grand Rapids: Baker Academic, 2004), 393–436.
2. G. K. Beale and Benjamin L. Gladd, *Hidden but Now Revealed: A Biblical Theology of Mystery* (Downers Grove, IL: InterVarsity, 2014), 35; Benjamin L. Gladd, "Mystery," *Dictionary of*

All the NT occurrences are eschatological in nature and in some way linked to the OT.[3]

The roots of usage appear to be in the book of Daniel, where the term functions distinctively as a translation for the Aramaic *rāz*, which means *mystery* (Dan. 2:18–19, 27–30, 47[2x]; cf. 4:9[6]).[4] In Daniel 2, King Nebuchadnezzar has a troubling dream about a towering statue, of which he has partial knowledge (2:31–35), and then he looks to Daniel for the interpretive revelation that includes full knowledge (2:36–45). The "mystery [LXX = *mystērion*]" that God revealed to Daniel (2:19) included both the initial dream and its interpretation, as the God in heaven "who reveals mysteries [*mystēria*] . . . made known to King Nebuchadnezzar what will be in the latter days" (2:28; cf. 2:47).

Mystery in the Old Testament[5]

At key points, the OT affirms the concept that there were levels of "mystery" in its meaning that God would reveal to some only in the latter days associated with the new covenant and the Messiah. First, with respect to the rebel majority, Moses declared, "To this day the LORD has not given you a heart to understand or eyes to see or ears to hear" (Deut. 29:4[3]). They were "stubborn" (9:6, 13; 10:16; 31:27), "unbelieving" (1:32; 9:23; cf. 28:66), and "rebellious" (9:7, 24; 31:27; cf. 1:26, 43; 9:23), and after Moses's death, their defiance would only escalate in the Promised Land (31:16). Consequently, the Lord would pour his covenant curses upon them (31:17, 29; cf. 28:15–68). He would not overcome their crookedness and twistedness (32:5; Acts 2:40; Phil. 2:15) until the covenant-mediatory prophet like Moses would rise to whom they would listen (Deut. 18:5; cf. Matt. 17:5). In the age of restoration, God would change the remnant's hearts and enable their love (Deut. 30:6), and in that day, which is now realized in the new covenant and the church (cf. Rom. 2:29; 2 Cor. 3:6), Moses's message in Deuteronomy would finally be heard and heeded: "And you will turn and you will hear the voice of the LORD and do all his commandments that I am commanding you today" (Deut. 30:8, DeRouchie's translation).

---

the New Testament Use of the Old Testament, eds. G. K. Beale, D. A. Carson, Benjamin L. Gladd, and Andrew David Naselli (Grand Rapids: Baker Academic, forthcoming).

3. Beale and Gladd, *Hidden but Now Revealed*, 321, 325–26; Gladd, "Mystery" (cf. Matt. 13:11; Mark 4:11; Luke 8:10; Rom. 11:25; 16:25; 1 Cor. 2:1, 7; 4:1; 13:2; 14:2; 15:51; Eph. 1:9; 3:3–4, 9; 5:32; 6:19; Col. 1:26–27; 2:2; 4:3; 2 Thess. 2:7; 1 Tim. 3:9, 16; Rev. 1:20; 10:7; 17:5, 7).

4. Benjamin L. Gladd, *Revealing the Mysterion: The Use of Mystery in Daniel and Second Temple Judaism with Its Bearing on First Corinthians*, BZNW 160 (Berlin: De Gruyter, 2008); Beale and Gladd, *Hidden but Now Revealed*, 29–46; Gladd, "Mystery."

5. See also Jason S. DeRouchie, *How to Understand and Apply the Old Testament: Twelve Steps from Exegesis to Theology* (Phillipsburg, NJ: P&R, 2017), 417–19. For more on these texts and the biblical-theological significance of the mystery concept, see Jason S. DeRouchie, "The Mystery Revealed: A Biblical Case for Christ-Centered Old Testament Interpretation," *Them* 44, no. 2 (August 2019): 226–48.

Second, Israel's spiritual disability continued in Isaiah's day, as the people were characterized by "deep sleep" and the inability to "read" God's word; it was as if Yahweh's written word through Isaiah was a sealed scroll to them: "Astonish yourselves and be astonished; blind yourselves and be blind! . . . For the LORD has poured out upon you a spirit of deep sleep. . . . And the vision of all this has become to you like the words of a book that is sealed. When men give it to one who can read, saying, 'Read this,' he says, 'I cannot, for it is sealed'" (Isa. 29:9–11; cf. Rom. 11:7–8). Under the judgment of God (Isa. 6:9), Isaiah's audience could not fully understand God's word. But Yahweh promised a day when "the deaf shall hear the words of a book . . . and the eyes of the blind shall see" (29:18). Because God instructed Isaiah to write his words in a book for a perpetual witness and because his own audience could not grasp these words, his book-writing was principally for later generations that would have eyes to see (30:8). These future generations would all "be taught by the LORD" (54:13), which Jesus stressed God was fulfilling in drawing people to him (John 6:44–45). To these would be given "the secret [*mystērion*] of the kingdom of God, but for those outside everything is in parables, so that 'they may indeed see but not perceive, and may indeed hear but not understand, lest they should turn and be forgiven'" (Mark 4:11–12; citing Isa. 6:9–10).

Third, Yahweh told Jeremiah that his writing was specifically intended for the restored community of God. "Write in a book all the words that I have spoken to you. For behold, days are coming, declares the LORD, when I will restore the fortunes of my people, Israel and Judah, says the LORD, and I will bring them back to the land that I gave to their fathers" (Jer. 30:2–3). The reason Jeremiah needed to write his words in a book was because the future generations would need them. And it would only be in those latter days that readers would truly comprehend what the prophet was writing. "The fierce anger of the LORD will not turn back until he has executed and accomplished the intentions of his mind. *In the latter days you will understand this.* At that time, declares the LORD, I will be the God of all the clans of Israel, and they shall be my people" (Jer. 30:24–31:1, emphasis added). The last clause is repeated later in the chapter in relation to the new covenant, and this shows that the "latter days" are none other than those associated with the church age, wherein God declares, "I will put my law within them, and I will write it on their hearts. And I will be their God, and they shall be my people" (31:33; cf. Luke 22:20; Heb. 8:8–12; 10:16). In this day, the forgiveness of all in the covenant would mean that "no longer shall each one teach his neighbor and each his brother, saying, 'Know the LORD,' for they shall all know me, from the least of them to the greatest" (Jer. 31:34; cf. Heb. 10:17). In Jeremiah, knowing God relates to joining him in living out steadfast love, justice, and righteousness (Jer. 9:24; 22:15–16). John stresses how *all* who are in Christ enjoy this knowledge (1 John 2:20–21, 27–29). Even for prophets like Jeremiah, there were certain levels of meaning associated with his words that only those associated with the new covenant would understand.

Fourth, God told Daniel that all the kingdom revelation he received he was to seal up in a book until the appointed time of disclosure to the wise: "But you, Daniel, shut up the words and seal the book, until the time of the end. Many shall run to and fro, and knowledge shall increase. . . . Go your way, Daniel, for the words are shut up and sealed until the time of the end. Many shall purify themselves and make themselves white and be refined, but the wicked shall act wickedly. And none of the wicked shall understand, but those who are wise shall understand" (Dan. 12:4, 9–10). The hiddenness of the OT's meaning is temporary for the remnant ("those who are wise") but permanent for the rebels ("the wicked").

These OT texts from Deuteronomy, Isaiah, Jeremiah, and Daniel identify two distinct groups who could not fully understand the prophets' messages. The rebel majority could not (due to God's punishment) and would not (due to their sinfulness) hear or heed any of the prophets' words (esp. Deut. 29:4[3]; Isa. 29:10–11). The remnant understood some things (Dan. 10:1), but the Lord would not disclose all things to them (12:8). Instead, they were among the "prophets and righteous people" who "longed to see what you see, and did not see it, and to hear what you hear, and did not hear it" (Matt. 13:17; cf. Luke 10:24). Yahweh's OT seers, sages, and sovereigns anticipated the latter days when the Lord would grant more complete revelation to the wise (Jer. 30:29; Dan. 12:10).

Mystery in the New Testament

God did not allow the majority of those in the old covenant to understand his prophets' words, and as a judgment, the people's blindness continued forward into the days of Christ (Isa. 6:9–10; Mark 4:12; cf. Matt. 13:13–15). But fulfilling what the OT predicts (e.g., Deut. 30:8; Isa. 29:18; Jer. 30:29; Dan. 12:10), Jesus's teaching and work began disclosing to his disciples truths that remained distant from the crowds: "To you has been given the secret [*mystērion*] of the kingdom of God, but for those outside everything is in parables" (Mark 4:11). The "mystery," therefore, remained permanently hidden for some (cf. 1 Cor. 2:8–9 with Isa. 64:4; Eph. 1:17–18) but only temporarily hidden for others (see Dan. 12:8–9, 12; Matt. 11:25).[6]

And what was this "mystery"? In the Synoptic Gospels, the "mystery" (Mark 4:11) or "mysteries" of the kingdom (Matt. 13:11; Luke 8:10) relate to

---

6. Gladd notes, "Temporary hiddenness operates on a redemptive-historical plane and concerns the unveiling of end-times events, whereas permanent hiddenness refers to the persistent inability to understand revelation even after the mystery has been revealed." Gladd, "Mystery"; cf. Carson, "Mystery and Fulfillment," 432; Beale and Gladd, *Hidden but Now Revealed*, 60–63.

the unexpected, gradual, already-but-not-yet fulfillment of God's end-time reign. While many OT texts clearly anticipate that Yahweh's reign will come through his anointed servant-king (e.g., Gen. 49:8–10; Num. 24:17–19; Isa. 9:6–7; 11:10; 52:13–15; Dan. 2:44; 7:13–14; Zech. 14:9), the same texts do not as plainly identify an extended period when the remnant that is part of God's kingdom will coexist with the rebel community (cf. Ps. 110:1; Zeph. 3:8–20).[7]

In Paul's epistles, which comprise twenty-one of the term's NT occurrences, the revealed "mystery" or "mysteries" refer to insight into God's end-time purposes (1 Cor. 4:1; 13:2; 14:2; Eph. 1:9) most directly associated with more fully understanding Christ and the gospel (Rom. 16:25; 1 Cor. 2:1, 7; Eph. 3:3–4, 9; 6:19; Col. 2:2; 4:3; 1 Tim. 3:9, 16). This knowledge included grasping better what the gospel implies for end-time suffering (2 Thess. 2:7) and a multi-stage resurrection (1 Cor. 15:51). It also included appreciating what the gospel implied for the people of God both as a multiethnic adopted community (Rom. 11:25; Eph. 3:3; Col. 1:26–27) and in relation to Christ (Eph. 5:32).[8] Some elements in the gospel's advance are ironic and somewhat unexpected, as in how the God-man reigns in death (1 Cor. 1–2; cf. Isa. 52:13–53:12; Dan. 9:25–26; Zech. 12:10; 13:1), how the Gentiles serve as gospel agents to Jews (Isa. 11:25–26; cf. Deut. 32:21; Jer. 3:16–18; 30:8–10), and how Gentiles join with Jews as full heirs of all God's promises apart from the Mosaic law (Eph. 3:3–4, 9; cf. Isa. 56:3–8; Jer. 3:14–17; Zech. 14:16–19). Through Christ's person and work, God reveals the meaning of every mystery and by this brings clarity to theology, soteriology, ecclesiology, eschatology, and the like.

Finally, in Revelation, "mystery" occurs four times. "The prophets" of old (like Daniel in 11:29–12:13) announced that the "mystery of God would be fulfilled" (Rev. 10:7). This "mystery" relates to the nature of the church (1:20) and the self-destructive nature of Babylon (17:5, 7), both elements that Paul's letters also identify (see above).

Israel's spiritual blindness and deafness would be healed only through Jesus. "The [Jews'] minds were hardened. For to this day, when they read the old covenant, that same veil remains unlifted, because only through Christ is it taken away" (2 Cor. 3:14; cf. John 5:39–40; Rom. 11:7–8). Apart from Jesus, the Jews could not fully see and savor the beauty of God in the OT, but with the coming of Christ, the veil is lifted and the greater glory of the new covenant gives clarity to the meaning and purpose of the old covenant texts.

---

7. For more, see Beale and Gladd, *Hidden but Now Revealed*, 56–83. See also the synthesis in Gladd, "Mystery."

8. For a full survey of these texts in Paul, see Beale and Gladd, *Hidden but Now Revealed*, 85–259; cf. Carson, "Mystery and Fulfillment," 412–25. For a briefer synthesis, see Gladd, "Mystery."

What Mystery Implies for Doing Biblical Theology

A striking element in Romans 16:25–26 is that the very "mystery" that is now revealed in and through Christ is also now being made known to all nations *through* the OT itself (cf. Rom. 1:2). Thus, Paul can also say, "But now the righteousness of God has been manifested apart from the law *to which the Law and the Prophets testify*" (3:21, DeRouchie's translation, emphasis added). Similarly, in Ephesians 3:4–5 Paul writes, "You can perceive my insight into the mystery [*mystērion*] of Christ, which was not made known to the sons of men in other generations as [*hōs*] it has now been revealed." On this text Benjamin Gladd notes, "The term 'as' [*hōs*] is key here, for it seems to indicate that OT authors had *some* insight into the unveiled mystery that was disclosed to Paul."[9] Reflecting on such passages, G. K. Beale and Gladd identify that "full or 'complete' meaning is actually 'there' in the Old Testament text; it is simply partially 'hidden' or latent, awaiting a later revelation, whereby the complete meaning of the text is revealed to the interpreter."[10] Similarly, D. A. Carson observes, "Paul thinks of the gospel he preaches as simultaneously something that has been predicted in times past, with those predictions now fulfilled, and something that has been hidden in times past, and now revealed."[11] These truths have at least three implications for doing biblical theology.

First, the presence of mystery in Scripture requires that we interpret the OT through the light and lens of Christ. In Schreiner's words, "We read the scriptures both front to back and back to front. We always consider the developing story as well as the end of the story."[12]

The OT is filled with declarations, characters, events, and institutions that bear meaning in themselves, but the coming of Christ enhances and clarifies that meaning (cf. John 2:20–22; 12:13–16). It is as if the OT gives us the start of a pattern in which we read "2" followed by "4," but we need the NT to clarify what comes next (2, 4, ?). If the NT identifies that the OT finds its fulfillment in Christ as the digit "6," then we know not only the final answer but also that the OT problem was "2 + 4." If, however, the NT establishes that the next digit is "8," then we know both the answer and that the OT problem was "2 x 4."[13] The coming of Christ supplies both the answer key and the algorithm that clarify how the divine author desired all along for us to read the OT.[14]

---

9. Gladd, "Mystery" (emphasis original); cf. Beale and Gladd, *Hidden but Now Revealed*, 159–73.

10. Beale and Gladd, *Hidden but Now Revealed*, 330.

11. Carson, "Mystery and Fulfillment," 425.

12. Thomas R. Schreiner, "Preaching and Biblical Theology," *SBJT* 10, no. 2 (Summer 2006): 28.

13. We could also find in the NT "−2" (2 − 4), or "16" (2^2, 4^2), etc.

14. Moo and Naselli rightly assert, "The most basic of all NT 'hermeneutical axioms' . . . is the authors' conviction that the God who had spoken in the OT continued to speak to them and that it was this final divine context for all of Scripture that determines the meaning of any particular text." Douglas J. Moo and Andrew David Naselli, "The Problem of the

In this respect, some have helpfully compared Scripture to "double narratives" like detective stories. Peter Leithart writes:

> Detective novels tell two stories at once: the story on the surface and the real story unveiled to the gathered suspects in the final chapter. Once the detective gives his solution to the crime, the reader cannot go back to the first narrative; the second completely overshadows it. . . . Under the circumstances, reading backwards is not merely a preferred reading strategy; it is the only sensible course of action for a reasonable person.[15]

I am not saying that the mysteries of the OT were something that the most enlightened saints could have fully solved. No, only God could reveal the mysteries that he hid there, and he does so partially to some in the OT age but only fully through Christ. Whether God revealed a mystery directly by vision, dream, or impression (as in Daniel's case; see Dan. 2:19) or indirectly through their own searching and inquiring carefully (1 Peter 1:10–11), the remnant understood some of God's mysteries, and those who did not understand were culpable before God. Other mysteries, however, God chose not to disclose until Jesus came, and this fact identifies that the Bible's last "chapter" (the NT) supplies us the necessary lens for reading the initial three-fourths the way God intends us to read it. Through Christ we can see and savor elements in the OT's plotline, content, and structure that were there all along but that were not clear apart from him.

Second, the nature of mystery as partially hidden but now more fully revealed motivates us to identify the organic connections between the mystery itself and its revelation. The OT prophets likely recognized in some ways the future, end-time, messianic nature of their proclamations, even though the NT authors would be the ones to supply the complete meaning of the mystery. So in texts like Romans 16:26 and Ephesians 3:4, the meaning of the "mystery" now revealed in and through Christ was already present to some extent *in* the OT itself. And as Beale and Gladd note, "Since this new meaning was

---

New Testament's Use of the Old Testament," in *The Enduring Authority of the Christian Scriptures*, ed. D. A. Carson (Grand Rapids: Eerdmans, 2016), 737.

15. Peter J. Leithart, *Deep Exegesis: The Mystery of Reading Scripture* (Waco, TX: Baylor University Press, 2009), 66, following historian David Steinmetz. Leithart sees later texts actually altering the very nature of an earlier text's meaning. Leithart, *Deep Exegesis*, 40, 43. In contrast, we are more comfortable speaking of layers of meaning and about how later interpreted events or messages *illuminate*, *enhance*, and *extend* the single meaning God intended from the beginning but which was only realized progressively through greater revelation and realized fully with the tribulation and triumph of Jesus Christ. Such a view alone maintains the organic link between type and antitype and the unified, omniscient, and omnipotent working of the single divine author.

really 'there' in the Old Testament, the original context is never completely severed. Certainly, the meaning of some Old Testament quotations is 'newer' or more creative than others, but if the biblical model of mystery is upheld, the original context is to some degree retained."[16]

Jesus identifies this organic continuity when he claims, "Your father Abraham rejoiced that he would see my day. He saw it and was glad" (John 8:56). Similarly, Daniel "understood the word and had understanding of the vision" (Dan. 10:1; cf. 9:23). Furthermore, the writer of Hebrews stressed, "These all died in faith, not having received the things promised, but having seen them and greeted them from afar" (Heb. 11:13). Often the OT prophets envisioned the very form we now enjoy, though perhaps more like an acorn anticipates a great oak.[17] They not only saw the shadow but also in many ways embraced the substance that is Christ (Col. 2:16–17; cf. Heb. 8:5; 10:1). God's work in their lives supplied them "light" for seeing truths God did not disclose to others, but it was not enough to clarify everything. The lens of salvation history climaxing in Jesus would be necessary for full disclosure.[18] As Beale states,

> When there is a divine understanding that transcends the conscious intention of the human author, the divine understanding is still organically related to the human author's understanding or "willed type." What God knew more fully than the prophet consciously knew would be an interpretive implication that would fit within the human author's "willed type," and, if asked later, the prophet would say, "Yes, I see how that is the wider, thicker meaning of what I intended originally to say." We must say that in every case God had a more exhaustive understanding than biblical authors had of what they wrote.[19]

Even if the OT authors were not always fully aware of all that God was speaking through them, they at least retrospectively would have affirmed the trajectories that later biblical authors identify.

---

16. Beale and Gladd, *Hidden but Now Revealed*, 335.
17. Beale writes, "Contrary to the consensus opinion both inside and outside evangelical scholarship, Old Testament authors may have had some inkling of how the meaning of their texts would be later understood in what would appear to us to be surprising interpretations." G. K. Beale, "The Cognitive Peripheral Vision of Biblical Authors: J. Gresham Machen Chair Installation Lecture," *WTJ* 76 (2014): 283; Beale and Gladd, *Hidden but Now Revealed*, 359.
18. While I believe the norm was that the OT prophets grasped at least the seed of what they were proclaiming, they may not have always understood—whether like Daniel (Dan 12:8) or like the disciples who failed to grasp Christ's statements about his passion until after his death and resurrection (Mark 6:51–52; Luke 2:50; 9:45; 18:31–34; 24:16; John 12:16).
19. Beale, "Peripheral Vision of Biblical Authors," 283; Beale and Gladd, *Hidden but Now Revealed*, 358.

Third, the presence of mystery that needs revealing helps clarify how God wrote the OT for Christians. There are elements in the OT that the OT prophets themselves knew people would not understand until the new covenant era (e.g., Jer. 30:29; Dan. 10:12). Indeed, the prophets wrote for the *future* generations who would have ears to hear (Isa. 30:8–9 with 29:18; Jer. 30:1–2). It is from this perspective that Paul claims God gave the OT for *new* covenant believers. For example, just after identifying Christ as the referent in Psalm 69, Paul emphasizes, "For whatever was written in former days was written *for our instruction*, that through endurance and through the encouragement of the Scriptures we might have hope" (Rom. 15:4, emphasis added; cf. 4:23–24; 1 Cor. 10:11).[20] For Paul, the OT was *Christian* Scripture and fully applicable to believers when read through the light and lens of Christ. Since the OT is part of the Christian Scriptures, we should follow the pattern of the NT authors by using the OT to know God and savor Christ (cf. e.g., 1 Cor. 5:13; Eph. 6:2–3; 1 Tim. 5:17–18; 1 Peter 1:15–16).

When Paul states that the OT "was written" for our instruction, he is not explicit as to whether the OT human authors understood this. Peter, however, made this clear:

> Concerning this salvation, the prophets who prophesied about the grace that was to be yours searched and inquired carefully, inquiring what person or time the Spirit of Christ in them was indicating when he predicted the sufferings of Christ and the subsequent glories. *It was revealed to them that they were serving not themselves but you*, in the things that have now been announced to you through those who preached the good news to you by the Holy Spirit sent from heaven, things into which angels long to look. (1 Peter 1:10–12, emphasis added)

The human authors of the OT knew that their inspired words were principally not for them but for those living after Christ came. The presence of mystery in the OT supports this truth, for only NT believers would fully understand the various symbols and patterns in the OT. The light of Christ supplies us the needed spiritual sight for understanding the things of God (1 Cor. 2:12–13; 2 Cor. 3:14), and the lens of Christ's life, death, and resurrection provides the needed perspective for reading the OT meaning to its fullness (Matt. 5:17–18; Mark 4:11; Rom. 16:25–26). God wrote the OT for Christians, and God enables Christians to more fully grasp both the meaning and intended effect of the initial three-fourths of the Christian Scriptures.

---

20. For a careful supporting analysis of Paul's claim in Romans 15:4, see George W. Knight III, "The Scriptures Were Written for Our Instruction," *JETS* 39 (1996): 3–13.

Summary

Mystery (*mystērion*) is a technical term in the NT that identifies an end-time event that was partially hidden to OT authors and more fully revealed only through Christ. A proper approach to biblical theology requires that we account for mystery for at least three reasons: (1) The presence of mystery pushes us to interpret the OT through the light and lens of Christ as the NT reveals. (2) The reality of a mystery that is only partially hidden requires that we interpret the Old and New Testaments carefully to determine the precise nature of the mystery that is now revealed. (3) Since we need the NT to arrive at the full meaning of the OT, the initial three-fourths of the Christian Bible is indeed written for *us*, upon whom the end of the ages has come (1 Cor. 10:11) and who enjoy the regenerating and illuminating work of Christ's Spirit (Rom. 16:25–26; 1 Cor. 2:13–14; 2 Cor. 3:14).

REFLECTION QUESTIONS

1. In what ways does the relationship of the Old and New Testaments express both continuity and discontinuity?

2. How does the story in Daniel 2 of Nebuchadnezzar's statue-vision inform our understanding of the biblical term "mystery"?

3. What are some ways that Moses, Isaiah, Jeremiah, and Daniel identify that the OT would only be fully understood in the NT age?

4. In what way does reading a "double narrative" like a detective novel compare and contrast with our reading of Scripture? Why is it important to read our Bible both front to back *and* back to front?

5. How might studying the concept of mystery inform Paul's statements that God wrote the OT Scriptures for instructing Christians (Rom. 15:4; 1 Cor. 10:11) and Peter's statement that God revealed to the OT prophets that "they were serving not themselves but you" (1 Peter 1:12)?

What Is a Biblical Theology of the Covenants?

Jason S. DeRouchie

The concept of *covenant* (Hebrew *bĕrît*; Greek *diathēkē*) is common in Scripture and the ancient world. We call the two main divisions of the Bible the Old and New *Testaments*—that is, *covenants*. "Covenant" is the Bible's term for "a chosen [as opposed to natural or biological] relationship in which two parties make binding promises to each other," often with God as the witness.[1] That is, at the core of covenant is a nonbiological, oath-bound relationship like those in clan alliances (Gen. 14:13), personal agreements (Gen. 31:44), international treaties (Josh. 9:6; 1 Kings 15:19), national agreements (Jer. 34:8–10), and loyalty agreements (1 Sam. 20:14–17), including marriage (Mal. 2:14).[2] It is through the covenants that God reverses the ruinous effects of sin and introduces his saving reign into the world.

We can picture the interrelationship of the covenants as an hourglass, with the most universal scope occurring at the two ends and the work of Christ at the center. The Adamic-Noahic, Abrahamic, Mosaic, and Davidic covenants are all named in light of the covenant head or mediator through whom God entered into a relationship with his chosen ones. The *old* Mosaic covenant and era of punishment contrasts with the *new* covenant in Christ,

---

1. Thomas R. Schreiner, *Covenant and God's Purpose for the World*, Short Studies in Biblical Theology (Wheaton, IL: Crossway, 2017), 13. Hugenberger writes similarly that "a covenant, in its normal sense, is an elected, as opposed to natural, relationship of obligation under oath." Gordon P. Hugenberger, *Marriage as a Covenant: Biblical Law and Ethics as Developed from Malachi* (Grand Rapids: Baker Books, 1994), 11; cf. Peter J. Gentry and Stephen J. Wellum, *Kingdom through Covenant: A Biblical-Theological Understanding of the Covenants*, 2nd ed. (Wheaton, IL: Crossway, 2018), 164–66.
2. Peter J. Gentry and Stephen J. Wellum, *Kingdom through Covenant: A Biblical-Theological Understanding of the Covenants*, 2nd ed. (Wheaton, IL: Crossway, 2018), 162–63.

which climaxes all of God's purposes in history (see Jer. 31:31–34; Heb. 8:6–13).

	Covenants	Stages of Redemptive History	Major Literary Divisions	
			Narrative	Commentary
Old Testament	Adamic/Noahic	1. Creation, fall, and flood	Law	
	Abrahamic	2. Patriarchs		
	Mosaic (Old)	3. Exodus, Sinai, & wilderness		
	Davidic	4. Conquest & kingdoms (united and divided)	Former Prophets	
				Latter Prophets
				Former Writings
		5. Exile and initial restoration	Latter Writings	
New Testament	Christ / Jesus	6. Christ's work	Gospels	
		and the Church age	Acts	
	New			General Epistles
				Pauline Epistles
				and Hebrews
		7. Christ's return and kingdom consummation	Revelation	

Fig. 22.1. The History of Redemption in the Context of Scripture

Jesus the Messiah fulfills all five covenants:

- Jesus fulfills the *Adamic-Noahic covenant*, obeying where Adam failed (Rom. 5:18–19; cf. Matt 4:1–11; Luke 4:4–13) and entering as Savior into the world for which the Noahic covenant ensured the context (Gen. 9:9–11). Jesus is the Son of Man, last Adam, and image of God (Mark 10:45; 14:62; 1 Cor. 15:45; 2 Cor. 4:4).

- Jesus fulfills the ultimate goals of the *Abrahamic covenant*. He is the offspring of Abraham and agent of universal blessing (Gen. 22:17b–18; Acts 3:25–26; Gal. 3:16), and he secures a Yes to every promise and full inheritance rights to all who believe, whether Jew or Gentile (2 Cor. 1:20, 22; Gal. 3:29; Eph. 1:3–14).

- Jesus fulfills the *Mosaic (old) covenant*. He represents Israel and stands as God's Son, Yahweh's servant, the embodiment of wisdom, the one who fulfilled the law's demands, and the substance of all covenant shadows (Exod. 4:22–23; Isa. 49:3, 5–6; Matt. 3:17; 11:2, 19; 12:42; 13:54; John 2:19–21; Acts 3:25–26; Rom. 5:19; Col. 2:17; Heb. 9:9–12; 10:1).

- Jesus fulfills the *Davidic covenant*. He is the King of the Jews and Son of David (Matt. 2:1; 21:9; Luke 1:32–33).

• Jesus fulfills the *new covenant*. He is the prophet like Moses who was to come and the only true mediator between God and humans (Deut. 18:15, 18; Luke 7:16; 22:20; Acts 3:22–26; 7:37; 1 Tim. 2:5; Heb. 8:6; 9:15; 12:24).

What follows surveys how these covenants progress, integrate, and climax in Christ.

Adamic-Noahic Covenant

Adam's Headship in the Covenant with Creation
The Bible's earliest chapters depict nothing less than the results of God's choosing to initiate a kinship-type bond with his creation through the representative headship of Adam (see Gen. 5:1–3; Jer. 33:20, 25).[3] This elected relationship includes both God's sustaining provision (Gen. 1:29–30) and humanity's conditional responsibility to fulfill their commission of serving as God's image-bearing priest-kings (1:28; 2:15–18). Through Adam's failure to listen to God's word and to protect and lead his wife (3:1–6), he transgressed this covenant (see Isa. 43:27; Hos. 6:7) with the result that God cursed the earth and condemned Adam and all his descendants to spiritual and physical death (Gen. 2:17; cf. Isa. 24:4–6).

As a result of Adam's rebellion, the Lord "subjected [the creation] to futility" but did so "in hope" (Rom. 8:20). Indeed, before God announced that he would punish Adam (Gen. 3:17–19), he cursed the serpent and identified the deceiver's ultimate destruction under the foot of a deliverer (3:15). By naming his wife "Eve" (*ḥawâ*), which resembles the Hebrew term for "life" (*ḥay*), Adam appears to profess his faith in the promise that the coming Savior would overcome the curse of death. God follows this act by clothing his royal priests with the garments of animal skins, likely because a substitutionary sacrifice is necessary for the Lord to mercifully and justly reestablish relationship and partnership with them (3:20–21).[4]

Covenant Affirmation through Noah
Rebellious humanity expands, and Yahweh preserves a remnant of those calling on his name.[5] Yet, because of human wickedness (Gen. 6:5, 13), the

---

3. It is clear that a covenant is described, though the word is not used. Comparably, although 2 Samuel 7 never explicitly says that God made a "covenant" with David, the context indicates it, and other passages teach it (2 Sam. 23:5; Pss. 89:3; 132:11–12).

4. See Meredith G. Kline, "Investiture with the Image of God," *WTJ* 40 (1977): 39–62; William N. Wilder, "Illumination and Investiture: The Royal Significance of the Tree of Wisdom in Genesis 3," *WTJ* 68 (2006): 51–69.

5. See Jason S. DeRouchie, "The Blessing-Commission, the Promised Offspring, and the *Toledot* Structure of Genesis," *JETS* 56, no. 2 (2013): 219–47.

Lord sent a great flood that resulted in the death of "everything on the dry land in whose nostrils was the breath of life" (7:22). He saved only eight people, the head of whom was Noah, who "found favor [i.e., grace] in the eyes of the LORD" (6:8) and who in turn "walked with God" and "was a righteous man, blameless in his generation" (6:9). Yahweh promised to "establish [his] covenant with [Noah]" (6:18), an "everlasting covenant between God and every living creature" (9:16; cf. 8:22). More specifically, following the flood, the Lord declared, "Behold, I establish my covenant with you and your off-spring after you, and every beast of the earth with you . . . that never again shall all flesh be cut off by the waters of the flood" (9:9–11). What God was obligating humanity to do recalled his earlier command to the first couple to fill the earth with his image (1:27–28; 9:1, 7). The sign of the covenant was his rainbow in the clouds, which symbolically appears to portray that Yahweh's war-bow was raised and that a season of common grace was now falling on the world (9:12–17).

A substitutionary blood-sacrifice was necessary for the Lord to declare, "I will never again curse the ground because of man. . . . Neither will I ever again strike down every living creature as I have done" (8:21). The burnt offering of clean animals was a "pleasing aroma" to Yahweh (8:20), and it moved him to affirm his covenant with creation initiated with Adam (thus, the Adamic-Noahic covenant [singular]).[6] Because even among the survivors of the flood "the intention of man's heart is [still] evil from his youth" (8:21; cf. 6:5), Yahweh's blood-bought grace alone could justly allow him to commit to make "his sun rise on the evil and on the good" and to send "rain on the just and on the unjust" (Matt. 5:45). That is, the symbolic and predictive nature of the substitutionary sacrifice of clean animals after the flood anticipated the atoning work of Jesus. This fact identifies that what God would ultimately ac-complish through Christ purchased the very context of common grace that allows for saving grace to become operative.

Abrahamic Covenant

After the flood, humans continued to rebel against God by exalting themselves, so Yahweh confused their languages and dispersed some seventy families across the globe (Gen. 11:8–9; cf. ch. 10). Into this context of curse, however, he set apart one family through whom he purposed to ultimately re-verse the global curse and reconcile the world to himself.[7] The Lord commis-sioned Abram to "go" to the land of Canaan and "be a blessing" (Gen. 12:1–3).

---

6. Some of the ways God developed his covenant with creation between the Adamic and Noahic eras include his introducing fear into humanity's dominion (Gen. 9:2), his sanc-tioning animal life as food (9:3; cf. 1:29), his including the defense of the sanctity of human life in his reaffirming the mandate to take dominion (9:6), and his promising to sustain the new order as marked by the covenant sign of the rainbow (9:12–17).

7. Cf. DeRouchie, "Blessing-Commission," 235.

The commission itself foreshadows the covenant that God would later formally "cut" (15:18) and then "affirm" (17:7, 19, 21). While rarely apparent in English translations, Genesis 12:1–3 includes two coordinated commands, each followed by one or more conditional promises and the latter including an ultimate promissory result of global blessing.[8] The passage foresees two major stages in salvation history that would grow out of the Abrahamic promises.

	DeRouchie's Modified ESV		**ESV**
	And the Lord said to Abram	1	Now the Lord said to Abram,
Mosaic covenant fulfills stage 1	"Go from your country and your kindred and your father's house to the land that I will show you,	b	"Go from your country and your kindred and your father's house to the land that I will show you.
	so that I may make you into a great nation,	2	And I will make of you a great nation,
	and may bless you,	b	and I will bless you
	and may make your name great.	c	and make your name great,
New covenant fulfills stage 2	Then be a blessing,	d	so that you will be a blessing.
	so that I may bless those who bless you,	3	I will bless those who bless you,
	but him who dishonors you I will curse,	b	and him who dishonors you I will curse,
	with the result that in you all the families of the ground may be blessed."	c	and in you all the families of the earth shall be blessed."

Fig. 22.2. Two Translations of Genesis 12:1–3

Stage one relates to Abraham becoming the father of one nation in the land. God fulfilled this stage with the Mosaic covenant and Israel's nationhood in the Promised Land, which they would claim only after four hundred years of affliction as sojourners in a foreign place (i.e., Egypt) (15:13). God gave Israel the land of Canaan for the twelve tribes during the days of Joshua (Josh. 11:23; 21:43–45; cf. Gen. 17:8), but it is not until the days of kings David and Solomon that Israel controls the entire realm from the River of Egypt to the Euphrates River (2 Sam. 7:1; 1 Kings 4:20–21; cf. Gen. 15:18).

God fulfilled stage two with the new covenant community reconciled in Christ. Genesis 17 contrasts Abraham's fatherhood of a single covenant nation in Canaan (17:7–8) with his becoming "a father of a multitude of nations" (17:4–6), which fulfills the promise in 12:3 and 15:5. Specifically, building off the promise of a singular "offspring" in 3:15, God would raise up an "offspring" from Abram's loins and multiply him like the stars (15:3–5; cf. 22:17).

---

8. For this understanding of the structure of Gen. 12:1–3, see Paul R. Williamson, *Sealed with an Oath: Covenant in God's Unfolding Plan*, NSBT 23 (Downers Grove, IL: InterVarsity, 2007), 78–79; DeRouchie, *Understand and Apply the Old Testament*, 209–11; Gentry and Wellum, *Kingdom through Covenant*, 266–70.

He would be named through Isaac (21:12; cf. 17:19, 21), would conquer the gate of his enemies, and would be the agent through whom all nations on the earth would be blessed (22:17–18). Earlier, God refers to both the limited "Canaan" and the larger suzerain state with the singular "land" (15:18; 17:8), but what God anticipates in Genesis 22:17–18 is larger—what he later promised to Isaac in the movement from "land" to "lands" (26:3–4). Thus, God would overcome the world's curse, and Abraham would become "heir of the world" (Rom. 4:13).

The "land, offspring, and blessing" that God promises reverse the curses he issued in Genesis 3:14–19.[9] The pain in childbirth (3:16) will give rise to a nation (12:2) from whom the curse-overcoming offspring will rise (22:17–18). From the same cursed ground that burdens life (3:17–19) will rise the realm of a kingdom in which God's people will enjoy a lasting relationship with the Lord (12:7; 15:7). And the overall curse on the world (3:14, 17; 4:11; 5:29; 9:25; cf. 8:21) will be destroyed when God blesses through his royal deliverer (22:17–18; cf. 3:15) the very "families/clans" he dispersed after the flood (12:3; cf. 10:32).

Mosaic Covenant

The Mosaic Covenant Fulfills Stage One of the Abrahamic Covenant

After the exodus, Israel arrives at Mt. Sinai, where Yahweh charges the people to respond to his salvation by heeding his voice, keeping his "covenant," and being his treasured possession amid the world so that they might ultimately serve the Lord as "a kingdom of priests and a holy nation" (Exod. 19:5–6).[10] God called Israel to mediate and display his worth and beauty to their neighbors through lives of surrendered loyalty—something that could happen only by the Lord's presence igniting holiness (33:16; cf. Lev. 9:23– 10:3; 20:8; 21:8; 22:32). "Covenant" in Exodus 19:5 points both backward to the Abrahamic covenant (Exod. 6:4) and forward to the Ten Words (i.e., the Ten Commandments) in 20:1. This link identifies that Yahweh's dealing with Israel through Moses fulfills stage one of the Abrahamic covenant promises. Moses pleads with God to preserve rebellious Israel since God promised to multiply the patriarchs' offspring and land (Exod. 32:13; Deut. 9:27). The prophet consistently treats the covenant he is mediating as an outworking of the Abrahamic covenant promises (e.g., Deut. 1:8; 6:10; 9:5; 29:13; 30:20).

---

9. James M. Hamilton Jr., "The Seed of the Woman and the Blessing of Abraham," *TynBul* 58 (2007): 253–73.

10. For a developed discussion of the structure of these verses that highlights why "be my treasured possession" is part of the protasis ("if" section) and not the apodosis ("then" section), see DeRouchie, *Understand and Apply the Old Testament*, 226–33. See also DeRouchie, *Understand and Apply the Old Testament*, 315–17.

The Mosaic Covenant Brings Death

Israel's problem was that at the core they were spiritually disabled and needed heart surgery (Deut. 10:16). They would enter into the Promised Land, rebel even more, and then experience God's just wrath through an exilic death (31:16–17, 27, 29). When Paul asserts, "the law is not of faith" (Gal. 3:12), he likely identifies that the period of the Mosaic covenant was not characterized in the majority by true believing.[11] Instead, the Mosaic covenant bore a "ministry of death" and a "ministry of condemnation" (2 Cor. 3:7, 9), multiplying sin (Rom. 3:20; 5:20), and establishing Israel and the world's need for the promised royal offspring deliverer (3:19).[12]

The Mosaic law demanded perfect obedience to *all* of its commands in order to enjoy righteousness, life, and blessing (Deut. 4:1; 6:25; 8:1; 28:1–2). That same law promised curses and death to all who disobeyed (27:26; 28:15). Because of these realities, the nation as a whole and its individual members should have recognized their deep neediness and that their only hope was God's reconciling them to himself through substitutionary atonement, which could be secured only through realizing their guilt and confessing their sin (e.g., Lev. 5:5–6; Num. 5:6–7).[13] If they were to enjoy any blessing, it would be solely because of God's grace and not because they earned it. It would be because the Lord's past pardoning of them would produce for them power to obey and purchase promises that would motivate.

The Mosaic Covenant Anticipates the New Covenant

Moses not only was convinced of the death-dealing nature of the covenant he mediated, but he also anticipated that after exile Yahweh would mercifully restore and transform his people. He would change hearts, enable love and obedience, defeat enemies, and secure life for the remnant (Deut. 4:30–31; 30:1–14). In this day of healing, all of Moses's teaching in Deuteronomy would still serve as a guide (30:8), but a prophet like Moses would supersede Moses's own role as covenant mediator (18:15, 18; cf. 1 Tim. 2:5; Heb. 9:15; 12:24). This prophet like Moses would also know Yahweh face-to-face and perform great signs and wonders (Deut. 34:10–12).

Davidic Covenant

In the midst of the Mosaic covenant era after Israel settled into the Promised Land, Yahweh built upon his promise of a coming royal Savior by

---

11. See Question 34.
12. See Jason S. DeRouchie, "From Condemnation to Righteousness: A Christian Reading of Deuteronomy," *SBJT* 18, no. 3 (Fall 2014): 87–118.
13. For more on the realization of guilt, see Leviticus 4:13, 22, 27; 5:2–5 for the sin offering and Leviticus 5:17; 6:4–5; and Numbers 5:7 for the guilt offering. For more on the confessions of sins, see Leviticus 5:5 for the sin offering; 16:21 for the scapegoat; 26:40 for covenant curses; and Numbers 5:6 for the guilt offering.

pledging to David an eternal kingdom (2 Sam. 7:8–16; 1 Chron. 17:7–14). While the narrative accounts do not call the event a "covenant," both David and others identify it that way (2 Sam. 23:5; Pss. 89:3, 28, 34, 39[4, 29, 35, 40]; 132:12). Scripture had already progressively revealed that God committed to raise up an offspring to deliver the world. This one would overcome the curse and come from the first woman (Gen. 3:15) and from the lines of Shem (9:26–27), Abraham (17:6, 16; 22:17–18), Isaac (17:19; 21:12), Jacob (35:11; Num. 24:17–19), and Judah (Gen. 49:8–10). God's covenant with David also revealed that this Savior would come from his royal line.

God echoed the Abrahamic covenant when he described what he had already done for David (2 Sam. 7:8–9) and promised what he would do for him in his lifetime (7:9–11a; cf. Ps. 89:21–23, 27[22–24, 28]). Yahweh then vowed that after the king's death he would build David a "house/dynasty" (2 Sam. 7:11–16): (1) David's own biological offspring would build a "house" for God's name, enjoy a lasting kingdom, and be counted as God's royal son (7:12–15), and (2) David's house, kingdom, and throne would remain steadfast and established forever (7:16). Because the text explicitly mentions the royal son's potential for sin (7:14) and because Solomon was convinced that his temple building stood in accord with God's promise that David's son would build Yahweh a "house" (1 Kings 8:18–20), Solomon initially fulfilled God's promise of a royal son. Nevertheless, Yahweh also promised a steadfast and established throne forever (2 Sam. 7:13, 16), and this could be fulfilled only through a sustained succession of Davidic kings in perpetuity or through a single monarch whose life and reign would never end.[14] The rest of Scripture teaches that God intended to raise up one king who would reign forever.

God's earliest promises focus primarily on a ruler through whom blessing would come to the world (Gen. 3:15; 22:17–18; cf. 49:8–10; Num. 24:7–9, 17–19; 1 Sam. 2:10, 35). The latter prophets then hoped for a coming monarch through whom God would reconcile many to himself (Isa. 9:7; 11:1–5; Jer. 23:5; Ezek. 37:24). The royal psalms also foreshadow the Davidic royal deliver, who will be Yahweh's "begotten son" (Pss. 2:7; 89:27[28]). He will receive Yahweh's everlasting blessing (21:6[7]; 45:2[3]; cf. 72:17), fulfill the Davidic covenant promises (89:28–37[29–38]; 132:11–12, 17–18), and be the heir of both the nations (2:8) and the Melchizedekian priesthood (110:1–4).[15]

---

14. Cf. Gentry and Wellum, *Kingdom through Covenant*, 479.
15. For more on the way the royal psalms portray the Messiah, see DeRouchie, *Understand and Apply the Old Testament*, 64–65; cf. J. Alec Motyer, *Look to the Rock: An Old Testament Background to Our Understanding of Christ* (Downers Grove, IL: InterVarsity, 1996), 23–38.

Peter identifies the Christ as the descendant whom God promised to sit on David's throne (Acts 2:30–31). The author of Hebrews views Jesus as fulfilling the promise, "I will be to him a father, and he shall be to me a son" (Heb. 1:5). And the rest of the NT stresses that Jesus's already-and-not-yet end-time reign realizes all Davidic kingdom hopes (Matt. 1:1; Luke 1:68–75; Rom. 1:1–4; Rev. 22:16).

New Covenant
The new covenant between God and his church in Christ realizes the hopes of all the previous ways God related to humans in Scripture. The OT promises the new covenant, and the NT fulfills it in bright, living color.

The Old Testament Terminology Associated with the New Covenant
From one perspective, the end-time relationship between Yahweh and his multi-ethnic, reconciled people in Christ includes Yahweh's *affirming* his original covenant promises to the patriarchs (i.e., "to establish a covenant"; Ezek. 16:60, 62, with Lev. 26:42). But in contrast to the temporary Mosaic covenant or to the wrath God had toward his people under this era, what Christ mediates is a *new, freshly initiated* covenant ("to cut a covenant"; Jer. 31:31; 32:40; Ezek. 34:25; 37:26).

In the OT, the adjective "new" describes "covenant" only in Jeremiah 31:31, which recounts the end-time relationship between God and humanity that Jesus inaugurates through his death and resurrection (Luke 22:20; 1 Cor. 11:25; Heb. 9:15). The newness of this covenant contrasts with the old Mosaic covenant—"the covenant that I made with their fathers on the day when I took them by the hand to bring them out of the land of Egypt, my covenant that they broke, though I was their husband" (Jer. 31:32). Paul distinguishes the "new covenant," for which he is a minister and which bore a "ministry of righteousness," from the "old covenant," which bore a "ministry of death" and a "ministry of condemnation" (2 Cor. 3:6–7, 9, 14). In relation to the outworkings of the Abrahamic covenant promises, the author of Hebrews notes that the Mosaic covenant was the "first covenant" and that the "new covenant" was the "second"; because of Christ, the "new" is "better" than the "old," which is now becoming "obsolete and growing old" (Heb. 8:6–8, 13).

The Way the Old Testament Depicts the New Covenant Community
The prophets teach that this transformed "Israel" of God would bear a multi-ethnic makeup that would fulfill the Lord's promise to bless the world through Abraham (Isa. 54:1–3; Jer. 4:1–2; Ezek. 16:60).[16] Specifically, some

---

16. See Question 24. See also Jason S. DeRouchie, "Counting Stars with Abraham and the Prophets: New Covenant Ecclesiology in OT Perspective," *JETS* 58, no. 3 (2015): 445–85;

from the nations will enjoy Yahweh's presence with ethnic Israelites in the new Jerusalem (Jer. 3:16–18; cf. Isa. 2:2–4; 4:2–6; Zech. 2:11; 8:22–23), all as a result of a new exodus led by the messianic, royal servant (Isa. 11:10–12; Hos. 3:5).[17] Sin once characterized the hearts of foreigners (Jer. 3:17) and Judeans alike (4:4; 9:26; 17:1), but now everyone in the new covenant will gain new, united, law-filled hearts (3:17; 31:33; 32:39; cf. Ezek. 11:19–20; 36:26–27). God will restore his relationship with them (Jer. 31:33). Every member of the covenant community will know, fear, and obey God because every member—from the least to the greatest—will experience blood-bought forgiveness (31:33–34; 32:39–40; cf. Isa. 43:25; 44:22; Ezek. 36:25–26, 33; Matt. 26:28). They will all be "the offspring of Israel" (Isa. 45:25; cf. 59:21) because they will be identified through adoption with Israel-the-person (Isa. 49:3; cf. 53:10), who will represent Israel as Yahweh's Spirit-filled deliverer and save some from both Israel-the-people and the other nations (11:1–2, 10; 42:1, 4, 6; 49:6).

The New Testament Witnesses How the New Covenant Is Realized

The NT identifies that Jesus's life, death, and resurrection inaugurates the new covenant and God's end-time reign that the OT anticipates (Matt. 26:28–29; cf. Mark 14:24–25; Luke 22:20).[18] The author of Hebrews writes, "Christ has obtained a ministry that is as much more excellent than the old as the covenant he mediates is better, since it is enacted on better promises" (8:6). Indeed, "in speaking of a new covenant, [God] makes the first one obsolete. And what is becoming obsolete and growing old is ready to vanish away" (8:13; cf. John 1:16–17; 2 Cor. 3:9–10).

The contrast of the old and new covenants parallels a number of other end-time old and new contrasts in the NT—for example, old wine in old wineskins versus new wine in fresh wineskins (Matt. 9:17; Mark 2:22; Luke 5:37–38), the old self versus the new self (Rom. 6:6; Col. 3:9–10; Eph. 4:22–24), oldness of the letter versus newness of the Spirit (Rom. 7:6; cf. 2:29; 2 Cor. 3:6), old leaven versus new leaven (1 Cor. 5:7–8), and old creation versus new creation (2 Cor. 5:17; Gal. 6:15). Furthermore, Paul highlights a series of theological contrasts that often parallel the old and new covenant distinction: law versus faith (Rom. 3:20, 28; 4:13–14; 9:30–10:8; Gal. 2:16–21; 3:1–14; Phil. 3:9), first Adam versus last Adam (Rom. 5:14, 18–19; 1 Cor. 15:22, 45), sin versus righteousness (Rom. 5:21; 6:20; 8:10), flesh versus Spirit (Rom. 8:4–13; Gal. 3:3; 4:29; 5:16–25; 6:8), letter versus Spirit (Rom. 2:29; 7:6; 2 Cor. 3:3, 6),

---

Jason S. DeRouchie, "Father of a Multitude of Nations: New Covenant Ecclesiology in Old Testament Perspective," in *Progressive Covenantalism: Charting a Course between Dispensational and Covenant Theologies*, eds. Stephen J. Wellum and Brent E. Parker (Nashville: B&H, 2016), 7–38.

17. Cf. 1 Cor. 3:16; 2 Cor. 6:16; Eph. 2:19–22; 1 Peter 2:4–5, 9; Rev. 5:9–10.

18. See Jason C. Meyer, *The End of the Law: Mosaic Covenant in Pauline Theology*, NAC Studies in Bible and Theology 7 (Nashville: B&H, 2009).

and slavery versus freedom (Gal. 4:21–5:1). All of these highlight two different ages and place Jesus's person and work as the decisive turning point in salvation history. In Christ, God fulfills what he promised. Christ realizes what the OT anticipates.

Jesus is a better covenant mediator than Moses (Heb. 8:6; 9:15; 12:24; cf. Deut. 18:15–16) because he offers a superior sacrifice (Heb. 9:6–10:18) that brings better results, better provision, and better promises. Through Jesus's perfect covenant-keeping unto death (Rom. 5:19, 2 Cor. 5:21; Phil. 2:8), he satisfies God's wrath against his elect (Rom. 5:9; 8:1; Gal. 3:13; Col. 3:14; Heb. 9:26) and secures for them eternal redemption, peace with God, righteousness, sanctification, and glorification (Rom. 5:1; 8:4, 30; Heb. 7:27; 9:12; 10:10, 14).

Summary
The historical covenants between God and his people progress in a way that holds together the Bible's storyline. Jesus fulfills each covenant. The Adamic-Noahic covenant with all creation results in the global problem of sin, curse, and alienation from God, but it also supplies the context of common grace through which saving grace could operate. The Abrahamic covenant clarifies how God will overcome curse with blessing, and it is worked out in two stages. The Mosaic covenant fulfills stage one of the Abrahamic covenant: the single nation, Israel, occupies the Promised Land. But their own spiritual stubbornness leads them to fail in their calling to mediate Yahweh's presence and display his holiness to the world by radically loving God and their neighbor. In the midst of Israel's rebellion, God reaffirms his commitment to create a multi-ethnic people for himself, and through the Davidic covenant he clarifies more specifically the royal line through which the messianic deliverer would rise. The new covenant fulfills stage two of the Abrahamic covenant, as the life, death, and resurrection of the Davidic descendant Christ Jesus secures blessing for all among the nations who by faith surrender to him—both Jews and Gentiles. Thus, through Jesus, Abraham becomes the father of a multitude of nations, and God overcomes the global curse stemming from the first man Adam through the perfect obedience of the last Adam, Christ.

REFLECTION QUESTIONS

1. What is the biblical meaning of the term "covenant"?

2. What are the five primary biblical covenants between God and people, and what are some ways that Jesus fulfills each one?

3. What is the function of the Adamic-Noahic covenant within salvation history?

4. What is the function of the Abrahamic covenant within salvation history, and how is this covenant worked out in two stages?

5. What is "new" about the new covenant, and how does the new covenant contrast with the "old" Mosaic covenant?

What Is a Biblical Theology of the Serpent?[1]

Andrew David Naselli

A pithy way to summarize the Bible's storyline is "Kill the dragon, get the girl!"[2] The storyline features three main characters:

1. The serpent (the villain—Satan)

2. The damsel in distress (the people of God)

3. The Serpent Slayer (the protagonist and hero—Jesus)

The serpent attempts to deceive and devour the young unmarried woman, but the Serpent Slayer crushes the serpent.

"Serpent" is an umbrella term that includes both snakes and dragons. Snakes and dragons are types of serpents. A serpent has two major strategies: *deceive* and *devour*. As a general rule, the form a serpent takes depends on its strategy. When a serpent attempts to deceive, it's a snake. When a serpent

---

1. See also Andrew David Naselli, *The Serpent and the Serpent Slayer*, Short Studies in Biblical Theology (Wheaton, IL: Crossway, 2020).

2. Joe Rigney coined that phrase (see Question 15). "Kill the Dragon, get the girl!" is not a misogynist saying or a cavalier cowboy phrase. It colorfully reflects classical literature like "Saint George and the Dragon" and the Bible itself. Jesus decisively defeated the Dragon, and he will conquer the Dragon and save his bride: "Husbands, love your wives, as Christ loved the church and gave himself up for her" (Eph. 5:25); "Come, I will show you the Bride, the wife of the Lamb" (Rev. 21:9). The metaphor doesn't communicate every nuance (e.g., God helps his people fight the Serpent), but it communicates a prominent biblical theme in a pithy way.

attempts to devour, it's a dragon. Snakes deceive; dragons devour. Snakes tempt and lie; dragons attack and murder. Snakes backstab; dragons assault.

Here's how the greatest story unfolds:

- The story begins with bliss. The damsel (i.e., initially Adam and Eve) enjoys a beautiful garden in a pristine world.

- But the serpent employs the first strategy: the snake deceives Eve.

- As the story develops, the serpent craftily alternates between deceiving and devouring.

- At the climax of the story, the dragon attempts to devour Jesus, but instead it merely bruises Jesus's heel while Jesus bruises the serpent's head.

- For the rest of the story (which is where we are living now), the dragon furiously attempts to devour the damsel.

- Jesus's mission: kill the dragon, get the girl.

We can trace that story under three headings: (1) the deceitful snake in Genesis 3; (2) snakes and dragons between the Bible's bookends; and (3) the devouring dragon in Revelation 12 and 20.

The Deceitful Snake in Genesis 3

The greatest story begins with God's creating the heavens and the earth as good. But a deceptive snake enters the garden. Ten observations about that snake are noteworthy:

1. The snake is deceitful. "The serpent was more crafty than any other beast of the field that the Lord God had made" (Gen. 3:1). In English, *crafty* means cunning or deceitful, but the Hebrew word is neutral. In Genesis, the word is initially ambiguous, but when you reread this story in light of the Bible's entire storyline, *crafty* is shown to be an excellent translation.

2. The snake is a beast that God created (Gen. 3:1). The snake is not the opposite of God. God does not have an archenemy who is independent and rivals his power.

3. The snake deceives by questioning God (Gen. 3:1–3), contradicting God (3:4–5), and tempting with worldliness (3:4–6; cf. Luke 4:1–13; 1 John 2:16).

4. The snake deceives Eve to rebel against God, and Adam follows Eve (Gen. 3:6, 13; cf. 2 Cor. 11:3; 1 Tim. 2:14). God commissioned his image-bearers to rule over the beasts of the field (Gen. 1:26–27), but instead his image-bearers committed treachery. Instead of obeying the King, they follow the snake. Eve was not alone. Adam "was with her" (3:6). So when Adam ate, he rebelled against God. He failed to lead and protect his wife. He should have killed the serpent.

5. As a result of the snake's deceit, Adam's and Eve's sins separate them from God (Gen. 3:7–13).

6. As a result of the snake's deceit, God curses the snake and promises a snake crusher (Gen. 3:14–15). God cursed not only the snake but also the snake's offspring—with "enmity" (3:15). The rest of the Bible's storyline traces the ongoing battle between the snake's offspring and the woman's offspring. The first seed of the serpent is Cain, who kills his brother Abel (4:1–16). Humans are either children of God or children of the devil (Matt. 13:38–39; John 8:33, 44; Acts 13:10; 1 John 3:8–10).

Instead of continuing through Abel, the seed of the woman continues through Seth (Gen. 4:25). That line continues through Noah (6:9) and then through Abraham, Isaac, Jacob, and Judah (chs. 11–50) and eventually through David all the way to Jesus the Messiah and his followers. The woman's offspring can refer to a group of people (the people of God collectively—cf. Rom. 16:20) and to a particular person (the Messiah—cf. Gal. 3:16). Although the snake will bruise the Messiah's heel (Jesus dies on a tree), Jesus is the ultimate seed of the woman who will mortally crush the snake (cf. Gal. 3:16; Heb. 2:14–15; 1 John 3:8).

7. As a result of the snake's deceit, God punishes Eve and Adam (Gen. 3:16–19).

8. As a result of the snake's deceit, God clothes Adam and Eve with garments of skin (Gen. 3:7, 9–11, 21).

9. As a result of the snake's deceit, God banishes Adam and Eve from the garden of Eden (Gen. 3:22–24).

10. The snake is Satan. Genesis 3 does not explicitly identify the snake as Satan, but when we read Genesis 3 in light of the whole Bible, we must identify the snake as Satan (cf. Rom. 16:19–20; 2 Cor. 11:3; Rev. 12:3, 9, 10, 12; 20:2).

Snakes and Dragons between the Bible's Bookends

Serpents occasionally symbolize good (e.g., Matt. 10:16), but they usually symbolize evil. Starting with Genesis 3, the Bible connects the serpent to sin and the curse. More specifically, serpents symbolize God's enemies—Satan and his offspring.

> 1. Satan is the ultimate serpent. He tempts God's people, but Jesus helps his people when Satan tempts them. God is sovereign over Leviathan (see Job 41), and God will slay the dragon (Isa. 27:1). Consequently, serpents will no longer be deadly (Isa. 11:6–9; 65:17, 25).

> 2. Egypt and its Pharaoh are a dragon in the seas (Ezek. 32:2). Egypt is a snake, a Leviathan, a sea monster. The dragon murders babies (Exod. 1:8–22), and in the exodus God delivers his people from the Egyptian serpent. Later when God's people complain about missing Egypt, God sends poisonous snakes among them and provides a curse-bearing bronze snake (Num. 21:4–9). God describes Egypt as a toothless dragon (Isa. 30:1–3, 6–7) whom he will judge (Jer. 46:22; Ezek. 29:3–9; 32:2–9).

> 3. Wicked leaders in Canaan and Moab are serpent heads to crush. Jael drives a peg into Sisera's temple (Judges 4:17–24; 5:24–27). A woman crushes Abimelech's skull (Judges 9:52–57). Saul crushes Nahash the snake (1 Sam. 11:1–2, 5–11). And David crushes Goliath the giant dragon (1 Sam. 17:1–11, 41–54).

> 4. The king of Babylon is a sea monster (Jer. 8:16–17; 51:34–35).

> 5. King Herod is a murderous dragon (Matt. 2:13–18; cf. Exod. 1:8–22).

> 6. Pharisees and Sadducees are a hypocritical brood of vipers (Matt. 3:7–12; 12:33–37; 23:29–36). They are like their spiritual daddy—the serpent (cf. John 8:44). What they teach is poisonous, and God will condemn them.

> 7. False teachers are intruding snakes (esp. Rom. 16:17–20; 2 Cor. 11:2–4, 13–15).

The Devouring Dragon in Revelation 12 and 20

The story culminates in Revelation 12 and 20. Thirteen observations about the dragon are noteworthy:

1. The dragon is the ancient serpent (Rev. 12:9–17; 20:2). Six labels apply to the same evil person: (1) the dragon, (2) the ancient serpent—alluding to Genesis 3; (3) the devil—that is, the slanderer; (4) Satan—that is, the adversary; (5) the deceiver; and (6) the accuser of our brothers.

2. The dragon is a murderer (Rev. 12:3). The dragon is red, which symbolizes blood to connote that the dragon is a murderer.

3. The dragon is powerful (Rev. 12:3). The dragon has great power and ruling authority that extends over the entire earth (12:9).

4. The dragon plans to devour the Messiah (Rev. 12:1–4; cf. Ps. 2:9; Rev. 2:27; 19:15).

5. The dragon fails to devour the Messiah (Rev. 12:4).

6. The dragon and his angels get thrown down to earth (Rev. 12:7–10). Satan used to have access to God in the midst of other angels to accuse God's people (see Job 1–2), but now Satan can no longer do that. God's angels threw Satan and his demons down to earth when Jesus decisively defeated Satan at the cross (John 12:31; Col. 2:15).

7. The dragon is conquered on the basis of the blood of the Lamb and the word of their testimony (Rev. 12:11–12). God's people participate in crushing the dragon based on Jesus the Messiah's being crushed for their sins (cf. Isa. 53:5, 10; Acts 2:23–24; 4:27–28).

8. The dragon furiously persecutes God's people (Rev. 12:1–2, 6, 12–17). We interpret the woman to symbolize the people of God and the 1,260 days to symbolize a period of intense suffering for God's people before God delivers them. The dragon is raging because he knows he doesn't have long (12:12). He knows that Christ has decisively defeated him, so he is taking out his rage on Christ's church by attempting to deceive them (with lies and false teaching) and to devour them (with persecution).

9. The dragon cannot destroy God's people (Rev. 12:6, 14–16). We interpret the wilderness to symbolize a place where God tests, protects, and miraculously nourishes his people.

10. The dragon empowers the beast (Rev. 13:1–4). The dragon forms a counterfeit trinity to rival the real Trinity (see 16:13; 20:10): (1) the

dragon—that is, Satan; (2) the first beast, which rises out of the sea (13:1–4); and (3) the second beast, which rises out of the earth—the false prophet (13:11–18).

11. The dragon is bound for a thousand years (Rev. 20:1–6). Jesus is coming back to slay the dragon and save his bride! God is more powerful than the dragon. The dragon cannot bind God, but God can send one of his angels to bind the dragon.

12. The dragon attempts to deceive the nations (Rev. 12:7–9; 20:2–3, 7–10).

13. The dragon is tormented forever in the lake of fire and sulfur (Rev. 20:9–10). Never again will the dragon, that ancient serpent, accuse or deceive or persecute God's people. The dragon will consciously experience fiery torment forever. God wins!

Summary

The story of the Bible begins with bliss. Adam and Eve enjoy a beautiful garden in a pristine world. But the snake deceives Eve, and Adam follows Eve instead of killing the snake.

As the story develops, the serpent craftily alternates between deceiving and devouring. The serpent is the ultimate snake and dragon, and he empowers his offspring. Those little snakes and dragons include Egypt and its Pharaoh, wicked leaders in Canaan and Moab, the king of Babylon, King Herod, Pharisees and Sadducees, and false teachers.

At the climax of the story, the dragon attempts to devour Jesus, but instead it merely bruises Jesus's heel while Jesus crushes the serpent's head. For the rest of the story (including our part in the story right now), the dragon furiously attempts to devour Jesus's bride and offspring. But the dragon will not succeed because Jesus will accomplish his mission to kill the dragon and get the girl.

REFLECTION QUESTIONS

1. Why do you think it is that we typically love a good dragon-slaying story (e.g., Saint George and the dragon or Tolkien's *The Hobbit*)?

2. On what basis can we be sure that the snake in Genesis 3 and the dragon in Revelation 12 refer to the same evil person?

3. How does Genesis 3:15 help us understand the Bible's storyline?

4. How should we think about the serpent now?

5. How should we think about Jesus in light of the "Kill the dragon, get the girl" storyline?

What Is a Biblical Theology of the People of God?

Jason S. DeRouchie

The people of God are humans who are related to the Lord through covenant, who identify him as King, and whom God uniquely grants the opportunity to display his greatness by embracing his claim on their lives. Genesis to Revelation testifies that God is committed to shape a global people for himself under his rule.

God Commissions Humanity, Promises a Deliverer, and Distinguishes Remnant and Rebel

The first couple was the prototypical "people," whom God called to represent, reflect, and resemble him as their sovereign Creator and to image his glory to the ends of the earth (Gen. 1:28; cf. Num. 14:21; Ps. 72:19; Isa. 11:9; Hab. 2:14). They served as *royal* sons because God charged them to jointly "subdue" and "have dominion" over the earth (Gen. 1:28). They served in a *priestly* role because God charged them to "work" and "keep/guard" his land (2:15, 18; cf. e.g., 3:23–24; Num. 3:4, 7–8).[1] But rather than operating as God's royal priests, they rebelled (Gen. 3:1–13). Before declaring how he would punish them, Yahweh God promised that a deliverer would one day overcome the evil one as the divine image-bearer and king-priest (3:15). He alone would reverse the curse, so humanity's hope now rested on him.

The exile from the garden of Eden resulted in two opposing lines of descent that Genesis highlights in linear genealogies (5:1–32; 11:10–26) and

---

1. Outside of Gen. 2:15 and 3:23–24, the only other places where the Hebrew verbs *'bd* ("serve/minister") and šmr ("guard") occur together are in association with the ministry of the Levites at the central sanctuary (cf. Num. 8:26; 18:5–6; 1 Chron. 23:32; Ezek. 44:14).

segmented genealogies (10:1–32; 25:12–18; 36:1–43).[2] The first line was a remnant who enjoyed God's grace (6:8), called on his name (4:26; cf. 13:4), walked with him (5:22, 24; 6:9), and hoped in his promised deliverer (5:29; cf. 9:26–27; 15:6). The other line features rebels who are against God and his ways but who stand as the long-range target of his blessing (12:3).[3]

God Commissions Abraham and Promises an Offspring That Will Bless All Nations

Into this cursed world, God uses the linear genealogy that runs from Seth to Terah in Genesis 11:10–26 to raise up Abra(ha)m. Though this man's wife was barren (Gen. 11:30), Yahweh calls him to "go" to a promised land so that the Lord may in turn make him into a great nation (12:1–2; cf. 18:18; 35:11; 46:3). From his own loins, Abraham would have an "offspring" who would ultimately become as numerous as the dust of the earth (13:16; 28:14), the stars of the sky (15:5; 22:17; 26:4), and the sand on the seashore (22:17; 32:12[13]).

While at one level this offspring would be a nation inhabiting the Promised Land (17:7; 35:12), the offspring would also be a single representative, perfectly obedient, warrior king who would rise from the tribe of Judah (18:19; 49:8–10; cf. 3:15; Num. 24:17–18). His kingdom would grow as he would possess enemy gates (Gen. 22:17; 24:60), and only in his day would Abraham move from being a father of a single nation to a father of a multitude of nations, with God's blessing working through him to reach all nations (22:17–18; cf. 26:4; 28:14).

God Commissions Israel and Points to the Nation's Royal Representative

Yahweh reiterated the Abrahamic promises of seed, land, and blessing to the patriarch's son Isaac and then again to his grandson Jacob, whose own sons became the twelve tribes of Israel. It was this group whom God first designated "my people" (Exod. 3:7, 10; 5:1; etc.): "I will take you to be my people, and I will be your God, and you shall know that I am the LORD your God, who has brought you out from under the burdens of the Egyptians" (6:7; cf. Lev. 26:12).[4]

Yahweh was Israel's royal "father" (Deut. 32:6)[5] or "king" (Exod. 15:18; Num. 23:21; Deut. 33:5),[6] and he designated his "people" as his communal

---

2. Linear genealogies follow the pattern, "A gave birth to B and others; B gave birth to C and others," etc. Segmented genealogies are shaped as "A gave birth to B, C, and D; B gave birth to . . . ; C gave birth to . . . ; D gave birth to . . . ."
3. See Jason S. DeRouchie, "The Blessing-Commission, the Promised Offspring, and the *Toledot* Structure of Genesis," *JETS* 56, no. 2 (2013): 237–42.
4. Cf. Jer. 7:23; 11:4; 24:7; 30:22; 31:33; 32:38; Ezek. 11:20; 14:11; 34:30; 36:28; 37:23, 27; Zech. 8:8; 2 Cor. 6:16; Heb. 8:10.
5. Cf. Isa. 63:16; 64:8; Jer. 3:4, 19; Mal. 1:6.
6. Cf. 1 Chron. 16:31; Pss. 29:10; 47:2, 6–8[3, 7–9]; 48:2[3]; 74:12; 93:1–2; 95:3; 96:10; 97:1; 99:1; Isa. 43:15; 52:7; Jer. 10:7; Zech. 14:16; Mal. 1:14; Matt. 5:35.

"firstborn son" (Exod. 4:22–23; cf. Deut. 1:31; 8:5; 14:1).[7] Once Israel arrived at Mount Sinai, Yahweh formalized his covenant with them. If they would but surrender to his precepts and live as his treasured possession, they would serve as "a kingdom of priests and a holy nation" (Exod. 19:5–6). God originally called humans to serve as royal and priestly sons (compare Gen. 5:1–3 with 1:26–28 and 2:15), and here God calls Israel as a nation to mediate and display his greatness to the world. By Israel's living completely for God's glory through lives of dependence, the nations would take notice (Deut. 4:5–8), God would exalt Israel (28:1), and Yahweh would be magnified on a global scale (26:19).

Significantly, Moses, the prophetic covenant mediator, knew that Israel would not fulfill what God called them to do. During his forty-year tenure as their leader, Moses noted that both the exodus generation and the one following it were "stubborn" (Exod. 32:9; 33:3, 5; 34:9; Deut. 9:6, 13; 10:16; 31:27), "unbelieving" (Num. 14:11; Deut. 1:32; 9:23; cf. 28:66), and "rebellious" (Num. 20:10, 24; 27:14; Deut. 9:7, 24; 31:27; cf. 1:26, 43; 9:23). Thus, he stressed, "The LORD has not given you a heart to understand or eyes to see or ears to hear" (Deut. 29:4[3]), and "I know that after my death you will surely act corruptly and turn aside from the way that I have commanded you" (31:29).

Nevertheless, in words reminiscent of God's promises to Abraham in Genesis 12:3, Moses also recalled Balaam's oracle that, just as Yahweh the king led Israel in the first exodus (Num. 23:21–22), so too would he raise up an earthly, exalted king who would lead his people in a second exodus and overcome all enemy hostility (24:7–8). God would bless those who bless this king, and God would curse those who curse this king (24:9). This royal figure would be like a star rising out of Israel in the latter days, and he would rule over nations (24:14, 17–19). Thus, a remnant would survive the dissolved Mosaic covenant. God would restore them to the land and alter their hearts, and they would heed his voice (Deut. 30:1–14), as God would speak through his new prophetic covenant mediator (18:15–18; cf. 34:10–12).

The Servant-People Rebel, but God Promises a Servant-Person Who Will Save and Have Offspring

Israel's history in the land went just as Moses foresaw. "The people served the LORD all the days of Joshua, and all the days of the elders who outlived Joshua," but then "there arose another generation after them who did not know the LORD or the work that he had done for Israel" (Judg. 2:7, 10). In asking for "a king to judge [them] like all the nations" (1 Sam. 8:5), they were doing nothing less than rejecting their royal father, God himself (8:7). And throughout the united and divided monarchies, the people progressively turned from Yahweh by despising his covenant and failing to heed

---

7. Cf. Ps. 103:13; Prov. 3:12; Jer. 31:9, 20; Hos. 11:1.

his prophets (2 Kings 17:7, 13–15). Therefore, the Lord declared, "My people are destroyed for lack of knowledge; because you have rejected knowledge, I reject you from being a priest to me. And since you have forgotten the law of your God, I also will forget your children" (Hos. 4:6).

In the midst of such darkness, Yahweh remained committed to shape a global people under his rule. Just as he called David to "be shepherd of my people Israel" (2 Sam. 5:2), so he promised him,

> I will raise up your offspring after you, who shall come from your body, and I will establish his kingdom. He shall build a house for my name, and I will establish the throne of his kingdom forever. I will be to him a father, and he shall be to me a son. . . . And your house and your kingdom shall be made sure forever before me. Your throne shall be established forever. (2 Sam. 7:12–14, 16)

The Lord predicts a reigning son of God who would have a kingdom and lasting dynasty (cf. Ps. 2:7–8; Acts 13:33; Heb. 1:5; 5:5). This son fulfills what God promised: a curse-overcoming royal deliverer—the offspring of the woman (Gen. 3:15) and the offspring of Abraham through whom he would bless the world (22:17–18; cf. 49:8–10; Num. 24:17–19).

The prophets after David developed this hope of a reigning Davidic "son" of God whose kingdom would span the nations. In this king's day (Hos. 3:5), those whom the Lord once declared "Not My People" will now be called "Children of the living God" and "You are my people" (Hos. 1:9–10; 2:1; cf. Rom. 9:25–26; 1 Peter 2:10).

Of all the prophets, Isaiah does the most to clarify the multiethnic, trans-formed makeup of the future people of God and does so by contrasting them with old covenant Israel and closely associating them with a child-king he tags "my servant." On the one hand, speaking of Isaiah's contemporaries, Yahweh asserted, "Children have I reared and brought up, but they have re-belled against me" (Isa. 1:2; cf. 30:9). In contrast to this servant-*people*, God promised to raise up a royal servant-*person* who would operate as the "arm of Yahweh" to bring salvation to the world (59:16–17; cf. 53:1–2).

This servant-king's identity would be closely tied to God's (7:14; 9:6), and he would reign eternally on David's throne with universal authority (9:6–7; 11:1, 10; 55:3–4). Yahweh's Spirit would empower him (11:2; 42:1; 61:1), and he would rule from God's holy mountain, work justice and peace, and draw nations to himself (11:1–10; cf. 2:2–4) by leading a second exodus (11:11–12:6; 52:11–12). This royal servant-person would be named "Israel," thus identi-fying his representative role over his people (49:3). His mission would include not only reconciling to God some from the people of Israel but also saving some from all the nations of the earth (49:6). He would serve as both a cov-enant for the people and a light for the nations (42:6; 49:6, 8), and he would render justice to the oppressed (42:4; cf. 9:7; 11:4) and instruct the coastlands (42:4; 50:4, 10; cf. 2:3; 54:13). He would give sight to the blind (42:7; cf. 42:16), free the captives (42:7; 49:9; 61:1; cf. 49:25–26), sustain the weary (49:10; 50:4), heal the broken (61:1; cf. 42:3), and proclaim good news of peace, happiness, and salvation to the longing (52:7; 61:1). He would be God's righteous one (50:8; 53:11; cf. Jer. 23:6; 1 John 2:1), and his path to triumph (Isa. 52:13) and to proclaiming the good news of Yahweh's reign (52:7) would be through great tribulation. He would offer himself as a substitutionary sacrifice for the many, bearing the iniquities of many nations and counting righteous many peoples (52:14; 53:11; cf. Rom. 5:19; 2 Cor. 5:21). Knowing that he would see these "offspring" following his death (Isa. 53:10–11; cf. Heb. 12:2) would motivate him to bear God's curse on behalf of the many and thus secure their salvation (cf. Gal. 3:13–14). Thus, "In the LORD all the offspring of Israel [i.e., the servant-person] shall be justified and shall glory" (Isa. 45:25; cf. 59:21). That the servant-person would have "offspring" is significant, seeing as Jesus never married and never had biological children. Hence, the "offspring" in view must be a spiritual progeny with no necessary ties to biology (cf. 1 Cor. 4:15; Gal. 4:18–19).[8]

The servant-person "Israel" would represent Yahweh and serve as the groom who would deliver his bride-city Jerusalem. He would redeem her with an everlasting love and establish her with an everlasting covenant (Isa. 54:8, 10; 62:23; 66:7–11; cf. Gal. 4:21–27). As the "servant," he would generate priestly "servants" (Isa. 54:17; cf. 65:13–16; 66:21–22)—some who were once foreigners (56:6) and some from Israel's twelve tribes (63:17). Thus, the servant-person's "offspring will possess the nations and will people desolate cities" (54:3), and they too would be empowered by God's Spirit (44:3; cf. 32:15). Yahweh would teach them (54:13; cf. Jer. 31:34; John 6:44–45), and they would be gathered to dwell forever at the newly created Jerusalem as "the offspring of the blessed of the LORD" (Isa. 65:18, 23; cf. 66:22). In that day, Yahweh will declare, "Blessed be Egypt my people, and Assyria the work of my hands, and Israel my inheritance" (Isa. 19:25). Psalm 87 captures well this imagery when it declares that peoples from Egypt, Babylon, Philistia, Tyre, and Cush will be residents of the new Jerusalem with new birth certificates that declare, "This one was born in her" and "this one was born there" (Ps. 87:4–6; cf. Gal. 4:26–27).

---

8. Jason S. DeRouchie, "Counting Stars with Abraham and the Prophets: New Covenant Ecclesiology in OT Perspective," *JETS* 58, no. 3 (2015): 445–85; Jason S. DeRouchie, "Father of a Multitude of Nations: New Covenant Ecclesiology in Old Testament Perspective," in *Progressive Covenantalism: Charting a Course between Dispensational and Covenant Theologies*, eds. Stephen J. Wellum and Brent E. Parker (Nashville: B&H, 2016), 7–38.

Jesus Christ Is the Offspring of Abraham and Servant-Son of God, and the Church Is His Servant-Offspring

As we enter the NT, Yahweh has punished the old covenant people through exile yet replanted a remnant of them back in the Promised Land. That is the context for the rising of the hoped-for Davidic ruler through whom God would reconcile the elect of the nations to himself. Thus, Matthew cites the prophecy in Micah 5:2: "And you, O Bethlehem, in the land of Judah, are by no means least among the rulers of Judah; for from you shall come a ruler who will shepherd my people Israel'" (Matt. 2:6). By recalling the first exodus of God's corporate "son" from Egypt, Matthew identifies that Joseph and Mary's flight with Jesus from Bethlehem in some way "fulfilled" Hosea's words, "Out of Egypt I have called my son" (2:15; cf. Hos. 11:1).[9] Implicit here is that this child-king divine Son now represents God's people. Those who identify with this Son are the new covenant people of God.

Specifically, this new family would be characterized by following Jesus (Matt. 10:38; 16:24; 19:21), doing his will (12:50), and heeding his teaching (17:5; 28:20; cf. Isa. 42:4; 50:4, 10). Along with claiming Jewish sheep, Jesus would fulfill the OT predictions of shepherding a multiethnic flock: "I have other sheep that are not of this fold. I must bring them also, and they will listen to my voice. So there will be one flock, one shepherd" (John 10:16). "Jesus would die for the nation, but not for the nation only, but also to gather into one the children of God who are scattered abroad" (11:51–52). Jesus called this end-time community of believers "my church" (Matt. 16:18; cf. 18:17), a common title from the OT for the gathered assembly of God's people (e.g., Deut. 4:10; 31:30; Josh. 8:35; Judg. 20:2; 1 Chron. 28:8; 2 Chron. 23:3). Jesus promised to build and protect his "church" (Matt. 16:18; John 10:27–30), and he commissioned his followers to make more disciples of all nations, under his authority and in the power of his presence (Matt. 20:18–20; Acts 1:8).

The book of Acts recalls "how God first visited the Gentiles, to take from them a people for his name" (Acts 15:14), and the Lord designated them along with the other early Christians "my people" (18:10). Both the church's multi-ethnic makeup (Rom. 9:25–26) and temple-identity (2 Cor. 6:16; Eph. 2:19–20) fulfilled explicit OT promises of her existence. When Jesus declared that he was inaugurating the new covenant (Luke 22:20), he was directly fulfilling for his church what Jeremiah predicted: "I will put my laws into their minds, and write them on their hearts, and I will be their God, and they shall be my people" (Heb. 8:10; cf. Jer. 31:33). Jesus reverses Israel's state: "Once you were not a people, but now you are God's people; once you had not received mercy, but now you have received mercy" (1 Peter 2:10; cf. Hos. 1:6, 9, 10, [2:1]; 2:23).

The church refers to those *in Christ*.

---

9. See Question 32.

> Christ redeemed us from the curse of the law by becoming a curse for us . . . so that in Christ Jesus the blessing of Abraham might come to the Gentiles . . . through faith. . . . Now the promises were made to Abraham and to his offspring . . . referring to one . . . who is Christ. . . . There is neither Jew nor Greek, there is neither slave nor free, there is no male and female, for you are all one in Christ Jesus. And if you are Christ's, then you are Abraham's offspring, heirs according to promise. (Gal. 3:13–14, 16, 28–29; cf. Rom. 3:21–24; 4:11)

Similarly, "No one is a Jew who is merely one outwardly, nor is circumcision outward and physical. But a Jew is one inwardly, and circumcision is a matter of the heart, by the Spirit" (Rom. 2:28–29; cf. Deut. 30:6; Ezek. 36:27).[10] And again, "It is not the children of the flesh who are the children of God, but the children of the promised are counted as offspring" (Rom. 9:8). At one time the Gentiles were

> separated from Christ, alienated from the commonwealth of Israel and strangers to the covenants of promise, having no hope and without God in the world. But now in Christ Jesus you who once were far off have been brought near by the blood of Christ. For he himself is our peace, who has made us both one and has broken down in his flesh the dividing wall of hostility by abolishing the law of commandments expressed in ordinances, that he might create in himself one new man in place of the two, so making peace, and might reconcile us both to God in one body through the cross, thereby killing the hostility. (Eph. 2:12–16)

Today the only people of God are those in Christ, and because Jesus represented Israel, even bearing the name (Isa. 49:3), the church is now "the Israel of God" (Gal. 6:16; cf. Matt. 19:28; James 1:1; 1 Peter 1:1).[11] The church does not replace Israel; she becomes Israel through identifying with the ultimate Israelite, Jesus. And every member of the church, whether Jew or Greek, slave or free, male or female, now enjoys oneness in Christ and the full inheritance of all God promised to Abraham (Gal. 3:28–29; cf. Matt. 3:9–10). The makeup of God's people moved from Adam, as God's son and head of all humanity, to Israel, as God's corporate son, to Jesus, as God's Son, who stands as the ultimate human and represents Israel and in whom all identified by faith

---

10. For other instances where ethnic Israelites/Jews are not counted as true Israelites, see 1 Cor. 10:1–5, 18; Phil. 3:2–3; Rev. 2:9; 3:9.
11. See G. K. Beale, "Peace and Mercy upon the Israel of God: The Old Testament Background of Gal. 6,16b," *Bib* 80 (1999): 204–23; G. K. Beale, *A New Testament Biblical Theology: The Unfolding of the Old Testament in the New* (Grand Rapids: Baker Academic, 2011), 722–23.

become God's people. Christ is the "head" (i.e., authority) (Eph. 1:22; 5:23; Col. 2:17–19), and the church is his "body" (Rom. 12:5; 1 Cor. 10:16; 12:27). He is the bridegroom (Mark 2:18–20), and the church, identified with the new Jerusalem, is his bride (Rev. 21:2, 9; 22:17; cf. Gal. 4:26). God's people now are members of his household (Gal. 6:10; Eph. 2:19–20; 1 Tim. 3:15; Heb. 3:6; 1 Peter 2:5; 4:17). Through our relationship with Christ the Son (see Heb. 3:2–6), the Lord of the universe becomes our "father," and we become his "sons and daughters"—his "children" (2 Cor. 6:18; 1 John 3:1; cf. Matt. 6:9; Eph. 3:14).

In the NT, the term "church" usually applies to individual Christian congregations (e.g., Rom. 16:5; 1 Cor. 1:2; 1 Thess. 1:1; 2 Thess. 2:1) or to collections of such congregations in geographical regions (e.g., 1 Cor. 16:1, 19; Gal. 1:2; 1 Thess. 2:14). Sometimes the term applies to all Christians on earth (e.g., 1 Cor. 15:9; Gal. 1:13) or even to all those for whom Christ died throughout all ages—all those whom God "chose in him before the foundation of the world" (Eph. 1:4) and who are now seated with Christ in the heavenly places (2:6; cf. 1:22; 2:6; 3:10; 5:23–27, 29, 32; Col. 1:18; 3:1–2). Thus, "Christ loved the church and gave himself up for her" (Eph. 5:25). Before Christ came, all the true saints were saved on *credit*, with the sure hope that their debt of sin would be paid through his substitutionary, victorious work (cf. Matt. 13:17; Luke 10:24; John 8:56; Heb. 11:13, 39–40). But now that Christ has come, the people of God are saved on *debit*, for Jesus cancelled "the record of debt that stood against us . . . nailing it to the cross" (Col. 2:14).

In the heavenly Jerusalem, in which we have been raised and are now seated with Christ (Eph. 2:6; cf. Col. 3:1), the heavenly beings are singing this song of praise to "the Lion of the tribe of Judah, the Root of David" who has conquered by becoming a sacrificial "Lamb": "Worthy are you . . . for you were slain, and by your blood you ransomed people for God from every tribe and language and people and nation, and you have made them a kingdom of priests to our God, and they shall reign on the earth" (Rev. 5:9–10). In the future day when the great priest-king will eradicate all evil and establish his kingdom on earth, "a great multitude that no one could number, from every nation, from all tribes and peoples and languages, standing before the throne and before the Lamb, clothed in white robes, with palm branches in their hands" will cry out with a loud voice, "Salvation belongs to our God who sits on the throne, and to the Lamb!" (7:9–10). And the multiethnic church—the eternal people of God—will serve God in his temple, be sheltered by his presence, and enjoy every provision, "for the Lamb in the midst of the throne will be their shepherd, and he will guide them to springs of living water, and God will wipe away every tear from their eyes" (7:15–17; cf. Isa. 25:8; Rev. 21:4).

Summary

From creation to consummation God is shaping a global people for himself under his rule. In response to Adam's rebellion, the Lord promised to raise up a deliverer who would overcome the curse with blessing and reconcile a people to himself. Yahweh set apart Abraham and ultimately Israel as the agents through whom this royal-priestly figure would rise. And while God's people Israel rebelled and were punished through exile, the Lord preserved a faithful remnant who hoped in the promise of a coming servant-person named "Israel," who would save many from both Israel and the rest of the nations. The NT highlights that all Jews and Gentiles who by faith unite with Christ make up the church, the lasting people of God, all of whom will fully and eternally inherit what God promised Abraham.

REFLECTION QUESTIONS

1. Who are "the people of God" in Scripture?

2. In what way is the concept of royal and priestly sonship carried on from the role of Adam in the garden of Eden through the identity and calling of Israel to the person and work of Christ and the makeup of his church, culminating in the new Jerusalem?

3. In what ways are the people of God in the Mosaic old covenant similar to and different from the people of God in the new covenant?

4. What difference does Jesus make in the nature or makeup of God's people?

5. If Jesus, who as a man never married or had children, is God's servant-person and named "Israel" (Isa. 49:3), and if he is called to save some from both Israel the people and the rest of the nations (49:6), and if this servant-person has "offspring," all of whom in Yahweh "shall be justified and shall glory" (45:25; cf. 53:10; 59:21), what are the implications for the makeup of God's people today? For help, consider Galatians 3:28–29.

What Is a Biblical Theology of the Law?

Jason S. DeRouchie

Scripture normally uses the term "law" to speak of the body of written commandments in the Mosaic covenant that together call people to love God and neighbor (Matt. 7:12; 22:37–40; Rom. 13:8–10). Hence, Paul asserts, "The law, which came 430 years afterward, does not annul a covenant previously ratified by God, so as to make the promise [made to Abraham] void" (Gal. 3:17). Paul also stressed that he was not "under the law [of Moses]" yet was not "outside the law of God but under the law of Christ" (1 Cor. 9:20–21; cf. Rom. 6:14). What, then, is a biblical theology of the law, and how should Christians relate to the law of Moses?

Antecedents to the Mosaic Law

While God never formalized the Adamic-Noahic and Abrahamic covenants with a written code, he did stipulate in these covenants how to live and relate with him. In the covenant with creation, God charged the human heads to multiply and to rule in ways that would reflect, resemble, and represent him on the earth (Gen. 1:28; 9:1, 7). Humans would image God by serving, guarding, helping, and loving in accordance with their roles (2:15, 18, 23–24). And, after humanity rebelled, they would continue to image him by calling on his name (4:26), walking with him (5:22; 6:9), and dependently trusting in his blood-bought promises (3:21; 8:20) of a royal deliverer (3:15) and of a sustained context from which this person would arise (8:20–22; 9:10–11). They needed to value his image in others (9:5–6) and care more about Yahweh's name than their own (4:26; 11:4).

When Adam disobeyed, God cursed the world and promised death to everyone after him. Thus, "sin indeed was in the world before the law was given" (Rom. 5:12–13; cf. Gen. 2:17). Isaiah notes the terrible results: "The earth lies defiled under its inhabitants; for they have transgressed the laws, violated the statutes, broken the everlasting covenant. Therefore a curse devours the

earth, and its inhabitants suffer for their guilt" (Isa. 24:5–6; cf. Jer. 25:30–38).
Yahweh used a flood to punish in the days of Noah because "the wickedness
of man was great in the earth" (Gen. 6:5), and then the pride of the Tower of
Babel moved the Lord to disperse the rebel families over the globe (11:8–9).

Yahweh commissioned Abram to "go" to the Promised Land and there
to "be a blessing," ultimately so that through him all the cursed families of
the ground could be blessed (12:1–2, DeRouchie's translation). Abram was to
"walk" before the Lord and to "be blameless" in order that God might fulfill
the covenant promises (17:1–2). Indeed, only by commanding "his children
and his household after him to keep the way of the LORD by doing righteousness and justice" would God "bring to Abraham what he [had] promised him"
(18:19). The patriarch believed Yahweh for his offspring promise, and God
counted Abraham's faith as if it were righteousness (15:6). The patriarch's will-
ingness to sacrifice his own son as an act of trusting the Lord's promise grew
out of this faith (22:10–12; cf. 17:19; 21:12). Because Abraham "did" as Yahweh
commanded and "obeyed" his voice, God vowed that he would indeed raise
up the offspring who would restore blessing to the world (22:16–18). In all,
Abraham's fear-filled obedience flowing from faith established him as a model
covenant-keeper for the Israelites. Yahweh identifies this role when he spoke
of the patriarch as if he had kept the law: "Abraham obeyed my voice and kept
my charge, my commandments, my statutes, and my laws" (26:4–5; cf. Deut.
11:1; 26:17; Rom. 4:11, 13; Heb. 11:8, 13).

The Mosaic Law's Ministry of Death

Old Testament Perspectives on the Mosaic Law

Yahweh redeemed Israel from slavery in Egypt, and at Mount Sinai he
entered into a formal covenant relationship with his people that included a
written code.[1] The Lord said, "If you will indeed obey my voice and keep
my covenant, . . . you shall be to me a kingdom of priests and a holy nation"
(Exod. 19:5–6). The Ten Words on the tablets of stone included "the law and
the commandment," which God gave to instruct his people (24:12). He also
gave them numerous other laws, all of which are summarized in the supreme
command: "Hear, O Israel: The LORD our God, the LORD is one. And you shall
love the LORD your God with all your heart and with all your soul and with
all your might" (Deut. 6:4–5; cf. 10:12–13). Love for God is the spring from
which love for neighbor flows (10:12, 19; cf. Lev. 19:18). And loving God and
neighbor is *what* God called Israel to do; the Ten Words and all the additional
"statutes and rules" clarify *how* God's people were to do it (see Deut. 4:25;
12:1; 26:16).

---

1. For more on the theme of this section, see Jason S. DeRouchie, "From Condemnation to
   Righteousness: A Christian Reading of Deuteronomy," *SBJT* 18, no. 3 (Fall 2014): 87–118.

Yahweh called the priests "to distinguish between the holy and the common, and between the unclean and the clean," and "to teach the people of Israel all the statutes that the LORD had spoken to them by Moses" (Lev. 10:10–11). He also charged Israel, "You shall be holy to me, for I the LORD am holy and have separated you from the peoples, that you should be mine" (Lev. 20:26; cf. 19:2; 20:7; 21:8). Through surrender to God's law, Israel would serve as a witness to the nations, mediating Yahweh's presence and displaying his holiness (Exod. 19:5–6; Deut. 4:5–6).

Yahweh set before Israel blessings and curses, contingent on whether they would obey his law (Deut. 11:26–28; 30:15–20; cf. Lev. 26:3–39; Deut. 28). The people would enjoy life and righteousness, if they could perfectly keep *all* his commandments (Lev. 18:5; Deut. 5:29; 6:2, 25; 8:1; 28:1; etc.). Nevertheless, Israel was "stubborn" (Exod. 32:9; 33:3, 5; 34:9; Deut. 9:6, 13; 10:16; 31:27), "unbelieving" (Num. 14:11; Deut. 1:32; 9:23), and "rebellious" (Num. 20:10, 24; 27:14; Deut. 9:7, 24; 31:27). And both Yahweh and Moses identified that the people's wickedness would only increase in the Promised Land. This would result in God's destroying them and sending them into exile (Deut. 4:25–28; 31:16–17, 27–29; cf. 32:5), just as he had done with Adam (Isa. 43:27; Hos. 6:7).

Recognizing their sinful state and anticipating his ultimate saving gift, Yahweh, who alone sanctifies (Exod. 31:13; Lev. 20:8; 22:32; Ezek. 37:28), supplied Israel substitutionary sacrifice as a means for encountering his glory and experiencing the awakening of holiness (Lev. 9:3–4, 6, 23–24; 10:3). Sacrifice could atone for Israel, but only if they realized their guilt and confessed their sin (Lev. 5:5–6; Num. 5:6–7; cf. Jer. 36:3). However, for the majority, God did not overcome their resistance. As Moses asserted, "To this day the LORD has not given you a heart to understand or eyes to see or ears to hear" (Deut. 29:4[3]). While God directed them to wholeheartedly embrace his call to love (6:5–6), and while he charged them, "Circumcise . . . the foreskin of your heart, and be no longer stubborn" (10:16), sin rather than the law was "engraved on the tablet of their heart" (Jer. 17:1). Rebellion rather than forgiveness characterized the old covenant era (31:32; cf. 31:34). While from one perspective, God delivered at Sinai "right rules and true laws, good statutes and commandments" (Neh. 9:13), from another very real perspective Yahweh "gave them statutes that were not good and rules by which they could not have life" (Ezek. 20:25). The result was their ruin, as history would show (cf. 2 Kings 17:13–15, 18; Dan. 9:11).

New Testament Perspectives on the Mosaic Law

Paul said that in the Mosaic law we have "the embodiment of knowledge and truth" (Rom. 2:20), and "the law is holy, and the commandment is holy and righteous and good" (7:12). Nevertheless, "the very commandment that promised life proved to be death to me" (7:10).

In the Lord's purposes, the old law-covenant bore a "ministry of death" and "a ministry of condemnation," which stands against the new covenant's "ministry of righteousness" (2 Cor. 3:7, 9). God hardened the majority of Israel (Rom. 11:7–8; cf. Deut. 29:4[3]; Isa. 29:10; 44:18), and he used the Mosaic law to multiply transgression (Rom. 5:20; Gal. 3:19), to expose sin (Rom. 3:15), and to bring wrath (4:15). He did this in order to reveal to all the world that "by works of the law no human being will be justified in his sight" (3:20) and also to prove through Christ's coming that he is both "just and the justifier of the one who has faith in Jesus" (3:26), whether Jew or Gentile (cf. 9:22–24).

When Paul said, "the law is not of faith" (Gal. 3:12), he likely meant that the age of the law was characterized by doing rather than believing as the means to righteousness (see Question 34). He states, "Israel, who pursued a law that would lead to righteousness, did not succeed in reaching that law. Why? Because they did not pursue it by faith, but as if it were based on works" (Rom. 9:31–32).

The Age of Faith and the Law of Christ

Old Testament Predictions of Something Better
Along with bemoaning Israel's state and fate under the old covenant, the OT prophets anticipated an end-time work of God that would transform the hearts of the people and include the Mosaic law's lasting relevance. When Yahweh first called Moses to construct a tabernacle and worship according to a pattern in heaven (Exod. 25:9, 40; 26:30; 27:8), there was a built-in assumption that Israel's symbolic system of worship would become obsolete if shadow ever moved to substance (Col. 2:16–17) and if the system's pattern ever came to earth (Heb. 9:11–12; cf. John 2:19–21). As Yahweh declared through Zechariah, the priesthood was but a "sign" or pointer to God's royal and priestly servant who would build a new temple-palace for God and "remove the iniquity of this land in a single day" (Zech. 3:8–9; 6:12–13).

Furthermore, Moses promised that, following the exile "in the latter days," Yahweh's mercy would move his people to turn to him and to listen to his voice so that they would "keep all his commandments that I am commanding you today" (Deut. 30:8; cf. 4:30–31). That is, in the day that the Lord would circumcise their hearts so that his people would love him with all their heart and soul (30:6; cf. 30:10), Deuteronomy would still matter, and people would follow Moses's instruction, now channeled through the prophetic covenant mediator who would be like but better than him (18:15). This covenant-keeping would be possible because the commandment Moses was commanding them would, in that day, not be too hard or too difficult, but "the word will be very near you. It will be in your mouth and in your heart, so that you can do it" (30:11–14, DeRouchie's translation; cf. Rom. 10:6–8).[2]

Isaiah also anticipated that "in the latter days" nations and peoples would stream to the transformed Zion in order for Yahweh to teach them his ways and that they might walk in his paths, "for out of Zion shall go the law" (Isa. 2:2–3; cf. Mic. 4:1–2). All those there "will be called holy" (Isa. 4:3), as they live loyally under the Spirit-empowered new David, the royal servant, who will reign in justice and righteousness (9:6–7; 11:2–5; 42:1–4; cf. 51:4) and teach in a way that sustains others (50:4). Yahweh identifies that there was a righteous remnant who were taught (8:16) and "in whose heart is my law" (50:7; cf. Pss. 37:31; 40:8[9]; 119:11), but one day "the deaf shall hear the word of a book" (29:18) and every member of the multiethnic, blood-bought community "shall be taught by the LORD" (Isa. 54:13; cf. 53:10; 54:3). In that day "the righteous one" (cf. 50:8–9) would "make many to be accounted righteous, and he shall bear their iniquity" (53:11; cf. 50:8–9).[3]

Jeremiah, too, anticipated that in the days after Yahweh restored his once faithless children to Zion, he would give them "shepherds after my own heart, who will feed you with knowledge and understanding" (Jer. 3:15; cf. 23:4). At that time some who were once God's "evil neighbors" will "be built up in the midst of my people" because "they will diligently learn the ways of my people," whereas he will destroy any nation that refuses to "listen" (12:14, 16–17; cf. 3:16–18). Some ethnic Israelites will be saved and dwell securely as the Davidic king reigns justly and righteously (23:5–6), and foreigners will join them and "serve the LORD their God and David their king" (30:9). It will

---

2. The subordinate conjunction "for" at the head of Deuteronomy 30:11 strongly ties verses 11–14 with the future prediction that precedes and suggests that the verbless clauses throughout the paragraph should all be translated as futures. For this reading of Deuteronomy 30:11–14, see, for example, J. Gary Millar, *Now Choose Life: Theology and Ethics in Deuteronomy*, NSBT 6 (Downers Grove, IL: InterVarsity, 1998), 94, 174–75; Stephen G. Dempster, *Dominion and Dynasty: A Biblical Theology of the Hebrew Bible*, NSBT 15 (Downers Grove, IL: InterVarsity, 2003), 118–21; Patrick A. Barker, *The Triumph of Grace in Deuteronomy: Faithless Israel, Faithful Yahweh in Deuteronomy* (Carlisle, UK: Paternoster, 2004), 182–98; Steven R. Coxhead, "Deuteronomy 30:11–14 as a Prophecy of the New Covenant in Christ," *WTJ* 68 (2006): 305–20; Bryan D. Estelle, "Leviticus 18:5 and Deuteronomy 30:1–14 in Biblical Theological Development: Entitlement to Heaven Foreclosed and Proffered," in *The Law Is Not of Faith: Essays on Works and Grace in the Mosaic Covenant*, eds. Bryan D. Estelle, J. V. Fesko, and David VanDrunen (Phillipsburg, NJ: P&R, 2009), 127–37; DeRouchie, "From Condemnation to Righteousness," 117–18; and Colin James Smothers, "In Your Mouth and in Your Heart: A Study of Deuteronomy 30:12–14 in Paul's Letter to the Romans in Canonical Context" (PhD diss., Southern Baptist Theological Seminary, 2018).

3. See Charles E. Hill, "God's Speech in These Last Days: The New Testament Canon as an Eschatological Phenomenon," in *Resurrection and Eschatology: Theology in Service of the Church; Essays in Honor of Richard B. Gaffin Jr.*, eds. Lane G. Tipton and Jeffrey C. Waddington (Phillipsburg, NJ: P&R, 2008), 203–54.

be this transformed "Israel" with whom Yahweh will cut a "new covenant," putting "my law within them" and writing "it on their hearts" (31:33; cf. Heb. 8:10; 10:16). And the result will be that every covenant member, from the least to the greatest, will know the Lord, for, as he says, "I will forgive their iniquity, and I will remember their sins no more" (Jer. 31:34; cf. 33:8; Heb. 10:17). Thus, Yahweh would distinguish the new covenant from the old by forgiving and internalizing his law within *every* member.

Ezekiel also envisions that, under the royal servant David, Yahweh will grant the restored community both a new heart and his Spirit, resulting in their life. The Lord would cause them "to walk in my statutes" and "to obey my rules" (Ezek. 36:26–27; 37:14, 24; cf. 11:19–20).

New Testament Perspectives on the New Era of Faith and the Law of Christ

The coming of Christ marked the major turning point in redemptive history.[4] Paul identified the Mosaic covenant as a temporary, enslaving economy that brought death and that God has now replaced by freedom in Christ and the age of faith (Rom. 7:6, 10–11; 10:4; 2 Cor. 3:7, 9; Gal. 3:23–26). On its own, the Mosaic law could not give life (Gal. 3:21). But in Christ Jesus "God has done what the law, weakened by the flesh, could not do. By sending his own Son in the likeness of sinful flesh and for sin, he condemned sin in the flesh, in order that the righteous requirement of the law might be fulfilled in us, who walk not according to the flesh but according to the Spirit" (Rom. 8:3–4). Christ mediates a better covenant with better promises (Heb. 8:6, 13; cf. 7:12; 10:9), and the glorious grace and truth coming to us through Jesus Christ has now superseded the grace and the glory of the Mosaic law (John 1:16–17; cf. 2 Cor. 3:7–11).

In the age of faith, Christians are part of the new covenant and not the old, which means that the Mosaic law no longer *directly* and *immediately* guides or judges how God's people behave (cf. Acts 15:10; Gal. 4:5; 5:1–12; Eph. 2:14–16).[5] We are "not under law but under grace" (Rom. 6:14–15); we are "not outside the law of God but under the law of Christ" (1 Cor. 9:20–21; cf. Gal. 6:2), the latter of which James terms "the perfect law," "the law of liberty," and "the royal law" (James 1:25; 2:8, 12). Our direct guidance comes from Jesus, to whom we are to listen and obey (Matt. 17:5; 28:19). He is the prophetic new covenant mediator like and better than Moses (Deut. 18:5; Acts 3:22–26; cf. 1 Tim. 2:5; Heb. 9:15), and he is Isaiah's servant-king, whose instruction would guide the end-time age (Isa. 2:3; 42:4; 51:4). His commandments, both from his mouth (John 14:15, 21; 15:10) and through his apostles (1 Cor. 7:25;

---

4. See also Jason S. DeRouchie, *How to Understand and Apply the Old Testament: Twelve Steps from Exegesis to Theology* (Phillipsburg, NJ: P&R, 2017), 428–36.
5. So too Douglas J. Moo, "The Law of Christ as the Fulfillment of the Law of Moses: A Modified Lutheran View," in *Five Views on Law and Gospel*, ed. Wayne G. Strickland, Counterpoints (Grand Rapids: Zondervan, 1996), 343, 375.

14:37; 2 John 6, 9; cf. John 14:26; 15:26–27; 1 Cor. 11:23; Gal. 1:2), are God's directives for the church that guide our lives (John 14:15, 21; 15:10; 1 Cor. 7:19; 1 John 3:23–24; 5:2–3). We endure by keeping God's commandments and holding fast to the testimony of Jesus (1 Tim. 6:13–14; Rev. 12:17; 14:12).

Christ as the Lens for Reappropriating the Mosaic Law
In the new covenant age, when Gentile believers without the written law "do what the law requires, . . . they show that the work of the law is written on their hearts" (Rom. 2:14–15; cf. Jer. 31:33).[6] And again, when a Gentile Christian "keeps the precepts [pl. of *dikaiōma*] of the law," he reveals that he is a true "Jew," for his heart is circumcised by the power of the Spirit (Rom. 2:26, 28–29; cf. Deut. 30:6; Ezek. 36:27). It is also this law-"fulfillment" that the apostle says we accomplish when we love our neighbor (Rom. 13:8, 10).

Although the Mosaic law does not *directly* legally bind Christians, we do not throw out the law. While the NT authors do indeed both *repudiate* and *replace* the old covenant law, in another very real sense, they *reappropriate* it both as prophecy that anticipates the gospel of Jesus and as wisdom intended to guide NT saints in our pursuit of God.[7] The Mosaic law, therefore, bears both a revelatory and pedagogical significance for the Christian.[8] Such is evident in the way that all the OT laws are treated as profitable and instructive (e.g., Rom. 13:9; 1 Cor. 9:7–9; Eph. 6:1–3; 1 Tim. 5:18; 1 Peter 1:15–16), yet only through the mediation of Christ. "All Scripture . . . is profitable for teaching, for reproof, for correction, and for training in righteousness," including the OT (2 Tim. 3:16; cf. Rom. 4:23; 15:4; 1 Cor. 10:11).

Jesus affirmed the law's lasting relevance, yet in a way that highlights both continuity and discontinuity between the Mosaic law and the law of Christ (cf. Luke 16:16). At the beginning of the Sermon on the Mount, he asserts that he did not "come to abolish the Law or the Prophets . . . but to fulfill them. For truly, I say to you, until heaven and earth pass away, not an iota, not a dot, will pass from the Law until all is accomplished" (Matt. 5:17–18).

---

6. For this reading of Romans 2:14–15, see Simon J. Gathercole, "A Law unto Themselves: The Gentiles in Romans 2.14–15 Revisited," *JSNT* 85 (2002): 27–49; A. B. Caneday, "Judgment, Behavior, and Justification according to Paul's Gospel in Romans 2," *Journal for the Study of Paul and His Letters* 1 (2011): 153–92; Thomas R. Schreiner, *Romans*, 2nd ed., BECNT (Grand Rapids: Baker Academic, 2018), 125–35. For an alternative reading that Romans 2:14–15 speaks of non-Christian Gentiles doing part of the law, see Thomas R. Schreiner, *Romans*, BECNT (Grand Rapids: Baker Academic, 1998), on 2:14; Douglas J. Moo, *The Letter to the Romans*, 2nd ed., NICNT (Grand Rapids: Eerdmans, 2018), on 2:14. Both views agree that, in light of human sinfulness, God does not justify people based on their works.

7. Brian S. Rosner, *Paul and the Law: Keeping the Commandments of God*, NSBT 31 (Downers Grove, IL: InterVarsity, 2013), esp. 208–9, 217.

8. On these distinctions, see David A. Dorsey, "The Law of Moses and the Christian: A Compromise," *JETS* 34 (1991): 325, 331.

When Jesus said that he came "to fulfill," he likely meant that he actualizes in his teaching and work what the OT foresaw.[9] All the Law and the Prophets pointed to a radical life of love for God and neighbor (7:12; 22:40), and this is what Jesus embodied, called for, and empowered. Christ saw a deep continuity between his teaching and that of Moses.[10] He called people to "do" and "teach" the very commands of the old covenant *but only* in light of how he fulfilled the law (5:19).[11]

When we view Jesus as the lens for considering the lasting validity of Moses (fig. 24.1), we recognize that Christ *maintains* some laws so that they look the same within the law of Christ as they did in the law of Moses (e.g., love God and neighbor; never commit adultery, murder, theft, etc.). At one level Jesus intensifies these laws in that his own life supplies believers an unparalleled pattern for living the Godward life (Phil. 2:5–7; Heb. 12:1–3; 1 Peter 2:21; 1 John 2:6) and an unparalleled power for the same (Rom. 1:16; 1 Cor. 1:18), specifically through his blood-bought pardon (Rom. 6:6–7, 22; 8:10) and promises (Rom. 8:32; 2 Cor. 1:20; 2 Peter 1:4). Nevertheless, Christian obedience to these instructions is very comparable to what OT believers would have looked like carrying out the laws.[12]

In contrast, when other laws hit the lens of Christ, they get "bent" in various ways. Consider these examples:

- When Christ fulfills the Mosaic law of the Sabbath (e.g., Deut. 5:12), he *transforms* it into sustained rest for the people of God (Matt.

---

9. For an exceptional word study of *plēroō*, see Vern S. Poythress, *The Shadow of Christ in the Law of Moses* (Phillipsburg, NJ: P&R, 1991), 363–77; cf. 267. For a similar approach to Matt. 5:17–19, see Douglas J. Moo, "Jesus and the Authority of the Mosaic Law," *JSNT* 20 (1984): 3–49; Douglas J. Moo, "The Law of Moses or the Law of Christ," in *Continuity and Discontinuity: Perspectives on the Relationship between the Old and New Testaments: Essays in Honor of S. Lewis Johnson Jr.*, ed. John S. Feinberg (Westchester, IL: Crossway, 1988), 203–218, 373–76; Poythress, *Shadow of Christ in the Law of Moses*, 263–69; Douglas J. Moo, "Law," in *Dictionary of Jesus and the Gospels*, eds. Joel B. Green and Scot McKnight (Downers Grove, IL: InterVarsity Press, 1992), 456–58; Moo, "Law of Christ as the Fulfillment of the Law of Moses"; Tom Wells and Fred G. Zaspel, *New Covenant Theology: Description, Definition, Defense* (Frederick, MD: New Covenant Media, 2002), 77–159; and D. A. Carson, "Matthew," in *Matthew–Mark*, 2nd ed., Expositor's Bible Commentary 9 (Grand Rapids: Zondervan, 2010), 172–79.

10. Moo, "Law of Christ as the Fulfillment of the Law of Moses," 314.

11. So too Moo, "Jesus and the Authority of the Mosaic Law," 28; Poythress, *Shadow of Christ in the Law of Moses*, 267–69; Moo, "Law," 458; Moo, "Law of Christ as the Fulfillment of the Law of Moses," 353; Wells and Zaspel, *New Covenant Theology*, 127; Carson, "Matthew," 179; and DeRouchie, *Understand and Apply the Old Testament*, 428–32.

12. For a study in how the law of Christ maintains the Mosaic law related to gender identity, see Jason S. DeRouchie, "Confronting the Transgender Storm: New Covenant Reflections on Deuteronomy 22:5," *JBMW* 21, no. 1 (2016): 58–69.

11:28–12:8). In Jesus, the kingdom rest to which the Sabbath pointed reaches its end-time realization.[13]

- Similarly, when Christ fulfills the Mosaic law regarding parapet building (Deut. 22:8), we find the application *extended* in a way that necessitates care for neighbor in every way one structures a living environment. Love for neighbor has no bounds, so long as it honors the Lord.

- Finally, when Christ fulfills the Mosaic law associated with unclean food (e.g., Lev. 20:25–26), he *annuls* it, declaring all foods clean (Mark 7:19; cf. Acts 10:14–15; Rom. 14:20). Even though he rescinded the earlier diet restrictions, we can still benefit from these commands by considering what they tell us about God and how they magnify Jesus's work. But we do not keep these laws in any way.

We must assess every law on its own terms in order to properly discern how it applies today.[14]

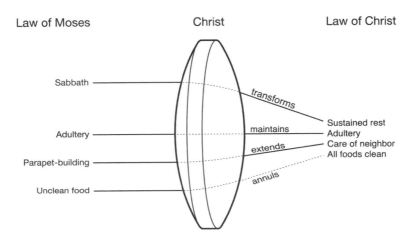

Fig. 25.1. The Law's Fulfillment through the Lens of Christ[15]

---

13. See Question 26.
14. For examples of how we see the Mosaic law being reappropriated in the law of Christ, see DeRouchie, *Understand and Apply the Old Testament*, 439–59.
15. I thank my student Benjamin Holvey, who initially inspired this lens illustration.

The Lasting Relevance of the Mosaic Law for Christians

There are at least three ways in which the Mosaic law continues to bear lasting relevance for believers today. First, the law portrays *the character of God*. The Lord asserted, "You shall . . . be holy, for I am holy" (Lev. 11:35), and the way Israel would fulfill this charge was by heeding God's commands. "So you shall remember and do all my commandments, and be holy to your God" (Num. 15:40; cf. Exod. 19:5–6). Paul stressed, "The law is holy, and the commandment is holy, righteous, and good" (Rom. 7:12), and Peter said, "As he who called you is holy, you also be holy in all your conduct, since it is written, 'You shall be holy, for I am holy'" (1 Peter 1:16–17). When we read the law of Moses, we get a glimpse into the very character of our great God.

Second, the law anticipates *Christ*. The divine Son of God embodies every OT ethical ideal. Jesus Christ is the ultimate king (Deut. 17:18–20) and "righteous one" who bears the iniquity of the guilty (Isa. 53:11; cf. 1 John 1:9–2:1). He was perfectly obedient (Rom. 5:19; Phil. 2:8; Heb. 5:8) and sinless (John 8:46; 14:30; 1 Peter 2:22; 1 John 3:5; Heb. 7:26), and for those in him, his life of perfect surrender frees from the law's condemning power and supplies for us all the righteousness that the law required. At the cross God cancelled "the record of debt that stood against us with its legal demands" (Col. 2:13–14; cf. Gal. 3:13). This he accomplished by counting our sins to Jesus, by pouring out his wrath against Jesus in our stead, and by counting Jesus's righteousness as ours (Isa. 53:11; Rom. 5:18–19; 2 Cor. 5:21; Heb. 9:28). Therefore, Christians can use the OT laws to move us to magnify all God is for us in Jesus.

Third, the law clarifies *the makeup of love and wise living*. Jesus said that "all the Law and the Prophets" depend on the dual commands to love God and love neighbor (Matt. 22:37–40). Stressing how love for neighbor really proves whether we love God, Jesus went further: "Whatever you wish that others would do to you, do also to them, for this is the Law and the Prophets" (7:12). Paul, too, emphasized, "The whole law is fulfilled in one word: 'You shall love your neighbor as yourself'" (Gal. 5:14). Significantly, not just a "moral" subset of the law but all the law—every commandment—is fulfilled in the call to love (Rom. 13:8–10).[16] From this perspective, while the Mosaic law does not bear

---

16. For an evaluation of the proposed threefold division of the law, see Dorsey, "Law of Moses and the Christian," 329–31; Poythress, *Shadow of Christ in the Law of Moses*, 283; Jerram Barrs, *Delighting in the Law of the Lord: God's Alternative to Legalism and Moralism* (Wheaton, IL: Crossway, 2013), 314; D. A. Carson, "The Tripartite Division of the Law: A Review of Philip Ross, *The Finger of God*," in *From Creation to New Creation: Essays on Biblical Theology and Exegesis*, eds. Daniel M. Gurtner and Benjamin L. Gladd (Peabody, MA: Hendrickson, 2013), 223–36; William W. Combs, "Paul, the Law, and Dispensationalism," *Detroit Baptist Seminary Journal* 18 (2013): 26–28; Rosner, *Paul and the Law*, 36–37; Jason C. Meyer, "The Mosaic Law, Theological Systems, and the Glory of Christ," in *Progressive Covenantalism: Charting a Course between Dispensational and Covenant Theologies*, eds. Stephen J. Wellum and Brent E. Parker (Nashville: B&H, 2016), 87–89; Stephen J. Wellum, "Progressive Covenantalism and the Doing of Ethics,"

direct or immediate guidance in a Christian's life, it does supply us a pattern for how deep and wide love for God and neighbor is to impact our lives.[17] Just as Moses could portray Abraham's true life of faith as a keeping of the law (Gen. 26:5; cf. Deut. 11:1; 1 Kings 2:3; 2 Kings 17:13, 34), so too Israel's law supplied a contextual paradigm of the values God desires for all peoples in all times (cf. Exod. 19:5–6; Deut. 4:5–8).[18]

Summary

Most often, "law" in Scripture points to the Mosaic law, which operated within the old covenant to identify and multiply sin and to condemn Israel. Jesus and the NT authors repudiate the Mosaic law, replace it with the law of Christ, and then reappropriate it through Christ in order to give us glimpses of God's character and the perfect righteousness of Christ and to guide believers in wisdom and love (so, too, Rosner). The Mosaic law does not *directly* bind the Christian in a legal manner, but we treat all the OT laws as profitable and instructive when we read them through the lens of Christ. And because Jesus fulfills different laws in different ways, we consider each law on its own in light of Christ's work. The result is that some laws are maintained, whereas others are transformed, extended, or annulled.[19]

---

in *Progressive Covenantalism*, 218–21; DeRouchie, *Understand and Apply the Old Testament*, 436–39.

17. For examples of a principlizing approach to OT law, see Walter C. Kaiser Jr., *Toward Old Testament Ethics* (Grand Rapids: Zondervan, 1983); Walter C. Kaiser Jr., "A Principlizing Model," in *Four Views on Moving Beyond the Bible to Theology*, ed. Gary T. Meadors (Grand Rapids: Zondervan, 2009), 19–50; J. Daniel Hays, "Applying the OT Law Today," *BSac* 158, no. 1 (2001): 21–35; Barrs, *Delighting in the Law of the Lord*, 315–26. In our view, we must include a redemptive-historical lens in order to engage in a principlizing approach faithfully.

18. For more on the principlizing-paradigmatic approach to the Mosaic law, see C. J. H. Wright, *Old Testament Ethics for the People of God* (Downers Grove, IL: InterVarsity, 2004), 62–74, 182–211, 314–25; cf. W. Janzen, *Old Testament Ethics: A Paradigmatic Approach* (Louisville: Westminster John Knox, 1994); E. A. Martens, "How Is the Christian to Construe OT Law?" *BBR* 12, no. 2 (2002): 199–216; Peter T. Vogt, *Interpreting the Pentateuch: An Exegetical Handbook*, Handbooks for Old Testament Exegesis (Grand Rapids: Kregel, 2009), 42–48; Daniel I. Block, "Preaching Old Testament Law to New Testament Christians," in *The Gospel according to Moses: Theological and Ethical Reflections on the Book of Deuteronomy* (Eugene, OR: Cascade, 2012), 104–46, esp. 133–36. In our view, we must employ a redemptive-historical, christological lens if we are to engage a principlizing-paradigmatic approach faithfully.

19. For an exceptional book on the Christian's relationship to the Mosaic law, see Thomas R. Schreiner, *40 Questions About Christians and Biblical Law* (Grand Rapids: Kregel, 2010).

REFLECTION QUESTIONS

1. What covenants preceded the Mosaic law, and how do these covenants influence our understanding of right relationship with God through obedience and faith?

2. Describe in your own words the Old and New Testaments' perspectives on the Mosaic law's ministry of death and condemnation and the new covenant's era of faith and ministry of righteousness. Use Scripture references.

3. In what ways do the NT authors repudiate, replace, *and* reappropriate old covenant law?

4. How does Jesus maintain, transform, extend, and annul old covenant laws? Find examples for each.

5. What significance do OT laws have for Christians today, and how should we appropriate them in our pursuit of Christ?

What Is a Biblical Theology of the Sabbath?

Andrew David Naselli

This question is a subset of the previous one: "What Is a Biblical Theology of the Law?" The old covenant required God's people to keep the Sabbath, but God's people today are under the new covenant and not the old covenant.[1] So how do those under the new covenant relate to the Sabbath commandment in the old covenant?[2]

Some believe that God's command to keep the Sabbath *maintains* from the old covenant to the new covenant (either maintaining on Saturdays or maintaining by transitioning from Saturdays to Sundays), but we believe that Christ *transforms* the Sabbath commandment.[3] Those who believe that the Sabbath *maintains* include those holding to Seventh-day Adventism and

---

1. See Question 25. See also Douglas J. Moo, "The Law of Christ as the Fulfillment of the Law of Moses: A Modified Lutheran View," in *Five Views on Law and Gospel*, ed. Wayne G. Strickland, Counterpoints (Grand Rapids: Zondervan, 1996); Thomas R. Schreiner, *40 Questions About Christians and Biblical Law* (Grand Rapids: Kregel, 2010).

2. See also D. A. Carson, ed., *From Sabbath to Lord's Day: A Biblical, Historical, and Theological Investigation* (Grand Rapids: Zondervan, 1982); Andrew G. Shead, "Sabbath," in *New Dictionary of Biblical Theology*, eds. T. Desmond Alexander and Brian S. Rosner (Downers Grove, IL: InterVarsity, 2000), 745–50; Jason S. DeRouchie, *How to Understand and Apply the Old Testament: Twelve Steps from Exegesis to Theology* (Phillipsburg, NJ: P&R, 2017), 449–53; and Thomas R. Schreiner, "Good-Bye and Hello: The Sabbath Command for New Covenant Believers," in *Progressive Covenantalism: Charting a Course between Dispensational and Covenant Theologies*, eds. Stephen J. Wellum and Brent E. Parker (Nashville: B&H, 2016), 159–88. Contra G. K. Beale, *A New Testament Biblical Theology: The Unfolding of the Old Testament in the New* (Grand Rapids: Baker Academic, 2011), 775–801.

3. On how Christ fulfills OT promises, see Jason S. DeRouchie, "Is Every Promise 'Yes'? Old Testament Promises and the Christian," *Them* 42, no. 1 (April 2017): 34–44. See Question 37. On how Christ fulfills OT commands, see DeRouchie, *Understand and Apply the Old Testament*, 427–59.

covenant theology,[4] and those who believe that Christ *transforms* the Sabbath include those holding to progressive covenantalism and dispensationalism.[5] We can trace the Sabbath theme through the Bible in three periods: (1) before the old covenant, (2) under the old covenant, and (3) under the new covenant.

The Sabbath before the Old Covenant

The story of God's creating the world does not use the word *Sabbath*, but it does refer to a time of rest, which is what *Sabbath* refers to. God created the universe in six days, and he rested on the seventh (Gen. 1:1–2:3; cf. Exod. 20:11). God did not rest because he was tired or lazy. His six days of work and one day of rest set a work-rest pattern for humans (Exod. 20:11; cf. Gen. 7:4, 10; 8:10, 12) and identified his sovereignty over the world (cf. Ps. 132:7–8, 13–14).

But God did not command Adam or any of the patriarchs to refrain from working on the Sabbath (i.e., the seventh day—Saturday). The first time God commanded people to keep the Sabbath was shortly before he gave the Mosaic law.

After God delivered the Israelites from Egypt but before he gave them the Ten Commandments and the rest of the old covenant, God provided bread from heaven for his people in the wilderness (Exod. 16). God instructed the people to gather the bread each day and to take only one omer (i.e., about two quarts or two liters) per person. If people gathered more than that, it would breed worms and stink. But the rules were different for gathering the bread on Friday (i.e., the day before the Sabbath):

> On the sixth day [i.e., Friday] they gathered twice as much bread, two omers each. And when all the leaders of the congregation came and told Moses, he said to them, "This is what the LORD has commanded: 'Tomorrow is a day of solemn rest, a holy Sabbath to the LORD; bake what you will bake and boil what you will boil, and all that is left over lay aside to be kept till the morning.'" So they laid it aside till the morning, as Moses commanded them, and it did not stink, and there were no worms in it. Moses said, "Eat it today, for today is a Sabbath to the LORD; today you will not find it in the field. Six days you shall gather it, but on the seventh day, which is a Sabbath, there will be none."
>
> On the seventh day some of the people went out to gather, but they found none. And the LORD said to Moses, "How long will you refuse to keep my commandments and my laws? See! The LORD has given you the Sabbath; therefore on the sixth day he gives you bread for two days. Remain each of you in his place; let no one go out of his

---

4. See Question 18.
5. See Questions 19 and 17. The best debate book on the Sabbath is Christopher John Donato, ed., *Perspectives on the Sabbath: 4 Views* (Nashville: B&H, 2011).

place on the seventh day." So the people rested on the seventh day. (Exod. 16:22–30)

Four observations are noteworthy:

1. Keeping the Sabbath appears to be new for God's people at this point in history. There is no evidence that prior to this event they religiously refrained from working on the Sabbath.

2. When the people in the wilderness broke the Sabbath, Moses rebuked them. But later under the old covenant, the penalty for breaking the Sabbath was death (Num. 15:32–36).

3. The Sabbath—a day of rest—was a gift. It was a present that God gave the Israelites, and the Israelites dishonored God when they did not value God's good gift.

4. The Sabbath was a way to sanctify God's people by testing whether they would trust him to sufficiently provide for them. God's people dishonor him when they disregard what he commands because they think they are smarter than God.

The Sabbath under the Old Covenant

The old covenant forbids God's people to work on Saturdays:

> Remember the Sabbath day, to keep it holy. Six days you shall labor, and do all your work, but the seventh day is a Sabbath to the LORD your God. On it you shall not do any work, you, or your son, or your daughter, your male servant, or your female servant, or your livestock, or the sojourner who is within your gates. For in six days the LORD made heaven and earth, the sea, and all that is in them, and rested on the seventh day. Therefore the LORD blessed the Sabbath day and made it holy. (Exod. 20:8–11)

> Above all you shall keep my Sabbaths, for this is a sign between me and you throughout your generations, that you may know that I, the LORD, sanctify you. You shall keep the Sabbath, because it is holy for you. Everyone who profanes it shall be put to death. Whoever does any work on it, that soul shall be cut off from among his people. Six days shall work be done, but the seventh day is a Sabbath of solemn rest, holy to the LORD. Whoever does any work on the Sabbath day shall be put to death. Therefore the people of Israel shall keep the Sabbath, observing the Sabbath throughout their generations, as a

covenant forever. It is a sign forever between me and the people of Israel that in six days the LORD made heaven and earth, and on the seventh day he rested and was refreshed. (Exod. 31:13–17)

Six days work shall be done, but on the seventh day you shall have a Sabbath of solemn rest, holy to the LORD. Whoever does any work on it shall be put to death. You shall kindle no fire in all your dwelling places on the Sabbath day. (Exod. 35:2–3)

Six days shall work be done, but on the seventh day is a Sabbath of solemn rest, a holy convocation. You shall do no work. It is a Sabbath to the LORD in all your dwelling places. (Lev. 23:3)

While the people of Israel were in the wilderness, they found a man gathering sticks on the Sabbath day. And those who found him gathering sticks brought him to Moses and Aaron and to all the congregation. They put him in custody, because it had not been made clear what should be done to him. And the LORD said to Moses, "The man shall be put to death; all the congregation shall stone him with stones outside the camp." And all the congregation brought him outside the camp and stoned him to death with stones, as the LORD commanded Moses. (Num. 15:32–36)

You shall remember that you were a slave in the land of Egypt, and the LORD your God brought you out from there with a mighty hand and an outstretched arm. Therefore the LORD your God commanded you to keep the Sabbath day. (Deut. 5:15)

Six observations are noteworthy:

1. The Sabbath command protected vulnerable people such as servants and sojourners (Exod. 20:10; Deut. 5:14). The head of a household was responsible to ensure that every member of his household rested on Saturday.

2. The Sabbath command required God's people to cease working—no plowing or harvesting (Exod. 34:21), kindling a fire (35:3), gathering sticks (Num. 15:32–36), or buying goods or food (Neh. 10:31; 13:15–22). But it did not require them to gather to worship. Israelites were free to assemble to worship on the Sabbath, but the essence of the Sabbath command was not to worship but to rest.

3. Keeping the Sabbath was "a sign" of the (temporary) old covenant (Exod. 31:13, 17). A covenant's sign lasts only as long as the covenant, and it is not binding on those who are not under that covenant.[6]

4. Breaking the Sabbath command under the old covenant was a criminal offense with the penalty of death (Exod. 31:15; 35:2; Num. 15:32–36). That is far more severe than the rebuke Moses gave the Sabbath-breakers in Exodus 16:27–29.

5. The ground for the Sabbath command in Exodus 20:11 is that God created the world in six days and rested on the seventh. But it does not follow that because God roots the Sabbath command in creation that therefore the Sabbath command is universally binding—specifically, that it is binding on God's people under the new covenant. There is no evidence that God required his people to cease working on the Sabbath prior to Exodus 16, and the New Testament reveals that the Sabbath command no longer applies to God's people under the new covenant (see below).

6. When Moses restates the Ten Commandments in Deuteronomy 5, the ground for the Sabbath command differs from Exodus 20:11. The

---

6. See also DeRouchie, *Understand and Apply the Old Testament*, 450–51:

The sign of the Sabbath . . . served to remind Israel of her identity and purpose as a people in relation to the whole world. . . . For God, the culmination of the creation week was a rest born not of laziness but of sovereignty, in which the Great King, having established the sacred space of his kingdom, sat enthroned, enjoying peace with all that he had made (Gen. 2:1–3; cf. Ps. 132:7–8, 13–14). While mankind's rebellion at the fall did not remove God's right and authority over all things, it did alter the state of universal peace or rest. Thus, within the Pentateuch, the 6 + 1 pattern of creation is used not simply as a portrait of what was but as an image of what should be, and this ideal becomes directly attached to the Israelites' commission to honor God among the nations (Ex. 19:4–6; Deut. 4:5–8; 26:18–19) and for their royal representative to operate as the instrument of curse-reversal and global blessing (Gen. 12:3; 18:18; 27:17b–18; 26:4; 28:14). The Sabbath was to serve as a weekly reminder to the community that Israel's calling (as a people and, ultimately through the Messiah) was to stand as the agent through whom God's sovereignty would be celebrated once again on a global scale. It is in this context that Moses stresses in the Ten words that "the seventh day is a Sabbath *to the* LORD" (Deut. 5:14); it was ultimately kept in order to see God exalted over all. For Israel, then, the Sabbath represented a future reality to which both Israel and the world were to hope. . . . Jesus' redeeming work brought Israel's global Sabbath mission to fulfillment. He is the one through whom the world is blessed (Gen. 22:17b–18; Acts 3:25–26; Gal. 3:8, 14), and by his victorious resurrection he inaugurated the end-times Sabbath rest as a culmination of his new-creation work. Jesus stands superior to Moses (Heb. 3:1–6), and those of us in him have already entered rest, even though we await its full consummation (4:3–10).

ground is that God delivered the Israelites from the Egyptians (Deut. 5:15). That implies that the Egyptians oppressed the Israelites to work without sufficient rest. The Israelites knew what it was like for an oppressor to victimize them by forcing them to work without breaks, and God graciously reminded the Israelites that his command to rest on the Sabbath was a gift for their good. The Sabbath reminded the Israelites that God delivered them from cruel forced labor in Egypt.

The Sabbath under the New Covenant

Jesus transforms how those under the new covenant relate to the Sabbath.

Typology: The Rest God Gave His Old Covenant People on Saturdays Is a Type, and the Rest Jesus Gives His New Covenant People Every Day Is the Antitype[7]

The only one of the Ten Commandments that the New Testament does not repeat is the one about observing the Sabbath day. Why? The other nine commandments maintain under the new covenant as part of the law of Christ, but Jesus transforms the Sabbath commandment.

Jesus was "born under the law" (Gal. 4:4) and thus observed the Sabbath during his earthly ministry prior to the cross. But Jesus taught that he is the Lord of the Sabbath. He offered true rest to his followers and flouted the extra rules about the Sabbath that the Pharisees insisted were necessary to obey God:

> "Come to me, all who labor and are heavy laden, and I will give you rest. Take my yoke upon you, and learn from me, for I am gentle and lowly in heart, and you will find rest for your souls. For my yoke is easy, and my burden is light."
>
> At that time Jesus went through the grainfields on the Sabbath. His disciples were hungry, and they began to pluck heads of grain and to eat. But when the Pharisees saw it, they said to him, "Look, your disciples are doing what is not lawful to do on the Sabbath." He said to them, "Have you not read what David did when he was hungry, and those who were with him: how he entered the house of God and ate the bread of the Presence, which it was not lawful for him to eat nor for those who were with him, but only for the priests? Or have you not read in the Law how on the Sabbath the priests in the temple profane the Sabbath and are guiltless? I tell you, something greater than the temple is here. And if you had known what this means, 'I desire mercy, and not sacrifice,' you would not have condemned the guiltless. For the Son of Man is lord of the Sabbath." (Matt. 11:28–12:8)

---

7. On typology, see Question 8.

"Healing on the Sabbath is intriguing," explains Schreiner, "for it points back to the seventh day of creation (Gen 2:1–3) and forward to the new creation where the world is free of death and disease. Jesus's healings on the Sabbath signal the inauguration of the kingdom, anticipating a world where there is no disease and death."[8]

Three main boundary markers distinguished Jews in New Testament times: (1) food laws, (2) circumcision, and (3) Sabbath. All three are connected to what God required his people to do under the old covenant, and all three are no longer necessary for God's people to follow under the new covenant.[9] Paul rebukes the Galatians for legalistically observing Jewish holy days (which included the Sabbath): "You observe days and months and seasons and years!" (Gal. 4:10).

The Sabbath command under the old covenant is a type that Jesus fulfills and that culminates in the new heaven and new earth. That is why Paul wrote, "Let no one pass judgment on you in questions of food and drink, or with regard to a festival or a new moon or a Sabbath. These are a shadow of the things to come, but the substance belongs to Christ" (Col. 2:16–17). Hebrews 10:1 makes a parallel argument: "Since the law has but a shadow of the good things to come instead of the true form of these realities, it can never, by the same sacrifices that are continually offered every year, make perfect those who draw near." Under the old covenant, God's people had to offer sacrifices, but under the new covenant, God's people no longer offer sacrifices because Jesus fulfills that type as the once-for-all-time sacrifice to which the sacrifices pointed. Similarly, under the old covenant, God's people had to keep the Sabbath, but under the new covenant, God's people no longer have to keep the Sabbath because Jesus fulfills that type by giving the ultimate rest. "Believers should not revert back to the type of the Sabbath any more than they should revert to the type of OT sacrifices."[10]

The Sabbath *now* versus the Sabbath *in the new heaven and new earth* parallels the already–not yet aspects of the kingdom of God now versus later. Right now God's people under the new covenant enjoy a quality of rest in Christ that those under the old covenant did not enjoy, and that rest is just a foretaste of the ultimate rest they will enjoy in the new heaven and new earth. Jesus inaugurated this rest when he first came to earth, and he will culminate this rest when he returns:

> For if Joshua had given them rest, God would not have spoken of another day later on. So then, there remains a Sabbath rest for the

---

8. Schreiner, "Good-Bye and Hello," 173.
9. See Schreiner, "Good-Bye and Hello," 174–80.
10. Schreiner, "Good-Bye and Hello," 165.

people of God, for whoever has entered God's rest has also rested from his works as God did from his.

Let us therefore strive to enter that rest, so that no one may fall by the same sort of disobedience. (Heb. 4:8–11; cf. 3:14)

For Christians today, *every* day is a day of Sabbath rest in Jesus. We have already entered the Sabbath rest that Jesus secured, and we will fully enter that rest in the future. At this point in the history of salvation, we can rest in Jesus now in a way that no one else could prior to Jesus's first coming. Jesus gives the weary rest because he is "lord of the Sabbath" (Matt. 11:28–30; 12:8).

Adiaphora: How Christians Treat the Sabbath Is a Matter of Conscience[11]

Observing the Sabbath is one of the adiaphora for Christians—that is, it is a disputable matter, a matter of conscience (Rom. 14:1, 5–6). Issues such as adultery or murder are not disputable matters, but at this stage in salvation history, observing the Sabbath is a disputable matter. Christians who think that obeying God entails observing the Sabbath have a weak conscience on this issue—that is, they are theologically incorrect on this issue. Those with a strong conscience on this issue must not look down on or despise sabbatarians as legalistic (Rom. 14:1–15:7).

Some Christians think that certain activities are sinful to do on Sunday—eating at a public restaurant, shopping at a grocery store, watching a football game, playing a football game, mowing your lawn, doing schoolwork, working for pay, and so on. Such issues should not divide fellow church members. They are matters of conscience, so Christians with less strict convictions about how to treat Sundays should respect those with stricter convictions (again see Rom. 14:1–15:7).

But the theologically correct position is that Sunday is not the Christian Sabbath. And as with other matters of conscience, it is heretical for a person to insist that observing the Sabbath is necessary to be a Christian. That distorts the gospel by legalistically adding to it.

The Lord's Day: Churches Historically Worship Together on Sundays

Israel followed a 6 + 1 pattern (the "1" = the Sabbath), but the early church followed a 1 + 6 pattern (the entire "1 + 6" = the Sabbath). Israel worked six days and rested one, and churches worshipped together on Sundays—the first day of the week (Acts 20:7; 1 Cor. 16:2). Why Sunday? Almost certainly because Jesus rose from the dead "on the first day of the week" (Matt. 28:1; Mark 16:2, 9; Luke 24:1; John 20:1). Sunday is resurrection day—"the Lord's day"

---

11. See Andrew David Naselli and J. D. Crowley, *Conscience: What It Is, How to Train It, and Loving Those Who Differ* (Wheaton, IL: Crossway, 2016), 84–117.

(Rev. 1:10). But it does not follow that (1) Sunday is the Christian Sabbath[12] or (2) it is sinful for a church to worship on a day of the week other than Sunday.[13]

Wisdom: Humans Should Follow the Pattern of Working Six Days and Resting One

God established at creation the principle of working six days and resting one, and it is wise for humans to follow that pattern. A weekly day of rest is a gift from God to refresh us. We rest so that we can run. And resting helps us increasingly depend on God to meet our needs (cf. Ps. 127:2). But the new covenant does not require Christians to treat Sunday the way the old covenant required God's people to treat Saturday (technically, Friday sundown to Saturday sundown). A Christian has freedom about when to rest one day each week.

Summary

We can trace the Sabbath theme through the Bible in three periods: (1) before the old covenant, (2) under the old covenant, and (3) under the new covenant. God required all of his people to keep the Sabbath only under the old covenant. Resting on Saturdays under the old covenant is a type, and experiencing the rest that Jesus gives his new covenant people is the antitype.

REFLECTION QUESTIONS

1. How does Hebrews 10:1 help us interpret Colossians 2:16–17?

2. Are you a sabbatarian (i.e., a Christian who strictly observes Sunday as the Sabbath)? Why or why not?

3. How did Jesus's person and work transform the command to keep the Sabbath?

4. How should you relate to fellow Christians who disagree with your view on the Sabbath?

5. Do you think humans should follow the pattern of working six days and resting one? Why?

---

12. Sabbatarianism developed not in the early church but in medieval times. See the four chapters by Richard Bauckham in Carson, *From Sabbath to Lord's Day*, 221–341.
13. E.g., our friends who lead Redeemer Church of Dubai in the United Arab Emirates choose to meet on Fridays because that is first day of the weekend and the day set aside for worship in their Muslim country.

What Is a Biblical Theology of the Temple?

Andrew David Naselli

The temple theme is so rich that G. K. Beale wrote a 458-page biblical theology of the temple.[1] Beale argues for this thesis: "The Old Testament tabernacle and temples were symbolically designed to point to the cosmic eschatological reality that God's tabernacling presence, formerly limited to the holy of holies, was to be extended throughout the whole earth. Against this background, the Revelation 21 vision is best understood as picturing the final end-time temple that will fill the entire cosmos."[2] The first nine chapter titles in Beale and Mitchell Kim's *God Dwells among Us: Expanding Eden to the Ends of the Earth* summarize how the temple theme progresses through the Bible:

---

1. G. K. Beale, *The Temple and the Church's Mission: A Biblical Theology of the Dwelling Place of God*, NSBT 17 (Downers Grove, IL: InterVarsity, 2004). Beale's book is a good example of what it looks like to trace a major theme from Genesis to Revelation. Beale and a co-author condensed his longer work into a more accessible 211-page book: G. K. Beale and Mitchell Kim, *God Dwells among Us: Expanding Eden to the Ends of the Earth* (Downers Grove, IL: InterVarsity, 2014). See also G. K. Beale, *A New Testament Biblical Theology: The Unfolding of the Old Testament in the New* (Grand Rapids: Baker Academic, 2011), 592–648. We are grateful to Beale for influencing how we trace the temple theme through the Bible. For a similar approach to Beale's that is even more accessible than the Beale and Kim volume, see J. Daniel Hays, *The Temple and the Tabernacle: A Study of God's Dwelling Places from Genesis to Revelation* (Grand Rapids: Baker, 2016). See also Andrew David Naselli, *How to Understand and Apply the New Testament: Twelve Steps from Exegesis to Theology* (Phillipsburg, NJ: P&R, 2017), 243–50. See that resource for illustrations of the tabernacle and court; the tabernacle tent; Solomon's temple; Zerubbabel's temple; Herod's temple, the temple mount, and the temple complex in the time of Jesus; and Golgotha in relation to the temple mount.

2. Beale, *Temple and the Church's Mission*, 25.

1. Eden as a Temple: The Context of Genesis 1–2
2. Expanding Eden: The Call in Genesis 1:26–28
3. Eden Lost? The Call to the Patriarchs after the Fall
4. Eden Remixed: The Tabernacle in a Context of Sin
5. Eden Restored: Promise of the Expansion of Eden in the Prophets
6. Eden Rebuilt: Jesus as the New Temple in the Gospels
7. Eden Expanding: The Church as the New Temple
8. Eden's Ministry: Serving as Priests in the New Temple
9. Eden Completely Expanded: The New Heavens and New Earth in Revelation 21:1–4

There are at least eleven significant points along the temple trajectory in the Bible's storyline. It starts at the very beginning in the garden of Eden.[3]

The Garden of Eden

The parallels between Genesis 1–3 and Revelation 21–22 are amazing.[4] The Bible has brilliant bookends, and part of those bookends is the temple theme. When God creates the heavens and the earth in Genesis 1–2, the earth is his dwelling place. Before the fall, God regularly fellowships with Adam and Eve. From the point of the fall onward, God's dwelling place is associated with heaven, and he "comes down" to earth. The garden of Eden is the first temple (cf. Ezek. 28)—"the temple-garden," "a divine sanctuary."[5] It's the place where humans meet God. There are all sorts of parallels between (1) the garden of Eden, and (2) the tabernacle and temple.[6]

The Tabernacle

The tabernacle court was a rectangle about half as big as a football field. When you entered it, you would see directly in front of you the bronze altar for burnt offerings. Behind that was the bronze basin, a big cleaning bowl resembling a massive birdbath. Behind that was the tabernacle itself.

The tabernacle was a large rectangular tent about forty-five feet long by fifteen feet wide. This tent had two rooms. The first room was twice as large as the second; it was a rectangle about thirty feet long by fifteen feet wide, and the second room just beyond it was a perfect fifteen-foot cube. (Remember that: it's in the shape of a cube. That'll be important later.)

---

3. That is why Andy and Jenni Naselli named their fourth daughter Eden Celeste. Her name reflects a biblical theology of the temple—from the garden of Eden to the celestial city.
4. See Question 35.
5. T. Desmond Alexander, *From Eden to the New Jerusalem: An Introduction to Biblical Theology* (Grand Rapids: Kregel, 2013), 20–21.
6. Cf. L. Michael Morales, *Who Shall Ascend the Mountain of the Lord? A Biblical Theology of the Book of Leviticus*, New Studies in Biblical Theology 37 (Downers Grove, IL: InterVarsity Press, 2015), 40–42.

The first room was called the Holy Place. After you entered the Holy Place through the large outer veil, you would see directly in front of you at the other end of the room the altar of incense. On your left was a beautiful burning golden lampstand, and on your right the table for the bread.

But what about the room in the back shaped like a cube? That was the Most Holy Place or the Holy of Holies. This room kept the ark of the covenant, which two elaborate gold cherubim surrounded. This room was God's throne room, and only the high priest entered the Most Holy Place once a year to make atonement for the people.

When priests served in the Holy Place, a large barrier kept them from seeing into the Most Holy Place. It wasn't sheetrock or a cement wall. It was the inner veil. The veil protected Israel from the brightness of God's glory consuming them. The veil made it possible for God in his white-hot holiness to dwell among his unholy people.

God instructed the Israelites to skillfully weave cherubim into this veil (Exod. 26:31; cf. 36:35). And that's one of the big clues that signals that the Most Holy Place parallels the garden of Eden. Do you recall what God did after he expelled Adam and Eve from the garden of Eden? "He drove out the man, and at the east of the garden of Eden he placed the cherubim and a flaming sword that turned every way to guard the way to the tree of life" (Gen. 3:24). In a similar way, the cherubim woven into the inner veil symbolized that sinful humans could not enter this temple either.[7]

The Temple Solomon Built

This was the first temple in Jerusalem, and it was magnificent. The dimensions double those of the tabernacle: in the tabernacle the Holy Place was thirty feet long by fifteen feet wide, and the Most Holy Place was a fifteen-foot cube. In the temple the Holy Place was sixty feet long by thirty feet wide, and the Most Holy Place was a thirty-foot cube.

To go up to Jerusalem was to go where God lived. So it devastated Israel when the Babylonians demolished this temple when they destroyed Jerusalem in 586 BC. When Israel sank so low that they repeatedly forsook God and his covenant, God left the temple (see the progressive departure in Ezekiel 8–11).

The New Temple in Ezekiel 40–48

Christians interpret this passage in several different ways. We think Beale argues persuasively that Ezekiel 40–48 figuratively presents a real,

---

7. By the way, this is illustrating that biblical-theological themes connect with others. "Temple" connects with other themes such as sin, law, sacrifice, atonement, priest, the glory of God, covenant, kingdom, exile and exodus, city of God, people of God, holiness, justice, wrath, and worship. The themes intertwine.

heavenly, nonstructural, end-time temple that God will establish on earth.[8] But Christians should be able to agree that at minimum the new temple symbolizes God's presence with his people in the future.

The Temple Zerubbabel Built

After the Babylonian captivity, it took about twenty years for a group of Jews to slowly rebuild the temple. Haggai and Zechariah exhorted the people to finish the job, but the temple was pitiful compared to Solomon's magnificent temple. And God did not fill this temple with his glorious presence. This began a period of time called *Second Temple Judaism*. It refers to Jewish history and literature from the time that Zerubbabel completed the second temple (c. 516 BC) to when the Romans destroyed Herod's temple in AD 70.

The Temple Herod Built

King Herod took several decades to rebuild the temple to rival Solomon's temple in its grandeur. Zechariah the priest was inside this temple when he burned incense at the golden altar in the Holy Place (Luke 1:9).

Jesus and the Temple

At least six significant events in Jesus's life involve the temple:

1. Jesus, who is God, tabernacles among humans. "The Word became flesh and dwelt [i.e., tabernacled—from σκηνόω (*skēnoō*)] among us" (John 1:14).

2. Jesus visited the temple complex as a boy (Luke 2:39–52).

3. Jesus judged the temple at the beginning and end of his earthly ministry (cf. John 2:13–25 and Matt. 21:12–17).

4. Satan tempted Jesus to jump off the temple mount (Matt. 4:5–7; Luke 4:9–12).

5. Jesus claimed that his body is the temple (John 2:18–22).[9]

6. When Jesus died on the cross, the veil between the Holy Place and the Most Holy Place "was torn in two, from top to bottom" (Matt.

---

8. Beale, *Temple and the Church's Mission*, 335–64.
9. See Paul M. Hoskins, *Jesus as the Fulfillment of the Temple in the Gospel of John*, Paternoster Biblical Monographs (Milton Keynes, UK: Paternoster, 2006).

27:51).[10] The torn veil pictures what Jesus's death accomplished. That massive curtain blocked access to God, and Jesus removed the barrier. The veil was the type or shadow, and Christ's body was the antitype or the reality that the shadow anticipated. The only way to approach God was to go through the veil, and now that the veil is torn, the only way for us to approach God is through Jesus. Jesus's death makes it possible for people to go directly into God's presence (see Heb. 6:19–20; 10:19–22). The temple rituals and the Mosaic covenant are now obsolete.[11] Now Jesus is our temple, our priest, our sacrifice.[12]

The Church as God's Temple

Four passages are most significant: 1 Corinthians 3:16–17; 2 Corinthians 6:14–7:1; Ephesians 2:21–22; and 1 Peter 2:4–10. Because the church is God's temple, the church must be unified and pure.

The Individual Christian as the Holy Spirit's Temple

Paul rhetorically asks, "Do you not know that your body is a temple of the Holy Spirit within you, whom you have from God? You are not your own, for you were bought with a price. So glorify God in your body" (1 Cor. 6:19–20). If you are a Christian, then your individual body is the temple of the Holy Spirit.[13]

Think about that in light of the biblical-theological trajectory that we just traced. Under the old covenant, only the high priest could enter the Most Holy Place, and only once a year. Under the new covenant, your individual body is a temple of the Spirit of God himself. Amazing.

Side note: Who says that biblical theology isn't practical? Paul's main argument in 1 Corinthians 6:12–20 is that you should glorify God with your body by not committing sexual immorality. And one reason he gives for why you should not have immoral sex is that your body is a temple of the Holy Spirit. It's unthinkable to commit sexual immorality in the Most Holy Place. But now your body is the Most Holy Place. So don't defile it. Keep it pure because it's sacred space. Richard Hays is right: "Sex education in the church might begin by seeking to cultivate a deep awareness of the indwelling presence of God."[14]

---

10. See Daniel M. Gurtner, *The Torn Veil: Matthew's Exposition of the Death of Jesus*, SNTSMS 139 (Cambridge: Cambridge University Press, 2007).
11. See Questions 22 and 25.
12. See Timothy Keller, *King's Cross: The Story of the World in the Life of Jesus* (New York: Dutton, 2011), 48.
13. The temple in 1 Corinthians 6:19 could refer to the church as a whole (and not a Christian's individual physical body), but it almost certainly refers to an individual Christian's body.
14. Richard B. Hays, *First Corinthians*, IBC (Louisville: John Knox, 1997), 108.

The Heavenly Temple

The heavenly temple is prominent in Hebrews 8–10. And it's the setting for the drama that plays out in Revelation 4–20.

The New Jerusalem

Revelation 21 begins, "Then I saw a new heaven and a new earth, for the first heaven and the first earth had passed away, and the sea was no more. And I saw the holy city, new Jerusalem, coming down out of heaven from God" (Rev. 21:1–2). What are the dimensions of this city? "The city lies foursquare, its length the same as its width. And he measured the city with his rod, 12,000 stadia. Its length and width and height are equal" (Rev. 21:16). The city is a perfect cube. There is only one other cube in the Bible: the Most Holy Place in Israel's tabernacle and temple. And both cubes are overlaid with gold (1 Kings 6:20; Rev. 21:18). What do we make of all this symbolism? There is no longer a small section of the earth that is the Most Holy Place. *The entire new earth* is the Most Holy Place. The entire city is God's temple. The temple theme culminates here: "And I saw no temple in the city, for its temple is the Lord God the Almighty and the Lamb" (Rev. 21:22).

That is how the temple fits into the Bible's storyline.

Summary

The temple theme progresses through the Bible from the garden of Eden to the new Jerusalem. The Old Testament temple types climax in Jesus and consummate in the new Jerusalem when the entire new earth is God's temple.

REFLECTION QUESTIONS

1. How would you summarize the temple theme throughout the Bible in your own words?

2. How does the temple theme climax in Jesus?

3. How does the temple theme culminate in the new heaven and new earth?

4. How does the temple theme throughout Scripture practically apply to the church?

5. How does the temple theme throughout Scripture practically apply to individual Christians at this stage in the history of salvation?

What Is a Biblical Theology of Mission?

Jason S. DeRouchie

> *Blessed be the LORD, the God of Israel,*
> *who alone does wondrous things.*
> *Blessed be his name forever;*
> *may the whole earth be filled with his glory!*
> (Ps. 72:18–19)

> *All the nations you have made shall come*
> *and worship before you, O Lord,*
> *and shall glorify your name.*
> (Ps. 86:9)

> *Praise the LORD, all nations!*
> *Extol him, all peoples!*
> *For great is his steadfast love toward us,*
> *and the faithfulness of the LORD endures forever.*
> *Praise the LORD!*
> (Ps. 117:1–2)

With voices of hope, the psalmists looked forward to the day when all peoples of the planet would praise the Lord and relish his favor (e.g., Pss. 72:18–19; 86:9; 96:3; 117:1). Paul, as a servant of Messiah Jesus, identifies that the aim of the gospel is "to bring about the obedience of faith for the sake of [Christ's] name among all the nations"—a mission that defines the very makeup of the church (Rom. 1:5).[1] Three elements are noteworthy with respect to this aim.

First, the phrase "the obedience of faith" probably means "the obedience that always flows from faith."[2] Faith is the root and obedience the fruit; the two are never separated. Saving faith submits to Christ's lordship (see Rom. 6:17–18; 10:13–17).

Next, the target of the gospel mission is to see people saved and satisfied from "among *all* the nations." The good news that the reigning God saves and satisfies believing sinners through Christ's life, death, and resurrection is for the Libyan and the Bolivian, for the expats in Dubai and the mountain tribes in the Himalayas, for the Latinos in Miami and for the poor in rural Minnesota.

Finally, this passage tells us that missions is a means to white hot worship. As John Piper explains, "Missions is not the ultimate goal of the church. Worship is. Missions exists because worship doesn't."[3] One day the need for missions will pass away, but the redeemed will forever magnify the majesty and glory of God in Christ. Missions exists "for the sake of Jesus's name" (Rom. 1:5). There is no higher goal than seeing and savoring Jesus's glory among the peoples of the world.

Humanity's Original Commission and the Need for Curse-Overcoming Blessing

When God first made the world, he planted a garden-sanctuary, and in it he placed his image—a man and a woman, whom he commissioned to expand his garden temple by carrying his image to the ends of the earth (Gen. 1:27–28).[4] God commissioned humanity to reflect, resemble, and represent his greatness and glory on a global scale.

Our first parents initially rejected this calling by choosing to imitate the serpent in their rebellion. But God remained committed to magnifying himself in the universe, and he promised to overcome the curse through a royal deliverer—an offspring of the woman who would one day overpower

---

1. Kevin DeYoung and Greg Gilbert, *What Is the Mission of the Church? Making Sense of Social Justice, Shalom, and the Great Commission* (Wheaton, IL: Crossway, 2011).

2. So, e.g., Richard N. Longenecker, *The Epistle to the Romans: A Commentary on the Greek Text*, NIGTC (Grand Rapids: Eerdmans, 2016), 79–82; Thomas R. Schreiner, *Romans*, 2nd ed., BECNT (Grand Rapids: Baker Academic, 2018), 40; Douglas J. Moo, *The Letter to the Romans*, 2nd ed., NICNT (Grand Rapids: Eerdmans, 2018), 50–51.

3. John Piper, *Let the Nations Be Glad! The Supremacy of God in Missions*, 3rd ed. (Grand Rapids: Baker Academic, 2010), 15.

4. See especially G. K. Beale, *The Temple and the Church's Mission: A Biblical Theology of the Dwelling Place of God*, NSBT 17 (Downers Grove, IL: InterVarsity, 2004); G. K. Beale, "Eden, the Temple, and the Church's Mission in the New Creation," *JETS* 48 (2005): 5–31; T. Desmond Alexander, *From Eden to the New Jerusalem: An Introduction to Biblical Theology* (Grand Rapids: Kregel, 2008). See also Question 27.

the serpent and reestablish global blessing (Gen. 3:15). Later prophets identified how this person would fulfill God's promise and fill the whole earth with God's glory (Ps. 72:1–2, 17–19; Isa. 11:1–2, 9–10; cf. Num. 14:21; Hab. 2:14).

Sin escalated after Adam's fall and moved God to justly punish humanity through the flood. As Noah and his sons repopulated the world, Yahweh punished the proud at the Tower of Babel. Far from seeking to magnify God's name, people sought to elevate their own names, so the Lord dispersed them—seventy different family groups—and confused their languages throughout the world (Gen. 11:8–9). For God's blessing to overcome his curse, he would now need to address the sins of peoples (plural) and to call for surrender across language groups.

The Means for Curse-Overcoming Blessing: The Two-Stage Abrahamic Promise

Yahweh pledged to overcome the sin and language barriers through a descendant of one of the seventy families—Abraham:

> Now the LORD said to Abram, "Go from your country and your kindred and your father's house to the land that I will show you so that I may make of you a great nation, and may bless you, and may make your name great. And there, be a blessing, so that I may bless those who bless you, and him who dishonors you I may curse. And the result will be that in you all the families of the ground shall be blessed." (Gen. 12:1–3, DeRouchie's translation)

Growing out of his two commands to the patriarch to *go* and *be a blessing*, the Lord here promises Abraham a two-stage process to see the world's curse overcome. First, he would need to go to the land of Canaan, where God would make him into a great nation. God fulfilled that promise in the Mosaic covenant era. Second, Abraham, or one representing him, would need to be a blessing, so that God could ultimately overcome global curse and bring blessing to all the families who earlier spread around the earth (cf. 10:32). The Lord ultimately realized that promise in Christ and the new covenant.

God promised Abraham that he would become "the father of a multitude of nations" (17:4–6), but he also stressed that this move from being the father of one nation (Israel) to a multitude of nations would happen only when the royal deliverer would rise—one who would expand kingdom territory by possessing the gate of enemies and through whom all the nations would be blessed (22:17–18; cf. 26:3–4). Missions as we know it—carrying a message of reconciliation outward to the nations—would become operative only in the day when this king would arise and crush the powers of the serpent. Let's now consider each of these two stages as they play out in Scripture.

Stage 1a: Israel's "Come and See" Calling and the Failed Mosaic Covenant

During the Mosaic covenant age, many non-Israelites *became* Israelites—people such as the mixed multitude coming out of Egypt, Rahab the Canaanite, Ruth the Moabite, and Uriah the Hittite. While Israel as a people was, at some level, a multiethnic community, during the entire OT period Abraham remained the father of a single nation. And like Adam in the garden-sanctuary, God called this people his firstborn son (Exod. 4:21; cf. Gen. 5:1–3) and charged them to be priest-kings by representing, resembling, and reflecting him to a needy world. Others would see their good deeds, and those good deeds would direct them to the greatness of God.

Thus, Yahweh told Israel, "If you will indeed obey my voice and keep my covenant, you shall be my treasured possession among all peoples, for all the earth is mine; and you shall be to me a kingdom of priests and a holy nation" (Exod. 19:5–6). Through radically surrendered lives, Israel would mediate God's presence and display God's holiness to a needy world. Similarly, Moses wrote, "Keep [the statutes and the rules] and do them, for that will be your wisdom and your understanding in the sight of the peoples, who, when they hear all these statutes, will say, 'Surely this great nation is a wise and understanding people'" (Deut. 4:6).

Israel had a high calling to reflect God's worth by surrendering wholly to him. But this calling does not appear to have included the "go and tell" mission that Christians now have. Instead, Israel's limited "mission" to the nations involved only a calling to "come and see."[5] As the Israelites obeyed Yahweh, the nations would take notice and draw near to Yahweh's greatness. But Israel failed in their covenant loyalty, and their rebellion, like Adam's, ultimately resulted in the Lord's removing them from paradise, a reality that Moses anticipated (Deut. 31:27, 29) and the prophets affirmed (2 Kings 17:13–15, 23).

Stage 1b: Prophetic Visions of Hope and a Global Mission of Reconciliation

Nevertheless, even amid the failures of the Mosaic covenant, God raised up prophets like Isaiah who recalled the promises that God would bring good news and blessing to the whole world through a single royal deliver. This

---

5. On this, see especially Eckhard J. Schnabel, "Israel, the People of God, and the Nations," *JETS* 45 (2002): 35–57; Eckhard J. Schnabel, *Early Christian Mission*, 2 vols. (Downers Grove, IL: InterVarsity, 2004); and Kevin Paul Oberlin, "The Ministry of Israel to the Nations: A Biblical Theology of Missions in the Era of the Old Testament Canon" (PhD diss., Bob Jones University, 2006). This approach contrasts with that of Walter Kaiser, who treats Israel's "come and see" calling as if it were a "go and tell" mission and who often fails to distinguish OT texts that are predicting what will happen in the new covenant age from what was happening in the old covenant age. See Walter C. Kaiser Jr., *Mission in the Old Testament: Israel as a Light to the Nations*, 2nd ed. (Grand Rapids: Baker Academic, 2012).

servant-king would represent the people of Israel—even bearing its name—and through him some from Israel and the nations would enjoy lasting salvation: "You are my servant, Israel, in whom I will be glorified. . . . It is too light a thing that you should be my servant to raise up the tribes of Jacob and to bring back the preserved of Israel; I will make you as a light for the nations, that my salvation may reach to the end of the earth" (Isa. 49:3, 6). This royal servant would enjoy God's presence and would fulfill his mission to bring justice to the nations, engage in a ministry of mercy, and guide the lost (42:1–4; 51:4–5; 61:1–3). He would serve as a covenant mediator and would open the eyes of the blind and deliver the captive (42:6–7; 49:8–9). He would preach the good news of God's victory over evil and God's saving grace (52:7–10; 61:1–3), which he would secure through his own substitutionary sacrifice (53:5). Yahweh would make his royal servant an offering for humanity's guilt, and by this atoning work he would "sprinkle many nations," "make many to be accounted righteous," and "bear their iniquities" (52:15; 53:10–11; cf. Rom. 5:18–19; 2 Cor. 5:21).

Through the death and resurrection of this royal servant-person, Israel, a multitude of offspring-servants would rise who would carry on the servant-person's missional task (Isa. 49:3, 6): "In the LORD all the offspring of Israel shall be justified and shall glory" (45:25); "When his soul makes an offering for guilt, he shall see his offspring; he shall prolong his days; the will of the LORD shall prosper in his hand. Out of the anguish of his soul he shall see and be satisfied: by his knowledge shall the righteous one, my servant, make many to be accounted righteous, and shall bear their iniquities" (53:10–11). These would be "an offspring the LORD has blessed" (61:9), and they would "possess the nations" (54:3), including "servants" who would operate as priests from among the foreigners (56:6–8) and ethnic Israelites alike (56:6–8; 63:17; 66:20–21).

Stage 2a: The New Covenant and Jesus's Mission of Good News

Jesus is the very one Moses, Isaiah, and the other prophets anticipated—the one through whom all the world can be blessed. He is the singular royal "offspring of Abraham," and in him Jews and Gentiles, slave and free, males and females can become Abraham's true "offspring," full heirs of all the promises. Paul draws on the promises of Genesis 12:3; 22:18; and 28:4:

> The Scripture, foreseeing that God would justify the Gentiles by faith, preached the gospel beforehand to Abraham, saying, "In you shall all the nations be blessed." . . . In Christ Jesus the blessing of Abraham [has] come to the Gentiles. . . . Now the promises were made to Abraham and to his offspring . . . who is Christ. . . . And if you are Christ's, then you are Abraham's offspring, heirs according to promise. (Gal. 3:8, 14, 16, 29)

Furthermore, Jesus is Yahweh's royal servant who proclaims the good news of God's reign and brings light and salvation to the nations. Thus, he opened his ministry citing LXX Isaiah 61:1–2: "The Spirit of the Lord is upon me, because he has anointed me to proclaim good news to the poor. He has sent me to proclaim liberty to the captives and recovering of sight to the blind, to set at liberty those who are oppressed, to proclaim the year of the Lord's favor" (Luke 4:18–19 ; cf. Isa 42:7). Jesus directly fulfilled Isaiah's promise that the servant-person Israel would save people from both Israel and the nations (Acts 26:22–23; cf. Isa. 49:3, 6). With citations from the Law, Prophets, and Writings, Paul also noted that Jesus is the one in whom peoples from the nations are now hoping:

> For I tell you that Christ became a servant to the circumcised to show God's truthfulness, in order to confirm the promises given to the patriarchs, and in order that the Gentiles might glorify God for his mercy. As it is written, "Therefore I will praise you among the Gentiles, and sing to your name." And again it is said, "Rejoice, O Gentiles, with his people." And again, "Praise the Lord, all you Gentiles, and let all the peoples extol him." And again Isaiah says, "The root of Jesse will come, even he who arises to rule the Gentiles; in him will the Gentiles hope." (Rom. 15:8–12; cf. Ps. 18:49[50]; Deut. 32:43; Ps. 117:1; Isa. 11:10)

Stage 2b: Jesus's Mission Becomes the Church's "Go and Tell" Mission

The mission of the Messiah becomes the mission of his church. In Isaiah 49:6, God commissions the servant king to bring light to the nations, but in Acts 13:47, the Messiah's mission is *Paul's* mission: "The Lord has commanded us, saying, 'I have made you a light for the Gentiles, that you may bring salvation to the ends of the earth.'" Accordingly, in Isaiah 52:7 the messianic servant is the one with beautiful feet bringing the good news of salvation and God's reign ("how beautiful on the mountains are the feet of *him* who brings good news"), but in Romans 10 Paul makes the subject plural to identify that the church now carries on the Messiah's good news proclamation to the nations. "How then will they call on him in whom they have not believed? And how are they to believe in him of whom they have never heard? And how are they to hear without someone preaching? And how are they to preach unless they are sent? As it is written, 'How beautiful are the feet of *those* who preach the good news!'" (Rom. 10:14–15, emphasis added).

Whereas Yahweh called OT Israel to be a kingdom of priests and a holy nation (Exod. 19:5–6), he now both calls and empowers the church to live in a way that points to the greatness and glory of God. Hence, Jesus commanded, "Let your light shine before others, so that they may see your good works and give glory to your Father who is in heaven" (Matt. 5:16). Similarly, Peter proclaimed, "But you are a chosen race, a royal priesthood, a holy nation, a people for his own possession, that you may proclaim the excellencies of him who called you out of darkness into his marvelous light" (1 Peter 2:9).

Yet for the church of Jesus, the responsibility to obey in order that others may "come and see" God's worth is now matched by a "go and tell" mission. Indeed, our Lord has commissioned us to proclaim to all nations the good news that the reigning God eternally saves and satisfies believing sinners through the life, death, and resurrection of Jesus Christ (Matt. 28:18–20).

Filled with the very Spirit of the resurrected Christ (Acts 16:7), the church as God's temple-sanctuary is fulfilling Christ's promise: "You will receive power when the Holy Spirit has come upon you, and you will be my witnesses in Jerusalem and in all Judea and Samaria, and to the end of the earth" (Acts 1:8; cf. Isa. 32:15; 43:10; 49:6; see also 44:3; 59:21). In Christ, the new creation has dawned. God is now reestablishing right order, and his glory is increasingly filling the earth:

> Therefore, if anyone is in Christ, he is a new creation. The old has passed away; behold, the new has come. All this is from God, who through Christ reconciled us to himself and gave us the ministry of reconciliation; that is, in Christ God was reconciling the world to himself, not counting their trespasses against them, and entrusting to us the message of reconciliation. Therefore, we are ambassadors for Christ, God making his appeal through us. We implore you on behalf of Christ, be reconciled to God. For our sake he made him to be sin who knew no sin, so that in him we might become the righteousness of God. . . . We put no obstacle in anyone's way, so that no fault may be found with our ministry, but as servants we commend ourselves in every way. (2 Cor. 5:17–21; 6:3–4)

Stage 2c: The Present and Lasting Praise to the Reigning Savior and Satisfier of the Nations

The ultimate end of missions is passionate praise—magnifying God's greatness and glory in Christ through a multi-ethnic bride (see Eph 1:5–6). Paul's mission and the church's mission is "to bring about the obedience of faith for the sake of [Jesus's] name among all the nations" (Rom. 1:5). Even now in the heavens, those gathered around God's throne are singing praise to the Lion-Lamb king, whose death and resurrection delivered peoples from all nations: "Worthy are you . . . for you were slain, and by your blood you ransomed people for God from every tribe and language and people and nation, and you have made them a kingdom and priests to our God, and they shall reign on the earth" (Rev. 5:9–10). And in the future, those saved and satisfied "from all tribes and peoples and languages" will together cry out, "Salvation belongs to our God who sits on the throne, and to the Lamb!" (7:9–10).

If you have tasted and seen that God in Christ is good, the call of our lives is to know Christ and make him known. As we write this book, there remain 269 unengaged, unreached people groups in this world—those for whom not one person, church, or mission agency has taken responsibility to proclaim the good news through word and deed that the reigning God saves and satisfies believing sinners through Christ's life, death, and resurrection.[6] Approximately 5.7 billion people remain in darkness—spiritually lost and helpless, not knowing, not acknowledging, not adoring Christ as Savior and Lord.

You have an opportunity and responsibility to participate in a work of cosmic proportions—one that God has been developing since creation and that will climax in the global praise of Christ and the immeasurable joy of the redeemed on the new earth. We must either go or send, to be either a rope-holder or one who crosses cultures for the sake of the name. Jesus said, "The harvest is plentiful, but the laborers are few. Therefore pray earnestly to the Lord of the harvest to send out laborers into his harvest" (Luke 10:2). We enjoy the greatest power for the highest task. We are praying that God would let the readers of this book become more faithful goers and more faithful senders until missions is unnecessary and worship continues. What is your part in reaching the neighborhoods and nations for Jesus?

Summary

God is committed to displaying his glory to the ends of the earth. He originally commissioned his image-bearers to reflect, resemble, and represent him in a way that would allow his garden-sanctuary to expand. Humanity's rebellion, however, brought curse on the world and with that, on multiple families and languages. Through Abraham and his offspring, Yahweh purposes to let his blessing overcome curse on a global scale. Through the Mosaic covenant, he commissioned Israel to mediate his presence and display his holiness so that the nations might "come and see" his worth and beauty and be moved to follow. The nation failed at their calling, yet God purposed that a royal deliverer would rise who would appease Yahweh's wrath, secure righteousness, and reconcile the nations. In Christ, God calls and empowers the church to proclaim his excellencies ("come and see") and to seek the conversion of the nations for the sake of Christ's name ("go and tell"). This "go and tell" mission marks a redemptive-historical shift, in which Abraham has moved from being a father of one nation to a father of a multitude of nations. Furthermore, now in Christ the glory of God is spreading through the church to the ends of the earth and will culminate in universal praise in a day when missions will no longer be necessary.

---

6. Figures taken from www.finishingthetask.com.

REFLECTION QUESTIONS

1. What is the ultimate goal of the church, and how does it relate to missions?

2. What significance does the garden of Eden and the original mandate God gave Adam and Eve have for a biblical theology of mission?

3. In what ways is the mission of the church intimately related to the mission of Jesus?

4. How would you describe the redemptive historical shift from a "come and see" mission to both a "come and see" and "go and tell" mission for God's people? What texts would you point to in support of this shift?

5. In what ways does a biblical theology of mission personally affect you? What tangible ways can you better serve God's great commission as a goer or a sender?

What Is a Biblical Theology of the Land?

Oren R. Martin

The land God promised to Abraham begins the process of recapturing and advancing what humanity lost in Eden and what will not be fulfilled until a new and better Eden is regained. At every point throughout the OT, then, the Promised Land anticipates an even greater land to come. Although the territorial promise initially related to Israel's settlement in the land of Canaan, by divine design it also points to something more expansive, which the NT finally reveals. This chapter tracks the progression of the land promise through the biblical covenants until it reaches its fulfillment in the new creation in Christ.[1]

The Giving of the Land Promises

God's covenant with Abraham recovers the universal purpose of Adam in terms of both the blessing of offspring and land. The universal scope of Eden narrows to the land of Canaan, thus allowing Canaan to serve as a microcosm of what God intended for all of humanity, which in time would expand with the proliferation of Abraham's offspring. For example, when Genesis 22:17–18 and 26:3–4 are taken together, the immediate context of the Abrahamic covenant already points to a universal expansion of the territorial promise (more on this point below). In other words, the propagation of Abraham's offspring would result in inheriting the world, as Paul says in Romans 4:13, "For the promise to Abraham and his offspring that he would be heir of the world did not come through the law but through the righteousness of faith." However, this interpretation is not reinterpreting or spiritualizing the OT promise. Rather, it begins to establish the type or pattern that points both back to Eden

---

1. For a more comprehensive treatment of this argument, see Oren R. Martin, *Bound for the Promised Land: The Land Promise in God's Redemptive Plan*, NSBT 34 (Downers Grove, IL: InterVarsity, 2015). Permission has been granted to use and build upon portions of *Bound for the Promised Land* in this chapter.

and forward to the ultimate fulfillment of the promise that would eventually encompass the entire world.

Furthermore, in the Abrahamic covenant there are both national (Gen. 12:2, "nation") and international (17:4–6, "nations") components. For example, Genesis 15 is a covenant God made with Abraham and his "seed," and in Genesis 17, which reaffirms the covenant in chapter 15 after it was doubted in chapter 16, broadens the category of "seed." Also, God changes Abram's name to Abraham, for God made him "the father of a multitude of nations" (17:5). An intended ambiguity exists, then, for Abraham's "seed" *both* encompasses a multitude of nations (ch. 17) *and* relates to an individual descendant (22:17) who will mediate blessing to all the nations of the earth.[2]

When these texts are put together, we see that the ultimate inheritors of the patriarchal promises are not restricted to a national entity but extend to an international community. That is, God's programmatic agenda for humanity after Eden begins with the formation of a nation through Abraham and points forward to an international people, which is picked up later in the Prophets. No political borders, whether Israelite or otherwise, could exhaust the territorial promise, for the multiplication of descendants naturally expands the territorial borders until the earth is filled.

The Fulfillment of the Land Promises

Though there is significant progression and fulfillment of the land promises under leaders such as Moses, Joshua, David, and Solomon, it is the prophets who bring back into focus the Abrahamic promises and advance the pattern of fulfillment in various ways and stages, including both a physical and spiritual return with national and international results. For example, Isaiah describes Israel's return from exile in both imminent and distant ways, as well as in language resembling the exodus (e.g., Isa. 11:1–16; 35:1–10; 51:9–11; 52:11–12). The first return from exile is a physical release and return to the land that God's servant Cyrus will accomplish (42:18–43:21; 44:24–45:1; cf. Ezra 1:1–3). But though this return is another fulfillment of God's promised restoration, it in no way compares to the prophet's final vision. Indeed, a deeper captivity kept Israel from being fully restored. That is, though the people are taken out of idolatrous nations, Yahweh still needs to take idolatry out of the people. God's servant-king would accomplish this

---

2. One can already see hermeneutical warrant for Paul to pick up on this idea when interpreted in light of Christ (Gal. 3:16, 28–29). On this, see C. John Collins, "A Syntactical Note (Genesis 3:15): Is the Woman's Seed Singular or Plural?," *TynBul* 48 (1997): 139–47; T. Desmond Alexander, "Further Observations on the Term 'Seed' in Genesis," *TynBul* 48 (1997): 363–67; C. John Collins, "Galatians 3:16: What Kind of Exegete Was Paul?," *TynBul* 54, no. 1 (2003): 75–86; and Jason S. DeRouchie and Jason C. Meyer, "Christ or Family as the 'Seed' of Promise? An Evaluation of N. T. Wright on Galatians 3:16," *SBJT* 14, no. 3 (Fall 2010): 36–48.

restoration by bringing back Israel so that God's salvation may reach the nations (Isa. 49:1–53:12). Forgiveness will come through God's (individual) servant, who will deliver his (corporate) servant Israel (42:1–9; 49:1–6), redeem his people (9:2–7), rule over his people (11:1–5), and atone for sin by suffering, dying, and taking the punishment upon himself that they deserve (42:1–9; 49:5–6; 50:4–9; 52:13–53:12).

Furthermore, the servant's substitutionary atonement will initiate a new covenant that will enable both Israel *and* the nations to enjoy the blessings of both the Abrahamic and Davidic covenants (54:1–55:13; cf. 19:19–25). Such an international redemption had been God's plan since Abraham had received the word of promise. Moreover, a Davidic king will bless and rule the nations because God has made him leader and commander of the peoples (55:4–5). This connects to the servant king in Isaiah 53, whose offering of himself and whose resurrection enables him to fulfill God's Davidic covenant promises and to serve as the basis for the new or everlasting covenant. Astonishingly, not only does Isaiah identify the remnant of ethnic Israelites as the Lord's servants (Isa. 65:13–25), but he also employs the same designation for redeemed foreigners from the nations (56:6). Furthermore, in fulfillment of the Abrahamic covenant, the Lord will give his *name* and *blessing* to his servants in the land (65:13–16; cf. Gen. 12:3; 17:5; 22:18; 26:4). The servant-person's saving work, therefore, creates *servants*, and all—transformed Israelites and foreigners—will go to Jerusalem as God's holy mountain in a pilgrimage of worship (Isa. 2:2–4; 27:13; cf. Mic. 4:1–5).

But Isaiah proceeds to describe more splendidly the result of this new order. Isaiah 65:17–66:24 succinctly summarizes the end-time themes that occur throughout the entire book and elaborates on the hope of restoration to the city of Jerusalem and the land in otherworldly language that describes astounding realities (cf. Isa. 2:1–4; 4:2–6; 9:1–16; 11:1–10). When the various strands are drawn together, Isaiah's vision of final restoration involves new heavens and a new earth (65:17; 66:22), a new Jerusalem (65:18–19; cf. 4:2–6), and a holy mountain, Zion (65:25; cf. 2:1–4; 4:2–6). Moreover, in fulfillment of the promises to and covenant with Abraham, God will give them a new *name*, and they will receive *blessing* in the *land* by the God of truth (65:15–16). By the end of Isaiah, then, this temple-mountain-city is coextensive with the new heavens and new earth, which resounds with astonishing realities cast in terms of God's kingdom coming to and filling the earth.

In similar order, in Jeremiah God promises to take back his people if they return, and "then nations shall bless themselves in him, and in him shall they glory" (Jer. 4:1–2). This reference identifies how God would fulfill his promises to Abraham (e.g., Gen. 12:3; 22:18) if Israel would repent and glorify God. As in Isaiah, the prophet sees the nations being a part of the restoration of Israel and Judah, and the realization of this cosmological and teleological goal will

fulfill the Abrahamic promises (Jer. 12:14–17).[3] Furthermore, Jeremiah proclaims that Israel will return from exile in terms of a new exodus (16:14–15).

Then, in Jeremiah 30–33, Jeremiah unfolds the great promises of salvation and offers hope beyond the exile that will come in the form of a new
covenant and a return to the land.[4] Of particular importance is 31:38–40,
which concerns the rebuilding and expansion of Jerusalem. In addition to
the restoration of Davidic leadership (30:8–11), priesthood (31:14), and
people (31:31–34), the restoration of the city completes the glorious reversal
of Jeremiah's pronouncements of judgment. Though the city had been destroyed, the future age of redemption will see its restoration *and more*. Derek
Kidner comments, "The promise [in 31:38–40] is 'earthed' not merely in this
planet but in the familiar details of Israel's capital, naming rubbish dumps
and all. . . . But the vision outruns that exercise, in scale and in significance."[5]
Therefore, the new Jerusalem will be both different and expanded from the
old, and the rebuilt city will become the center of God's presence among his
people (3:14–18; cf. Isa. 65:17; 66:12; Rev. 21:3).

Jeremiah describes the restoration of both people and place in the future
and pins these hopes on a Davidic leader, a righteous branch who, interest-
ingly, combines both king and priest (33:14–18). This king-priest will secure a
new covenant for his people as certain as God's covenant with day and night;
he will make them dwell securely in the land and multiply the offspring of
David as numerous as the sands of the sea in fulfillment of his covenant with
Abraham (33:14–26). Moreover, Jeremiah 31:35–40 hints that this new covenant will operate within the contours of a new creation.

In similar fashion, Ezekiel, the last in the so-called Major Prophets, proph-
esies that the renewed people will be purified in heart and spirit, and they will
be one flock under a new David (Ezek. 34–37). As a result, "the nations will

---

3. Jeremiah 12 intriguingly speaks of an exile, not just for Judah but also for Yahweh's evil
   neighbors "who touch the heritage that I have given my people Israel to inherit" (12:14).
   Astonishingly, in verse 15, after Yahweh plucks up each people from their land, he will again
   have compassion on them, and he will "bring them in again each to his heritage and each
   to his land." And in the end, when Yahweh brings all the exiles home, if the nations learn to
   swear by Yahweh's name, "then they shall be built up in the midst of my people" (v. 16).

4. Jeremiah is the only text in the OT that specifically speaks of the "new covenant." However,
   Walter Kaiser is correct in seeing the concept of the new covenant in other passages despite
   the omission of the exact phrase. He writes, "Based on similar content and contexts, the
   following expressions can be equated with the new covenant: the 'everlasting covenant' in
   seven passages (Jer 32:40; 50:5; Ezek 16:60; 37:26; Isa 24:5; 55:3; 61:8), a 'new heart' or a
   'new spirit' in three or four passages (Ezek 11:19; 18:31; 36:26; Jer 32:39 [LXX]), the 'covenant of peace' in three passages (Isa 54:10; Ezek 34:25; 37:26), and 'a covenant' or 'my covenant' which is placed 'in that day' in three passages (Isa 49:8; 59:21; Hos 2:18–20)—making
   a grand total of sixteen or seventeen major passages on the new covenant." Walter C. Kaiser
   Jr., "The Old Promise and the New Covenant: Jeremiah 31:31–34," *JETS* 15 (1972): 14.

5. Derek Kidner, *The Message of Jeremiah*, BST (Downers Grove, IL: InterVarsity, 1987), 111.

know that I the LORD make Israel holy, when my sanctuary is among them forever" (37:28). Whereas God had been a sanctuary to the exiles "for a little while" (11:16), now his presence will be with them forever. He will make a new covenant (36:16–38), which will deal with their sin and finally reconcile them to Yahweh, so that he can say, "They will be my people, and I will be their God" (37:23, 27). In order for this restoration to come, however, God must create a holy people from nothing. And to be sure, he will accomplish his new creation. Indeed, Ezekiel uses the language of resurrection to illustrate the promise of Israel's return to a new life in her own land from the deathlike existence of exile (37:11–14). In other words, the restoration to the land is linked with the resurrection motif. The dead shall be brought to life so that they too may participate in the restoration. But Ezekiel's vision of restoration does not stop with Israel. Like similar passages throughout the writing Prophets, Ezekiel indicates that the restoration will have international significance (16:59–63).

Ezekiel continues with his program by envisioning in chapters 40–48 a rebuilt temple with revitalized worship. That is, first a new humanity is (re)created (ch. 37) and then placed in a new temple-Eden. The climactic vision in chapters 40–48 describes the fulfillment of the promises of chapters 1–39. In a significant passage, Ezekiel 37:25–28 pulls together various strands of the new place for God's people and prepares the way for even more glorious promises in chapters 40–48 (cf. 37:25–28 and 43:7–9). It is significant, then, that Ezekiel ends with a vision of a purified land with boundaries situated around a new temple complex. More specifically, Ezekiel 47:1–12 contains an abundance of Edenic imagery and describes a paradisiacal temple that extends to encompass the entire land. Significantly, Ezekiel uses similar language as Jeremiah regarding a measuring line extending the boundaries outward (Ezek. 47:3; Jer. 31:39; cf. Zech. 2). Thus, the promise concerning the renewed Israel living in the land under a new David is fulfilled in the vision of a temple, recreating an Edenic context, the boundaries of which are coterminous with the land.

From a canonical perspective, then, Revelation presents this worldwide temple as the new heaven and new earth—the new Jerusalem—in light of the fulfillment of Christ, the true temple.[6] For the NT writers, this prophecy became a brilliant way of speaking of what God had now achieved in and through Jesus. Paradoxically, although Ezekiel's vision had focused so much upon the temple, it found its ultimate fulfillment in that city where there was no temple, because its temple is the Lord God Almighty and the Lamb

---

6. It is beyond the scope of this chapter to provide a detailed analysis of all the allusions of Ezekiel 40–48 in Revelation 21–22. Suffice it to say, Revelation 21–22 further interprets the yet-future fulfillment of Ezekiel by collapsing temple, city, and land into one end-time picture, thus describing how God fulfills his covenant promises. See G. K. Beale, *The Temple in the Church's Mission: A Biblical Theology of the Dwelling Place of God*, NSBT 17 (Downers Grove, IL: InterVarsity, 2004), 348–53.

(Rev. 21:22).[7] Ezekiel, then, in line with the other prophets, describes astounding hope for the future that includes transformed land and human nature—a new and better Eden enlarged with one immense river of life and many trees of life.

The NT reveals that what was promised in the OT is fulfilled through the person and work of Christ, the son of David, the son of Abraham, the son of Adam, the son of God. Jesus—the obedient Israelite—inaugurates the kingdom through his death and resurrection and finally delivers his people from the exile of sin (Matt. 2:15; Col. 1:13–14). Matthew interprets the end-time land promises through the lens of various typological and universalized texts in the OT (Matt. 5:5; Ps. 37). Through Christ's work, he makes a new covenant people—who belong to the new creation and are temples of the living God (2 Cor. 5:17; 6:16)—united to him by faith, the true temple (John 1:14; 2:19–22). This new people, the church of Jesus Christ made up of both Jew and Gentile, await their final home. In this way it can be said that Abraham would "inherit" the world (Rom. 4:13) without contravening or spiritualizing OT promises.[8] This new heaven and new earth is cast in terms of a paradisiacal garden-temple-city (Rev. 21–22; cf. Isa. 65–66; Ezek. 40–48). In other words, the variegated realities of the OT land promises—the expansive city, temple, and land—reach their *telos* in the new creation that Christ wins.[9] In this sense, then, what believing Israel obtains is far greater than the land of Canaan, for they—along with the nations—will inherit the whole earth in fulfillment of God's gracious and irrevocable promises. It is important to note, however, that the church of Jesus Christ, composed of both Jew and Gentile, does not necessarily eliminate a future salvation for ethnic Israelites (Rom. 9–11). However, this future salvation is obtained only through faith in Jesus Christ as a surprising display of God's faithfulness and grace, and both saved Jews and Gentiles will together enjoy the land inheritance of the new earth.

---

7. Peter W. L. Walker, *Jesus and the Holy City: New Testament Perspectives on Jerusalem* (Grand Rapids: Eerdmans, 1996), 313.

8. While there is no explicit statement in the OT that Abraham would become heir of the world, the idea is there. Of particular importance is Genesis 26:3–4, where the unique plural "lands," when read in conjunction with the oath to which it alludes in Genesis 22:17–18, makes clear that Abraham's seed will possess/inherit the gate of his enemies. See Douglas J. Moo, *Romans*, 2nd ed., NICNT (Grand Rapids: Eerdmans, 2018), 299–300; Thomas R. Schreiner, *Romans*, 2nd ed., BECNT (Grand Rapids: Baker, 2018), 235–36. This, together with Genesis 22:17, provides exegetical footing for Paul's assertion that Abraham would inherit the world. Paul, then, is demonstrating sound biblical exegesis, informed by Scripture's redemptive-historical storyline, by putting all three elements of the covenant together. In light of Christ, Abraham, Abraham's (singular) seed (Gal. 3:16), and Abraham's (corporate) offspring will inherit the world as people, both Jews and Gentiles, come to faith in Jesus Christ (3:29).

9. One could also explore the rich use of inheritance language in the NT in light of its OT background. For example, see Martin, *Bound for the Promised Land*, ch. 8.

Summary

Scripture's beginning and end show that God's cosmological goal is to establish his kingdom on earth. However, due to the fall of humankind into sin and death, the accomplishment of this goal is radically marred but not decimated, for God makes a promise (Gen. 3:15) that will providentially guide his redemptive means to their divinely appointed end. In fact, he will reestablish his kingdom on earth through his graciously initiated covenants that reach their completion in and through the person and work of Christ, the last Adam. The land promised to Abraham picks up and advances what was lost in Eden and anticipates a better land to come that finds its fulfillment in the person and work of Christ, who as a result, the kingdom of the world will become the kingdom of our Lord and of his Christ, and he shall reign forever and ever (Rev. 11:15).

Let us be reminded, therefore, that our great and glorious Triune God fulfills his promises. In his ministry, Jesus announced that God was fulfilling his ancient promises to restore his people from exile and establish his universal and international kingdom. In this age, however, we live as sojourners and exiles who seek the city that is to come, whose designer and builder is God (Heb. 11:10; 13:14; 1 Peter 2:11). We should, therefore, live in faith with the anticipation in our lives and words until *that* day, when "the dwelling place of God is with man. He will dwell with them, and they will be his people, and God himself will be with them as their God" (Rev. 21:3).

REFLECTION QUESTIONS

1. How does a biblical theology of the land promise demonstrate God's faithfulness?

2. What OT evidence is there to conclude that God intended the land he promised to Abraham and gave to Israel to be more than the limited geographical area of Canaan?

3. How do the prophets pick up and advance the land promises?

4. How does the NT demonstrate the fulfillment of the OT land promises? What passages and themes (e.g., inheritance, rest) relate to it?

5. How does Revelation 21–22 fulfill the land promises?

What Is a Biblical Theology of Resurrection?

Jason S. DeRouchie

Next to God's original creation of humanity, Jesus's resurrection unto glory is the most decisive event in the history of humankind, for it brings the dawning of the new creation (2 Cor. 5:17) and validates that those in Christ are no longer imprisoned under sin, the payment for which is death (Rom. 6:23; 1 Cor. 15:17). The OT Scriptures foresaw "that the Christ should suffer and on the third day rise from the dead" (Luke 24:46; cf. John 20:9; Acts 17:2–3; 1 Cor. 15:4; cf. Luke 24:7) and that "by being the first to rise from the dead, he would proclaim light" both to the Jews and the Gentiles (Acts 26:22–23). So, where does the OT anticipate the third-day resurrection? Closely assessing NT texts that cite or allude to specific OT texts gives us an initial clue to how those living at the dawn of the new creation were seeing how the OT anticipates the resurrection of the Messiah and of the just and unjust alike.

New Testament Citations and Allusions of Old Testament Resurrection Texts

The Sadducees did not believe in the resurrection.[1] In contrast, Jesus argued that God "is not the God of the dead, but of the living" since that is what God implied when he proclaimed to Moses, "I am the God of Abraham, and the God of Isaac, and the God of Jacob" (Mark 12:26–27; cf. Exod. 3:6). Similarly, when Jesus asserted his God-given authority to judge, he alluded to Daniel 12:2: "An hour is coming when all who are in the tombs will hear his voice and come out, those who have done good to the resurrection of life, and those who have done evil to the resurrection of judgment" (John 5:28–29).

---

1. See Mitchell L. Chase, "The Genesis of Resurrection Hope: Exploring Its Early Presence and Deep Roots," *JETS* 57 (2014): 467–71.

Later, when Paul defended himself before Felix in Caesarea, he alluded to the
same OT text when he claimed that those of the Way (i.e., Christians) "have
hope in God . . . that there will be a resurrection of both the just and the unjust" (Acts 24:14–15).

In Acts, both Peter and Paul identified that Psalm 16:10–11 directly
foretells Christ's resurrection (Acts 2:25–31; 13:34–35). Peter cites Psalm
16:10—"you will not abandon my soul to Hades, or let your Holy One see
corruption"—and explains that David "foresaw and spoke about the resurrection of the Christ" (Acts 2:27, 31). Paul also cited Psalm 2:7 and Isaiah 55:3:

> And we bring you the good news that what God promised to the fa-
> thers, this he has fulfilled to us their children by raising Jesus, as also
> it is written in the second Psalm, "You are my Son, today I have be-
> gotten you." And as for the fact that he raised him from the dead, no
> more to return to corruption, he has spoken in this way, "I will give
> you the holy and sure blessings of David." Therefore he says also in
> another psalm, "You will not let your Holy One see corruption." For
> David, after he had served the purpose of God in his own generation,
> fell asleep and was laid with his fathers and saw corruption, but he
> whom God raised up did not see corruption. (Acts 13:32–37)

Finally, 1 Corinthians 15:54–58 recalls both Isaiah 25:8 and Hosea 13:14 to
argue how God must transform the perishable, mortal bodies of dead and
living believers into imperishable, immortal bodies to triumphantly defeat
death:

> When the perishable puts on the imperishable, and the mortal puts
> on immortality, then shall come to pass the saying that is written:
> "Death is swallowed up in victory." "O death, where is your victory? O
> death, where is your sting?" The sting of death is sin, and the power of
> sin is the law. But thanks be to God, who gives us the victory through
> our Lord Jesus Christ. Therefore, my beloved brothers, be steadfast,
> immovable, always abounding in the work of the Lord, knowing that
> in the Lord your labor is not in vain.

Whereas Isaiah declared that Yahweh would "swallow up death forever" and
thus identify himself as the anticipated savior (Isa. 25:8–9), the immediate
context of God's original queries through Hosea offered little hope: "Shall I
ransom them [i.e., Ephraim] from the power of Sheol? Shall I redeem them
from Death? O Death, where are your plagues? O Sheol, where is your sting?
Compassion is hidden from my eyes" (Hos. 13:14). God would not remain
distant forever, however, for he tore them so that he could ultimately heal
them (6:1–2). He would move them to seek Yahweh their God and David their

king (3:5) and would heal their apostasy as they would find shelter under the shadow of their royal representative (14:4–8). Thus, the victory of our Lord Christ would overcome the sting of death—just as Paul declared.

Potential Third-Day Resurrection Typologies in the Old Testament

None of the above OT texts that the NT points to includes any mention of a *third-day* resurrection, yet both Jesus (Luke 24:46) and Paul (1 Cor. 15:4) stress that the prediction of Christ's being raised on the third day was "written" and was "in accordance with the Scriptures."[2] It seems likely, therefore, that we should look for typologies that foreshadow a third-day resurrection event, and when we broaden our perspective here, a number of other texts become possible sources for the NT claims. We will look at them moving from back to front through the canon.

First, Jesus paralleled his own coming resurrection with Jonah's resurrection-like deliverance from the belly of the fish: "For just as Jonah was three days and three nights in the belly of the great fish, so will the Son of Man be three days and three nights in the heart of the earth" (Matt. 12:40; cf. Jon. 1:17–2:10[2:1–11]). Jesus appears to read the Jonah story typologically, seeing it as both pointing to his exaltation through trial and clarifying how his resurrection would signal salvation through judgment.

Second, building on his earlier predictions of the exile's end (e.g., Hos. 3:5), Hosea declared that the end of Israel's exile would be like a resurrection after three days:

> Come, let us return to the LORD; for he has torn us, that he may heal us; he has struck us down, and he will bind us up. After two days he will revive us; on the third day he will raise us up, that we may live before him. Let us know; let us press on to know the LORD; his going out is sure as the dawn; he will come to us as the showers, as the spring rains that water the earth. (Hos. 6:1–3)

Significantly, the prophets are clear that the Christ would represent Israel by bearing the people's name and saving representatives from both the nation and the other nzations (Isa. 49:3, 6). At the end of his book, Hosea himself appears to make this connection between the one and the many when he relates a plural people with a singular "Israel," under whose shadow they will find refuge (Hos. 14:4–8 in the Hebrew, seen in the ESV footnotes; cf. Zech.

---

2. See Nicholas P. Lunn, "'Raised on the Third Day according to the Scriptures': Resurrection Typology in the Genesis Creation Narrative," *JETS* 57 (2014): 523–35; Stephen G. Dempster, "From Slight Peg to Cornerstone to Capstone: The Resurrection of Christ on 'the Third Day' according to the Scriptures," *WTJ* 76 (2014): 371–409; Joel R. White, "'He Was Raised on the Third Day according to the Scriptures' (1 Corinthians 15:4): A Typological Interpretation based on the Cultic Calendar in Leviticus 23," *TynBul* 66 (2015): 103–19.

3:7–9). Thus, in Christ's resurrection on the third day, the true Israel in him rises to life.[3]

Third, in the NT, Christ portrays his death as a baptism (Luke 12:50), and the NT authors portray the judgments of both the flood (1 Peter 3:20–21) and the Red Sea (1 Cor. 10:2) as baptisms. Because the initial Passover sacrifice marks Israel's birth as a nation (i.e., a new creation) and because Moses highlights only three stopping points en route to the parting of the Red Sea (Num. 33:3–8; cf. Exod. 12:37; 13:20; 14:2), some propose that the Red Sea crossing likely happened three days after this new creation.[4] While the evidence that Israel crossed the Red Sea only three days after the Passover is questionable, the great exodus event still points typologically to Christ's resurrection as a new creation.[5] Indeed, on the mount of Jesus's transfiguration, Moses and Elijah identified Jesus's coming work in Jerusalem as an "exodus" (Luke 9:30–31, ESV = "departure"), thus signaling that Jesus fulfilled the second exodus that the prophets anticipated (e.g., Isa. 11:10–12:6; Jer. 23:7–8; Zeph. 3:19–20).

Fourth, it was "on the third day" of his journey to sacrifice his son that Abraham promised his servants, "I and the boy will go over there and worship and come again to you" (Gen. 22:4–5). Reflecting on this story, the writer of Hebrews declares of the patriarch, "He considered that God was able even to raise him from the dead, from which, figuratively speaking, he did receive him back" (Heb. 11:19). Thus, the substitutionary sacrifice that saved Isaac's life (22:13) and the youth's own deliverance pointed ahead to the greater offspring who would triumph only through great tribulation.

---

3. For the significance of this text in the backdrop of the NT's assertion that the third day resurrection of Jesus was "according to the Scriptures," see esp. Dempster, "From Slight Peg to Cornerstone to Capstone," 404–9.

4. See Lunn, "Raised on the Third Day," 527–30.

5. While the exodus clearly anticipates Christ's resurrection, I question that this saving event anticipates his *third-day* resurrection. This is because Moses appears to portray the journey to the Red Sea (= *Yam Suph*) as being much more extensive. First, he actually notes that Israel set out "the day after the Passover" (Num. 33:3), which supplies only two more days to get in three camping spots. Second, we know that "God led the people around by the way of the wilderness toward the Red Sea [= *Yam Suph*]" (Exod. 13:18). "The way of the wilderness" is best identified as the caravan road stretching eastward across the middle of the Sinai Peninsula from the base of the Nile Delta to the Gulf of Aqaba. If this Gulf is indeed the location of *Yam Suph* and the place of the Sea crossing (which seems likely from texts like Exod. 23:21; Deut. 21:1; 1 Kgs. 9:26; Jer. 49:20–21), then the journey was probably closer to two weeks than three days. While a well-known travel route, "the way of the wilderness" was still through the wilderness, and the only specific reason that Moses would need to list specific camping sites was (1) if something important happened there or (2) if the campsite was in close proximity to a known location. In all likelihood, the three camp sites were *not* Israel's only three respite points en route to the Sea. For more on the Gulf of Aqaba as the place of the Red Sea crossing, see Duane A. Garrett, *A Commentary on Exodus*, Kregel Exegetical Library (Grand Rapids: Kregel, 2014), 104–35.

Fifth, the NT portrays both baptism (e.g., Rom. 6:4–5; Col. 2:12) and sprouting seeds (e.g., 1 Cor. 15:35–38) as images of resurrection. As such, we may see the earliest anticipations of Jesus's third-day resurrection in the fact that the first sprouts came forth out of the watery chaos on the third day following the original creation (Gen. 1:11–13).[6] Jesus is the "seed" that first dies and then bears much fruit (Gen 3:15; John 12:23–24).

Other Old Testament Resurrection Texts

Other passages in the OT foreshadow or predict future resurrection.[7] For example, with Israel's exile and following restoration in view, Yahweh declared through Moses, "See now that I, even I, am he, and there is no god beside me; I kill and I make alive; I wound and I heal; and there is none that can deliver out of my hand" (Deut. 32:39; cf. 1 Sam. 2:6; 2 Kings 5:7). Because "healing" always *follows* "wounding," God's "making alive" after "killing" envisions that he would resurrect his people from death. Kenneth Turner has noted that by using words like "perish," "destroy," "annihilate," and the like, Moses in Deuteronomy portrays Israel's exile as a "death," by which the nation as Yahweh's elect son and servant "loses her identity, history, and covenant relationship with Yahweh. Restoration from exile, then, is a resurrection from death to life."[8] And because Jesus Christ as *Israel the person* represents *Israel the people* (Isa. 49:3, 6), his bodily resurrection following his bearing the curse-judgment (Gal. 3:13) inaugurates his fulfilling of this promise.

Living in the midst of exile, Ezekiel envisioned how Yahweh would fulfill the resurrection he predicted through Moses. Whereas covenant obedience could have led to life (Lev. 18:5; Ezek. 20:11, 13, 21), Israel's covenant rebellion resulted in the nation's exilic death, so God portrayed them as dried up bones filling a field (Ezek. 37:1; cf. Jer. 8:1–2). Nevertheless, Yahweh promised, "Behold, I will cause breath to enter you, and you shall live" (Ezek. 37:5).

---

6. Cf. Mitchell L. Chase, "'From Dust You Shall Arise': Resurrection Hope in the Old Testament," *SBJT* 18, no. 4 (Winter 2014): 11; Lunn, "Raised on the Third Day," 532–34.

7. See Chase, "'From Dust You Shall Arise,'" 9–29; Chase, "Genesis of Resurrection Hope," 467–80; Lunn, "Raised on the Third Day," 523–35; Dempster, "From Slight Peg to Cornerstone to Capstone," 371–409.

8. Kenneth J. Turner, "Deuteronomy's Theology of Exile," in *For Our Good Always: Studies on the Message and Influence of Deuteronomy in Honor of Daniel I. Block*, eds. Jason S. DeRouchie, Jason Gile, and Kenneth J. Turner (Winona Lake, IN: Eisenbrauns, 2013), 190, 194. He further notes, "The people will continue to exist physically in exile; yet, as a single entity, Israel is said to 'perish' or 'be destroyed.' So, it is not Israel as an historical or socioreligious people, but Israel as Yahweh's elect son and servant (Deut 1:31, 7:6, 14:1) that is put to death. Exile constitutes the death of Israel as a nation in covenant—a covenant comprised of a dynamic relationship between Yahweh, the nation, and the land. Whatever existence continues, it is discontinuous with the past." Turner, "Deuteronomy's Theology of Exile," 194; cf. Kenneth J. Turner, *The Death of Deaths in the Death of Israel: Deuteronomy's Theology of Exile* (Eugene, OR: Wipf & Stock, 2011).

This resulted in his supplying them with human form and breathing into them the breath of life, so that "they lived and stood on their feet, an exceedingly great army" (37:10). The vision anticipated how God would "raise you from your graves" and put "my Spirit within you"; they would not only live but be God's very temple (37:13–14; cf. 36:27). Thus, "My dwelling place shall be with them, and I will be their God, and they shall be my people" (37:27; cf. 2 Cor. 6:16).

Earlier, building on his claim that Yahweh would "swallow up death forever" (Isa. 25:8; cf. 1 Cor. 15:54), Isaiah declared, "Your dead shall live; their bodies shall rise. You who dwell in the dust, awake and sing for joy!" (Isa. 26:19). The fourth Servant Song unpacks how God awakens those bodies and enables them to exult. Isaiah first highlighted the servant-person's resurrection when he identified his seeing offspring *after* his substitutionary sacrifice: "It was the will of the LORD to crush him; he has put him to grief; when his soul makes an offering for guilt, he shall see his offspring; he shall prolong his days; the will of the LORD shall prosper in his hand" (53:10). We then hear Yahweh declare, "Out of the anguish of his soul he shall see and be satisfied; by his knowledge shall the righteous one, my servant, make many to be accounted righteous, and he shall bear their iniquities" (53:11). Because Yahweh declared his servant-person righteous (cf. 50:8), this righteous one would be able to bear the sins of many in death, and through his victorious resurrection all those in him—his spiritual progeny—would be declared righteous. Yahweh's servant person was "Israel" (49:3), and "in the LORD all the offspring of Israel shall be justified and shall glory" (45:25).

Beyond Psalm 2:7 and 16:9–11 noted above (cf. Acts 2:25–31; 13:32–35), the Psalter points to the resurrection multiple times. For example, we learn that "the upright shall behold [Yahweh's] face" (Ps. 11:7), and the psalmist declares in hope, "When I awake, I sahll be satisfied with your likeness" (17:15). Similarly, the very one forsaken of God and afflicted to the point of death (22:1–21[2–22]) promises to proclaim God's name to his brothers (22:22[23]), which implies resurrection (cf. Matt. 28:10; Rom. 8:29; Heb. 2:12). Furthermore, before the Lord "shall bow all who go down to the dust," which highlights a future beyond the grave for those who die (Ps. 22:29[30]). The sons of Korah end Psalm 48 with the testimony of the faithful that God "will guide us beyond death" (ESV footnote). They then assert in Psalm 49 that the proud "are appointed for Sheol" but that "the upright [ones] shall rule over them in the morning" (49:14[15]). With the voice of the royal representative, they declare, "God will ransom my soul from the power of Sheol, for he will receive me" (49:15[16]). At the very least, such assertions point to a spiritual resurrection. Similarly, the psalmist points to life after death when he writes, "You who have made me see many troubles and calamities will revive me again; from the depths of the earth you will bring me up again" (71:20). And Asaph contrasts the terrifying end of the proud (73:17–22) with God's commitment to bring the humble to glory and to be their strength and portion *forever* (73:24–26).

Finally, both Job and the Preacher in Ecclesiastes point to the hope of resurrection. Job questions, "If a man dies, shall he live again?" He seems to answer in the affirmative, for he then states, "All the days of my service I would wait, till my renewal should come" (Job 14:14). And again, "For I know that my Redeemer lives, and at the last he will stand upon the earth. And after my skin has been thus destroyed, yet in my flesh I shall see God" (19:25–26). At the end of Job's trial-filled life, which included the death of his ten children (1:2, 18–19), he had another "seven sons and three daughters" (42:13). But because "the Lord gave Job twice as much as he had before" (42:10), the text may imply the spiritual resurrection of his earlier children, similar to the way Jesus spoke of Yahweh's declaring, "I am the God of Abraham"—not "of the dead, but of the living" (Matt. 22:32).[9] The Preacher was convinced that death would come to all, both those who are good or those who are evil (Eccl. 9:2–3), and that "there is a righteous man who perishes in his righteousness, and there is a wicked man who prolongs his life in his evildoing" (7:15). Nevertheless, "Though a sinner does evil a hundred times and prolongs his life, yet I know that it will be well with those who fear God, because they fear before him" (Eccl. 8:12–13). The Preacher was certain in a future hope beyond the grave for the righteous.

Resurrection in the New Testament

To highlight that Jesus fulfills what the OT anticipates (cf. Luke 24:46–47; Acts 10:43; 26:22–23; Rom. 3:21; 1 Cor. 15:3–4; 1 Peter 1:10–11), each of the four Gospels concludes with stories of Jesus's bodily resurrection from the dead (Matt. 28:1–10; Mark 16:1–8; Luke 24:1–12; John 20:1–10), and the rest of the NT portrays this as the watershed event that alters the course of world history.[10] Jesus's resurrection happens on the first day of the week (John 20:1, 19), thus symbolizing the inauguration of the new creation (1 Cor. 15:20, 23; 2 Cor. 5:17). It establishes Jesus Christ as the Righteous One (1 Tim. 3:16; cf. Isa. 50:8; 53:11; 1 John 2:1) and the Lord and Judge of the universe (Matt.

---

9. On this proposal, see, e.g., Franz Delitzsch, *Job*, trans. Francis Bolton, Commentary on the Old Testament 4 (Grand Rapids: Eerdmans, 1988), s.v. Job 42:13; John E. Hartley, *The Book of Job*, NICOT (Grand Rapids: Eerdmans, 1988), 542; Robert L. Alden, *Job*, NAC 11 (Nashville: B&H, 1993), 413.

10. See esp. N. T. Wright, *The Resurrection of the Son of God*, Christian Origins and the Question of God 3 (London: SPCK, 2003). For a brief synthesis of his view, see N. T. Wright, "Resurrection Narratives," in *Dictionary for Theological Interpretation of the Bible*, ed. Kevin J. Vanhoozer (Grand Rapids: Baker Academic, 2005), 675–76; N. T. Wright, "Resurrection of the Dead," in Vanhoozer, *Dictionary for Theological Interpretation of the Bible*, 676–78. For more on the doctrine of resurrection, see the entire issue of *SBJT* 18, no. 4 (Winter 2014).

28:18; Acts 2:36; 10:42; 17:31; Rom. 1:4; 14:9). It secures justification for all who believe (Rom. 4:25; 6:8–11; 1 Cor. 15:17), initiates the spread of the good news (Rom. 1:16–17; Gal. 1:11–12) and a Spirit-empowered global mission of salvation (Matt. 28:19–20; John 20:19–22; Acts 1:8), and supplies the necessary lens for understanding the OT (John 2:20–22; 12:13–16; 20:9). Jesus's resurrection creates for all in him a living hope for "an inheritance that is imperishable, undefiled, and unfading" (1 Peter 1:3–5), and it provides hope for the entire created order that it will be renewed (Rom. 8:18–25; cf. Col. 1:20)—"Christ the firstfruits, then at his coming those who belong to Christ" (1 Cor. 15:23). In his resurrected body, at least prior to his ascension, Jesus retained physical signs of his execution so as to validate his identity (Luke 24:39; John 20:20, 25, 27; Acts 1:3), but he could remain unrecognized until he chose to disclose himself (Luke 24:16, 31; John 20:14, 16; 21:4, 12). He could walk and dialogue with others (Luke 24:15–17; John 20:15), vanish and appear at will (Luke 24:31, 36–37; John 20:19, 26), be touched (Luke 24:39; John 20:17, 27), and eat and drink (Luke 24:30, 42–43; Acts 10:41). He was rightfully worshipped, and he visibly ascended to heaven (Luke 24:51–52; Acts 1:9).

Jesus compared God's power to raise the dead (e.g., Deut. 32:39; 1 Sam. 2:6; 2 Kings 5:7) with his power to overcome spiritual death by presently giving people eternal life (John 3:16; 5:21, 24–26); such initial "resurrection" gives certainty of consummate resurrection following physical death, first spiritually and then bodily (5:28–29; 11:25–26; 14:2–3). Paul, too, notes that, although "we were dead in our trespasses," God has already "made us alive together with Christ . . . and raised us up with him and seated us with him in the heavenly places in Christ Jesus, so that in the coming ages he might show the immeasurable riches of his grace in kindness toward us in Christ Jesus" (Eph. 2:5–7). Believers are, thus, *already* experiencing a spiritual resurrection, and Christians who die before Christ's second appearing enter into a state of conscious rest in the presence of Jesus (Luke 23:43; John 14:2–3; 2 Cor. 4:14; Phil. 1:23). But when Christ does return, those who already experienced initial spiritual resurrection will then be given new supernatural bodies that will never wear out (Rom. 8:11; Phil. 3:20–21; 1 Thess. 4:16–17).

As noted above, Scripture anticipates "a resurrection of both the just and the unjust" (Acts 24:15; cf. Dan. 12:2; Matt. 25:46; John 5:28–29). This is what Revelation 20:12 refers to when it asserts, "And I saw the dead, great and small, standing before the throne, and books were opened. Then another book was open, which is the book of life. And the dead were judged by what was written in the books, according to what they had done" (cf. Matt. 25:31–32; 2 Cor. 5:10). Scholars continue to disagree on the meaning and proper temporal referents of Revelation 20:1–6, which mentions "the first resurrection" and "the second death" (20:5–6). While the text is not explicit, the ordinals "first" and "second" imply at least a "second" and "first" for both resurrection and death. Furthermore, "the first resurrection" likely applies only to believers ("blessed and holy is the one who shares in the first resurrection!" 20:6) and refers to the spiritual life already enjoyed by believers who die (cf. Luke 23:43; Phil. 1:23).[11] In contrast, "the second death" will apply only to nonbelievers ("over such [i.e., those who experience the first resurrection] the second death has no power," Rev. 20:6) and relates to the eternal state of the unregenerate in the lake of fire (20:14).[12] The note that "the rest of the dead did not come to life" (20:5) refers to the unbelievers who, after physical death, remain "dead in [their] trespasses and sins" (Eph. 2:1) but who will rise at the final judgment.[13] See figure 30.1.

	Believers	Nonbelievers
First resurrection	Spiritual (immediate)	—
First death	Physical	Physical
Second resurrection	Physical	Physical
Second death	—	Spiritual (eternal)

Fig. 30.1. Death and Resurrection in Revelation 20

Christ's resurrection impacts the Christian's present ethics and future hope. Paul says, "If then you have been raised with Christ, seek the things that are above, where Christ is, seated at the right hand of God" (Col. 3:1). Similarly, the apostle notes, "We were buried . . . with him by baptism into death, in order that, just as Christ was raised from the dead by the glory of the Father, we too might walk in newness of life. . . . So you also must consider yourselves dead to sin and alive to God in Christ" and must not let "sin therefore reign in your mortal body" (Rom. 6:4, 11–12; cf. 1 Cor. 6:12–20; 2 Cor. 5:15). Our identification with Christ in his resurrection demands that we live as part of the new creation.

Related to this, God's reconciling us should move us to help others be reconciled with God (2 Cor. 5:17–19), for Christ's resurrection now gives our

---

11. See Meredith G. Kline, "The First Resurrection," *WTJ* 37 (1975): 366–75; and Meredith G. Kline, "The First Resurrection: A Reaffirmation," *WTJ* 39 (1976): 110–19. As noted above, both John and Paul identify that the "first resurrection" is actually inaugurated at conversion (John 5:21, 24; Eph. 2:6; Col. 3:1) and consummated when, following physical death, persons presently exiled enter their heavenly citizenship (Luke 23:43; John 14:2–3; 2 Cor. 4:14; Phil. 1:23), awaiting the reunion with their bodies at the "second resurrection" (John 5:28–29; Phil. 3:20–21).

12. See G. K. Beale, "The Millennium in Revelation 20:1–10: An Amillennial Perspective," *CTR* 11, no. 1 (2013): 29–62.

13. Both John and Paul identify that physical death is merely the consummation of the "first death" that was already inaugurated at conception through a person's identification with Adam (Rom. 5:12, 18–19) and the spiritual death lived out in the land of the living (John 3:18, 36; 4:24–26; Eph. 2:1, 5).

preaching, faith, and labors eternal purpose (1 Cor. 15:14, 58). Jesus's resurrection awakens confidence in the life to come (15:23), and what we hope for tomorrow changes who we are today (2 Peter 1:4). We are empowered to radical mission and radical joy amid a world of chaos and suffering because we know that when Christ returns, our new body will be raised in glory and power and will bear the very image of the man of heaven, the divine Son (1 Cor. 15:43–44, 49; cf. Phil. 3:20–21). Come, Lord Jesus!

Summary

The OT anticipates the (third day) resurrection of God's people following an exilic death (e.g., Deut. 32:39; Hos. 6:2; Dan. 12:2), and it clarifies that the new life of the community will be multiethnic in nature and will result from the representative suffering servant's own triumph over death (Isa. 53:10–11; Ps. 16:10). Jesus Christ's resurrection on the third day fulfills what the OT predicts (Luke 24:46–47; 1 Cor. 15:4), establishes him as the reigning king (Rom. 1:4; Matt. 28:18), inaugurates the new creation (1 Cor. 15:20, 23; 2 Cor. 5:17), justifies the many (Rom. 4:25), calls believers to walk in newness of life (6:4; Col. 3:1), births a global mission (Matt. 28:19–20; John 20:19–22; Acts 1:8; Rom. 1:16–17; Gal. 1:11–12), and supplies hope to all believers of their own resurrection (Rom. 8:11; 1 Cor. 15:43–44, 49; Phil. 3:20–21; Heb. 9:27–28). It also should stress to nonbelievers that they will indeed meet the heavenly judge face-to-face (Dan. 12:2; Matt. 25:46; John 5:28–29).

REFLECTION QUESTIONS

1. What are some reasons why the resurrection of Jesus is the most decisive event in the history of humankind?

2. According to Jesus, what in Moses's encounter with the burning bush supports a belief in the resurrection (Mark 12:26–27)?

3. Jesus said, "It is written that the Christ should suffer and on *the third day* rise from the dead" (Luke 24:46), and Paul claimed that Jesus "was raised on *the third day* in accordance with the Scriptures" (1 Cor. 15:4). What are some of the OT texts that may anticipate a "third day" resurrection?

4. How does Revelation 20 clarify our understanding of death and resurrection?

5. What are some ways that the resurrection of Jesus impacts our present ethics and future hope?

PART 4

Illustrating Biblical Theology: The Use of Earlier Scripture in Later Scripture

How Does Isaiah 12:2 Use Exodus 15:2?

Jason S. DeRouchie

> *You will say in that day:* . . .
> *"Behold, God is my salvation;*
> *I will trust, and will not be afraid;*
> *for the LORD God is my strength and my song,*
> *and he has become my salvation.* . . .
> *Sing praises to the LORD, for he has done gloriously;*
> *let this be made known in all the earth."*
> (Isa. 12:1–2, 5)

> *I will sing to the LORD, for he has triumphed gloriously;*
> *the horse and his rider he has thrown in to the sea.*
> *The LORD is my strength and my song,*
> *and he has become my salvation.*
> (Exod. 15:1–2)

The exodus is one of the key themes that ties all of Scripture together.[1] The prophets regularly utilize the imagery of the exodus to depict the great

---

1. See, for example, J. Gordon McConville, "Exodus," in *New International Dictionary of Old Testament Theology and Exegesis*, ed. Willem A. VanGemeren (Grand Rapids: Zondervan,1997), 4:601–605; Rikki E. Watts, "Exodus," in *New Dictionary of Biblical Theology*, eds. T. Desmond Alexander and Brian S. Rosner (Downers Grove, IL: InterVarsity, 2000), 478–87; Stephen G. Dempster, "Exodus and Biblical Theology: On Moving into the Neighborhood with a New Name," *SBJT* 12, no. 3 (Fall 2008): 4–23; Thomas Richard Wood, "Exile and Exodus," in *Zondervan Biblical Theology Study Bible*, ed. D. A. Carson (Grand Rapids: Zondervan, 2018), 2347–49; Bryan D. Estelle, *Echoes of Exodus: Tracing a Biblical Motif* (Downers Grove, IL: InterVarsity, 2017); Alastair J. Roberts and Andrew Wilson, *Echoes of Exodus: Tracing Themes of Redemption through Scripture* (Wheaton, IL: Crossway, 2018).

restoration associated with the Messiah and the new covenant,[2] and the NT authors identify Christ's work as fulfilling what the OT anticipates in relation to the end times.[3] Luke 9:30–31 makes this point: "Moses and Elijah . . . appeared in glory and spoke of [Jesus's] departure [= *exodus*], which he was about to accomplish in Jerusalem."

Perhaps more than any other OT prophet, Isaiah depicts the end-time ingathering as a second exodus. For example, in Isaiah 12:1–6 he incorporates some of Israel's song at the sea from Exodus 15:1–18 in his testimony of what the multiethnic community will sing when Yahweh gathers them in from the ends of the earth. We will analyze how Isaiah uses Exodus 15 by following the six steps we outline in Question 9.

The Context of Isaiah 12:2

Isaiah 12:1–6 speaks with prophetic certainty and portrays how both the collective group (12:1–2) and the individual (12:3–6) will responsively celebrate that Yahweh delivered them in a great second exodus. The overall unit runs from 11:1 to 12:6:

I.   The Spirit-Empowered Savior Rises (11:1–9)
     A.   The Promise of His Rise (11:1–5)
     B.   The Impact of His Rise (11:6–9)
II. The Redeemed Celebrate God as Their Salvation (11:10–12:6)
     A.   The Gentile Nations Hope in the Savior (11:10)
     B.   Yahweh Saves and His People Celebrate (11:11–12:6)
          1.   Yahweh Saves a Multiethnic People through a Second Exodus (11:11–16)
          2.   The Inhabitants of Zion Celebrate Yahweh's Salvation (12:1–6)
               a.   The Collective Response (12:1–2)
               b.   Each Individual's Response (12:3–6)

---

2. Rikki E. Watts, "Consolation or Confrontation? Isaiah 40–55 and the Delay of the New Exodus," *TynBul* 41 (1990): 31–59; Gary Yates, "New Exodus and No Exodus in Jeremiah 26–45: Promise and Warning to the Exiles in Babylon," *TynBul* 57 (2006): 1–22; Rikki E. Watts, "Exodus Imagery," *Dictionary of the Old Testament: Prophets*, eds. Mark J. Boda and J. Gordon McConville (Downers Grove, IL: InterVarsity Press, 2012), 205–14.
3. Rikki E. Watts, *Isaiah's New Exodus and Mark*, WUNT 2/88 (Tübingen: Mohr Siebeck, 1997); David W. Pao, *Acts and the Isaianic New Exodus*, WUNT 2/130 (Tübingen: Mohr Siebeck, 2000); Thomas Richard Wood, "The Regathering of the People of God: An Investigation into the New Testament's Appropriation of the Old Testament Prophecies concerning the Regathering of Israel" (PhD diss., Trinity Evangelical Divinity School, 2006); Douglas S. McComiskey, "Exile and Restoration from Exile in the Scriptural Quotations and Allusions of Jesus," *JETS* 53 (2010): 673–96; Daniel Lynwood Smith, "The Uses of 'New Exodus' in New Testament Scholarship: Preparing a Way through the Wilderness," *CurBR* 14 (2016): 207–43.

> i. Calling for Individual Praise (12:3–5)
> ii. Calling for Collective Praise (12:6)

Following visions of an end-time ingathering to God's presence (2:2–4; 4:2–6) and of a messianic child king who would rule the world (7:14; 9:1–7), Isaiah 11 opens by declaring that "a shoot from the stump of Jesse . . . shall bear fruit," "the Spirit of the LORD" shall rest on him like a moving temple, and he will be an agent of justice on the whole earth (11:1–5; cf. 4:5; 6:13). Beasts (or nations) that once were hostile against one another will now be at peace, all the while led by a child and located at the mountain of God (11:6–9). Thus, the multiethnic people who will be drawn to Yahweh's presence and exalt him in the "latter days" will be linked directly to the global reign of the child-king working justice, righteousness, and peace on the earth. The various visions are working together to depict the same end-time reign of God through his messianic royal servant.

But how will this eschatological reign develop? Isaiah 11:10–11 supplies two parallel "and it shall come about in that day" statements that unpack how Yahweh will raise up the Davidic ruler as a "signal for the peoples" and will "extend his hand yet a second time to recover the remnant that remains of his people." Hence, some from "the nations" and "the banished of Israel" and "dispersed of Judah" will experience a second exodus (11:12). "The LORD will utterly destroy the tongue of the Sea of Egypt, and will wave his hand over the River with his scorching breath, and strike it into seven channels, and he will lead people across in sandals. And there will be a highway from Assyria for the remnant that remains of his people, as there was for Israel when they came up from the land of Egypt" (11:15–16).

Isaiah uses images of the original exodus to depict how Yahweh will deliver his multiethnic people in the end times. The prophet follows these declarations by including two parallel predictions of the redeemed praising Yahweh for saving them. The first is singular, cites Exodus 15:2, and declares how the collective group will in that day give thanks and trust in God, who has proven himself the great Savior (Isa. 12:1–2). The second is plural, may allude to Exodus 15:1 and 3, and details how each member of the saved community will charge both one another (Isa. 12:3–5) and the collective group in Zion (12:6) to exalt in Yahweh and to praise and proclaim his great name and deeds in all the earth.[4]

---

4. Isaiah 12:3–5 uses the masculine plural and, therefore, addresses each individual of the redeemed community. Isaiah 12:6 uses the feminine singular and points to the city Zion as a whole (portrayed as a woman).

The Context of Exodus 15:2

The song of the sea in Exodus 15:1–18 poetically celebrates Yahweh's redeeming of his people from the clutches of Egypt, and it testifies to one step in God's fulfilling what he earlier declared to Pharaoh: "For this purpose I raised you up, to show you my power, so that my name may be proclaimed in all the earth" (9:16). Egypt, too, grew to know Yahweh's supremacy (14:17–18, 25), as did numerous other nations and generations (18:11; Josh. 2:9–11; 9:10; 1 Sam. 4:8; Neh. 9:9–10).

The song follows the detailed prose account in 12:37–14:31, and it praises Yahweh as saving Warrior and eternal King: "Your right hand, O LORD, glorious in power, your right hand, O LORD, shatters the enemy. In the greatness of your majesty you overthrow your adversaries; you send out your fury; it consumes them like stubble" (15:6–7). And again, "Who is like you, O LORD, among the gods? Who is like you, majestic in holiness, awesome in glorious deeds, doing wonders?" (15:11).

The "testimony" section that opens the song and includes verses 1–2 uses first-person speech and speaks of Yahweh in the third person. Isaiah draws his citation (Exod. 15:2) and allusions (15:1, 3) from portions of the song that supply reason to praise Yahweh.

I.   The Testimony of Praise to King Yahweh as Saving Warrior (15:1c–5)

      A.   Declaring Praise to Yahweh (15:1c)

      B.   The Reason for Praise to Yahweh (15:1d–5)

           1.   Yahweh has highly exalted himself by destroying the Egyptian army in the sea (15:1de).

           2.   Yahweh my God has become my salvation (15:2).

           3.   Yahweh has proven himself a warrior by destroying Pharaoh and his army in the sea (15:3–5).

II.   The Utterance of Praise to King Yahweh as Saving Warrior (15:6–17)

      A.   Praise to Yahweh for His Enemy-Overcoming Power in Relation to the Egyptians (15:6–10)

           1.   Asserting Yahweh's enemy-overcoming power (15:6–7a)

           2.   Expressing Yahweh's enemy-overcoming power (15:7b–10)

                a.   Yahweh's piling of the waters (15:7b–8)

                b.   The enemy's pride in destruction (15:9)

                c.   Yahweh's drowning of the enemy (15:10)

      B.   Praise to Yahweh for His Saving Work Shown through His Superiority over the Gods of the Nations (15:11–17)

           1.   Asserting Yahweh's superiority over the gods of the nations (15:11)

2. Expressing Yahweh's superiority over the gods of the na-
    tions (15:12–17)
    a. Yahweh's saving work shown through his over-
        coming the gods of Egypt (15:12–13)
    b. The nations' dread of Yahweh the Saving Warrior
        (15:14–16)
    c. Yahweh's commitment to plant his redeemed people
        in his mountain sanctuary (15:17)

III. The Declaration of Praise for King Yahweh's Eternal Reign
     (15:18)

The Exodus narrative suggests that Moses and Israel initially sang this
song directly after Yahweh delivered them at the sea but well before they ever
arrived at the Promised Land and before any of the global terror described in
15:13–17 could have taken place. Verse 13 identifies that the exodus-deliverance
has made Israel's arrival at Yahweh's Edenic sanctuary so certain that they can
speak about it as already accomplished, but verse 17 shows that the fulfillment
is still future from the perspective of the singers. Moreover, Miriam's prophetic words in this song (see 15:20) treat the original exodus event typologically by arguing from the greater to the lesser: if Yahweh rescued Israel from
the clutches of the greatest power on earth, certainly he will also deliver them
from all other human powers until he settles them in complete rest within his
garden-temple (cf. Rom. 8:31–32). Even before the word had time to get out,
"the peoples have heard; they tremble" (Exod. 15:14). Philistia, Edom, Moab,
Canaan—all stand in terror in light of the saving power of God displayed
on Israel's behalf. Peter Gentry captures the significance: "The exodus is a
model or pattern of future salvation from the very beginning. The first time
[Israel] sang this song, they were using the crossing of the Red Sea as a model
or pattern of how God would bring them successfully through the desert to
Canaan."[5]

Relevant Uses of Exodus 15 Elsewhere in Scripture[6]

Psalm 118:14 is the only other place the OT cites Exodus 15:2a, and
Psalm 118:28 then cites Exodus 15:2b (cf. Pss. 18:1–2[2–3]; 59:17[18]; 118:14;
140:7[8]). In a context that celebrates the enduring nature of Yahweh's steadfast love to those who take refuge in him, the psalmist proclaims, "The LORD

---

5. Peter J. Gentry, *How to Read and Understand the Biblical Prophets* (Wheaton, IL: Crossway,
   2017), 89; cf. Norbert Lohfink, "The Song of Victory at the Red Sea," in *The Christian
   Meaning of the Old Testament*, trans. R. A. Wilson (Milwaukee: Bruce, 1994), 67–86.
6. In chapter 9, the pattern for inquiry moved to extrabiblical literature at this point, but that
   was assuming we were studying the NT's use of the OT. Here, however, we are focusing on
   the OT's use of the OT, and we will restrict our inquiry to how Isaiah used Exodus 15, how
   other biblical authors used Exodus 15, and how NT authors may have engaged Isaiah 12.

is my strength and my song; he has become my salvation. . . . You are my God, and I will give thanks to you; you are my God; I will extol you." Frank-Lothar Hossfeld and Erich Zenger, therefore, assert, "The whole song in Exod 15:1–18 is the hermeneutical horizon within which Psalm 118 is to be understood."[7]

The book of Exodus alludes to the garden of Eden several times. That influences how we read Exodus 15 and clarifies how later Scripture appropriates the song. Adam was God's "son" (Gen. 5:1–3) and king-priest whom God called to "serve" and "guard" his garden-temple (2:15; cf. Num. 3:7–8; 8:26; 18:7) and to "subdue" and "have dominion" over the earth (Gen. 1:26, 28), all to display God's greatness. When the serpent, who embodied all that was evil and hostile to God, tempted Adam and Eve to sin, Adam, the divine son, should have slain him, but the first man's failure gave rise to the Lord's promise to do just this through a greater Son, an offspring of the woman, who would triumph over the serpent through his own tribulation (Gen. 3:15). Similarly, Israel was God's "firstborn son" (Exod. 4:22–23), whom God called to be a kingdom of priests and a holy nation (19:6) out of Yahweh's holy mountain abode (15:13, 17). In a way that recalls the promise of the serpent's destruction, Yahweh portrays Pharaoh as a "serpent," whom he would catch and overcome, ultimately at the sea (cf. the parallel phrases "put out the hand" in Exod. 3:19–20; 4:2–3; 9:15–16).[8] "I will get glory over Pharaoh and all his host, his chariots, and his horsemen" (14:17).

Later OT authors identify motifs of creation and conquest fused together in the song of Moses, with Yahweh standing as the great Warrior who redeems his son Israel from the serpent-king Pharaoh in order to lead his people back to his Edenic holy mountain. Isaiah, in order to awaken Yahweh to bring his promised end-time deliverance, asserts:

> Was it not you who cut Rahab [i.e., Egypt] in pieces, who pierced the dragon? Was it not you who dried up the sea, the waters of the great deep, who made the depths of the sea a way for the redeemed to pass over? And the ransomed of the LORD shall return and come to Zion with singing; everlasting joy shall be upon their heads; they

---

7. Frank-Lothar Hossfeld and Erich Zenger, *Psalms 3: A Commentary on Psalms 101–150*, ed. Klaus Baltzer, trans. Linda M. Maloney, *Hermeneia* 19c (Minneapolis: Fortress, 2011), 239.

8. This link with the serpent is enhanced by the fact that the serpent was the symbol of Pharaoh's power in Lower Egypt, where Israel was enslaved. Pharaoh believed his kingdom was protected by the cobra-goddess, Wadjet, so he wore an image of the serpent on his headdress. See John H. Walton, "Serpent," *Dictionary of the Old Testament: Pentateuch*, eds. T. Desmond Alexander and David W. Baker (Downers Grove, IL: InterVarsity Press, 2003), 736. And for more on the theme of serpent in biblical theology, see Question 23 and Andrew David Naselli, *The Serpent and the Serpent Slayer*, Short Studies in Biblical Theology (Wheaton, IL: Crossway, 2020).

shall obtain gladness and joy, and sorrow and sighing shall flee away. (Isa. 51:9–11; cf. 27:1; Ezek. 29:3; 32:2)

Similarly, Job declared, "By his power [God] stilled the sea; by his understanding he shattered Rahab. By his wind the heavens were made fair; his hand pierced the fleeing serpent" (Job 26:12–13; cf. Pss. 74:13–14; 78:53–54).[9]

The book of Revelation recalls the song of the sea. With likely typological echoes of the plagues Yahweh brought against Egypt, John sees "seven angels with seven plagues" by which "the wrath of God is finished" (Rev. 15:1; cf. Deut. 7:19; 30:7; Mic. 7:10–17).[10] Here "those who had conquered the beast and its image" are gathered by "the sea of glass" singing "the song of Moses, the servant of God, and the song of the Lamb" (Rev. 15:2–3). The OT identified the sea as the serpent's watery abode (Ps. 74:12–15; Isa. 51:9–11; Ezek. 32:2), but through Christ's sacrificial death and victorious resurrection, he has now quieted the sea as the fires of God's judgment burn (Rev. 4:6; 15:2; cf. Dan. 7:10–11). And as at the original exodus where Israel praised Yahweh on the banks of the Red Sea for saving them from the serpent-king Pharaoh, John sees the church singing a revised "song of Moses" on the banks of the quieted waters following the decisive victory of the Lamb over the ultimate enemy.

The mention of "the song of Moses" seems to recall both the song of the sea in Exodus 15:1–18 and the later song of Moses in Deuteronomy 32:1–43, which also describes Yahweh's defeat of all enemy powers and his end-time deliverance of his people.[11] Nevertheless, the actual words of the song in Revelation 15:3–4 come not from Exodus 15 but from other OT passages that themselves are reflecting on the song in Exodus 15. As G. K. Beale notes, "Later OT interpretations of the first exodus have been selected to explain the new exodus, which has happened on a grander scale than the first, to praise God for the redemption and the implicit scene of judgment pictured in v. 2."[12] The saints are singing a "new song" (cf. Rev. 5:9–10; 14:3) that echoes the earlier music but focuses praise on the Lamb who has conquered.

---

9. For numerous other references in Job that suggest the book arose after the formation of the Pentateuch, see Christopher B. Ansberry, "The 'Revealed Things': Deuteronomy and the Epistemology of Job," in *For Our Good Always: Studies on the Message and Influence of Deuteronomy in Honor of Daniel I. Block*, eds. Jason S. DeRouchie, Jason Gile, and Kenneth J. Turner (Winona Lake, IN: Eisenbrauns, 2013), 307–25.

10. For more on the typological link between plagues of Egypt and Revelation 15:1–16:21, see G. K. Beale, *The Book of Revelation: A Commentary on the Greek Text*, NIGTC (Grand Rapids: Eerdmans, 1999), 787.

11. So too Beale, *Revelation*, 794.

12. Beale, *Revelation*, 794. Beale identifies likely allusions to Exod. 15:11; 34:10; Deut. 28:59–60 LXX, 32:4; Pss. 85(86):9–10 LXX; 110(111):2–4, 6 LXX; Jer. 10:7.

Textual Issues

Using "Yah," the abbreviated form of "Yahweh," Moses begins Exodus 15:2, "The LORD is my strength and my song, and he has become my salvation." Without any citation formula, Isaiah identifies these exact words as part of the end-time music of the redeemed community, though he inserts the full form of the divine name after the abbreviation, resulting in the ESV's translation, "The LORD GOD is my strength and my song, and he has become my salvation" (Isa. 12:2). Beyond this, Isaiah 12:4 matches the sense of Exodus 15:3 in exalting Yahweh's "name" ("The LORD is a man of war; the LORD is his name"; cf. 15:11). Furthermore, Moses stresses that one reason he will sing is that Yahweh has "triumphed gloriously." Isaiah may allude to this when he predicts that the redeemed will call their contemporaries to praise Yahweh, "for he has done gloriously" (Isa. 12:4, using the nominal form of the same root found twice in Exod. 15:1).

Isaiah's Hermeneutical Warrant for Using Exodus 15:1–2

The "day" in which Yahweh will become the song of his people (Isa. 12:2) is the "day" of the Spirit-empowered king (11:10), when "the LORD will extend his hand yet a second time to recover the remnant that remains of his people" (11:11). It is also the day when "the LORD will utterly destroy the tongue of the Sea of Egypt . . . and he will lead people across in sandals. And there will be a highway from Assyria . . . as there was for Israel when they came up from the land of Egypt" (11:15–16). Isaiah is portraying the future redemption in terms that recall the first exodus event, and this backdrop substantiates the idea that Isaiah is indeed citing and alluding to Exodus 15:1–3 in Isaiah 12:1–6.

Isaiah's treatment of the original exodus is typological and follows the pattern Moses himself employs when he saw Yahweh's victory over the great enemy serpent-king as a sign that all future deliverances were sure to come.[13] Jeremiah 23:7–8 applies the exodus event in a similar way: "Behold, the days are coming, declares the LORD, when they shall no longer say, 'As the LORD lives who brought up the people of Israel out of the land of Egypt,' but 'As the LORD lives who brought up and led the offspring of the house of Israel out of the north country and out of all the countries where he had driven them.' Then they shall dwell in their own land" (cf. 16:14–15). Comparably, after recalling the original exodus through the lens of corporate solidarity ("Out of Egypt I have called my son," Hos. 11:1), Hosea envisions both a return to captivity (11:5) and a second exodus (11:10–11) that both Yahweh and the new David will lead (3:5).[14] Similarly, Yahweh announces through Zechariah:

---

13. Gentry, *Read and Understand the Biblical Prophets*, 89.
14. See Question 32.

I will whistle for them and gather them in, for I have redeemed them. . . . I will bring them home from the land of Egypt, and gather them from Assyria. . . . He shall pass through the sea of troubles and strike down the waves of the sea, and all the depths of the Nile shall be dried up. The pride of Assyria shall be laid low, and the scepter of Egypt shall depart. I will make them strong in the LORD, and they shall walk in his name. (Zech. 10:8, 10–11)

All of these texts portray the end-time restoration as the antitype of the original exodus.

Isaiah's Theological Use of Exodus 15:2

The original exodus from Egypt of Yahweh's corporate "son" Israel is the most foundational salvific event in the OT. The portrayal of Pharaoh as a serpent-king (Exod. 3:19–20; 4:2–3; 9:15–16; cf. Ps. 74:13–14; Isa. 51:9–11; Ezek. 29:3; 32:2) allows the original exodus to recall the redemptive promise that the first woman's offspring would bruise the head of the serpent, thus overcoming the curse and bringing blessing from God to the world (Gen. 3:15; cf. 22:17–18).

Because Moses himself treats the exodus event as a typological pattern for future deliverance (Exod. 15:12–16), the prophets naturally used exodus imagery to portray the future end-time redemption that God promised and that was associated with his messianic king. Isaiah predicted that in the Messiah's day—the day of the second exodus—Yahweh's people would praise and thank him because "the LORD GOD is my strength and my song, and he has become my salvation" (Isa. 12:2; cf. Exod. 15:2). Revelation 15:1–4 fulfills that "new song" (cf. Rev. 5:9–10; 14:3): those of us surviving the Lord's wrath will once again stand next to a quieted sea while singing "the song of Moses, the servant of God, and the song of the Lamb." Through his life, death, and resurrection, Jesus representatively inaugurated a new exodus on behalf of God's people (Luke 9:30–31; cf. Matt. 11:5 with Isa. 35:5–6; 61:1–2; Mark 1:1–3 with Isa. 40:3). The result is that those in him "go out" and "separate" from the world (2 Cor. 6:17; cf. Isa. 52:11), following the Lord en route to the consummated new creational rest (Heb. 4:8; cf. Matt. 11:28).

Summary

After employing numerous images of the first exodus to depict Yahweh's end-time, international ingathering, Isaiah declares that in that day the redeemed will sing a song of praise to the Lord (Isa. 12:1–2, 3–6). The testimony of those rescued will recall the original song at the sea when Israel praised Yahweh as saving Warrior and eternal King. Significantly, Exodus portrays Pharaoh as a serpent, thus recalling the garden of Eden, and within the original song, Moses himself uses Yahweh's saving of Israel from the clutches of the serpent-king as a typological pointer to future deliverance. This sets the stage for prophets like Isaiah to use exodus imagery (e.g., Isa. 11:10–16; Jer. 23:7–8) and even the very words of the song at the sea (Isa. 12:2; cf. Exod. 15:2) when portraying the deliverance that Jesus would secure on behalf of the many, who with Christ would crush the serpent's head (Rom. 16:20; Col. 2:15). And the saints will then stand at a quieted sea singing praise to the conquering Lion-Lamb, using language reminiscent of the first exodus salvation (Rev. 15:1–4).

REFLECTION QUESTIONS

1. What are some ways that the theme of "exodus" ties all of Scripture together?

2. What is the original context of both Exodus 15:2 and Isaiah 12:2, and how does this information influence our understanding of Isaiah's use of Moses's writing?

3. What support is there that Moses himself saw the original exodus event as a typological pattern for future deliverance?

4. In what way does Scripture employ the original exodus as a typological pattern for future deliverance?

5. How would you synthesize Isaiah's use of Exodus 15:2 in Isaiah 12:2?

How Does Matthew 2:15 Use Hosea 11:1?

Jason S. DeRouchie

And [Joseph] rose and took the child and his mother by night and departed to Egypt and remained there until the death of Herod. This was to fulfill what the Lord had spoken by the prophet, "Out of Egypt I called my son."
(Matt. 2:14–15)

When Israel was a child, I loved him,
and out of Egypt I called my son.
(Hos. 11:1)

One of the most challenging examples of the NT's use of the OT is how Matthew 2:15 appropriates Hosea 11:1: "[Joseph] remained there [i.e., Egypt] until the death of Herod. This was to fulfill what the Lord had spoken by the prophet, 'Out of Egypt I called my son'" (Matt. 2:15).[1] Matthew claims that the events in Matthew 2:13–15 fulfill Hosea 11:1. That is why God directed the holy family to depart Bethlehem, go to Egypt, and return to the holy land only after Herod's death.

Many scholars cite this text as a prime example of the NT's complete lack of respect for the meaning and context of the OT. They claim that Hosea 11:1 is simply a historical reflection and that Matthew wrongly reads it as prophecy that Jesus fulfills. They also claim that Hosea 11:1 refers to Israel the nation coming out of Egypt and that Matthew wrongly applies it to Jesus. But Matthew is actually using the OT in a way that is faithful to its original

---

1. See also DeRouchie, *How to Understand and Apply the Old Testament*, 374–79.

context.[2] We will analyze how Matthew uses Hosea 11:1 by following the six steps we outline in Question 9.

The Context of Matthew 2:15

Matthew 2 picks up after the birth of Christ (Matt. 1:18–25) and relates events that led to his growing up in Nazareth. The visit of the wise men (2:1–12) arouses paranoia in King Herod (2:3–8), which results both in the holy family's temporarily departing Egypt (2:13–15) and Herod's slaughtering the young of Bethlehem (2:16–18). Upon Herod's death, the holy family returns to the holy land but settles in Nazareth (2:19–23). Our particular quotation comes in the midst of a series of fulfillment texts reaching back to Micah 5:2 (Matt. 2:6), Hosea 11:1 (Matt. 2:15), and Jeremiah 31:15 (Matt. 2:18). Specifically, the citation explains why the holy family departed Bethlehem for Egypt before the narrative of their return.

The Context of Hosea 11:1

Hosea 4–14 unpacks the nature of Yahweh's lawsuit against Israel. Hosea states his thesis in 4:1: "There is no faithfulness or steadfast love, and no knowledge of God in the land." He briefly expands on this point (4:2–3) and then unpacks "no knowledge" (4:4–6:3), "no steadfast love" (6:4–11:11), and "no faithfulness/truth" (11:12–14:8).

Hosea 11:1 comes at the end of the second of these units. It recalls the nation of Israel's feeble state when God first redeemed them from Egypt: "Out of Egypt I called my son." Referring to Israel as God's communal "son" recalls Exodus 4:22–23, where the Lord calls Israel his "firstborn son." Hosea then unpacks the people's sustained covenant rebellion that will result in their exile to Assyria: "They shall not return to the land of Egypt, but Assyria shall be their king" (11:5).[3] Nevertheless, because of God's deep "compassion" (11:8), "they shall go after the LORD; he will roar like a lion; when he roars, his children shall come trembling from the west; they shall come trembling like birds from Egypt, and like doves from the land of Assyria, and I will return them to their homes, declares the LORD" (11:10–11).

---

2. See Duane A. Garrett, *Hosea, Joel*, NAC 19A (Nashville: B&H, 2001), 220–22; Derek Drummond Bass, "Hosea's Use of Scripture: An Analysis of His Hermeneutics" (PhD diss., Southern Baptist Theological Seminary, 2008), 217–24; Robert L. Plummer, "Righteousness and Peace Kiss: The Reconciliation of Authorial Intent and Biblical Typology," *SBJT* 14, no. 2 (Summer 2010): 54–61; G. K. Beale, "The Use of Hosea 11:1 in Matthew 2:15: One More Time," *JETS* 55 (2012): 697–715; G. K. Beale, "The Use of Hosea 11:1 in Matthew 2:15: Inerrancy and Genre," in *The Inerrant Word: Biblical, Historical, Theological, and Pastoral Perspectives*, ed. John MacArthur (Wheaton, IL: Crossway, 2016), 210–30.

3. Hosea 11:5 could also be a rhetorical question: "Will they not return to the land of Egypt? And Assyria will be their king" (DeRouchie's translation).

Hosea 11 begins with Israel's first exodus (11:1; cf. 2:15; 12:13; see also 12:9; 13:4) and ends with Israel's second exodus—their return from Egypt and Assyria (11:10–11; cf. 7:11, 16; 8:13; 9:3, 6). The use of Egypt in 11:11 with respect to a fresh redemption recalls the first redemption and suggests that Hosea himself is interpreting the first exodus typologically by following the pattern Moses himself set for the exodus in Exodus 15:14–16.[4] In Exodus, Moses and the people treat the future victory over the Canaanites as if it had already happened, simply because God had delivered them from the Egyptians. That is, Moses viewed God's redeeming Israel from Egypt as a type of all future deliverances (cf. Rom. 8:32). The climax of God's delivering his people would be the work of Abraham's offspring to overcome the gate of his enemies and establish global blessing (Gen. 22:17–18; cf. 3:15).

Along with reading the original exodus as a type that pointed to the day when God would restore his people in a second exodus, Hosea already linked that future restoration to a latter-day Davidic king: "Afterward the children of Israel shall return and seek the LORD their God, and David their king, and they shall come in fear to the LORD and to his goodness in the latter days" (Hos. 3:5 cf. Gen 49:1, 8–10; Num 24:14, 17–19; Deut 4:29–30). That passage raises the question, "What role would the future David play in the second exodus?"

Hosea 11:10–11 further encourages that question (emphasis added): "They shall go after the LORD; he will roar *like a lion*; when *he roars*, his children shall come trembling from the west; they shall come trembling like birds *from Egypt*, and like doves from the land of Assyria, and I will return them to their homes, declares the Lord." That passage likely alludes to Numbers 23:21–24 and 24:7–9, the only passages that associate God's delivering Israel "from Egypt" with the imagery of a lion. Further, many scholars see the OT background of the "king of the Jews" and "his star" in Matthew 2:2 to be Numbers 24:17: "I see him, but not now; I behold him, but not near: a star shall come out of Jacob, and a scepter shall rise out of Israel; it shall crush the forehead of Moab and break down all the sons of Sheth."[5]

---

4. Blomberg argues, "The original event need not have been intentionally viewed as forward-looking by the OT author" (Craig L. Blomberg, "Matthew," in *Commentary on the New Testament Use of the Old Testament*, eds. G. K. Beale and D. A. Carson [Grand Rapids: Baker Academic, 2007], 8). But that is exactly how Hosea treats it. What could further support Hosea's typological reading is if Hosea 11:5 declares that Israel will *not* return to Egypt (see previous footnote and context) but then portrays Israel's end-time restoration as nothing less than returning from Egypt. For similar typological readings of Hosea 11 itself, see Garrett, *Hosea, Joel*, 222; Beale, "Hosea 11:1 in Matthew 2:15: One More Time," 703–5.

5. See CD 7:18–26 and 4QTest. 9–13 for examples in Judaism of reading Num 24:17 as pointing to a messianic deliver. For Balaam's prophecy as key background to "his star" in Matthew 2:2, see, e.g., Michael J. Wilkins, Matthew, NIVAC (Grand Rapids: Zondervan, 2004), 95;

At first glance, the "lion" in Hosea 11:10–11 appears to be Yahweh, who delivers his trembling people from their adversity. Nevertheless, closely associating Yahweh with his king in 3:5 suggests that God's roar could come through his royal human agent.

Numbers 23:21–24 treats the people of Israel in the first exodus as a lion, with the "king" most likely being Yahweh, but possibly Moses (cf. Exod. 2:14; Acts 7:35).

> He has not beheld misfortune in Jacob, nor has he seen trouble in Israel. The Lord their God is with them, and the shout of a *king* is among them. God brings them *out of Egypt* and is for them like the horns of the wild ox. For there is no enchantment against Jacob, no divination against Israel; now it shall be said of Jacob and Israel, "What has God wrought!" Behold, a people! As a *lioness* it rises up and as a *lion* it lifts itself; it does not lie down until it has devoured the prey and drunk the blood of the slain. (Num. 23:21–24)

In contrast, Numbers 24:7–9 points to a future exodus that Yahweh's king—now called a lion—will lead. "God will bring him out of Egypt" and use him to crush either "Agag" (24:7), future king of the Amalekites (24:20; cf. 1 Sam.15:3, 8) and image of God-hostility, or "Gog," the end-time personification of evil (as rendered in the Septuagint; cf. Ezek. 38–39; Rev. 20:8).

> Water shall flow from his buckets, and his seed shall be in many waters; *his king* shall be higher than Agag [Gog?], and his kingdom shall be exalted. God brings him *out of Egypt* and is for him like the horns of the wild ox; he shall eat up the nations, his adversaries, and shall break their bones in pieces and pierce them through with his arrows. He crouched, he lay down like a *lion* and like a *lioness*; who will rouse him up? Blessed are those who bless you, and cursed are those who curse you. (Num. 24:7–9) The NIV unhelpfully translates the singular forms as plural.

Following the pattern in Exodus 15, Numbers also appears to be treating the first exodus as typological of an end-time exodus that a lion-king will lead. Yahweh God guides this lion-king, who represents his lion-people.

John Nolland, The Gospel of Matthew: A Commentary on the Greek Text, NIGTC (Grand Rapids: Eerdmans, 2005), 111; John Sailhamer, *The Meaning of the Pentateuch: Revelation, Composition, and Interpretation* (Downers Grove, IL: InterVarsity Press, 2009), 521 n.100. See also 2 Pet 1:19; Rev 22:16; cf. Rev 2:28.

Relevant Uses of Hosea 11:1 Elsewhere in Scripture or in Extrabiblical Jewish Literature

Outside Matthew 2:15, we find no other explicit links to Hosea 11:1. Furthermore, there are no clear passages in extrabiblical Jewish literature that apply Hosea 11:1. But there are many second exodus motifs.[6]

Textual Issues

Matthew's translation ("Out of Egypt I called my son") aligns more closely with the Hebrew MT than with the Greek Septuagint, which reads "and out of Egypt I summoned his children" (i.e., the children of the king). While not present in the MT, the Septuagint's use of the pronoun "his" refers to Israel's king, who is present both in Numbers 23:21 and 24:7, to which Hosea 11:10–11 alludes, and in the context of Matthew 2:2, with reference to Jesus as the one "born king of the Jews."

Matthew's Hermeneutical Warrant for Using Hosea 11:1

Following the pattern of Hosea himself and Moses before him, Matthew uses typology. Hosea refers to the first exodus as type for the antitypical end-time second exodus, which Christ ultimately leads (cf. Luke 9:31). In Beale's words, "The first exodus was seen by Hosea and, more clearly, by Matthew as a historical pattern pointing to the reoccurrence of the same pattern later in Israel's history."[7] As the "king of the Jews," Jesus represents the nation, and his departing "Egypt" as a child is one more intermediary type in the progression of redemptive history that climaxes in his bringing about the great second exodus on behalf of his people.

Matthew's Theological Use of Hosea 11:1

The way Matthew uses Hosea 11:1 is but one of a whole series of OT quotations that declare that Jesus, the Messiah-king, climactically fulfills the OT. Some scholars struggle with the way Matthew places the citation here and did not link it with the family's return from Egypt to Israel in 2:19–23. Craig Blomberg believes the apostle desired to "create five discrete pericopes concerning five fulfillments of prophecy" and, therefore, separated it from its more natural location.[8] In contrast, G. K. Beale believes that the OT citation is not oddly placed; it identifies that Matthew is replicating an OT pattern of leaving Egypt, returning to Egypt, and then leaving Egypt again (e.g., 1 Kings 11:40; Jer. 26:21–23; 44:12–15; cf. 2 Kings 25:26; Jer. 41:16–18; 43:1–7). That

---

6. See T. R. Hatina, "Exile," *Dictionary of New Testament Background*, eds. Craig A. Evans and Stanley E. Porter (Downers Grove, IL: InterVarsity Press, 2000), 348–49.
7. Beale, "Hosea 11:1 in Matthew 2:15: One More Time," 705. Similarly, Garrett notes, "[Matthew's] application of the typological principles to Hos 11:1 is in keeping with the nature of prophecy itself and with Hosea's own method." Garrett, *Hosea, Joel*, 222.
8. Blomberg, "Matthew," 7.

pattern is apparent in Hosea 11 itself: past exodus (v. 1), return (v. 5), and second exodus (v. 11). In this light, Beale believes Israel's original exodus in Hosea 11:1 included in its purview Israel's future reentering into Egypt. Matthew's narrating the family's journey to Egypt in Matthew 2:15 inaugurates the pattern, and then his noting in 2:21 that they returned to Israel fulfills a later stage in the pattern.[9]

Beale's reading is legitimate. But Matthew could instead be speaking metaphorically. He may identify ancient Egypt as a place of bondage with Judea of Jesus's day.[10] In Leithart's words,

> The meaning of the quotation is lost unless we see that Herod is acting like Pharaoh, killing Israelite children; that his court trembles at the announcement to Jesus' birth, as Pharaoh's court was in fear of the plagues; that Herod consults his court magicians, as Pharaoh did. . . . Jesus is the miracle child born from the seed of Abraham, who escapes from Pharaoh, who passes through the sea, who ascends a mountain to teach the law, et cetera.[11]

Beale questions this view because it requires "Egypt" in the quote to have a different referent than the actual geographical "Egypt," which Matthew refers to in 2:13–14, 19.[12]

Regardless, the typological link between Christ and the people of Israel is but one of many in Matthew's Gospel that identifies Jesus recapitulating Israel's history with successes they did not enjoy. Hence, Jesus's exodus from "Egypt" (Matt. 2:15) parallels Israel's flight; his journey through the waters of baptism (3:16–17) recalls Israel's crossing through the Red Sea; his forty days in the wilderness during which he was tempted (4:1–11) points back to Israel's forty years in the desert; his teaching on the mountain (e.g., 5:1) alludes to Moses's giving of the law, and so on.[13]

Hosea 11:1 is an ideal choice for a support text for at least three reasons. First, Hosea himself treats the first exodus of national Israel (God's "son") as typological of the end-time second exodus (see above). So, Matthew is simply following Hosea's lead.

---

9. Beale, "Hosea 11:1 in Matthew 2:15: One More Time," 707–8.

10. See especially Joel Kennedy, *The Recapitulation of Israel: Use of Israel's History in Matthew 1:1–4:11*, WUNT 2/257 (Tübingen: Mohr Siebeck, 2008), 313–14; Peter J. Leithart, *Deep Exegesis: The Mystery of Reading Scripture* (Waco, TX: Baylor University Press, 2009), 64–66.

11. Leithart, *Deep Exegesis*, 64–65.

12. Beale, "Hosea 11:1 in Matthew 2:15: One More Time," 706n26.

13. See esp. William L. Kynes, *A Christology of Solidarity: Jesus as the Representative of His People in Matthew* (Lanham, MD: University Press of America, 1991); Kennedy, *Recapitulation of Israel*; cf. W. D. Davies and Dale C. Allison Jr., *A Critical and Exegetical Commentary on the Gospel according to Saint Matthew*, 3 vols., ICC (London: T&T Clark, 2004), 1:262–64.

Second, Hosea already employed imagery of corporate solidarity by identifying the nation as God's singular "son." His language recalls Exodus 4:22–23, where Israel the nation is first tagged God's "firstborn son." The Exodus text itself looks back to Genesis 5:1–3, where Adam is God's first son, and it anticipates texts like 2 Samuel 7:14 and Psalm 2:7, which highlight Israel's messianic king as the son of God. As with Adam, God called Israel his corporate son to display his image and worth to the world (Exod. 19:5–6; Lev. 11:45; Deut. 6:5) as they awaited in hope for the (royal) offspring who would overcome evil and reconcile the world to God, thus restoring a state of blessing (Gen. 3:15; 22:17–18; 49:8, 10). Like Adam, Israel the nation was placed into its own land-paradise (Exod. 15:17), and like Adam, they would lose it due to their sin. Yet the prophets are united in their conviction that the hope of the Messiah-led kingdom endured and that Israel's representative would one day rise and lead them out of bondage into freedom.

Beyond Numbers 24:7–8 and Hosea 3:5, other texts directly associate the messianic royal figure with the second exodus and great end-time ingathering. For example, the Spirit-empowered Davidic child-king (Isa. 9:7; 11:1–2) will "stand as a signal for the peoples," and "in that day the Lord will extend his hand yet a second time to recover the remnant. . . . He will raise a signal for the nations and will assemble the banished of Israel and gather the dispersed of Judah from the four corners of the earth. . . . And there will be a highway from Assyria for the remnant that remains of his people, as there was for Israel when they came up from the land of Egypt" (11:10–12, 16).[14] Similarly, Jeremiah predicted,

> Behold, the days are coming, declares the LORD, when I will raise up for David a righteous Branch, and he shall reign as king and deal wisely, and shall execute justice and righteousness in the land. In his days Judah will be saved, and Israel will dwell securely. . . . Therefore, behold, the days are coming, declares the LORD, when they shall no longer say, "As the LORD lives who brought up the people of Israel out of the land of Egypt," but "As the LORD lives who brought up and led the offspring of the house of Israel out of the north country and out of all the countries where he had driven them." Then they shall dwell in their own land. (Jer. 23:5–8)

Third, Hosea already connected the antitypical second exodus with the reign of God and his Davidic royal son. "Afterward the children of Israel shall return and seek the LORD their God, and David their king, and they shall come in fear to the LORD and to his goodness in the latter days" (Hos. 3:5). "They shall go after the LORD; he will roar like a lion; when he roars, his children shall come trembling from the west; they shall come trembling like birds

---

14. See Question 31.

from Egypt, and like doves from the land of Assyria, and I will return them to their homes, declares the LORD" (Hos. 11:10–11). These parallels emphasize the close tie that Hosea saw between the ultimate second exodus and the Messiah's representative kingship.

Summary

Matthew 2:15 treats the statement in Hosea 11:1 ("Out of Egypt I called my son") as typologically predicting the Christ child's exodus from "Egypt." Egypt could be either metaphorical Judea under Pharaoh-like Herod or the actual geographical location to which Joseph and his family fled. Matthew's approach identifies his understanding of both corporate solidarity (the one representing the many) and typology (Christ is Israel), which directly parallels Hosea's own redemptive-historical hermeneutic. Specifically, by pointing to the original exodus, the prophet speaks of Israel as God's redeemed "son" (Hos. 11:1) and then anticipates their re-enslavement to (11:5) and future deliverance from Egypt (11:10–11). The latter passage recalls Balaam's oracles, in which God leads his victorious lion-king "out of Egypt" in a second exodus (Num. 24:7–8). That parallels God's earlier leading of his lion-people "out of Egypt" in the original exodus (24:22, 24). And because Hosea already linked Yahweh and his Davidic ruler with the second exodus in Hosea 3:5, the Lord's delivering his people from Egypt and Assyria in 11:10–11 implies that Yahweh's royal representative is present. Hence, Matthew is simply doing careful exegesis and theology by identifying Jesus's "exodus" as foreshadowing his greater "exodus" at the cross (Luke 9:29–30), through which he would lead many out of the grips of the curse.

REFLECTION QUESTIONS

1. How does Matthew 2:15 relate to its immediate surroundings in the book of Matthew?

2. How does Hosea 11:1 fit into the book of Hosea as a whole, and how does Hosea employ the theme of the exodus?

3. What are the concepts of "corporate solidarity" and "typology," and how are both Hosea and Matthew utilizing these concepts similarly and differently in the statement, "Out of Egypt I have called my son"?

4. What is Matthew's hermeneutical warrant for using Hosea 11:1 in Matthew 2:15?

5. How would you synthesize Matthew's theological use of Hosea 11:1 in Matthew 2:15?

How Does Romans 11:34–35 Use Isaiah 40:13 and Job 41:11a?

Andrew David Naselli

Paul asks three rhetorical questions in Romans 11:34–35:

1. [Isa. 40:13a] "For who has known the mind of the Lord,

2. [Isa. 40:13b] or who has been his counselor?"

3. [Job 41:11a] "Or who has given a gift to him that he might be repaid?"

We will analyze how Paul uses Isaiah 40 and Job 41 in Romans 11:34–35 by following the six steps we outline in Question 9.[1]

The Context of Romans 11:34–35

The theological message of Romans is that the gospel reveals how God is righteously righteousing (i.e., justifying) unrighteous individuals—both Jews and Gentiles—at this stage in the history of salvation. Romans 9–11 is—from a literary standpoint—critical but not central to Paul's unfolding argument. Romans 9:6–11:32 vindicates God's righteousness in his past, present, and future dealings with Israelites.[2] The uncontainable praise for God in Romans 11:33–36 naturally flows out of and euphorically concludes chapters 9–11. Responding primarily to the revealed nature of God's ways, Paul praises

---

1. This answer condenses Andrew David Naselli, *From Typology to Doxology: Paul's Use of Isaiah and Job in Romans 11:34–35* (Eugene, OR: Pickwick, 2012). See that book for more details (references to extrabiblical Jewish literature, secondary literature, etc.).
2. See also Jared M. Compton and Andrew David Naselli, eds., *Three Views on Israel and the Church: Perspectives on Romans 9–11*, Viewpoints (Grand Rapids: Kregel, 2019).

God for being deep (11:33), incomprehensible (11:34a), without counselors (11:34b), without creditors (11:35), and supreme (11:36). See the argument diagram in figure 33.1.

11:33	[1] Oh, the depth of the riches	33–36 responds to 9:1–11:32; 33 = three exclamations about God
b	and wisdom	
c	and knowledge of God!	
d	[2] How unsearchable are his judgments	
e	[3] and how inscrutable his ways!	Supports 33 (three rhetorical questions quote the OT)
11:34	[1] "For who has known the mind of the Lord,	
b	[2] or who has been his counselor?"	
11:35	[3] "Or who has given a gift to him	
b	that he might be repaid?"	Supports 33–35 (three prepositional phrases)
11:36	For [1] from him	
b	and [2] through him	
c	and [3] to him are all things.	Inference of 33–36c (doxology)
d	To him be glory forever. Amen	

Fig. 33.1. Argument Diagram of Romans 11:33–36

The Context of Isaiah 40:13 and Job 41:11a

Isaiah's theological message is that people should trust the Holy One of Israel because he is the incomparable King and Savior. Isaiah 40–66 emphasizes that God will comfort and restore his people, and Isaiah 40 exalts God's incomparability to demonstrate that he can easily restore his people. Isaiah 40:13 exclaims that no one gives God advice, and it evokes God's unrivaled wisdom and incomparable greatness.

Job's theological message is that people should respond to innocent, unexplained suffering by trusting God because he is supremely wise, sovereign, just, and good. The way God interrogates Job in Job 38:1–42:6 is significant for at least four reasons: (1) God is too small in Job's eyes; (2) Job is too large in his own eyes; (3) God is not obligated to give Job anything, not even answers to his questions; and (4) only God is all-wise. God makes two arguments in Job 41:10–11. First, God argues from the lesser to the greater to teach Job a lesson on humility. If Job would be terrified to stand before Leviathan, he should be even more terrified to demand a trial with God and stand before him. Second, God argues from the greater to the lesser to teach Job a lesson on ownership. Because God created Job, God owns Job, and because God owns Job, God does not owe Job anything.

Relevant Uses of Isaiah 40:13 and Job 41:11a in Extrabiblical Jewish Literature

The apparent ways that extracanonical Jewish literature quotes and alludes to Isaiah 40:13 have at least two themes. First, humans cannot fully understand God's thoughts and ways, especially in salvation history. Second, the only humans who can acquire a degree of God's wisdom are those to whom God reveals himself. These themes are also present in both Isaiah 40:13 and Romans 11:34.

There is both continuity and discontinuity between the uses of Isaiah 40:13 in Jewish literature and in Romans 11:34. The continuity is that Paul writes within a rich Jewish heritage that understands all these texts that praise God for his thoughts and ways. The discontinuity is what triggers Paul's praise: Paul reflects on God's sovereign ways in salvation history with reference to God's saving Jews and Gentiles.

The few uses of Job 41:11a in extracanonical Jewish literature are not significant for understanding how Paul uses Job 41:11a in Romans 11:35. But the use of Leviathan in Jewish literature is at least partially consistent with the larger cosmic realities present in Job 40–41.

Textual Issues

There are not any significant textual issues in these three passages. The textual integrity of Isaiah 40:13, Job 41:11, and Romans 11:34–35 is unassailable. Although some question whether Paul directly cites Isaiah 40:13 and Job 41:11a in Romans 11:34–35, the external and internal evidence strongly favors that Paul directly quotes them and slightly adapts them.

Paul's Hermeneutical Warrant for Using Isaiah 40:13 and Job 41:11a

Of the many possible hermeneutical warrants explaining why New Testament authors use the Old Testament the way they do, two apply to how Paul uses Isaiah 40 and Job 41 in Romans 11:34–35: (1) the larger Old Testament contexts, and (2) typology, a core component of the canonical approach. By quoting Isaiah 40:13 and Job 41:11a in Romans 11:34–35, Paul typologically connects Isaiah 40 and Job 38:1–42:6 with Romans 9–11 in order to exalt God's incomprehensibility, wisdom, mercy, grace, patience, independence, and sovereignty.

When Paul quotes Isaiah 40:13 and Job 41:11a, he includes their larger Old Testament contexts. That reveals a remarkable typological connection between the two Old Testament passages and the end of Romans 11. The subjects in all three contexts (Job and the Israelites) have been experiencing God's blessing, but God takes that away to some degree in a way that they think is unfair. After questioning God's righteousness while asserting their own, God reveals truth to them that they find difficult and unsatisfying. But they must repent of their flawed view of God and of themselves and trust God before they experience God's restored blessing to an even greater degree and in an unexpected way. God's salvation-historical plan demonstrates that he is wise, kind, and sovereign.

Paul's Theological Use of Isaiah 40:13 and Job 41:11a

The three rhetorical questions in Romans 11:34–35 communicate three of God's characteristics that correspond to his ways in salvation history, and each of them carries simple and profound theological implications.

1. God is incomprehensible in the sense that no one can *fully* understand him (Rom. 11:34a). At least four theological implications follow: (1) humans cannot understand everything; (2) God is not obligated to explain anything; (3) Christians must humbly believe and cherish what God has revealed; and (4) God deserves praise for what he does and does not explain.

2. God is without counselors (Rom. 11:34b). At least two theological implications follow: (1) humans should not try to give God advice, and (2) God deserves praise for not needing advice.

3. God is without creditors (Rom. 11:35). At least two theological implications follow: (1) humans should not try to place God in their debt, and (2) God deserves praise for not owing anything to anyone.

These three characteristics share at least two implications: (1) God's attributes are humbling to humans, and (2) God is gloriously praiseworthy. These characteristics and their implications tie perfectly into Romans 11:36, the climactic ending of Romans 9–11: "For from him and through him and to him are all things. To him be glory forever. Amen." All three of God's characteristics in Romans 11:34–35 are rooted in God's sovereignty (11:36a) and culminate in doxology (11:36b).

Summary

In Romans 11:34–35, Paul quotes Isaiah 40:13 and Job 41:11a. Paul brilliantly cites those two passages because in their literary contexts, the situation of the Israelites in Isaiah 40 and the situation of Job in Job 41 typologically connect with the situation of the Israelites in Romans 9–11. The way God wisely, kindly, and sovereignly deals with his people moves his people to praise him (Rom. 11:36). Paul moves from typology (Rom. 11:34–35) to doxology (Rom. 11:36).

REFLECTION QUESTIONS

1. Why is it important to understand the literary context of Romans 9–11 in order to analyze how Paul uses the OT in Romans 11:34–35?

2. How is understanding the broader literary context of Isaiah 40 and Job 41 important for understanding how Paul uses Isaiah 40:13 and Job 41:11a in Romans 11:34–35?

3. What does Paul imply when he describes God as incomprehensible, without counselors, and without creditors?

4. When you analyze Romans 11:34–35, why should you marvel that God's attributes are humbling?

5. When you analyze Romans 11:34–35, why should you marvel that God is uniquely praiseworthy?

How Does Galatians 3:12 Use Leviticus 18:5?

Jason S. DeRouchie

Now it is evident that no one is justified before God by the law, for "The righteous shall live by faith." But the law is not of faith, rather "The one who does them shall live by them."
(Gal. 3:11–12)

You shall therefore keep my statutes and my rules; if a person does them, he shall live by them: I am the LORD.
(Lev. 18:5)

In Galatians 3, the apostle Paul draws on several OT texts to support his reading of salvation history as culminating in Christ. One of those texts is Leviticus 18:5. Paul appropriates Leviticus 18:5 to support that "no one is justified before God by the law" (Gal. 3:11) and that "the law is not of faith" (3:12; cf. Rom. 10:5). Is the apostle actually viewing Habakkuk's claim that "the righteous shall live by faith" (Hab. 2:4) as counter to what Moses declares in Leviticus 18:5? Did not Moses himself celebrate the life of faith (Gen. 15:6) and grieve over Israel's lack of it (Num. 14:11; Deut. 1:32; 9:23)? What are we to make of how Paul uses Leviticus 18:5 in Galatians 3:12? We will analyze this question by following the six steps we outline in Question 9.

The Context of Galatians 3:12

In Galatians 2:16 Paul distinguishes two possible means of justification: "works of the law" and "faith in Jesus Christ." "Works of the law" refer to doing what the Mosaic covenant requires—actions by which "no one will be justified" (2:16);[1] "faith in Jesus Christ" is the only means for right standing with God (2:16) and is linked to "believing" (2:16), "life" (2:19–20), "grace" (2:21), "the Spirit" (3:2–3), and "hearing with faith" (3:2, 5). Faith in Jesus is the only way to become a "child" of Abraham (3:1–6; cf. 3:26, 29).

In 3:7–29 Paul builds on that understanding of justification and identity to clarify that only through faith in Christ does God declare us righteous and do we inherit all that he promised Abraham. Positively, all people of faith, including Gentiles, are blessed with Abraham (3:7–9). Negatively, those who relate to God by works of the law are cursed (3:10–14).

More specifically, relying on doing the law brings curse (3:10), and such activity fails to secure justification (3:11–12). In 3:11, Paul quotes Habakkuk 2:4: "The righteous shall live by faith." Believing—not doing—is the means to life. In Galatians 3:12, Paul quotes Leviticus 18:5: "The one who does them shall live by them." Paul assumes that Israel failed to keep the law and that consequently they experienced exilic death and desperately need Jesus. Paul concludes the unit by identifying how those of faith can enjoy justification and the Abrahamic blessing—solely by the redemption Christ secured by his obedient, substitutionary, curse-bearing work (Gal. 3:13–14).

The Context of Leviticus 18:5

Leviticus 11–26 clarifies how Israel was to pursue holiness as a means for living in the light of Yahweh's holy presence. Israel was on a journey between two realities—their former enslavement in "the land of Egypt" from which God redeemed them and their entry into "the land of Canaan" to which he was bringing them (18:3). Such past and future grace provides Israel's context for pursuing holiness and fulfilling what God prohibited and commanded. In light of their deliverance and future hopes, the Lord charges them two times, "You *shall not do*" like the Egyptians or Canaanites (18:3, emphasis added), who follow corrupt practices like sexual immorality (18:6–20, 22–23) and idolatry through child sacrifice (18:21). God then clarifies what they *should do*: "You shall follow my rules and keep my statutes. . . . You shall therefore

---

1. For this understanding of the phrase "works of the law" (*erga nomou*) in Rom. 3:20, 28, and Gal. 2:16[3x]; 3:2, 5, 10, see Thomas R. Schreiner, "Works of the Law," in *Dictionary of Paul and His Letters*, eds. Gerald F. Hawthorne and Ralph P. Martin (Downers Grove, IL: InterVarsity, 1993), 974–78; Thomas R. Schreiner, *40 Questions About Christians and Biblical Law*, 40 Questions, ed. Benjamin L. Merkle (Grand Rapids: Kregel, 2010), 41–45; cf. Douglas J. Moo, *Galatians*, BECNT (Grand Rapids: Baker Academic, 2013), 158–60. For this understanding of the phrase "faith of Christ" (*pistis Christou*), see Moisés Silva, "Faith versus Works of Law in Galatians," in *The Paradoxes of Paul*. vol. 2 of *Justification and Variegated Nomism*, eds. D. A. Carson, Peter T. O'Brien, and Mark A. Seifrid, WUNT 2/181 (Grand Rapids: Baker Academic, 2004), 217–48; Schreiner, *40 Questions About Christians and Biblical Law*, 133–38; cf. Moo, *Galatians*, 38–48.

keep my statutes and my rules; if a person does them, he shall live by them: I am the LORD" (18:4–5).

Three observations are pertinent here. First, the Mosaic covenant is built upon a principle of retribution that Yahweh designed to motivate holy living in the present. What people hope for or fear tomorrow should change who they are today (cf. 2 Peter 1:4). Thus, Moses promises blessings (Lev. 26:3–13; Deut. 28:1–14) and curses (Lev. 26:14–19; Deut. 27:11–26; 28:15–68) to stimulate Israel's loyalty. By perfectly keeping the *whole* law, Israel could enjoy life and good things, but disobedience would result in death and evil things (Deut. 11:26–28; 30:15–19).[2] People needed to surrender to God with *all* their heart and soul (4:29; 6:5; 10:12; 11:13; 13:3; 26:16; cf. 30:2, 6, 10). And if they would surrender to God's standard of "righteousness" (*ṣédeq*, 16:20) and obey his whole commandment manifest in the various statutes and rules, the Lord would preserve their lives (6:24), they would enjoy the status of "righteousness" (*ṣĕdeqâ*, 6:25), and they would secure lasting "life" (8:1; 16:20; 30:16).

Second, while Yahweh was Israel's God in the sense that he had redeemed them through the exodus and uniquely claimed them as his own through covenant (cf. Deut. 4:32–35), the rest of the OT, including the Pentateuch, identifies the ruinous state and fate of the majority. While Yahweh would have regarded life-encompassing obedience as "righteousness" (*ṣĕdeqâ*, 6:25), they were far from such status, with their own wickedness resembling that of the nations whom they were called to dispossess (9:4–7; cf. 9:27). By Leviticus 18, the people have already tested God seven times since leaving Egypt, and they would soon rebel a total of ten times (Num. 14:21–23).[3] Thus, Moses calls them "stubborn" (Exod. 32:9; 33:3, 5; 34:9; Deut. 9:6, 13; 10:16; 31:27), "unbelieving" (Num. 14:11; Deut. 1:32; 9:23), and "rebellious" (Num. 20:10, 24; 27:14; Deut. 9:7, 24; 31:27). He also promises that their insolence would only increase in the Promised Land (Deut. 31:16), resulting in curses climaxing in an exilic death (31:17, 29; cf. 28:15–68). While the Lord redeemed the nation from Egypt, he did not regenerate most of their hearts, and while he gave them the law on tablets of stone, they remained spiritually disabled with sin etched on their inner being (see Deut. 29:4[3]; Jer. 17:1). The cry, "Do this law so that you may live!" came to a primarily *unregenerate* community. The majority of old covenant Israel were not eternally saved, and the covenant they were in bore a ministry that would only multiply sin (Rom. 3:20; 5:20; Gal. 3:19) and lead to their death and condemnation (2 Cor. 3:7, 9; cf. 2 Kings 17:13–18; Rom. 11:7–10; Heb. 3:16–19).

---

2. Deuteronomy stresses the need to keep all (*kōl*) the laws (see Deut. 5:29, 31, 33; 6:2, 24–25; 8:1; 10:12; 11:8, 22, 32; 12:13, 28, 32; 13:18; 15:5; 17:10, 19; 19:9; 26:14, 18; 27:1; 28:1, 14, 15, 58; 30:8; 31:5, 12; 32:46).

3. For the ten testings, see: (1) Exod. 14:11–12; (2) 15:24; (3) 16:2–3; (4) 16:20; (5) 16:27; (6) 17:1–2; (7) 32:1–6; (8) Num. 11:1; (9) 11:4; (10) 14:1–4.

Third, neither faith nor forgiveness characterized the era of the Mosaic covenant. In this covenant, Moses never explicitly called for faith, though he affirmed its necessity (cf. 2 Chron. 20:20). What he did call for was wholehearted, perfect commandment keeping in order to enjoy life and righteousness (emphasis added): "You shall follow my rules and keep my statutes. . . . If the person *does* them, he shall live by them" (Lev. 18:5). "The *whole* commandment that I command you today you shall be careful to do, that you may live and multiply, and go in and possess the land that the LORD swore to give to your fathers" (Deut. 8:1, emphasis added; cf. 6:24–25; 11:32; 26:18; 28:1). Moses stressed that Abraham believed God (Gen. 15:6) and that this faith moved him to obey (e.g., 22:16–18; 26:3–5). Moses even treated the patriarch as a model Israelite and covenant keeper before the law (26:3–5).[4] The old covenant mediator also celebrated that Israel temporarily believed in both him and Yahweh through the exodus (Exod. 15:31). Nevertheless, he grieved deeply that both he and Israel did not continue to believe in God while in the wilderness (Num. 14:11; 20:12; Deut. 1:32; 9:23); the results were tragic (cf. Heb. 3:16–19). This very faithlessness of the exodus generation continued as the dominant motif throughout the people's tenure in the Promised Land and into the exile. Thus, Nehemiah cites Leviticus 18:5, "And you warned them in order to turn them back to your law. Yet they acted presumptuously and did not obey your commandments, but sinned against your rules, which *if a person does them, he shall live by them.* . . . Therefore you gave them into the hand of the peoples of the lands" (Neh. 9:29–30, emphasis added). Rather than enjoying life, Israel experienced death, due in part to their lack of faith (see 2 Kings 17:13–14, 18).

Jeremiah highlights the substantial lack of saving forgiveness in the Mosaic covenant when he contrasts the old covenant with the new and better one that would include a democratized knowledge of God only *because* "I will forgive their iniquity, and I will remember their sins no more" (Jer. 31:34). Nehemiah highlights the way God continued to mercifully pardon his people throughout their history (Neh. 9:17, 19, 27–28, 31). But still their hearts remained cold, and the death of exile became their lot. The perfect obedience that laws like Leviticus 18:5 demanded was a God-dependent obedience, but since no one could remain perfectly dependent, if anyone was to enjoy life, it would only be by Yahweh declaring them right by faith (cf. Gen. 15:6; Isa. 53:11; Rom. 4:5). Only Jesus ultimately secures the life that the law promised. He does so by obeying perfectly—his "one act of righteousness leads to justification and life for all men" (Rom. 5:18). Yet the majority of the Israelite community did not live in the context of spiritual reconciliation with God; they were covenant partners outwardly but rebels inwardly.

---

4. R. W. L. Moberly, *The Old Testament of the Old Testament: Patriarchal Narratives and Mosaic Yahwism*, OBT (Minneapolis: Fortress, 1992), 144–45; cf. John H. Sailhamer, "The Mosaic Law and the Theology of the Pentateuch," *WTJ* 53 (1991): 241–61.

Walter Kaiser asserts that, because "one of the ways of 'doing' the law was to recognize the imperfection of one's life and thus to make a sacrifice for the atonement of one's sins," Leviticus 18:5 "is not referring to any offer of eternal life as a reward for perfect law-keeping."[5] In contrast, what the law demanded was complete fear, whole-hearted love, and absolute obedience in order to be declared right (Deut. 6:5; 10:12–13) and to enjoy lasting life (4:1; 8:1; 16:20; 30:16). When one recognized that he failed and cound not meet this demand, trusting God's substitutionary sacrifice was a means for reconciliation. But we must not lower the law's demand for total and perfect surrender, for this alone provides the context for Jesus Christ's faultless obedience that secures "justification of life" for the many (Rom. 5:18–19; 2 Cor. 5:21; Phil. 3:9).[6] If, as we have argued, most original recipients of Moses's words were unregenerate, a call to "do in order to live" would have resulted in nothing less than a type of legalism for the majority, as the "gracious character of the Levitical system" would be inoperative without the feeling of guilt, confession, and trust (Lev. 5:5–6; Num. 5:6–7).[7] Thus Paul alludes to Moses's charge in Deuteronomy 16:20 ("Righteousness, righteousness you shall pursue, so that you may live") in Romans 9:31–32: "Israel who pursued a law that would lead to righteousness did not succeed in reaching that law. Why? Because they did not pursue it by faith, but *as if it were based on works*." "Christ," therefore, "is the end of the law for righteousness to everyone who believes" (10:4). His arrival signals a transition from an age of death associated with the Mosaic covenant to an age of life enjoyed by a righteousness that comes by faith.

Relevant Uses of Leviticus 18:5 in the Rest of the Old Testament, Early Extrabiblical Jewish Literature, and Other New Testament Texts

Ezekiel graphically contrasts the failure of human "doing" in the Mosaic covenant with the divine and human "doing" within the future everlasting/new covenant.[8] Ministering in the midst of Judah's Babylonian exile, he cites Leviticus 18:5 to identify Judah's exile as a "death," which stood as the opposite of the life promised for obedience (Ezek. 20:11, 13, 21).[9] The prophet sees that Yahweh's purpose for the very good law (Neh. 9:13; cf. Rom. 2:20; 7:12) was to

---

5. Walter C. Kaiser, "Leviticus 18:5 and Paul: Do This and You Shall Live (Eternally?)," *JETS* 14, no. 1 (1971): 25; cf. Walter C. Kaiser, *The Promise-Plan of God: A Biblical Theology of the Old and New Testaments* (Grand Rapids: Zondervan, 2008), 80.

6. See Peter J. Gentry and Stephen J. Wellum, *Kingdom through Covenant: A Biblical-Theological Understanding of the Covenants*, 2nd ed. (Wheaton, IL: Crossway, 2018), 777–82.

7. The brief quote comes from Hamilton, whose perspective differs from the one this chapter proposes. James M. Hamilton Jr., "The One Who Does Them Shall Live by Them: Leviticus 18:5 in Galatians 3:12," *Gospel Witness* (2005): 10.

8. See Preston M. Sprinkle, "Law and Life: Leviticus 18:5 in the Literary Framework of Ezekiel," *JSOT* 31, no. 3 (2007): 275–93.

9. For other similar allusions, see Ezek. 18:5, 9, 17, 19, 21; 33:10, 13, 19; Amos 5:4.

destroy and thus identify the need for a better covenant and better mediator (Ezek. 20:25; cf. Gal. 3:21). Israel had become like the dried skeletons of a defeated army in a valley (37:1); this was where the Mosaic covenant had brought them. It bore a "ministry of death" and "ministry of condemnation" (2 Cor. 3:7, 9). In Paul's words, "The very commandment that promised life proved to be death to me" (Rom. 7:10).

Yet into this setting, Yahweh declares, "I will put my Spirit within you, and cause you to walk in my statutes and be careful to obey my rules" (Ezek. 36:27; cf. 11:19–20). And again, "I will put my Spirit within you, and you shall live" (37:14). Out of the valley of death would come resurrection, and what was not "done" in the age of the law covenant, the power of God's presence would now enable (37:24).[10] Thus, the OT itself explicitly contrasts (1) the old covenant as a failed, human deeds–based covenant, and (2) the coming better covenant that God would enable and that would be marked by faith (cf. Hab. 2:4).

During Israel's initial restoration from exile, Nehemiah recalled Leviticus 18:5 when pleading for mercy and when speaking of the way Yahweh pursued his people in the past: "And you warned them in order to turn them back to your law. Yet they acted presumptuously and did not obey your commandments, but sinned against your rules, which *if a person does them, he shall live by them*. . . . Therefore you gave them into the hand of the peoples of the lands" (Neh. 9:29–30, emphasis added). Rather than enjoying life by remaining loyal to God, Israel rebelled and experienced a justified death at the hands of God's agents of covenant curse.[11]

While not echoing Leviticus 18:5 directly, Malachi, the last of the OT prophets, spoke on Yahweh's behalf: "Remember the law of my servant Moses, the statutes and rules that I commanded him at Horeb for all Israel" (Mal. 4:1). Thus, until the prophet like Moses arose to mediate a new covenant (Deut. 18:15–18; 34:10–12), God's command to Israel remained "You shall . . . keep my statutes and my rules; if a person does them, he shall live by them."

By alluding to Leviticus 18:5, the Jews of the Qumran community (ca. 250 BC–AD 135) affirmed that curse awaited all who failed to keep the law and that God promised life for those who obey and who are redeemed (CD 3:15–16; 4Q266 f11:11–13). Other Jews believed that the "life" Leviticus 18:5 promised was both eschatological and eternal (Pss. Sol. 14:1–5; Tg. Onq. Lev. 18:5; Tg. Ps.-J. Lev. 18:5).[12]

---

10. See Sprinkle, "Law and Life," 290.
11. Significantly, Nehemiah 9 also appears to contrast the "doing" of the law of Moses (Neh 9:29–30) with the "faith" of Abraham (9:8). For a defense of Neh 9:8 referring to Abraham's "faith," see Michael B. Shepherd, *The Text in the Middle*, StBibLit 162 (New York: Lang, 2014), 38–39. I thank my research assistant Brian Verrett for directing me to this resource.
12. For more on Leviticus 18:5 in extrabiblical Jewish literature, see Preston M. Sprinkle, *Law and Life: The Interpretation of Leviticus 18:5 in Early Judaism and in Paul*, WUNT

In the Gospels, Jesus alludes to Leviticus 18:5:

> And behold, a lawyer stood up to put [Jesus] to the test, saying, "Teacher, what shall I do to inherit eternal life?" He said to him, "What is written in the Law? How do you read it?" And he answered, "You shall love the Lord your God with all your heart and with all your soul and with all your strength and with all your mind, and your neighbor as yourself." And he said to him, "You have answered correctly; *do this, and you will live.*" But he, desiring to justify himself, said to Jesus, "And who is my neighbor?" (Luke 10:25–29, emphasis added)

Knowledge is not enough to "inherit eternal life"; one must "do this" in order to "live." Nevertheless, for sinful humans, the quest for self-justification will always end in condemnation. We must ultimately look beyond ourselves to Jesus Christ, "the righteous," who is "the propitiation for our sins, and . . . for the sins of the whole world" (1 John 2:1–2).

The final NT citation of Leviticus 18:5 is in Romans 10:5, where Paul is arguing about the means for justification in ways very comparable to Galatians 3. Throughout Romans 9:30–10:13 Paul continually pits doing and believing as two opposing means for enjoying righteous status. Believing is the only option for fallen humans. Verses 5–8 contrast the fruitless attempt to gain righteousness "from the law" (10:5) with trusting Christ for righteousness (10:6–8). That is why "Christ is the end of the law for righteousness to everyone who believes" (10:4; cf. Phil. 3:9).[13] That is, the goal and end of the law is believing in Christ *because* the law covenant required an impossible perfect obedience to enjoy righteousness and life (cf. Lev. 18:5), whereas trusting Christ supplies by faith what is impossible otherwise (cf. Deut. 30:11–14). Paul can contrast Moses against Moses most likely because Leviticus 18:5 and Deuteronomy 30:11–14 address two different eras in salvation history. Leviticus 18:5 addresses the "doing" era of the Mosaic covenant, and Deuteronomy 30:11–14 predicts the "believing" era of the new covenant.[14]

2/241 (Tübingen: Mohr Siebeck, 2008), 1–130; Simon J. Gathercole, "Torah, Life, and Salvation: Leviticus 18:5 in Early Judaism and the New Testament," in *From Prophecy to Testament: The Function of the Old Testament in the New*, ed. Craig A. Evans (Peabody, MA: Hendrickson, 2004), 126–45.

13. Thomas R. Schreiner, *Romans*, 2nd ed., BECNT (Grand Rapids: Baker Academic, 2018), 535.

14. In contrast to contemporary English translations, the verbless clauses in Deuteronomy 30:11–14 are most naturally read as futures, continuing the *future* predictions begun in 30:1, the whole of which anticipates that what Moses is commanding "today" will have lasting relevance in the new covenant age (30:2, 8, 11). Deuteronomy 30:11–14 begins with the subordinate conjunction *ki* ("for, because") and provides the logical reason the people will turn to the LORD in the latter days (30:10). Paul is, therefore, identifying that Christ fulfills what Moses predicted in bringing an obedience that flows from faith. My research assistant Brian Verrett has helped me see further support in this by the fact that the phrase

Textual Issues

There is some minimal variation in wording between Paul's citation in Galatians 3:12 and his possible sources. Nevertheless, no substantial differences exist in meaning between the Hebrew and Greek treatments of Leviticus 18:5 and Paul's quotation.[15]

Paul's Hermeneutical Warrant for Using Leviticus 18:5

In Galatians 3:12 Paul appears to employ Leviticus 18:5 to contrast (1) the pattern for enjoying life and justification in the era of the Mosaic covenant from (2) the pattern that must characterize all who are in Christ in the new covenant era.[16] More specifically, in Galatians 3:11–12 Paul is noting how the respective periods in salvation history testify to two different possible ways to enjoy right standing before God: *doing* leads to life (Lev. 18:5) versus *believing* leads to life (Hab. 2:4).[17]

"obey/listen unto the voice" in Deuteronomy 30:8, 10 likely alludes to Genesis 22:18 when Abraham "obeyed/listened to the voice" of God by being willing to sacrifice Isaac. Abraham's obedience in Genesis 22:18 flowed from his faith (Gen. 15:6; Heb. 11:19), which in turn provides a model for the obedience of faith that Paul is arguing for in both Romans and Galatians.. On the future-oriented reading of Deuteronomy 30:11–14, see, for example, J. Gary Millar, *Now Choose Life: Theology and Ethics in Deuteronomy*, NSBT 6 (Downers Grove, IL: InterVarsity, 1998), 94, 174–75; Stephen G. Dempster, *Dominion and Dynasty: A Biblical Theology of the Hebrew Bible*, NSBT 15 (Downers Grove, IL: InterVarsity, 2003), 118–21; Patrick A. Barker, *The Triumph of Grace in Deuteronomy: Faithless Israel, Faithful Yahweh in Deuteronomy* (Carlisle, UK: Paternoster, 2004), 182–98; Steven R. Coxhead, "Deuteronomy 30:11–14 as a Prophecy of the New Covenant in Christ," *WTJ* 68 (2006): 305–20; Bryan D. Estelle, "Leviticus 18:5 and Deuteronomy 30:1–14 in Biblical Theological Development: Entitlement to Heaven Foreclosed and Proffered," in *The Law Is Not of Faith: Essays on Works and Grace in the Mosaic Covenant*, eds. Bryan D. Estelle, J. V. Fesko, and David VanDrunen (Phillipsburg, NJ: P&R, 2009), 127–37; Jason S. DeRouchie, "From Condemnation to Righteousness: A Christian Reading of Deuteronomy," *SBJT* 18, no. 3 (Fall 2014): 117–18; Colin James Smothers, "In Your Mouth and in Your Heart: A Study of Deuteronomy 30:12–14 in Paul's Letter to the Romans in Canonical Context" (PhD diss., Southern Baptist Theological Seminary, 2018).

15. See Moisés Silva, "Galatians," in *Commentary on the New Testament Use of the Old Testament*, eds. G. K. Beale and D. A. Carson (Grand Rapids: Baker Academic, 2007), 802–803; Douglas J. Moo, *Galatians*, BECNT (Grand Rapids: Baker Academic, 2013), 220–21.

16. Of Beale's twelve possible ways the NT authors hermeneutically use the OT, this is number four: "To indicate an analogical (/contrastive) or illustrative use of the Old Testament." G. K. Beale, *Handbook on the New Testament Use of the Old Testament: Exegesis and Interpretation* (Grand Rapids: Baker Academic, 2012), 67–71.

17. For a sound argument that Habakkuk 2:4 intentionally echoes Genesis 15:6 ("And [Abram] believed the LORD, and he counted it to him as righteousness") and that the Hebrew noun ʾĕmûnâ (= Greek *pistis*) in Habakkuk 2:4 is indeed best rendered "faith" rather than "faithfulness," see E. Ray Clendenen, "Salvation by Faith or by Faithfulness in the Book of Habakkuk?" *BBR* 24 (2014): 505–13; Shepherd, *The Text in the Middle*, 32–36. cf. Silva, "Galatians," 802.

The *doing* that the law in Leviticus 18:5 called for was completely conforming to how God defines right order: "Righteousness, righteousness you shall pursue, that you may live" (Deut. 16:20; cf. Rom. 9:30–31). However, "No one is justified before God by the law" because no person born in Adam was able to keep it and because the Mosaic law itself could only declare what ought to happen; it could not make it happen because human sinfulness weakened it (Rom. 8:3; Gal. 3:10, 21). Thus, when God gave his holy law to sinful people whose resistance he did not overcome (Deut. 29:4[3]), the law brought death and condemned (Rom. 7:10; 11:7–10; 2 Cor. 3:7, 9). In Paul's day, for the Jews to require "works of the law" as the means of justification was to go back to a death-dealing era in salvation history—an era that Christ's own curse-bearing, perfect obedience alone overcame and destroyed (Gal. 3:13–14).

Paul is reading Leviticus 18:5 in light of the death-dealing nature of the Mosaic covenant. God's revealed will within his holy law was that people exalt him through lives of surrender and by this enjoy the blessings that come with delighting in his presence ("do in order to live"). Nevertheless, these revealed purposes (i.e., what Israel *ought* to have done) contrasted with the Lord's more sovereign purposes for the law—namely, to multiply Israel's sin (Rom. 3:20; 5:20), to condemn them (2 Cor. 3:9), and by this to point them and the rest of the world to Christ as the only means for right standing with God (Rom. 10:4; cf. 3:19–22). Jesus alone fulfills the demands of the law and by this secures the promised justification unto life for all who believe (Rom. 5:18). Leviticus 18:5 falls within the redemptive-historical context of death (i.e., imperfect human doing apart from imputed righteousness brings destruction), and therefore it stands in contrast with the life of faith. Blessing and curse—life and death— were the options before the community (Deut. 11:26–28; 30:15–20).

Hamilton rightly recognizes that Paul in Galatians 3:12 is speaking from a redemptive-historical perspective, but we differ when he argues that the Mosaic era *was* one of faith but now is not considered so because of the coming of Christ.[18] Instead, Paul is identifying that because God gave the Mosaic covenant to a hard-hearted people, his call to "do this and live" became an impossible and, therefore, legalistic way of gaining salvation. The inability to keep the law perfectly should have pushed the Israelites to recognize Christ as "the end of the law for righteousness" (Rom. 10:4). That is, it should have moved them to join Abraham in hoping in the coming offspring (Gen. 15:1–6; 22:17–18; cf. John 8:56; Rom. 4:18–25) and to see the tabernacle, priests, and substitutionary animal sacrifices as mere pointers (Exod. 25:9; Zech. 3:8–9; Heb. 9:8–10; 10:1–10)

---

18. Hamilton, "One Who Does Them Shall Live," 10–12. Hamilton writes, "'Before faith came' Leviticus 18:5 meant that the one who *by faith* kept the Mosaic Covenant would live. Now that 'faith has come,' the Mosaic covenant is no longer in force, it has served its redemptive-historical purpose, with the result that anyone who seeks to live by it must keep all of its regulations flawlessly since its sacrifices are now abolished" (cf. Gal. 5:3). Hamilton, "One Who Does Them Shall Live," 12.

to God's future saving provision through his suffering servant, who would triumph through tribulation (Isa. 50:8–9; 53:11; cf. Gen. 3:15; Zech. 13:7–9). But instead, rather than attaining righteous status by faith (like many Gentiles in Paul's day were), Israel pursued righteousness not "by faith, but as if it were based on works" (9:32; cf. 9:30–33). The sacrifices in the old covenant provided a temporary and insufficient provision for sinners who believed, and the once-for-all sacrifice of Christ nullifies the need for any more sacrifices (Heb. 9:11–12, 25–28; 10:10).[19] Nevertheless, when Paul asserts, "I testify again to every man who accepts circumcision that he is obligated to keep the whole law" (Gal. 5:3), he is not claiming that this is only the case now that Christ has nullified the old covenant sacrifices.[20] He is asserting that the old covenant has *always* been associated with the need to keep the whole law (cf. Gal. 2:21), and one must either trust in Jesus who alone fulfilled the law completely or be condemned in light of human inability and the historical failure of the law.

Similar to this reading of Leviticus 18:5 and to Ezekiel's handling of that text in Ezekiel 20, Moses consistently urges Israel, "Do this so that you may live" (e.g., Deut. 4:1; 5:33; 8:1; 11:8–9; 16:20; 22:7; 30:19; 31:13; cf. Rom. 7:10). The only place in Deuteronomy where Moses speaks differently is when he predicts the new covenant era: "The LORD will circumcise your heart . . . to love the LORD your God with all your heart and with all your soul *for the sake of your life*" (Deut. 30:6, DeRouchie's translation). God is fulfilling that text in the church age (Rom. 2:29), and it is in this era alone that God would work in his people "for the sake of their life," thus securing for them what they could not secure on their own.

Paul's Theological Use of Leviticus 18:5 in Galatians 3:12

When Paul cites Leviticus 18:5 in Galatians 3:12, he is identifying how the Mosaic law-covenant brought death to all and that, therefore, "the law is not of faith." What characterized the Mosaic law was "works of the law," not believing. The call to "do in order to live" set a context for Christ's complete, whole-life obedience, even to the point of death (Rom. 5:18–19; Phil. 2:8). But that same call should have pushed sinful people to turn away from doing as a means to

---

19. Carson writes, "It is not at all clear that Paul would have admitted to any life-giving or salvific capacity in the Mosaic covenant: the law-covenant had quite different functions in the stream of redemptive history (Gal. 3). By the same token, judging by such passages as 1 Corinthians 5:7; 11:23–25; Romans 3:24–25; 8:3; 2 Corinthians 5:21; Paul would not have admitted to the atoning efficacy of the old covenant's sacrifices: sin's solution is the work of Christ. In other words, the center of gravity in Paul's thought is Christ, and the antecedent revelation points decisively to him and all that he brings." D. A. Carson, "Mystery and Fulfillment: Toward a More Comprehensive Paradigm of Paul's Understanding of the Old and New," in *The Paradoxes of Paul*, vol. 2 of *Justification and Variegated Nomism*, eds. D. A. Carson, Peter T. O'Brien, and Mark A. Seifrid, 2 vols., WUNT 2/181 (Grand Rapids: Baker Academic, 2004), 434.
20. Contra Hamilton, "One Who Does Them Shall Live," 12; cf. Schreiner, *40 Questions About Christians and Biblical Law*, 62.

righteousness and life (see Lev. 18:5; Deut. 6:25; 16:20) and to start looking to God for right standing and power to obey, which he promised to supply through substitutionary atonement (see Rom. 9:30–31). The Mosaic covenant bore a ministry of death and condemnation (2 Cor. 3:7, 9). It was characterized by a hard-hearted, faithless people who pursued righteousness apart from faith. All those in Christ must turn away from "works of the law" to faith in Christ because "it is evident that no one is justified before God by the law" (Gal. 3:11; cf. 2:16).

Summary

In order to support his claim in Galatians 3:11 that "no one is justified before God by the law," the apostle Paul asserts in 3:12, "The law is not of faith, rather 'The one who does them shall live by them'"—quoting Leviticus 18:5. Paul's point is that the era of the Mosaic covenant (which an era of faith has now superseded because of Christ) was as a whole characterized by faithlessness among the majority. And the failure to "abide by all things written in the Book of the Law, and do them" resulted in "a curse" (Gal. 3:10). Therefore, salvation history has proven that justification comes only by faith in Christ, whose perfect obedience climaxing in the curse-bearing cross event secured life and righteousness for all who believe, "so that in Christ Jesus the blessing of Abraham might come to the Gentiles" (3:13–14).[21]

REFLECTION QUESTIONS

1. What is the thrust of Paul's argument in Galatians 2–3 in which his citation of Leviticus 18:5 occurs?

2. What does the OT context of Leviticus 18:5 suggest Paul means in Galatians 3:12 by "the law is not of faith"?

3. What is significant about Ezekiel's vision of dry bones (Ezek. 37:1–14) after his identification in chapter 20 that Israel's history was marked by a failure to heed the statutes and rules, by which, "if a person does them, he shall live by them" (20:11, 13, 21)?

4. What hermeneutical warrant does Paul have for using Leviticus 18:5 in Galatians 3:12 the way he does?

5. How would you synthesize Paul's theological use of Leviticus 18:5 in Galatians 3:12?

---

21. For more on this question, see Jason S. DeRouchie, "The Use of Leviticus 18:5 in Galatians 3:12: A Redemptive-Historical Reassessment," *Them* 45, no. 2 (2020): 240–59.

How Do Genesis 1–3 and Revelation 21–22 Relate as the Bible's Bookends?

Andrew David Naselli

The Bible's bookends are beautiful. So many themes that begin in Genesis 1–3 culminate in Revelation 21–22. Figure 35.1 highlights more explicit themes in the order they appear in Revelation 21–22.[1]

Theme	Genesis 1–3	Revelation 21–22
Heaven and earth	"In the beginning, God created the heavens and the earth" (Gen. 1:1).	"I saw a new heaven and a new earth, for the first heaven and the first earth had passed away" (Rev. 21:1).
The sea	"And God said, 'Let the waters under the heavens be gathered together into one place, and let the dry land appear.' And it was so. God called the dry land Earth, and the waters that were gathered together he called Seas" (Gen. 1:9–10).	"And the sea was no more" (Rev. 21:1).
Garden-city temple	"And the LORD God planted a garden in Eden, in the east, and there he put the man whom he had formed" (Gen. 2:8).	"And I saw the holy city, new Jerusalem, coming down out of heaven from God, prepared as a bride adorned for her husband. . . . I saw no temple in the city, for its temple is the Lord God the Almighty and the Lamb" (Rev. 21:2, 22; see 21:9–27).

---

1. Some themes such as the Sabbath or the serpent culminate in the new heaven and new earth but are not explicit in Revelation 21–22.

Theme	Genesis 1–3	Revelation 21–22
Dwelling with God: exile and exodus	"And they heard the sound of the Lord God walking in the garden in the cool of the day, and the man and his wife hid themselves from the presence of the Lord God among the trees of the garden. . . . The Lord God sent him out from the garden of Eden to work the ground from which he was taken. He drove out the man" (Gen. 3:8, 23–24).	"Behold, the dwelling place of God is with man. He will dwell with them, and they will be his people, and God himself will be with them" (Rev. 21:3).
Pain and death	"I will surely multiply your pain in childbearing; in pain you shall bring forth children. . . . Cursed is the ground because of you; in pain you shall eat of it all the days of your life . . . till you return to the ground, for out of it you were taken; for you are dust, and to dust you shall return" (Gen. 3:16, 17, 19).	"He will wipe away every tear from their eyes, and death shall be no more, neither shall there be mourning, nor crying, nor pain anymore, for the former things have passed away. . . . The leaves of the tree were for the healing of the nations" (Rev. 21:4; 22:2).
Creating	"In the beginning, God created . . . " (Gen. 1:1).	"Behold, I am making all things new" (Rev. 21:5).
Beginning and end	"In the beginning, God . . . " (Gen. 1:1).	"I am the Alpha and the Omega, the beginning and the end. . . . I am the Alpha and the Omega, the first and the last, the beginning and the end" (Rev. 21:6; 22:13).
First and second death	"And the Lord God commanded the man, saying, 'You may surely eat of every tree of the garden, but of the tree of the knowledge of good and evil you shall not eat, for in the day that you eat of it you shall surely die.' . . . 'By the sweat of your face you shall eat bread, till you return to the ground, for out of it you were taken; for you are dust, and to dust you shall return'" (Gen. 2:16–17; 3:19).	"But as for the cowardly, the faithless, the detestable, as for murderers, the sexually immoral, sorcerers, idolaters, and all liars, their portion will be in the lake that burns with fire and sulfur, which is the second death" (Rev 21:8).
Marriage	"'It is not good that the man should be alone; I will make him a helper fit for him.' . . . Therefore a man shall leave his father and his mother and hold fast to his wife, and they shall become one flesh" (Gen. 2:18, 24).	"Come, I will show you the Bride, the wife of the Lamb" (Rev. 21:9).

Theme	Genesis 1–3	Revelation 21–22
Sacrifice	"And the LORD God made for Adam and for his wife garments of skins and clothed them" (Gen. 3:21).	"the Lamb" (Rev. 21:9, 14, 22, 23, 27; 22:1, 3)
Light	"Darkness was over the face of the deep. . . . And God said, 'Let there be light,' and there was light. And God saw that the light was good. And God separated the light from the darkness. God called the light Day, and the darkness he called Night. . . . And God said, 'Let there be lights in the expanse of the heavens to separate the day from the night. . . . And let them be lights in the expanse of the heavens to give light upon the earth.' And it was so. And God made the two great lights—the greater light to rule the day and the lesser light to rule the night—and the stars. And God set them in the expanse of the heavens to give light on the earth, to rule over the day and over the night, and to separate the light from the darkness" (Gen. 1:2–5, 14–18).	"And the city has no need of sun or moon to shine on it, for the glory of God gives it light, and its lamp is the Lamb. . . . There will be no night there. . . . And night will be no more. They will need no light of lamp or sun, for the Lord God will be their light" (Rev. 21:23, 25; 22:5).
Access to the garden-city temple	"He drove out the man, and at the east of the garden of Eden he placed the cherubim and a flaming sword that turned every way to guard the way to the tree of life" (Gen. 3:24).	"Its gates will never be shut by day—and there will be no night there. . . . Blessed are those who wash their robes, so that they may have the right to the tree of life and that they may enter the city by the gates. Outside are the dogs and sorcerers and the sexually immoral and murderers and idolaters, and everyone who loves and practices falsehood" (Rev. 21:25; 22:14–15).
Sinners in the garden-city temple	"So when the woman saw that the tree was good for food, and that it was a delight to the eyes, and that the tree was to be desired to make one wise, she took of its fruit and ate, and she also gave some to her husband who was with her, and he ate" (Gen. 3:6).	"But nothing unclean will ever enter it, nor anyone who does what is detestable or false, but only those who are written in the Lamb's book of life" (Rev. 21:27).
River	"A river flowed out of Eden to water the garden, and there it divided and became four rivers" (Gen. 2:10).	"To the thirsty I will give from the spring of the water of life without payment" (Rev. 21:6). "Then the angel showed me the river of the water of life, bright as crystal, flowing from the throne of God and of the Lamb through the middle of the street of the city" (Rev. 22:1–2).

Theme	Genesis 1–3	Revelation 21–22
The fruit-bearing tree of life	"And God said, 'Let the earth sprout vegetation, plants yielding seed, and fruit trees bearing fruit in which is their seed, each according to its kind,' on the earth.' And it was so. The earth brought forth vegetation, plants yielding seed according to their own kinds, and trees bearing fruit in which is their seed, each according to its kind. . . . And God said, 'Behold, I have given you every plant yielding seed that is on the face of all the earth, and every tree with seed in its fruit. You shall have them for food.' . . . And out of the ground the LORD God made to spring up every tree that is pleasant to the sight and good for food. The tree of life was in the midst of the garden, and the tree of the knowledge of good and evil" (Gen. 1:11–12, 29; 2:9).	"Also, on either side of the river, the tree of life with its twelve kinds of fruit, yielding its fruit each month" (Rev. 22:2).
Curse	"The LORD God said to the serpent, 'Because you have done this, cursed are you above all livestock and above all beasts of the field. . . . ' To the woman he said, 'I will surely multiply your pain in childbearing; in pain you shall bring forth children. Your desire shall be contrary to your husband, but he shall rule over you.' And to Adam he said, 'Because you have listened to the voice of your wife and have eaten of the tree of which I commanded you, "You shall not eat of it," cursed is the ground because of you; in pain you shall eat of it all the days of your life; thorns and thistles it shall bring forth for you; and you shall eat the plants of the field. By the sweat of your face you shall eat bread, till you return to the ground, for out of it you were taken; for you are dust, and to dust you shall return'" (Gen. 3:14–19).	"No longer will there be anything accursed" (Rev. 22:3).

Theme	Genesis 1–3	Revelation 21–22
God's presence	"And they heard the sound of the LORD God walking in the garden in the cool of the day, and the man and his wife hid themselves from the presence of the LORD God among the trees of the garden. . . . The LORD God sent [the man] out from the garden of Eden to work the ground from which he was taken. He drove out the man, and at the east of the garden of Eden he placed the cherubim and a flaming sword that turned every way to guard the way to the tree of life" (Gen. 3:8, 23–24).	"But the throne of God and of the Lamb will be in it" (Rev. 22:3).
Work	"'Let them have dominion over the fish of the sea and over the birds of the heavens and over the livestock and over all the earth and over every creeping thing that creeps on the earth. . . . Subdue [the earth], and have dominion over the fish of the sea and over the birds of the heavens and over every living thing that moves on the earth.' . . . There was no man to work the ground. . . . The LORD God took the man and put him in the garden of Eden to work it and keep it" (Gen. 1:26, 28; 2:5, 15).	"And his servants will worship [NIV: "serve"] him" (Rev. 22:3).
Shame	"And the man and his wife were both naked and were not ashamed. . . . [Adam] said, 'I heard the sound of you in the garden, and I was afraid, because I was naked, and I hid myself'" (Gen. 2:25; 3:10).	"They will see his face, and his name will be on their forehead" (Rev. 22:4).
Viceroys	"Then God said, 'Let us make man in our image, after our likeness. And let them have dominion over the fish of the sea and over the birds of the heavens and over the livestock and over all the earth and over every creeping thing that creeps on the earth.' . . . And God said to them, 'Be fruitful and multiply and fill the earth and subdue it, and have dominion over the fish of the sea and over the birds of the heavens and over every living thing that moves on the earth'" (Gen. 1:26, 28).	"They will reign forever and ever" (Rev. 22:5).

Theme	Genesis 1–3	Revelation 21–22
Clothing	"And the man and his wife were both naked and were not ashamed. . . . [Adam] said, 'I heard the sound of you in the garden, and I was afraid, because I was naked, and I hid myself.' [God] said, 'Who told you that you were naked?' . . . And the LORD God made for Adam and for his wife garments of skins and clothed them" (Gen. 2:25; 3:10–11, 21).	"Blessed are those who wash their robes, so that they may have the right to the tree of life and that they may enter the city by the gates" (Rev. 22:14–15).
Gold	"[The Pishon river] is the one that flowed around the whole land of Havilah, where there is gold. And the gold of that land is good" (Gen. 2:11–12a).	"The city was pure gold, like clear glass. … The street of the city was pure gold, like transparent glass" (Rev. 21:18, 21).
Jewels	"Bdellium and onyx stone are there" (Gen 2:12b).	"[One of the seven angels] showed me the holy city Jerusalem coming down out of heaven from God, having the glory of God, its radiance like a most rare jewel, like a jasper, clear as crystal. … The wall was built of jasper, while the city was pure gold, like clear glass. The foundations of the wall of the city were adorned with every kind of jewel. The first was jasper, the second sapphire, the third agate, the fourth emerald, the fifth onyx, the sixth carnelian, the seventh chrysolite, the eighth beryl, the ninth topaz, the tenth chrysoprase, the eleventh jacinth, the twelfth amethyst. And the twelve gates were twelve pearls, each of the gates made of a single pearl, and the street of the city was pure gold, like transparent glass" (Rev. 21:10–11, 18–21).

Fig. 35.1. Themes in Genesis 1–3 That Culminate in Revelation 21–22

At the beginning of Genesis, sin and death enter the world, and God banishes humans from his presence. At the end of Revelation, God banishes sin and destroys death, and he lives among his people in the Most Holy Place itself. The themes that start as little seeds in Genesis 1–3 sprout and grow into mature apple trees. Those themes climax in Christ and culminate when Christ returns and makes all things new.

D. A. Carson identifies twelve seminal themes in Genesis 1–3 that are significant for biblical theology:[2]

1. "God comes first." Genesis 1–3 presupposes God as first in both se "quence and status.

2. "God speaks; he is a talking God." God's first action in the Bible is to create the universe by speaking.

3. "Old creation, new creation." When the Bible later refers to the new heavens and the new earth, a renewed creation, and a new or second Adam, it presupposes a *first* heaven and earth and a *first* Adam.

4. "God makes everything, and he himself is unmade." This rules out pantheism, panentheism, gnostic dualism, deism, philosophical materialism, and ontological dualism.

5. "God makes everything good." Therefore, "there was nothing to hide," and "the source of moral evil is not God; it erupts from rebellion against God."

6. "Creation establishes human accountability to God." Humans are without excuse because God has revealed himself in creation.

7. "Let us make. . . . " In light of the rest of the Bible, this suggests that the one God is a plurality of persons—a triune God.

8. "The image of God." God rules, and he commissions his image-bearers to rule.

9. Five more "divine attributes and functions": (1) "God reigns; he is king." (2) "God is the ultimate Judge." (3) "God's meting out of the curses and punishments depicted in Gen 3 anticipates a Bible characterized by many judgments precisely because it is a Bible that reports so many sins." (4) "Gen 1–3 preserves signs of grace." (5) "The interplay between the sovereign good God and his creatures, briefly illuminated by the narrative in Gen 1–3, plays out in the rest of the Bible."

10. "The serpent." Revelation 12 specifically identifies the ancient serpent in Genesis 3 as Satan, the devil, the accuser of the brothers, the dragon.

---

2. D. A. Carson, "Genesis 1–3: Not Maximalist, but Seminal," *TJ* 39, no. 2 (2018): 143–63.

11. "Sacrifice?" When God makes garments of skin for Adam and Eve (Gen. 3:21), that seems to foreshadow animal sacrifices under the Mosaic covenant and the ultimate sacrifice at the cross that enables the new covenant.

12. "Major redemptive-historical structures." Genesis 1–3 is seminal for major themes such as covenant, Sabbath, temple, and seed.

Summary

Revelation 21–22 brilliantly bookends Genesis 1–3. More than twenty themes that begin in Genesis 1–3 culminate in Revelation 21–22 when the Alpha and Omega makes all things new.

REFLECTION QUESTIONS

1. In your own words, how does Revelation 21–22 bookend Genesis 1–3?

2. Do you think there are any other themes at the Bible's bookends that figure 35.1 does not display?

3. How would you trace the theme of marriage from Genesis to Revelation?

4. Pick another theme in figure 35.1. How does that theme climax in Christ and then culminate in Christ when Christ makes all things new?

5. When you meditate on how the Bible's bookends relate, how does that make you feel about the divine author who designed the story?

PART 5

Applying Biblical Theology

How Does Biblical Theology Help Us Teach and Preach the Old Testament?

Jason S. DeRouchie

"Preach the word" (2 Tim. 4:2)! That is what Paul charges Timothy immediately after the apostle asserts that the sacred Jewish Scriptures on which Timothy was raised (i.e., what we now call the Old Testament) are "able to make one wise for salvation through faith in Christ Jesus" and that "all Scripture is breathed out by God and profitable for teaching, for reproof, for correction, and for training in righteousness" (2 Tim. 3:15–16; cf. 1:5; Acts 16:1). There are at least eight ways biblical theology enables Christians to understand and herald the OT more faithfully.

1. Biblical Theology Helps Us Declare the Whole Counsel of God by Which We Develop a Christian Worldview

Biblical theology helps us see how and what a given OT book or passage contributes to the whole counsel of God, which is a necessary step in our teaching and preaching if we are to guard ourselves from God's wrath and help our people know their place in God's story. Before Timothy oversaw the Ephesian church, Paul had told the elders that he would not be guilty before the Lord if any of them fell away. Why? "I did not shrink back from declaring to you the whole counsel of God" (Acts 20:26–27; cf. Ezek. 33:8). He would have been an unfaithful shepherd if he failed to proclaim God's revealed purposes from creation to consummation that climax in Christ. By declaring the story of God's glory in Christ, he helped the Ephesians identify their part in the world's problem and see that Jesus alone provides the solution.

Biblical theology is concerned with how the whole Bible progresses, integrates, and climaxes in Christ. Christ is both the beginning and the end of God's purposes (Col. 1:16), so biblical theology is concerned with capturing "the whole counsel of God." The OT does not stand alone; it is the foundation of the NT. The OT saga ends in a way that demands a sequel, and the NT is that sequel. Christ realizes what the OT anticipates; Christ fulfills what the OT promises.[1] Because the gospel alone "is the power of God for salvation" (Rom. 1:16; cf. 1 Cor. 1:18), Christian teachers and preachers should engage in biblical theology by helping people recognize how a particular passage adds to or embellishes the Bible's overarching storyline and how it helps them see and savor all that God is for them in Christ.[2] Richly portraying Christ's saving power and all-satisfying beauty fortifies people with a big vision of God's supremacy and helps them recognize their deep need.

Adam offers the following questions to help expositors read ever biblical text in light of it greater biblical-theological framework:[3]

- How does this text fit into the progressive revelation that God gives in the Bible?
- Is it related to any major biblical themes?
- Is its theme one in which there is significant development between the OT and NT?
- What relationship does it have to the gospel?
- How does the gospel form a context for it?
- How does it relate to the revelation of Jesus Christ, to the promise or the fulfilment?
- Is it used or interpreted elsewhere in the Bible?
- In which major theological category does it occur, e.g. promise, law, prophecy, wisdom, instruction, blessing, curse, people of God, gospel?

---

1. As Goldsworthy notes, "The Old Testament ends with hope but not real substance to the fulfillments." Graeme Goldsworthy, "Biblical Theology and Hermeneutics," *SBJT* 10, no. 2 (Summer 2006): 13. Schreiner adds, "We must acknowledge progress of revelation from the OT to the NT. Such progress of revelation recognizes the preliminary nature of the OT and the definitive word that comes in the NT." Thomas R. Schreiner, "Preaching and Biblical Theology," *SBJT* 10, no. 2 (Summer 2006): 23.

2. In Schreiner's words, "All the varied material in both the Old and New Testaments can in some way be related to the plan and purpose of the one God of the whole Bible. . . . [Preachers] must preach in such a way that they integrate their sermons into the larger biblical story of redemptive history." Schreiner, "Preaching and Biblical Theology," 23, 25; cf. James M. Hamilton Jr., "Biblical Theology and Preaching," in *Text Driven Preaching: God's Word at the Heart of Every Sermon*, eds. Daniel L. Akin, David L. Allen, and Ned L. Mathews (Nashville: B&H, 2010), 197.

3. P. J. H. Adam, "Biblical Theology and Preaching," *New Dictionary of Biblical Theology*, eds. T. Desmond Alexander and Brian S. Rosner (Downers Grove, IL: InterVarsity Press, 2000), 108.

2. Biblical Theology Helps Us Consider the Canonical Context

Biblical theology helps us interpret OT texts in light of their God-intended canonical contexts.[4] There are certain features of canonical arrangement that must be accounted for when interpreting Scripture.[5] For example, the OT includes the initial three-fourths of the Bible's salvation-historical narrative unpacked progressively in a chain of books, and we must understand the various persons, events, and institutions highlighted within the story in light of the accounts already described in the earlier narration and in light of the story's climax in Christ.[6]

So a sermon series on Judges, for example, should both (1) explain the conquest account in Joshua and the instructions and warnings of Moses in Deuteronomy, and (2) show how the story sets the stage for the prophecy of Hannah (1 Sam. 2:10), the rise of David, and the coming of the ultimate king, Messiah Jesus, since "there was no king in Israel; everyone did what was right in his own eyes" (Judg. 17:6; 21:25).

Furthermore, as the ultimate author of Scripture, God used previous biblical texts to inform the vocabulary and worldview of the biblical authors. So, because Moses's law highly influenced the rest of the OT and because Yahweh's prophets were "searching" their Scriptures and "inquiring" about the "person and time" of the Messiah (1 Peter 1:10–11), we should read a book like Zephaniah in the light of any previously written Scripture he may have had available, whether Genesis, Deuteronomy, or Isaiah. Similarly, we should read Deuteronomy in the light of Genesis–Numbers, all of which Moses's final sermons assume.

Finally, the way a later biblical author appropriates an earlier Scripture passage more fully explains what that previous passage means by expanding what it signifies and even defining new referents.[7] For example, biblical theology lets us see that God's record of the flood and Red Sea water judgments intentionally clarify and foreshadow new covenant baptism (1 Cor. 10:2; 1 Peter 3:20–21).[8] And again, Hosea, Isaiah, and Jeremiah predict a second "exodus" (Hos. 11:1, 11; Isa. 11:11, 15–16; Jer. 16:14–15; 23:7–8), and Jesus refers to his crucifixion as an exodus (Luke 9:31). By these connections, God

---

4. See also Schreiner, "Preaching and Biblical Theology," 24–25; Hamilton, "Biblical Theology and Preaching," 198.

5. See Question 16.

6. For more on this, see D. A. Carson, "How Does a Thorough Knowledge of Biblical Theology Strengthen Preaching?," *SBJT* 10, no. 2 (Summer 2006): 89–90.

7. Hamilton rightly notes, "The Bible is laced with . . . intertextuality. The biblical authors learned key patterns from earlier texts, noticed repetitions of those patterns, and highlighted the repetition of such patterns in their accounts." Hamilton, "Biblical Theology and Preaching," 207.

8. See Meredith G. Kline, *By Oath Consigned: A Reinterpretation of the Covenant Signs of Circumcision and Baptism* (Grand Rapids: Eerdmans, 1968), 50–83.

fills out his intended meaning of the original record of the exodus. If we preach Exodus 14–15 without considering how biblical theology informs the text, we fail to grasp some of what God intended to communicate.

3. Biblical Theology Helps Us See the Mystery Revealed

Biblical theology helps fill out what enigmatic elements of the OT mean and clarifies how the OT was written for our instruction. The biblical authors were convinced that the OT writings were like sealed scrolls to the rebel majority, who had no eyes to read and no ears to hear (e.g., Isa. 29:10–11; cf. Deut. 29:4[3]).[9] While the prophets themselves knew much of what they were writing (e.g., Dan. 10:1; John 8:56; Acts 2:30–31; Heb. 11:13; cf. Matt. 13:17; Luke 10:24), even to them there were secrets left that only the new covenant work of Christ—his death and resurrection—would reveal (e.g., Jer. 30:24; Dan. 12:8–10; cf. John 2:20–22; 12:13–16). Thus, Paul could describe the gospel associated with Christ as "the revelation of the mystery that was kept secret for long ages but has now been disclosed and through the prophetic writings has been made known to all nations" (Rom. 16:25–26; cf. Isa. 29:18).

Along with the illuminating light that God's Spirit supplies to see kingdom truths (1 Cor. 2:14; cf. John 3:3), Christ's death and resurrection supply the necessary lens for reading old covenant materials (2 Cor. 3:14). This means that biblical theology is important for helping people more fully grasp what God intended to communicate in Jesus's Bible. Because elements of the OT could not and would not be understood until the church age (see Deut. 30:8; Isa. 29:18; Jer. 30:24; Dan. 12:8–10), biblical theology helps us better understand that "whatever was written in former days was written for our instruction" (Rom. 15:4; cf. 4:23–24; 1 Cor. 10:11). In Peter's words, "Concerning this salvation, the prophets who prophesied about the grace that was to be yours searched and inquired carefully, inquiring what person or time the Spirit of Christ in them was indicating when he predicted the sufferings of Christ and the subsequent glories. *It was revealed to them that they were serving not themselves but you*" (1 Peter 1:10–12, emphasis added).

4. Biblical Theology Helps Us Identify Types

Biblical theology also helps us identify how certain OT characters, events, and institutions predictively point ahead to and clarify the person and work of Christ. The escalating shift from type to antitype—from shadow to substance—progressively unfolds the whole counsel of God.[10] Thus, Adam, as the head and first human of the original creation, is a "type" for Jesus Christ, the head of the new covenant and first member of the new creation (Rom. 5:14; cf. 1 Cor. 15:20, 23). And where Adam failed and thus brings death to all, Jesus

---

9. See Question 21.
10. See Question 8.

succeeded and thus supplies life to many (Rom. 5:18–19; 1 Cor. 15:22, 45). So too, new covenant baptism "corresponds" to the flood judgment (1 Peter 3:20–21), and the various accounts of the Lord's punishing Israel in the wilderness serve as "an example" and "were written down for our instruction" (1 Cor. 10:11; cf. 10:6). Finally, OT legislation regarding "food and drink . . . festival or a new moon or a Sabbath" are all "a shadow of the things to come, but the substance belongs to Christ" (Col. 1:16–17).

Biblical theology helps us more fully recognize how certain figures, circumstances, or objects in the OT climax in Christ's person and work and how his life and passion draw on and complete a God-designed pattern. If we try to interpret the OT without accounting for what God later revealed, we may never recognize the role a given passage plays in the story of redemption.

5. Biblical Theology Helps Us Celebrate the Messiah and His Mission

Biblical theology helps us appreciate how a biblical book or passage contributes to the OT's message regarding the Messiah and the mission he would accomplish. While Jesus was convinced that many texts in his Bible directly bore witness about him (e.g., Luke 24:27, 44; John 5:39, 46; Rom. 1:1–3), he also claimed that *the whole* of the Hebrew Scriptures and not just a part portrayed a unified message that foretold, foreshadowed, and foresaw his tribulation and triumph as the Messiah and the mission his resurrection would generate: "Then he opened their minds to understand the Scriptures, and said to them, 'Thus it is written, that the Christ should suffer and on the third day rise from the dead, and that repentance and forgiveness of sins should be proclaimed in his name to all nations, beginning from Jerusalem'" (Luke 24:45–47; cf. Acts 26:22–23; 1 Peter 1:10–11).[11]

If Jesus asserts that numerous texts were about him and that all of Scripture together testifies to his life and work, the OT preacher must use biblical theology to clarify how and in what way(s) the specific passage magnifies the majesty of the Messiah and his deeds.[12] This is all the more true when we remember that *all* things, including the OT, were created *by* the Son and *for* the Son (Col. 1:16). Biblical theology helps us give Christ his due worship when we preach the OT.[13]

Paul preached the OT, and he could declare, "We preach Christ crucified" (1 Cor. 1:23), and again, "I decided to know nothing among you except Jesus Christ and him crucified" (2:2). Because all new covenant shepherds stand

---

11. See Carson, "Biblical Theology Strengthen Preaching?," 90–91.
12. Goldsworthy rightly notes, "Old Testament preaching should be undertaken in a way that shows how the whole Bible testifies to Christ." Goldsworthy, "Biblical Theology and Hermeneutics," 17, cf. 10.
13. See Question 4.

on the shoulders of Jesus and his apostles (Eph. 2:19–20; cf. Acts 2:42), we would do well to follow Paul's pattern of "testifying to the kingdom of God and trying to convince them about Jesus both from the Law of Moses and from the Prophets" (Acts 28:23).[14]

6. Biblical Theology Helps Us Apply Laws

Biblical theology helps new covenant believers know how to faithfully appropriate OT laws. *None* of the old covenant legislation *directly* binds a new covenant believer, but through the mediation of Christ *all* of the Mosaic laws should guide us *indirectly*.[15] The age of the law covenant was not characterized by faith (Gal. 3:12). However, by disclosing and multiplying sin and by condemning and imprisoning sinners (Rom. 3:20; 5:20; 2 Cor. 3:9; Gal. 3:23), it pointed to the need for Jesus, who is both the terminus and the goal of the law for righteousness to everyone who believes (Rom. 10:4).[16] With the coming of Jesus, Christians are still called to "do" and "teach" the commandments of Moses, but only in the light of Christ's fulfilling them (Matt. 5:17–19; cf. Deut. 30:8). "All Scripture is . . . profitable for teaching, for reproof, for correction, and for training in righteousness" (2 Tim. 3:16), and the Mosaic law matters for Christians in the way it models the breadth and depth of love and thus points to the internalized law of Christ (1 Cor. 9:20–21). Those who are true "Jews" and new creations, with transformed hearts by the Spirit (Rom. 2:29; 2 Cor. 5:17; Gal. 6:15), now "do," "keep," and "fulfill" the commandments of God as defined through the lens of Christ and with their faith working through love (Rom. 2:14–15, 26; 13:8–10; 1 Cor. 7:19; Gal. 5:6).

Biblical theology enables Christians to understand the lasting significance of specific Mosaic laws for today, and it invites expositors to preach from the whole of Scripture—the OT included—in ways that God intended to serve believers in this age. Teaching and preaching the OT law apart from the lens of Christ (i.e., without using biblical theology) assumes that all the old covenant commands continue without change this side of the cross, but some laws are transformed, extended, or annulled. Furthermore, failing to use biblical theology when interpreting the Mosaic law may lead to moralism

---

14. As Schreiner states, "If we believe . . . that the apostles were inspired and wise readers of the OT, then we have a pattern for reading all of the OT in light of the fulfillment accomplished in Jesus Christ. The storyline and structures of the OT all point towards him and are completed in him." Schreiner, "Preaching and Biblical Theology," 27. For more on faithfully seeing and savoring Christ in the OT, see the whole issue of *SBJT* 22, no. 3 (Fall 2018), titled *Preaching Christ from the Old Testament*, and the bibliography in Jason S. DeRouchie, *How to Understand and Apply the Old Testament: Twelve Steps from Exegesis to Theology* (Phillipsburg, NJ: P&R, 2017), 493–95.

15. See Question 25.

16. See Question 34.

or legalism that celebrates neither Jesus's justifying nor sanctifying work on our behalf.[17]

7. Biblical Theology Helps Us Claim Promises

Biblical theology helps new covenant believers know how to faithfully appropriate OT promises for the church. All of God's promises find their "yes" in Jesus (2 Cor. 1:20), but only through him can Christians appropriate them rightly.[18] Biblical theology is, therefore, a means for engendering greater hope, for it allows those living on this side of the cross to benefit from all the promises in both testaments as we pursue holiness (7:1; 2 Peter 1:4; 1 John 3:3) and endure through suffering (Ps. 119:50, 54; Rom. 5:3–5). Yet without biblical theology, we will too easily misuse promises.

For example, without biblical theology, we may mishandle old covenant blessings, which were conditioned on perfect obedience (e.g., Deut. 28:1–14). We might either relegate those blessings to the old covenant alone or wrongly apply them in an over-realized way to Christians in this already-but-not-yet age. All the promises God gave directly to his corporate "son" (Israel the servant people) become ours only because God's representative "Son" (Israel/Jesus the servant person—Isa. 44:1–3; 49:3, 6; Hos. 14:4–8) secured those promises for all in him. And while we already enjoy every spiritual blessing in Christ, the full inheritance is still to come (Eph. 1:3, 14; cf. 2 Cor. 1:20–22). "Now the promises were made to Abraham and to his offspring . . . who is Christ. . . . And if you are Christ's, then you are Abraham's offspring, heirs according to promise" (Gal. 3:16, 29). To properly preach many OT promises requires that we use biblical theology.

8. Biblical Theology Helps Us Grasp How God Justly Justifies

Biblical theology helps us understand how God justly justifies the ungodly, even those in the OT era. Throughout the OT a remnant of believers set their hope on God (e.g., Gen. 15:6; Ps. 32:1–2) and "died in faith, not having received the things promised, but having seen them and greeted them from afar" (Heb. 11:13). But had Jesus never come, no OT remnant would have existed, for the sacrifice of animals cannot ultimately take away sins (Heb. 10:4, 11). Further, there would be no righteousness to impute (Isa. 53:11; Rom. 5:18–19) with the result that the record of debt against sinful humanity with its legal demands would have remained (Col. 2:14). This was the point in Zechariah's night vision when Satan ("the Adversary") accused the high priest Joshua and ultimately Yahweh of iniquity (Zech. 3:1). Yet God argued that Joshua and his fellow priests were but "signs" that pointed forward to a greater priest, the Branch, by whose sacrifice the Lord would "remove the iniquity of

---

17. See also Schreiner, "Preaching and Biblical Theology," 27.
18. See Question 37.

the land in a single day" (3:8–9; cf. 12:10; 13:1). This is why Paul later asserts: "God put forward [Christ Jesus] as a propitiation by his blood, to be received by faith. This was to show God's righteousness, because in his divine forbearance he had passed over former sins. It was to show his righteousness at the present time, so that he might be just and the justifier of the one who has faith in Jesus" (Rom. 3:25–26). Biblical theology allows us to grasp how the sacred writings of the OT "are able to make you wise for salvation through faith in Christ Jesus" (2 Tim. 3:15).

Summary

Biblical theology helps us faithfully preach the OT. It helps us proclaim the whole counsel of God, appreciate the canonical context of a given passage, and gain the necessary revelation for understanding OT mysteries and how God wrote Jesus's Bible for Christians. Biblical theology helps us give Christ the glory he deserves, both through identifying how OT types foreshadow him and by properly magnifying how a given passage contributes to the overarching message of the Messiah's work and mission. And biblical theology helps us faithfully appropriate OT laws and promises and ascertain how God can use the OT to effectively save people through faith in Jesus.

REFLECTION QUESTIONS

1. Without looking, list the eight ways this chapter proposes biblical theology helps us teach and preach the OT.

2. Which of these eight ways is most exciting to you? Why?

3. Which of these eight ways is most new or convicting? Why?

4. How could biblical theology have better informed the last sermon you heard or the last passage you taught or preached?

5. What is the next passage you hope to understand, and how may biblical theology inform your study? What is the next text you plan to explain or herald, and what is one way that you could faithfully magnify Christ and his mission during your message?

QUESTION 37

How Should a Christian Relate to Old Testament Promises?

Jason S. DeRouchie

The apostle Peter declared, "God has granted to us his precious and very great promises, so that through them you may become partakers of the divine nature, having escaped from the corruption that is in the world because of sinful desire" (2 Peter 1:4; cf. Rom. 4:18–21; 15:13).[1] God's promises of blessing and curse (2 Peter 3:9, 14) play a vital role in helping believers grow in sanctification (cf. 2 Cor. 7:1; 1 John 3:2–3) and suffer with hope (Ps. 119:50). But which promises are for Christians? Paul asserts in 2 Corinthians 1:20, "*All* the promises of God find their Yes in [Jesus]," but is he talking only about NT promises or OT promises as well?

Later in the epistle, after Paul cites a list of OT promises (2 Cor. 6:16–18), he urges the Corinthian believers to pursue holiness "since we have these promises" (7:1). That is firm ground to believe that Paul intends "*all* the promises" to refer to God's promises in both the Old and New Testaments. But how can believers today faithfully appropriate OT promises?

As Christians, we need a framework for benefiting from God's ancient promises, yet in a way that does not produce abuses. What follows are four biblical principles that should shape our thinking, and then proposes biblical-theological guidelines for appropriating OT promises.

---

1. See also Jason S. DeRouchie, "Is *Every* Promise 'Yes'? Old Testament Promises and the Christian," *Them* 42, no. 1 (2017): 16–45.

Four Foundational Principles

Christians Benefit from OT Promises Only through Christ
Yahweh promised Abraham, "And your offspring shall possess the gate of *his* enemies, and *in your offspring* shall all the nations of the earth be blessed" (Gen. 22:17–18, emphasis added). The "his" refers to a masculine, singular descendant, whom later revelation identifies as Christ, and "in your offspring" highlights that only through identification with him would Gentiles enjoy God's blessing. This text and Genesis 12:3 supply the backdrop to Galatians 3:

> Know then that it is those of faith who are the sons of Abraham. And the Scripture, foreseeing that God would justify the Gentiles by faith, preached the gospel beforehand to Abraham, saying, "*In you* shall all the nations be blessed." So then, those who are of faith are blessed along with Abraham, the man of faith. . . . Christ redeemed us from the curse of the law by becoming a curse for us . . . so that *in Christ Jesus* the blessing of Abraham might come to the Gentiles. . . . Now the promises were made to Abraham and to his offspring . . . who is Christ. . . . And if *you are Christ's*, then you are Abraham's offspring, heirs according to promise. (Gal. 3:7–9, 13–14, 16, 29, emphasis added)

For Paul, only in Christ can anyone inherit the OT's promised blessings.[2] This is what Paul means when he declares that *in Christ* alone all of God's promises find their "yes" (2 Cor. 1:21).

Fig. 37.1. OT Promises Reach Believers Only through Christ

All Old Covenant Curses Become New Covenant Curses
As is explicit in the Abrahamic covenant (Gen. 12:3), the era of the new covenant includes God's promise to curse enemies. Thus, immediately after Moses predicts when Yahweh would "circumcise your heart and the heart of

---

2. For a helpful synthesis of promise, offspring, and inheritance in Galatians 3, see David Starling, "The Yes to All God's Promises: Jesus, Israel and the Promises of God in Paul's Letters," *RTR* 71, no. 3 (2012): 187–89.

your offspring, so that you will love the LORD" (Deut. 30:6), the prophet pronounces, "And the LORD your God will put all these curses on your foes and enemies who persecuted you" (30:7). Moses believed that in the age of new covenant heart circumcision (realized in the church—Rom. 2:28–29; Phil. 3:3), God will take the curses of Deuteronomy—the very curses that served as warnings to old covenant national Israel—and he will pour them out on the enemies of God's restored community.

The NT displays these curses as warnings against apostasy and against all who oppose God and his people (see Matt. 25:31–46; Luke 6:20–26; 2 Tim. 2:12; Heb. 10:26–27; cf. Gen. 12:3; Deut. 30:7). In Hebrews 10:29–30, the author cites the new covenant curse text in Deuteronomy 32:35 ("Vengeance is mine; I will repay") and declares that God will punish apostates who for a while looked as though they were a part of the new covenant but then turned on God (cf. 2 Peter 2:1).

Those in Christ will not experience curse in a punitive way, for Christ bears upon himself God's curse against all believers: "Christ redeemed us from the curse of the law by becoming a curse for us" (Gal. 3:13; cf. John 3:14–15; 2 Cor. 5:17; 1 Peter 2:24). "Since, therefore, we have now been justified by his blood, much more shall we be saved by him from the wrath of God" (Rom. 5:9). While we still experience God's fatherly discipline, no level of earthly discipline or consequence calls into question the eternal security of any believer. Instead, new covenant curses serve as a means of grace to the elect in order to generate within them reverent fear of God leading to greater holiness (cf. Lev. 26:18, 21, 23, 27; Rom. 2:4). For those heeding the covenant warnings, the curses become words of hope, as Christians rest confident that God will work justice in this age through the political state (Rom. 13:4; cf. 1 Thess. 4:6) or through death (Acts 5:5, 10; 12:23) and most ultimately through Christ's second appearing (2 Thess. 1:8–9) and final judgment (Matt. 25:31–32; John 5:28–29; Acts 24:15; 2 Cor. 5:10; Rev. 20:12).

As Part of the New Covenant, Christians Inherit the Old Covenant's Original and Restoration Blessings

In Leviticus and Deuteronomy, there are old covenant conditional promises of blessing (Lev. 26:1–13; Deut. 28:1–14) and curse (Lev. 26:14–39; Deut. 28:15–68). The condition is perfect obedience. There are also restoration blessings (Lev. 26:40–45; Deut. 30:1–14) that point in part to the era of the church age following the curse of exile. Paul declares, "Since we have these promises, beloved, let us cleanse ourselves from every defilement of body and spirit, bringing holiness to completion in the fear of God" (2 Cor. 7:1). One of the promises to which the apostle refers is in 2 Corinthians 6:16, which combines an old covenant original blessing in Leviticus 26:11–12 and a restoration blessing from Ezekiel 37:27.

2 Corinthians 6:16	Leviticus 26:1, 11–12	Ezekiel 37:27
What agreement has the temple of God with idols? For we are the temple of the living God; as God said, "**I will make my dwelling among them** and **walk among them, and I will be their God, and they shall be my people.**"	If you walk in my statutes and observe my commandments and do them . . . **I will make my dwelling among** you, and my soul shall not abhor you. And I will **walk among** you and **will be** your **God, and** you **shall be my people.**	My **dwelling** place shall be with **them, and I will be their God, and they shall be my people.**

The apostle draws the statements "I will make my dwelling among" and "I will walk among" directly from Leviticus 26:11–12. "And I will be their God, and they shall be my people" comes directly from Ezekiel 37:27. Because Israel did not fully obey what God instructed, the Mosaic covenant resulted in curse and condemnation, not blessing (2 Cor. 3:9). Nevertheless, Paul says that all those in Christ are enjoying that God has inaugurated his fulfilling of both the original and restoration blessings.[3] Most likely, the apostle understands that, when Christ perfectly obeyed the Father, he satisfied God's demands for absolute loyalty and thus secured blessing for the elect he represents (cf. John 15:10; Rom. 5:18–19; 8:4; Phil. 2:8; Heb. 5:8).

Two conclusions follow from how Paul applies OT promises in 2 Corinthians 6:16: (1) The restoration blessings of the old covenant include all the original blessings but in escalation and without the chance of loss. The way Ezekiel's new covenant promise reasserts the original old covenant blessings from Leviticus 26 supports this claim. (2) Through Christ, the original old covenant blessings *and* the restoration blessings have direct bearing on Christians. Paul appears to draw together both texts, which suggests not only their close tie in the OT but also that, along with the new covenant restoration blessings, the original old covenant blessings do indeed relate to believers.

---

3. Balla writes, "Since all of these OT references [in 2 Cor. 6:16–18] are direct verbal prophecies or are set in a direct verbal prophetic context, Paul sees them having inaugurated fulfillment in the Corinthian community. Consequently, the Corinthians are the beginning of the prophesied end-time tabernacle or temple, and they are part of the dawning fulfillment of Israel's restoration prophecies." Peter Balla, "2 Corinthians," in *Commentary on the New Testament Use of the Old Testament*, eds. G. K. Beale and D. A. Carson (Grand Rapids: Baker Academic, 2007), 773.

Through the Spirit, Some Blessings of the Christian's Inheritance Are Already Enjoyed, Whereas Others Are Not Yet

> Blessed be the God and Father of our Lord Jesus Christ, who has blessed us *in Christ* with every spiritual blessing in the heavenly places. . . . In him you also, when you heard the word of truth, the gospel of your salvation, and believed in him, were sealed with the promised Holy Spirit, who is the guarantee of our inheritance until we acquire possession of it, to the praise of his glory. (Eph. 1:3, 13–14, emphasis added)

In Christ believers enjoy "every spiritual blessing in the heavenly places." Most scholars believe this expression refers to the blessings "pertaining to or belonging to the Spirit"—that is, all the blessings that the Spirit of Christ secures for the saints, whether those *already* enjoyed like election, adoption to sonship, redemption, forgiveness, and sealing, or those *not yet* enjoyed like the full inheritance (Eph. 4:4–14).[4] Therefore, while *all* God's promises find their "yes" in Christ (2 Cor. 1:20), we enjoy some *already*, while others remain for the future (cf. 2 Cor. 1:22; 1 Peter 1:3–4).[5]

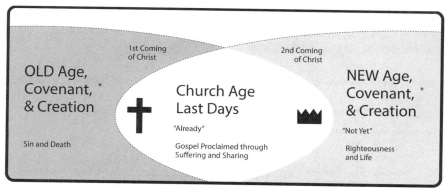

Fig. 37.2. The Overlap of the Ages[6]

4. E.g., Andrew T. Lincoln, *Ephesians*, WBC 42 (Dallas: Word, 1990), 19; Gordon D. Fee, *God's Empowering Presence: The Holy Spirit in the Letters of Paul* (Peabody, MA: Hendrickson, 1994), 666–67; Klyne R. Snodgrass, *Ephesians*, NIV Application Commentary (Grand Rapids: Zondervan, 1996), 46; Peter T. O'Brien, *The Letter to the Ephesians*, PNTC (Grand Rapids: Eerdmans, 1999), 95. F. F. Bruce distinguishes the "spiritual blessings" from "material," but I do not see this as justified in light of the reference in 1:14 to our full inheritance, which will include a transformed material creation. F. F. Bruce, *The Epistles to the Colossians, to Philemon and to the Ephesians*, NICNT (Grand Rapids: Eerdmans, 1995), 253.
5. We see the same already-but-not-yet tension when Peter cites Psalm 34:12–16 (LXX 33:13–17) in 1 Peter 3:9–12.
6. This image first occurred in Jason S. DeRouchie, ed., *What the Old Testament Authors Really Cared About: A Survey of Jesus' Bible* (Grand Rapids: Kregel, 2013), 39. Used by permission.

For Christians living today, the new covenant blessings are *already* our inheritance but *not yet* ours to enjoy in the fullness that we will in the age to come. In this overlap of the ages, our battle with sin is still evident, but God has freed believers so that sin no longer enslaves and condemns (Rom. 6:16–18; 7:25; 12:2). So too we still battle brokenness and decay, but such sufferings only develop our dependent faith in God and heighten our longing for the future (8:20–23; 2 Cor. 4:16–18). And while death looms over us all, Christ removes its sting, and death itself becomes the channel to great reward (Phil. 1:21; cf. Rom. 5:17; 6:23; Rev. 22:4).

Guidelines for Appropriating OT Promises as Christians

God's promises (old and new) are vital for Christians, and if we fail to appropriate OT promises, we will lose three-fourths of the life-giving words of truth that our trustworthy God has given us to nurture our hope. When Jesus "fulfills" the OT Law and Prophets, he is actualizing what Scripture anticipated and achieving what God promised and predicted (Matt. 5:17; cf. 11:13; Luke 16:16). But while every promise is indeed "yes" in Jesus (2 Cor. 1:20), and while every blessing is now ours *in Christ* (Gal. 3:14; Eph. 1:3), the way Jesus fulfills the various OT promises and secures them as "yes" for us is not static. So, we must approach biblical promises through a salvation-historical framework that has Jesus at the center—as a lens that gives focus to the lasting significance of all God's promises (see fig. 37.3).

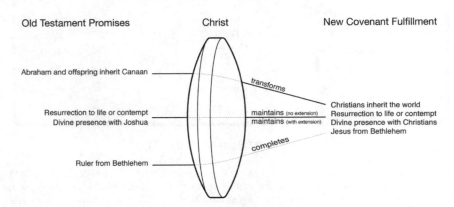

Fig. 37.3. Old Testament Promises through the Lens of Christ

Christ Maintains Some Old Testament Promises (No Extension)

Many of the promises that Christ *maintains* without any extension (i.e., without adding any further beneficiaries to the original promise) are explicit restoration promises that include a vision of a global salvation after Israel's exile. For example, "And many of those who sleep in the dust of the earth shall awake, some to everlasting life, and some to shame and everlasting contempt" (Dan. 12:2). Jesus likely alludes to that passage: "An hour is coming when all who are in the tombs will hear [the Son of Man's] voice and come out, those who have done good to the resurrection of life, and those who have done evil to the resurrection of judgment" (John 5:28–29; cf. 11:11, 25; 1 Cor. 15:20, 23). Daniel 12:2 gives Christians hope because "if we have been united with [Christ] in a death like his, we shall certainly be united with him in a resurrection like his" (Rom. 6:5).

Christ Maintains Some Old Testament Promises (with Extension)

While God maintains the nature of most OT promises on each side of the cross, when Christ fulfills some promises he extends the parties related to those promises. Consider how the NT applies Isaiah 49:6, which is part of the third Servant Song. Isaiah portrays the coming royal deliverer as speaking in the first person and declaring that the Lord called him from the womb, named him "Israel," and told him, "It is too light a thing that you should be my servant to raise up the tribes of Jacob and to bring back the preserved of Israel; I will make you as a light for the nations, that my salvation may reach to the end of the earth" (Isa. 49:1, 3, 6). Through the messianic servant-person, God would save not only ethnic Israelites but also some from the nations, thus fulfilling his earlier promises to Abraham (Gen. 12:3; 22:18). Paul emphasizes that both the prophets and Moses said that following the Messiah's death he "would proclaim light both to our people and to the Gentiles" (Acts 26:23). Jesus is, therefore, the most immediate referent to which Isaiah 49:6 points. But it also reaches further by referring to the mission of all who are in Christ. Paul extends this OT promise in his earlier words to the Jews at Antioch in Pisidia, where he declares with reference to him and Barnabas, "The Lord has commanded us, saying, 'I have made you a light for the Gentiles, that you may bring salvation to the ends of the earth'" (13:47). A promise related to the work of the servant Christ has now become a commission for all the servants identified with him.

| God promises that his servant-person would be a light to the nations.→ | Christ is this servant-light. → | Faith unites us to Christ. → | Union with Christ makes us servants with him. → | We join Christ as lights to the nations. |

Fig. 37.4. God Maintains the Promise of Serving as a Light While Extending It to All in Christ

Christ Completes Some Old Testament Promises

There are some OT promises that Christ has already fully *completed*. These promises prove to believers now that God will certainly keep the rest of his promises (Deut. 18:22; Ezek. 33:33; cf. Rom. 8:32). For example, the prophet Micah predicts that a long-prophesied ruler in Israel would rise from Bethlehem (Mic. 5:2), and Christ fulfilled that promise at his birth (Matt. 2:6). There is only one Christ, and he was born only once. Nevertheless, his birth was to spark a global return of "his brothers," and as king he would "shepherd his flock in the strength of the LORD," thus establishing lasting security and peace and enjoying a great name (Mic. 5:3–5). All these added promises continue to give Christians comfort and hope, and Christ's birth in Bethlehem validates for us that ultimately the whole world will exalt him.

Christ Transforms Some Old Testament Promises

Christ fulfills some OT promises by transforming them. That is, he develops both the promise's makeup and audience. These promises relate most directly to shadows that clarify and point to a greater substance in Christ or to OT patterns or types that find their climax or antitype in Jesus. For example, God promised Abraham and his offspring that they would inherit a tribal land (Gen. 17:8) with a kingdom extending from the border of Egypt to Mesopotamia (15:18). Christ transforms that promise in the new covenant to include the church's title to the whole world in the new earth (Rom. 4:13).[7]

More specifically, Yahweh told Abraham, "I will give to you and to your offspring after you the land of your sojournings, all the land of Canaan, for an everlasting possession" (Gen. 17:8). He also said, "To your offspring I give this land, from the river of Egypt to the great river, the river Euphrates" (15:18). In Genesis, the land promise is directly associated with Abraham's being the father of *one* nation, which we now know as Israel (12:1–2). Remembering his pledge to the patriarchs (Exod. 2:24; 6:8; Deut. 1:8; 6:10; 9:5; 30:20; 34:4), God fulfilled his land promise during the period of the Mosaic covenant, first by giving Canaan to the tribes in the days of Joshua (Josh. 11:23; 21:43–44) and then by letting Solomon's geopolitical state include the broader territory (1 Kings 4:20–21; cf. Gen. 15:18). Yet Genesis looked ahead to when Abraham would be the father of not just one nation but *nations* (17:4–6) and when the "land" (singular) would be extended to "lands" (plural) (26:3–4). It also envisioned that this new development would happen only when the singular, royal offspring would rise to extend the kingdom realm by possessing the gate of his enemies and by blessing all the earth's nations (22:17–18). Paul cites the Genesis land promises (Gen. 13:15; 17:8; 24:7) when he identifies Christ as the offspring to whom the promises were made (Gal. 3:16) and then declares that all in him, whether Jew or Gentile, slave or free, male or female, "are Abraham's offspring, heirs according to promise" (3:28–29). Only in relation to Christ do the promises of land, seed, and blessing reach their ultimate fulfillment, and *all* in Christ enjoy the full blessings (cf. Matt. 5:5; Eph. 6:3; Heb. 11:13–16).

---

7. See Question 29 for more detail.

Fig. 37.5. God Transforms the Promise of Land to Include the Whole World for All His People

Summary

Should Christians claim OT promises as our own? Yes, following these four foundational principles: (1) Christians benefit from OT promises only through Christ. (2) All old covenant curses become new covenant curses. (3) As part of the new covenant, Christians inherit the old covenant's original and restoration blessings. (4) Through the Spirit, Christians already enjoy some blessings of their inheritance but not yet others. Christians should appropriate God's OT promises by distinguishing between how Christ fulfills them—maintaining some without extension, maintaining others with extension, completing some, and transforming some.

REFLECTION QUESTIONS

1. Supply biblical support for the claim that God's promises play a vital role in helping believers grow in sanctification and suffer with hope.

2. How do old covenant curses relate to new covenant curses/warnings, and what role should the latter play in believers' lives?

3. What is the connection between old covenant original blessings and restoration blessings, and how do they relate to new covenant blessings?

4. Using Christ as a redemptive-historical lens, how would you explain the relationship of OT land promises to Christians?

5. How does the conviction that, in Christ, "all God's promises find their Yes" (2 Cor. 1:20) give believers hope for the Christian life?

How Should Biblical Theology Impact the Christian Life?

Oren R. Martin

The words "biblical theology" often kill conversations. When others ask what I (Oren) do, my attempt to explain clearly what I study and teach commonly brings interesting responses. Why? Because studying the Bible regularly evokes pictures of lifeless, obscure, and pretentious work practiced by those who want to win arguments about (but not win people to) Jesus. Why spend time studying something so seemingly outdated and out of touch with today? What does it have to do with real life? It has everything to do with real life (and death)! Because of the nature of Scripture (i.e., God's speaking committed to writing), biblical theology yields life-giving, joy-producing, faith-strengthening, love-increasing, and hope-sustaining fruit, for it teaches us to find our stories in the grand story of all that God is doing in Christ. Here are just a few ways that biblical theology impacts the Christian life.

Biblical Theology Helps Us Know God

Biblical theology plays an important role in knowing God since it fills that pursuit with content and meaning. Jesus said to his disciples, "And this is eternal life, that they might know you, the only true God, and Jesus Christ whom you have sent" (John 17:3). Eternal life begins not merely in the future but even in the present, for the resurrection and the life has entered into history to be with his people. Furthermore, this life is characterized by knowing the only true God, who is essentially identified with Jesus Christ (e.g., Rom. 9:5). These realities are simply staggering, for the eternal, transcendent God apart from us takes the initiative to be with us by becoming one of us, and in so doing makes it possible for us to fellowship with him—fellowship filled with abundant life.

In his classic work on knowing God, J. I. Packer makes the point that the more complex the object, the more complex is the knowing of it.[1] For example, it is easier to know an impersonal, abstract thing such as a painting than it is a living, personal thing such as a dog. In the case of human beings, however, knowledge becomes more difficult because they can withhold or hide what is in their hearts. Thus, "the quality and extent of our knowledge of them depends more on them than on us. Our knowing them is more directly the result of their allowing us to know them than of our attempting to get to know them."[2] Imagine, then, meeting someone who is above us in rank, intellect, knowledge, and skill—a school president meeting the leader of his or her country, an athlete meeting their favorite hall of famer, or a computer programmer meeting Bill Gates. In this case,

> The more conscious we are of our own inferiority, the more we shall feel that our part is simply to attend to him respectfully and let him take the initiative in the conversation. . . . We would like to get to know this exalted person, but we fully realize that this is a matter for him to decide, not us. If he confines himself to courteous formalities with us, we may be disappointed, but we do not feel able to complain; after all, we had no claim on his friendship. But if instead he starts at once to take us into his confidence, and tells us frankly what is in his mind on matters of particular undertakings he has planned, and asks us to make ourselves permanently available for this kind of collaboration whenever he needs us, then we shall feel enormously privileged, and it will make a world of difference to our general outlook. If life seemed footling and dreary hitherto, it will not seem so any more, now that the great man has enrolled us among his personal assistants. Here is something to write home about!—and something to live up to! Now this, so far as it goes, is an illustration of what it means to know God.[3]

The God of the universe, "the One who is high and lifted up, who inhabits eternity, whose name is Holy," says, "I dwell in the high and holy place, and also with him who is of a contrite and lowly spirit, to revive the spirit of the lowly, and to revive the spirit of the contrite" (Isa. 57:15). God, who is the fountain of life and in whose light we see light (Ps. 36:9[10]), sent the Son to come into the world to give life (John 10:10) and to shine in our hearts to give the light of the knowledge of the glory of God in the face of Jesus Christ (2 Cor. 4:6). This relationship is an astounding thing—that sinful human

---

1. J. I. Packer, *Knowing God* (Downers Grove, IL: InterVarsity, 1973), 30.
2. J. I. Packer, *Knowing God*, 31.
3. J. I. Packer, *Knowing God*, 31.

beings can know this God, be friends with him, and become his heirs and, in the Spirit, fellow heirs with Christ (Rom. 8:17). What a gift! And what does this gift of knowing God involve? Packer provides the answer:

> We must say that knowing God involves, first, listening to God's Word and receiving it as the Holy Spirit interprets it, in application to oneself; second, noting God's nature and character, as his word and works reveal it; third, accepting his invitations, and doing what he commands; fourth, recognizing, and rejoicing in, the love that he has shown in thus approaching one and drawing one into this divine fellowship.[4]

Biblical theology helps us know God because learning how to read the Scripture as God has given it, from Genesis to Revelation, helps us to better listen, receive, apply, note, accept, do, recognize, and rejoice in who God is for us in Christ by his Spirit. Such knowledge is too wonderful for us; it is high, and we cannot attain it by our own efforts. Nevertheless, God has graciously given it for our supreme good. So "let not the wise man boast in his wisdom, let not the mighty man boast in his might, let not the rich man boast in his riches, but let him who boasts boast in this, that he understands and knows me, that I am the LORD who practices steadfast love, justice, and righteousness in the earth. For I delight in these things, declares the LORD" (Jer. 9:23–24).

Biblical Theology Helps Us Gain Canonical Literacy

Biblical theology helps us gain what Kevin Vanhoozer calls canonical literacy, or canon sense. He writes,

> It is not enough to know facts about the Bible. What is needed is canon sense: the ability to interpret particular passages of Scripture in light of the whole Bible. Canon sense means knowing where we are in the flow of redemptive history. Canon sense means thinking not only about but *with* the Bible, to the point of being able to interpret one's own experience with the biblical categories, in light of the overarching story line of Scripture. Jesus did this with his own person and history. No one had canon sense more than Jesus himself. . . . It means being able to read one's own historical situation and life, in light of the world of the biblical text. Typology is an excellent means of doing this. As members of the New Testament church understood themselves via the events of Israel's history, so members of the contemporary church must understand themselves as participants in the same ongoing drama of redemption. The historical and cultural scenery may have changed, but Christians today are in the

---

4. J. I. Packer, *Knowing God*, 32.

same redemptive-historical context as the early Christians, poised in expectation between the first and second comings of Christ, still having to endure various kinds of opposition in the world.[5]

Reading God's Word is for all Christians and should not be reserved for academic specialists. Biblical theology encourages more productive Bible study as we learn how to read *with the Bible* the parts in light of the whole and how the whole connects to Christ. We must, therefore, become increasingly competent in knowing how God has acted to sum up all things in Christ (Eph. 1:9–10) so that we may live faithfully before him in every area of our lives.

Biblical Theology Reminds Us of the Already and Not Yet

Biblical theology reminds us that Jesus fulfills God's promises. The NT displays that God's highly anticipated Messiah arrives on the historical scene, and, true to prophetic form, he inaugurates a kingdom that cannot be shaken and that awaits its final consummation in the new heavens and new earth. Thus, themes, categories, and structures in the OT now connect to Jesus, who fulfills them. He is the obedient Son who performs a better exodus because he saves his people out of sin and into the place of redemptive blessing— now centered in him (Matt. 2:15). He is the true temple through whom we have better access to God (John 1:14; 2:21). Moreover, he gives rest to those who come to him (Matt. 11:28–30). Life that once abounded in Canaan now abounds in him, for he is the fruit-bearing vine, the resurrection, and the life (John 6:35; 11:25–26; 15:1–11). Yet, Christ fulfills the OT in a surprising way, for God's saving promises are inaugurated but not yet consummated. That is, the kingdom of God is "already but not yet." George Ladd writes,

> The Kingdom of God is the redemptive reign of God dynamically active to establish his rule among human beings, and . . . this Kingdom, which will appear as an apocalyptic act at the end of the age, has already come into human history in the person and mission of Jesus to overcome evil, to deliver people from its power, and to bring them into the blessings of God's reign. The Kingdom of God involves two great moments: fulfillment within history, and consummation at the end of history.[6]

The kingdom is present because the Messiah-King is present, but we will not see his reign fully realized until his second coming (see Heb. 2:8; 9:28).

---

5. Kevin J. Vanhoozer and Owen Strachan, *The Pastor as Public Theologian: Reclaiming a Lost Vision* (Grand Rapids: Baker, 2015), 114 (emphasis original).
6. George Eldon Ladd, *A Theology of the New Testament*, rev. ed. (Grand Rapids: Eerdmans, 1993), 89–90.

The already–not yet nature of the kingdom is important to remember in our Christian lives, for it guards against pessimism and optimism. On the one hand, we might be inclined toward pessimism, which can lead to hopelessness and despair. We are aware of and affected by sin both inside and outside of us, perhaps so aware that we sink into despondency and wonder if we will ever be freed from sin's presence. This outlook stems from an under-realized view of the end times—one that underestimates how much Christ accomplished in his first coming. But Scripture encourages us to have a different perspective by lifting our eyes to the serpent-crushing, sin-killing, death-defeating Christ and by enlarging our understanding of what God has already accomplished for us in him. Thus, biblical theology fuels hope and holy progress in our lives as we fix our eyes on him. On the other hand, we might be inclined toward optimism, which can lead to perfectionism and pride. This outlook stems from an over-realized view of the end times—one that thinks so much has happened through Christ's first coming that there remains nothing left for him to do. This belief can result in, for example, a spouse's or parent's impatience or demand for perfection. Biblical theology promotes progress without perfection until the perfect comes, so that we can be confident in the process of change while patient in waiting for it. Scripture reminds us that the covenant relationship for which we were created and saved will one day come in the new heaven and new earth, where our glorious Triune God will dwell with us, and we will be his people, and God himself will be with us as our God (Rev. 21:3). Thus, biblical theology fuels humility and dependence as we wait and work in faith until *that day.*

Biblical theology is also important for other areas—indeed every area!— of our lives in Christ. For example, corporate worship should reflect both the already and not yet, be patterned after heavenly worship, and reflect participation in heavenly worship (Col. 3:16; Rev. 4–5). More specifically, worship solemnly and joyfully exults in the forgiveness and salvation accomplished in Christ. Likewise, we should pray by approaching God on the basis of what he has done in Christ and by asking God for what he has promised to do (Matt. 6:9–14).[7] Obedience should be rooted in our death with Christ to sin and life with Christ in his resurrection (Rom. 6:1–14; Col. 3:1–4). In other words, it is because of God's sovereign and gracious work in redemption through Christ in the Spirit that we can become that new kind of people. Lastly, God's mission in the present time is carried out through his Spirit-indwelt people who proclaim the gospel and extend the boundaries of God's presence by calling people to repent of sin and to trust in Christ. This mission requires that all Christians, regardless of vocation, be a light of salvation to the ends of the earth (Matt. 28:18–20). By reading Scripture from promise to fulfillment,

---

7. For an excellent book on how to pray in light of Christ's person and work, see D. A. Carson, *Praying with Paul: A Call to Spiritual Reformation* (Grand Rapids: Baker, 2015).

from the parts to the whole, biblical theology yields abundant fruit in our Christian lives.

Summary

Biblical theology teaches us to understand our stories in the grand story of God's saving purposes in Christ. Doing biblical theology helps us to become biblically literate as we know God and make Christ known in our world. And in so doing, there is great reward in both this life and the life to come.

REFLECTION QUESTIONS

1. How would you describe the importance of biblical theology for the Christian life?

2. How has biblical theology helped you in your Christian life?

3. How does biblical theology help in sharing the gospel with others?

4. How can you grow and help others grow in discipleship in becoming more "canonically literate"?

5. Can you think of any other ways that biblical theology impacts the Christian life (e.g., teaching, counseling)?

How Can a Church Teach Biblical Theology?

Oren R. Martin

Biblical theology is not exclusively reserved for academia. In fact, the most fruitful place for biblical theology is the church. When Jesus asked his disciples, "Who do people say that the Son of Man is?" (Matt. 16:13), their faithful—or unfaithful—confession revealed their relation to him. The same is true for us. He is not merely an extraordinary prophet, gentle sage, or good teacher. No, he is the way, the truth, and the life, and no one comes to the Father except through him (John 14:6). People in our churches must be prepared to answer Jesus's question as well. May they faithfully confess, "You are the Christ, the Son of the living God" (Matt. 16:16).

Embedded in that confession is an entire biblical theology of Jesus's personhood, promise-fulfillment, and kingdom purposes. God the Son, the second person of the Trinity, became man in the person of Jesus Christ to deliver his people from the domain of darkness and to transfer us to his blessed kingdom. Therefore, it is vital that pastors and teachers proclaim the whole counsel of God, week by week, year by year, decade by decade, so that believers rightly confess and live in light of Christ's finished work. Together, believers learn about and live out these truths in the church, so why is it vital that churches teach *good* biblical theology?

Why Churches Should Teach (Good) Biblical Theology

First, everyone in your church has adopted a biblical theology. The question is whether or not they possess *good* biblical theology. Bad biblical theology distorts the biblical story of redemption. From beginning to end, through all of its grand literary diversity, God has spoken, and the Bible reveals in dramatic ways how God reigns, saves, and satisfies through covenant for his glory in Christ. Bad biblical theology takes the focus off of God's glory

373

in Christ and places it on other things—often us. For example, instead of seeing our fundamental problem as idolatrous rebellion against God, bad biblical theology points the finger at other things (e.g., injustice, miseducation, "really" bad people, low view of self). Though these problems should indeed be alleviated, they are not our fundamental problem in light of God's holiness. Rather, our fundamental problem is that *every person is alienated from God* and in need of his reconciling grace. Furthermore, a distortion of the core problem leads to a distortion of the actual solution. Instead of embracing the ultimate solution of turning from sin and trusting Christ's finished work on the cross, other solutions are viewed as viable (e.g., health, wealth, education, how-to and self-help advice). Good biblical theology equips people to live in the light of God's glory in Christ.

Second, biblical theology promotes the study of Scripture. Doing exegesis in light of the whole Bible bears remarkable fruit in the weekly ministries of the Word. When a church regularly makes its way through Scripture, new vistas open for people to see the stunning, life-changing beauty of God's Word. Things once hidden become known, shadows become realities, and black and white pictures gleam with the brilliant light of Christ. Eyes are opened and hearts enflamed when biblical-theological patterns fit together to form a mosaic—from the first Adam to the last Adam, from the worldwide promises to Abraham to the worldwide blessing in Christ, from the exodus from Egypt to the better redemption in Christ, from the sacrificial system to the spotless Lamb who takes away the sin of the world, from the presence of God in the temple to his presence in the Word who became flesh and "templed" among us, from the brokenness of creation to the rest inherent in the glorious new creation in Christ.

This illuminating change happened for me (Oren) and my wife as we sat under our pastor's teaching year after year. Tom Schreiner seamlessly moved back and forth between OT and NT, from Exodus to Revelation, Ecclesiastes to James, Isaiah to Galatians, Proverbs to Acts, Samuel to Romans. Through his weekly exposition, our hearts burned within us with the fire and beauty of God's faithfulness in Christ and his finished work. We learned how to more faithfully read our Bibles as we saw a better exodus accomplished by the true Son who delivered his people from the greater enemies of sin, Satan, and death. Things that formerly seemed like vanity now became meaningful under the sustaining power of Christ, who upholds the universe by the word of his power. Prophets like Moses, Samuel, and Isaiah, though instrumental in God's redemptive purposes, paled in comparison to the final prophet, Jesus, who perfectly spoke and kept God's Word. Through the church's weekly ministry, we were recipients of a Word that does not merely form but transform us in Christ's image. Mining the treasures of God's life-giving Word yields priceless and joyful treasures that cannot be taken away.

Third, biblical theology promotes the centrality of the gospel and anchors all of Scripture in the person and work of Christ. Like a moth to a flame, people constantly drift toward moralism and are tempted to rely on what they do rather than on what Christ has done. Good biblical theology reminds us that, yes, we are called to obey God and live holy lives, but true obedience comes only when we are united to the Holy One, who fulfilled the law *in our place*. In other words, Christians do not obey *in order* to earn God's acceptance in Christ, but rather *because* they have been accepted by God through faith in Christ (Col. 3:1–17). Good biblical theology does not end with, "Don't be like Adam, who disobeyed," or, "Be like David, who defeated the enemy in his life," but rather, "You cannot obey or put to death your greatest enemy apart from Christ, who did what you could not, so live by faith in him who loved you and gave himself up for you." Yes, call people to repentance and faith and obedience; and yes, hold up faithful examples like David and Daniel across Scripture (e.g., Heb. 11). But even the courage of David and Daniel could neither deliver themselves nor their hearers from sin. When we are made new in Christ and filled with the Holy Spirit, only then can we be the kind of people God has called, commanded, and empowered us to be: holy in Christ.

Finally, biblical theology guards against pragmatism. In an age of quick-fix, numbers-driven, platform-building fads, biblical theology tethers itself to the One who, although he was fully God, humbled himself by taking the form of a servant and becoming obedient to the point of death (Phil. 2:5–11). True Christian growth cannot be manufactured. The story of the Bible is the story of a great and glorious God, who lovingly sent his Son, who for the joy set before him endured the cross, despising the shame, and is now seated at the right hand of the throne of God (Heb. 12:2; cf. Ps. 110:1), in order to redeem a rebellious people estranged from him. People who find their individual stories written in this grand story of redemption may not get the quick fix they desire, but they can rest in the forgiveness of sins and eternal life they need. Good biblical theology displays discipleship shaped by a cross and made possible by the power of Christ's resurrection.

Therefore, it is vital that churches practice and model good biblical theology. The remainder of this chapter offers suggestions for how churches can teach good biblical theology.

How Churches Can Teach Biblical Theology

The most important element in teaching biblical theology is to practice what you preach. In other words, biblical theology is caught more often than taught; therefore, it is vital that the church model biblical theology in the regular preaching and teaching of the church. Here are two ways churches can model biblical theology when working its way through Scripture.

Churches can teach the "three views" of Scripture, which together supply a lens for seeing the entirety of Scripture as well as each book therein. The first approach is the *satellite* view. Like looking at the world from the perspective of a satellite, this view looks at the big picture of where a book or portion of Scripture is located in the unfolding storyline of Scripture. For example, where is Samuel, Psalms, or Hosea located in God's unfolding purposes, or in what covenantal context does it sit (e.g., Abrahamic, Mosaic, new)? This view teaches people to think in canonical terms of what came before and what comes after in order to better understand the passage at hand. For example, to correctly understand marriage, one must consider what God originally intended at creation and what happened after the fall into sin (Matt. 19:1–9). To understand that God justifies a person by faith in Christ apart from works of the law, understanding the progress of the Abrahamic and Mosaic covenants is crucial.

Second is the *street* view. Like a perspective from the street, this view "parks" outside the book and explains its introductory details (e.g., date, authorship, language, culture, genre). This view helps to understand the basic features of a book and its various emphases, again taking into account where it is in its overall place in Scripture.

The third approach is the *seated* view. Like having a perspective where you can take in all the details, one gains the seated view by going inside and living in the book through its exposition. The time it takes to preach or teach through a book depends on its size and the desired pace (e.g., verse by verse, literary unit by unit). When a preacher or teacher regularly approaches Scripture from these three views, churches learn how to understand various parts of Scripture in light of the whole.

Churches can also teach in more detail where each part of Scripture is situated in the unfolding drama of redemption. When teaching through a book or section of Scripture, it is vital to locate its place in the progressive unfolding of God's kingdom purposes, which began in Genesis 1 and culminate in Revelation 22. In Question 2, we offer one memorable model that uses the acronym KINGDOM:

1. Kickoff and Rebellion: Creation, Fall, and Flood
2. Instrument of Blessing: Patriarchs
3. Nation Redeemed and Commissioned: Exodus, Sinai, and Wilderness
4. Government in the Land: Conquest and Kingdoms
5. Dispersion and Return: Exile and Initial Restoration
6. Overlap of the Ages: Christ's Work and the Church Age
7. Mission Accomplished: Christ's Return and Kingdom Consummation

Another helpful overview is as follows:[1]

---

1. This overview is adapted from Vaughn Roberts, *God's Big Picture: Tracing the Storyline of the Bible* (Downers Grove, IL: InterVarsity, 2002).

1. The Prototypical Kingdom (Gen. 1–2)
2. The Perished Kingdom (Gen. 3)
3. The Promised King(dom) (Gen. 3:15)
4. The Progressing Kingdom (Noahic-Davidic covenants; Gen. 12–1 Kings 10)
5. The Parted Kingdom (Solomon-Exile)
6. The Prophesied King(dom) (The Latter Prophets)
7. The Present King(dom) (Gospels)
8. The Proclaimed King(dom) (Acts–Jude)
9. The Perfected Kingdom (Revelation)

Furthermore, churches can teach biblical theology from the nursery to the corporate gatherings. Here are some suggestions and resources:

1. Vary how you preach and teach through the Old and New Testaments in your weekly gatherings. For example, preach the whole message of the Bible in one sermon, the message of the OT in one sermon, the message of the NT in one sermon, the message of a section of Scripture in one sermon (e.g., Law, Prophets, Gospels, or Epistles), the message of a book in one sermon, or various themes.[2] Moreover, go back and forth between preaching OT and NT books as well as different genres.

2. In your liturgy or service of worship, include elements that move through creation, fall, redemption, and consummation (e.g., songs, Scripture readings). Furthermore, if preaching through an OT or NT book, choose a Scripture reading from the opposite Testament that corresponds to it (e.g., John 15 and Isaiah 5; Exodus 19 and Hebrews 12:18–24).

3. Introduce the big picture of the Bible in your membership class to show how life together in the church and its mission fit into God's broader redemptive purposes.[3]

4. Intentionally and strategically teach biblical theology in the age-graded ministries of the church. From nursery to youth, connect various parts

---

2. A great example of how to teach biblical theology in the weekly gathering of the church is Mark Dever at Capitol Hill Baptist Church, who has done many of these things in his tenure as pastor. Listen, for example, to his sermons (https://www.capitolhillbaptist.org), which he published as *The Message of the Old Testament: Promises Made* and *The Message of the New Testament: Promises Kept* (Wheaton, IL: Crossway, 2005, 2006). See also T. Desmond Alexander, Brian S. Rosner, D. A. Carson, Graeme Goldsworthy, eds., *New Dictionary of Biblical Theology: Exploring the Unity and Diversity of Scripture* (Downers Grove, IL: InterVarsity, 2000).

3. See, for example, Roberts, *God's Big Picture*.

of Scripture to the whole. If you use a curriculum that doesn't connect individual stories in Scripture to the person and work of Christ or that simply moralizes them (e.g., be like Abram, and go where God is leading you; don't be like Saul; be like David, and kill the giants in your life), then supplement by showing how the gospel connects to and fulfills them.[4]

5. In addition to pastors preaching and teaching, identify and equip qualified teachers to offer classes or seminars on biblical theology. There are numerous studies from which to choose.[5]

Summary

Biblical theology belongs in the church. Churches should work to help people see the priceless treasures of God's glory in Christ from all of Scripture. From young people to seasoned saints, churches can take advantage of existing resources to teach biblical theology throughout the various ministries of the church. As eyes are opened by the Spirit to the Christ who fulfilled the Law of Moses and the Prophets and the Psalms (Luke 24:44), may people see and be satisfied and say, "Our hearts burned within us while the Scriptures were opened to us" (24:32).

REFLECTION QUESTIONS

1. Why should churches teach biblical theology?

2. How can churches inadvertently teach bad biblical theology?

3. How can churches intentionally teach and model good biblical theology?

4. How does biblical theology guard and grow the church in Christ?

5. Can you think of ways that churches can teach biblical theology other than the ones this chapter identifies?

---

4. See, for example, David Helm, *The Big Picture Story Bible* (Wheaton, IL: Crossway, 2004); Roberts, *God's Big Picture*; Kevin DeYoung, *The Biggest Story: How the Snake Crusher Brings Us Back to the Garden* (Wheaton, IL: Crossway, 2015).

5. See, for example, Chris Bruno, *The Whole Story of the Bible in 16 Verses* (Wheaton, IL: Crossway, 2015); Nick Roark and Robert Kline, *Biblical Theology: How the Church Faithfully Teaches the Gospel* (Wheaton, IL: Crossway, 2018); T. Desmond Alexander and Brian S. Rosner, eds., *New Dictionary of Biblical Theology* (Downers Grove, IL: InterVarsity, 2000); Thomas R. Schreiner, *The King in His Beauty: A Biblical Theology of the Old and New Testaments* (Grand Rapids: Baker, 2013); D. A. Carson, *The God Who Is There: Finding Your Place in God's Story* (Grand Rapids: Baker, 2010).

What Should Motivate Us to Do Biblical Theology?

Oren R. Martin

The beginning of this book compared biblical theology to putting together a building block set. Each part of Scripture, when connected to the whole, fits together to form a grand story in Christ—and we participate in that story as God is making all things new. This endeavor, however, takes work. As Paul charged young Timothy in his ministry saying, "Think over what I say, for the Lord will give you understanding in everything" (2 Tim. 2:7), so there is a command and a promise for us in thinking God's thoughts after him as the Scripture reveals them. What, then, should motivate us to do biblical theology?

The Nature of Scripture Motivates Us to Do Biblical Theology

Scripture is a gracious and indispensable gift to God's people. Christians not only follow Christ, who is the way, the truth, and the life (John 14:6), but they are also fed by the words of him who is the resurrection and the life (John 11:25; Acts 5:20). God's words are for our instruction "that through endurance and through the encouragement of the Scriptures we might have hope" (Rom. 15:4). As John Murray rightly noted, the Bible not only reveals to us God's saving acts in history and interprets the meaning of those acts, "it is itself also an abiding and for us indispensable organ in the fulfillment of God's redemptive will."[1] In other words, Scripture itself is redemptive, which is why Jesus can pray, "Sanctify them in the truth; your word is truth" (John 17:17). Scripture is God's gracious means to bring about holiness in our lives, and holiness yields deep and abiding joy.

---

1. John Murray, "Systematic Theology, Second Article," in *The Collected Writings of John Murray*, vol. 4 (Edinburgh: Banner of Truth Trust, 1982), 4.

The Summit of Scripture Motivates Us to Do Biblical Theology

I (Oren) recall a hike up a trail in Rocky Mountain National Park that was both difficult and painful. What started in a warm sunny forest ended on a snowcapped peak. The relentless pace and ascent sent pain into muscles I never knew existed. But what awaited me on the other side of that demanding and agonizing climb was the most beautiful, breathtaking scenery I had ever witnessed. Had I not persevered, I would not have experienced the sheer joy of beholding those spectacular views.

Learning to read Scripture is like that hiking experience. Not every part is equally easy to understand. In fact, some parts of it are just hard to grasp due to distance in time, culture, language, and genres (even Peter thought there were some things in Paul's letters that were hard to understand! [2 Peter 3:16]). Furthermore, we are confronted with our sin and need for grace when looking into the mirror of Scripture. But awaiting us on the other side of that work is a summit that opens our eyes to the beauty of Christ and his work for us and our salvation. As we fix our eyes on Jesus, the author and perfecter of our faith, we are motivated to understand more and more of the riches in God's living and active Word. Learning to do biblical theology may not always be easy, but at the end it is always rewarding—after all, we are thinking about our great God and Savior!

My colleague Jim Hamilton wrote an article called "Biblical Theology and Preaching."[2] I have read the end of it several times through the process of writing this book because it motivates me to do biblical theology. Here is an excerpt from the book that motivates me, and I hope it motivates you too.

Can God's People Handle This?

Can God's people operate those complicated remote controls that come with everything from their new flat-screen TVs to their new cars? Can God's people use computers; navigate grocery stores; hold down jobs; and acquire homes, cars, toys, and all the stuff they jam into the garage?

Let me be frank: I have no patience for suggestions that preachers need to dumb it down. Preachers need to be clear, and they need to be able to explain things in understandable ways. But human beings do not need the Bible to be dumbed down. If you think that, what you really think is that God the Holy Spirit did not know what He was doing when He inspired the Bible to be the way it is. Not only does the suggestion that the Bible is more than God's people can handle

---

2. James M. Hamilton Jr., "Biblical Theology and Preaching," in *Text-Driven Preaching: God's Word at the Heart of Every Sermon*, eds. Daniel L. Akin, David L. Allen, and Ned L. Mathews (Nashville: B&H, 2010), 193–218.

blaspheme God's wisdom; it also blasphemes His image bearers. People are made in the image of God. Human beings are endowed with brains and sensibilities of astonishing capacity.

Do you want people to think that everything that is interesting or artistic or brilliant comes from the world? Dumb down the Bible.

Do you want them to see the complexity and simplicity of God? The sheer genius of the Spirit-inspired biblical authors? The beauty of a world-encompassing metanarrative of cosmic scope? Teach them biblical theology.

Do not discount the capacities of God's people. They may be stupid and uninformed when their hearts are awakened, but do not punish them by leaving them there. Show them literary artistry. Show them the subtle power of carefully constructed narratives. Show them the force of truth in arguments that unfold with inexorable logic. If they are genuine believers, they will want to understand the Bible. Show them the shouts and songs, the clamor and the clarity, the book of books. Let their hearts sing with the psalmist, weep with Lamentations, and ponder Proverbs. Give them the messianic wisdom of the beautiful mind that wrote Ecclesiastes. Preach the word!

Unleash it in all its fullness and fury. Let it go. Tie it together. Show connections that are there in the texts from end to end. Tell them the whole story. Give them the whole picture. Paint the whole landscape for them, not just the blade of grass.[3]

Incredible! These words motivate me to grow in doing biblical theology well, and I hope they have the same effect on you. Commit yourself to climb the summit of Scripture, and there you will see glory as you've never seen before—and God will satisfy you.

Summary

It is our hope and prayer that, as a result of reading this book, you are motivated to read your Bible again and again and again, and in so doing taste and see that the Lord is good (Ps. 34:8[9]). We pray you see more and more of the beauty and wonder of Jesus Christ in all that he has accomplished for us and our salvation. And just like those disciples on the road to Emmaus, when we grow in learning all that Christ fulfills that is written in the Law of Moses and the Prophets and the Psalms, we pray that your hearts burn hot within you with the life-giving fire of Christ (Luke 24:27, 32, 44). A billion years from now we will not say, "If only I had spent less time reading the Bible and more

---

3. Hamilton, "Biblical Theology and Preaching," 216–17.

time doing _____." May we spend our lives knowing and making known our great Triune God. Hallelujah, what a Savior![4]

REFLECTION QUESTIONS

1. What motivates you to do biblical theology?

2. How can you motivate others?

3. How can you grow in reading Scripture? Is there something in your life holding you back from experiencing the life-giving words of Scripture?

4. In what ways has biblical theology helped you understand the whole counsel of God?

5. How has biblical theology increased your confidence in God who keeps his promises in Christ by his Spirit?

---

4. If you are thinking, "How should I get started?" A good place is to carefully read the Bible along with some of the best resources on biblical theology. Here is a link to an annotated bibliography of 101 resources on biblical theology: https://www.zondervan.com/p/biblical-theology/bibliography/. Also see the *Zondervan Biblical Theology Study Bible*, ed. D. A. Carson (Grand Rapids: Zondervan, 2016).

Scripture Index